W9-BUT-310

THE RESEARCH GUIDE FOR THE DIGITAL AGE

A New Handbook to Research and Writing for the Serious Student

Francis A. Burkle-Young
Saundra Rose Maley

JENKS L.R.C.
GORDON COLLEGE
255 GRAPEVINE RD.
WENHAM, MA 01984-1895

University Press of America, Inc.
Lanham • New York • Oxford

GORDON COLLEGE
JENKS LRC
DISCARDED

Copyright © 1997 by
University Press of America,® Inc.
4720 Boston Way
Lanham, Maryland 20706

12 Hid's Copse Rd.
Cummor Hill, Oxford OX2 9JJ

All rights reserved
Printed in the United States of America
British Library Cataloguing in Publication Information Available

Library of Congress Cataloging-in-Publication Data

Burkle-Young, Francis A.
The research guide for the digital age : a new handbook to research and
writing for the serious student / by Francis A. Burkle-Young and
Saundra Rose Maley.
p.   cm.
Includes bibliographical references and index.
1. Report writing--Handbooks, manuals, etc. 2. Research--United
States--Handbooks, manuals, etc. 3. Report writing--Computer
network resources--Handbooks, manuals, etc. 4. Research--United
States--Computer network resources--Handbooks, manuals, etc. 5.
Online databases--Handbooks, manuals, etc.
I. Maley, Saundra. II. Title.
LB2369.B78   1997   808/.0221--dc21   97-16464 CIP

ISBN 0-7618-0779-9 (pbk: alk. ppr.)

⊖™ The paper used in this publication meets the minimum
requirements of American National Standard for information
Sciences—Permanence of Paper for Printed Library Materials,
ANSI Z39.48—1984

DEDICATION

We are grateful to be able to dedicate this book to three people who belong, forever, to the great chain of discovery and scholarship that represents, together with the highest in Art, the supreme triumph of civilization:

ELLEN LOUISE BURKLE YOUNG

(Pittsburgh, Pennsylvania: September 1, 1905 – Washington, D. C.: January 30, 1979) of the Smithsonian Institution and the Library of Congress. A researcher and scholar who overcame tremendous handicaps to contribute substantially to our knowledge of both the history of technology and the history of social philosophy. She was the editor and publisher of the *Jamestown Courier* and the author of more than forty articles in the fourteenth revised edition of the *Encyclopædia Britannica*.

SISTER BERNARD
OF THE SISTERS OF NOTRE DAME DE NAMUR
[CATHERINE BRIDGET DOUGHERTY]

(Philadelphia, Pennsylvania: September 16, 1893 – Stevenson, Maryland: April 29, 1971) of Saint Aloysius School, North Capitol Street, Washington. In nearly sixty years as a teacher, she dedicated herself to planting the seeds of sound research, rational thinking, and, above all, clear writing, to hundreds of pupils in her care. A noble exponent of the highest ideals of Mother Julie Billiart.

HERMANN EVERARD SCHÜSSLER, DR. THEOL.

(Rostock in Mecklenburg: April 24, 1929 – Bottmingen, B. L., Switzerland: August 14, 1975) Professor of History in Brown University and in the University of Maryland. A scholar and teacher of international renown who was, in every historical sense of the term, the full embodiment of the Christian gentleman. Author of *Georg Calixt: Theologie und Kirchenpolitik, eine Studie zur Okumenizitat des Luthertums* and *Der Primat der Heiligen Schrift als theologisches und kanonistisches Problem im Spatmittelalter*.

Table of Contents

PREFACE *1*

INTRODUCTION

How Research Will Set You Free *5*
Emancipating Yourself Through Knowledge *8*
The Term Paper As A Formal Essay *11*
What Will You Discover? *15*
Three Basic Assumptions for
Rational Thinking *18*

CHOOSING YOUR TOPIC *23*

GETTING STARTED: PART ONE *41*

The URL *51*
List of *FirstSearch* Databases *53*
Other Library Resources on the Internet *58*
Lynx's Keystroke Commands *65*
Bibliographies of Bibliographies and Research Guides *68*

GETTING STARTED: PART TWO *78*

Mining, Not Surfing, the 'Net *78*
I. DIALOG *79*
II. LEXIS/NEXIS *82*
III. WESTLAW *84*
IV. Other Large Commercial Services *85*
V. RLIN [Research Libraries's Information Network] *86*
VI. *Melvyl* *87*
VII. MEDLINE *87*
VIII. The Argus Clearinghouse *90*
IX. The December List *90*
X. ALTAVISTA *91*
XI. YAHOO *92*
XII. Wilson Indexes and Abstracts *93*

YOUR FIRST SOURCES *95*

Browsing the Shelves—Physically and Digitally *101*
Citation Searching *102*

THE ANNOTATED BIBLIOGRAPHY *107*

PRESERVING YOUR PAPER TRAIL *111*

How to Read *WorldCat* Display Screens *120*
A List of Labels for *WorldCat* *130*
How to Read Library of Congress LOCIS screens *132*

FINDING THE RIGHT PEOPLE *134*

Talk to an Expert *134*
Encyclopedia of Associations *139*
Dissertations Abstracts Online *143*
Texts in Foreign Languages *147*

ANALYSIS *151*

Occam's Razor *160*
Sherlock Holmes's Rule *162*
Hanlon's Corollary *167*
Logic for Analysis *168*
Constructing a Logical Argument *169*
Stage One: Premises *172*
Stage Two: Inference *173*
Stage Three: Conclusion *173*
Types of Logical Argument *173*
Implication in Detail *176*
Fallacies *178*

SYNTHESIS *183*

WRITING *196*

Preliminaries: Thesis Statement *196*
Preliminaries: Outline *198*
Nine Principles of Good Writing *206*

MINING THE INTERNET—AGAIN *226*

A SUMMING UP *227*

Remember the Principle of Self-Editing *228*
Clarity Above All *229*

ANNOTATING YOUR OWN TEXt *230*

Footnotes, and How to Use Them *230*
Bibliographical Footnotes *235*
Brief Biographical Footnotes *237*
Geographical Identification *239*
Descriptions of Objects *239*
Expand Information on a Secondary Topic *240*
Gloss Unusual Words or Expressions *240*
Document Contrasting Views *241*
Your Own Asides and Commentaries *244*
Relationships and Associations *245*
Translations to or from Another Language *246*
Cross-References *247*
Express Acknowledgments and Thanks *249*

ASSEMBLING THE FINAL PAPER *252*
A Sample Formating for Your Paper 254

CONCLUSION *257*

EPILOGUE: CONSIDERING PUBLICATION *262*

Where You Are Today *263*
Who Will Publish Your Work *263*
The Next Step *264*
Once Your Revision is Done *264*
What You Can Expect Next *265*
Getting Closer to Print *266*

APPENDICES

Appendix A

Some Sample Searches of Important Databases *268*
I. *WorldCat* *268*
II. Library of Congress Databases *279*
III. Establishing Subject Headings Online *287*
IV. Citation Searches with *Arts & Humanities Search* *293*
V. Searching *Dissertations Abstracts Online* *299*
VI. How to Browse Shelves Digitally *304*

Appendix B

A Sample Undergraduate Term Paper *309*

Appendix C

Logical Fallacies That You Must Avoid *336*

Appendix D

Abbreviations Used in Footnotes *358*

Appendix E

How to Evaluate Information on the 'Net *362*

FOR FURTHER READING *373*

INDEX *376*

Acknowledgments

First, we wish to acknowledge our debt to several scholars and teachers whose standards of excellence, and adherence to the methods that we describe in this book, have touched us directly or, in some cases, indirectly, through the guidance of those whom they taught: Hermann Everard Schuessler, to whom this book is dedicated, in part; Charles Richard Sanders, Lionel Stevenson; Joseph Lortz, founder and, for many years, the head of the Institut für Europäische Geschichte at the Johannes Gutenberg University at Mainz; R. W. B. Lewis, Charles Carroll Mish, Fra Raphael Brown, Elizabeth O. Cullen, Philip Bishop, Eugene Ferguson, Palma Romano, Hermine Herta Meyer, and, especially, James Arlington Wright.

Next, we would like to remember several of our teachers and mentors who gave us an understanding of the importance of rigorous scholarship, together with a devotion to intellectual honesty and openness: George Allan Cate, William S. Peterson, W. Milne Holton, Clifford McLean Foust, George Patrick Majeska, Michael J. Pelczar, Wilhelmina Jashemski, Harold Herman, Dickie A. Spurgeon; and Leonard I. Lutwack. Since this book is for the students who *are* the future, we wish to mention some of our students who have embraced these methods and who now embody the future of scholarship: Johanna C. Cullen, Joseph Michael Bizup, Jan Robert Danielsen, Christian Danielsen, John Montgomery Bishop, Mariusz Richard Grabek, Michael Doerrer, Robert L. Tillman, Bryan S. Miller, Nissrin M. Ezmerli, Chryssoula I. Kinna, Elaine C. Fajardo, Neal O. Paulsen, Marjan Yousefi, Michael Dennis Sawyer, Brian J. Moylan, Spencer James, Li Liu, Riccardo Vezzosi, and the late Frederick Blake Temple. These students, as their names reveal, came to us from every continent and from every ethnic background Their enthusiasm for serious scholarship and learning testifies to the real best fruit of diversity in our fast-shrinking world.

We also would like to thank Elaine Kallio who read this book in manuscript; and, for kind support and encouragement, Nancy Prothro Arbuthnot, Paul Andrew Love, and Richard E. Cullen.

We also wish to acknowledge two members of the staff of the Library of Congress who have aided materially in the antecendent research for this book. Bruce Martin, head of the Study Facilities Office, made the advantages of readerships available to us; and Thomas Mann, of the General Reference and Bibliography Division, who has helped us, not only with his bibliographic wisdom but also with his two notable volumes, *A Guide to Library Research Methods* and *Library Research Models, A Guide to Classification, Cataloging, and Computers.*

Thanks also to Ernest A. Braund, formerly with the Library of Congress, for reading the manuscript and offering several valuable emendations.

For substantial help in preparing the index, we wish to thank Juliet Bruce, George Allan Cate, Laurence S. Galvin, and Judith Cochran. Finally, a word of thanks to Danny Aube, who has, for many years, kept our computers running, without which we would have become mute.

Preface

WE DECIDED to write this book after many years of experience in the classroom as teachers of writing courses. Our professional lives have taught us that some of the critical and fundamental principles behind the research and writing of the college term paper have been, it seems, entirely forgotten. We do understand, of course, that the great decline in literacy that has been experienced in the United States over the past decades, has forced teachers in writing courses to spend a vast amount of their classroom time in teaching fundamental writing skills, including the simplest aspects of the grammar and punctuation of standard American English, which once were staples of the elementary school curriculum. Consequently, in the interest of ensuring an adequate degree of fundamental English expression, many professors have been forced to choose between having their students master the most important basic skills or having them receive an adequate introduction to the world of research and scholarship. Too often, this choice has relegated the latter to comparative obscurity. Thus it is that so many older members of college and university faculties bemoan the lack of "college content" in the courses they must teach.

We have noticed, on the modern campus, that only the older teachers, and practically no students, realize that the term paper, as a form of expository essay, is a very important part of that training in the life of scholarship which sets students free from the received intellectual authority which was, of necessity, imposed on them in childhood—that it is, if you like, the first truly adult writing in the life of everyone who experiences the process. Moreover, the antecedent techniques of research and analysis provide each student with a method by which information can be discovered, weighed on the scales of relative importance, and discussed in its own terms as well as in terms of its usefulness for others.

But this consideration of writing a term paper as a part of the process of intellectual growth and maturity is only one important reason for undertaking a fresh discussion of the subject today. A significant number of other texts have appeared over the past decades which also lead the freshman or sophomore student through the processes of doing research and analysis—both on the scientific

1

and the historical methods. Today, however, none of them offer an adequate introduction to the new technical methods for identifying, recovering, and assembling relevant research information. The recent rise to great importance of the major online union catalogues, such as *WorldCat* and the Library of Congress's SCORPIO and MUMS systems, together with the tremendous asset students now have by taking advantage of the interlibrary loan system, have changed forever the mechanical procedures of doing research for term papers, as they have for doing theses, dissertations, and scholarly articles. Similarly, the wide range of resources that are available now on the Internet, from archival catalogues to full-text presentations on the *World Wide Web*, also have enhanced significantly the process of doing research.

But there is yet more. Modern college undergraduates in America generally come to the classroom with no instruction at all in writing in the traditional, lucid, formal essay. Moreover, their ability to distinguish the important and vital from the unimportant and trivial is minimal. To many of them, the fact that George Washington was an eighteenth-century figure who wore false teeth is as important as his accomplishments in the French and Indian War, the American Revolution, the founding of the federal republic, and his terms as the first president of the United States. It often seems as if the great ocean of information which now surrounds us has washed away, or even drowned, the untrained mind's ability to distinguish relative importance among all this welter of organized noise. The process of analyzing information and then writing about the stream of causes and effects—one of the most elementary intellectual skills—offers a framework for all the other kinds of analyses which the rational adult must perform throughout life. After all, the chief duty of the modern mind is to select from the inexhaustable phenomena which pass before us in our lives those events which are most meaningful and relevant to us: a uniquely necessary "wise eclecticism."

Of course, the act of researching and writing the term paper also is every student's first real introduction to the world of scholarship. And without a growing community of scholars in all fields, not only academic progress but also economic and political progress is stunted. More often than not, today, students are left to discover the principal tenets of good scholarship in a haphazard way by themselves. Only the fortunate find a professor who will take the time with undergraduates to inculcate in them both a love of learning for its own sake and a realization of the importance of the life of the mind, not only to the person so persuaded but to the country at large, as well. By offering this small guide to college students, we hope to illustrate, clearly and logically, those principles of enquiry, curiosity, discovery, and enthusiasm which will vitalize their future academic careers and their lives as rational and thoughtful adults.

We also wish to say to our colleagues that we know very well that the methods we advocate in this book add a great burden to your teaching, in the additional time that you must spend to guide your students to sources and to help them to interpret those sources; and in additional scholarly labors of your own, because you must enter into the paths of discovery that your students find. We all know that thinking is hard work, and the first steps in both research and analysis are often irregular, hesitant, or confused. Consequently, the degree of guidance and personal involvement that is dictated by these older, traditional methods for introducing students to real scholarship will take from you precious hours which might well be devoted to your own scholarly pursuits. We do believe, however, that the rewards for the students, the illumination of the mind and the excitement of discovery, repay your substantial effort, both in and out of the classroom, and can make the act of learning mutual.

Introduction: How Research Will Set You Free

If you are reading these words, it is probable that you are about to write your first college term paper. If that is the case, you are at the beginning of a journey that will truly set you free, raise you from intellectual dependency to intellectual freedom, and place you firmly on the road to a genuine education. In reality, the first serious term paper that you write probably is your first experience in learning how to learn on your own—self education is, after all, not just the best education, it is the only education. If you master the standard skills and methods that are appropriate for this work, you can transfer them very easily to any field of inquiry—business, professional, academic, or everyday life.

Consider for a moment how you know what you think you know. Most of the information you received during your twelve years or more of schooling, and most of the information you acquired outside of the classroom, as well, was believable only in proportion to the degree of trust that you placed in the person who told you those things which you now hold to be "facts." This dependent trust in intellectual authority begins, of course, with the child's faith that what mother and father tell her is true. Later, this intellectual dependency widens to embrace the authorities of teachers and other adults. However, you had no real method by which to verify the truthfulness of those "facts." You were not concerned with finding primary source materials,[1] or printed versions of those materials, and you were given little chance to explore the full range of scholarship in any field, because facilities for discovering pathways to the truth, such as the interlibrary loan system and massive online bibliographies and catalogues, were not yet at your disposal. Consequently, only the perceived authority of the person who conveyed "facts" to you was the authority for those "facts." Even when you used textbooks in your formal classes, the authority embodied in those books rested upon their choice by your teachers and, only indirectly, on the scholarly reputations of the authors themselves.

---

[1]We will cover just what primary source materials are in some detail later in this volume. For the present, you can think of them as the original documents that you can find that are contemporary with the subject and time you are studying, or nearly so.

You were, in fact, schooled, not educated. All of that is about to change. Of course, neither your professors nor the college or university itself educates you. You educate yourself. By learning how to discover primary sources and how to use them to answer your own questions—the thesis of your term paper, in this case—you will have your first practice at the art of finding the best information to answer any question, whether a matter of business, a social or political issue, a matter of options for yourself later in life, or matters of more academic and scholarly inquiry.

The concept of the primary source is the most important single element in your understanding of how to do serious research on any topic. A primary source is one that was created at the same time, or nearly at the same time, as the event or personal experience that is the subject of your study. Primary sources will appear in two forms, unpublished and published, or printed. The former consists of documents that exist only in handwritten form—or, in the case of some later nineteenth century and twentieth century materials, in typescript—and encompass letters, diaries, journals, memoranda, public records, and other holographic manuscripts of all kinds. Published primary sources encompass two classes of works. First, they include all the documents about your subject that were printed at a time that is contemporaneous with the person or event you are scrutinizing. Among this class are contemporary newspaper articles, government documents, literary works, and other public writings by the subject of your research; as well as other printed materials that shed contemporary light on your topic, which may include drawings, plans, illustrations, films, recordings, musical scores, and other ephemeral items. The second class includes later scholarly editions of manuscript materials, typically, but not universally, done by academicians and published by scholarly and university presses.

Secondary sources are writings **about** the subject of your study. They include books and articles written after the event, and often embody commentary, criticism, and opinion. They are different because the relative importance of an event in the past may well be modified significantly by later events—the absolute future to the event you are studying. It is conventional wisdom to say that nothing can modify the facts of the past, and this is, self-evidently, true.

5

But later events can modify the significance and import of past facts so much that later knowledge and opinion completely alters the view that people hold about the earlier event. This may seem, at first glance, to be very confusing, but we can illuminate this with great clarity with a brief illustration. Today, we regard the date we call February 22, 1732,[2] as historically noteworthy. But we do so primarily because of the birth of George Washington, and not for other reasons. Needless to say, contemporary letters, newspaper and journal articles, and other surviving written relics of the time, make no mention at all of Washington's birth—for it had no contemporary significance, except for Captain Augustine Washington and his second wife, Mary Ball Washington, the happy parents, and some of their relatives and friends near Pope's Creek in Westmoreland County, Virginia, and some others at, or near, Captain Washington's other valuable property, Epsewasson.[3] Our understanding of the important things that happened on February 22, 1732, is very different from what most people who were alive on that date thought were the important events of the time. Thus, the passage of time—history—changes our perspective of the past, and validates new interpretations all the time.

There also are tertiary sources, which need not concern you very much in conducting your research. Tertiary sources are those

---

[2]In the Gregorian calendar. For George Washington and his parents, the date was February 11, 1732, under the Julian, or "Old Style," calendar, which Britain and its dependencies abandoned in 1752 in favor of the system we use today.

[3]Epsewasson is, in itself, another example of the principle we illustrate here. It belonged to Mildred, Augustine Washington's sister, who transferred it to her brother on May 26, 1726. When Augustine Washington died, April 12, 1743, the property was inherited by his eldest surviving son, Lawrence. He, in turn, had just come home from a two-year term of service in the Royal Navy, during which he had served in the West Indies in a squadron commanded by Vice-Admiral Edward Vernon (1684-1757). When he took possession of Epsewasson, he renamed it in honor of his naval commander and it became Mount Vernon. When Lawrence died, July 22, 1752, his four little children already were dead, and his wife, Anne Fairfax, was wealthy and soon to marry again. Consequently, he left the property to his twenty-year-old half-brother, George—who did not change the name Lawrence had given to the estate. Thus, all the people who were contemporary with the youth of George Washington, including the future president himself, knew the estate as Epsewasson, a name that is hardly familiar to anyone today. However, we think that probably there are few who do not know of Mount Vernon.

which are based exclusively on secondary sources. Their authors have relied on the principal secondary sources in the field in the process of preparing a digest or epitome of a subject. Many college textbooks and almost all general reference works, like encyclopedias, for example, are tertiary sources, whose secondary antecedents are to be found in the chapter or sectional bibliographies in them.

EMANCIPATING YOURSELF THROUGH KNOWLEDGE

We assert that the process of writing the first serious term paper begins the process of setting you free, because you will learn how you can answer any question that you care to ask of yourself through the methods of discovering and analyzing appropriate source materials.[4] When you hear and read debates about the biases of various news media, for example, you will no longer have to concern yourself deeply with such questions, because you will have the ability to search for, discover, and use primary information to answer important questions in both your public and private life.

We also wish to say that what we offer here is a set of methods which, if mastered thoroughly, will give you the skills you need to conduct any inquiry that you wish. Some of you will grasp these methods quickly, while others will do so only after long hours of laborious study followed by many hesitating experiments with the sources we discuss. To both sorts of students, we offer the following realization from our decades of study and research—the "ten hour rule." By this we mean that, though one student may master a particular piece of knowledge, or a specific skill, in one

---

[4]Nearly every government document, newspaper, film and filmed commentary, print, photograph, audio source, and digital file, as well as books and journals of all kinds, can be obtained through the methods of bibliographic scholarship combined with such aids to the student as the interlibrary loan system. For example, the annual *Budget of the United States* is available not only in print from the Government Printing Office in Washington, but also through interlibrary loan from dozens of suppliers; and it is available in full text at a number of sites on the Internet. You need not rely on your local newspaper to tell you what a president has proposed to spend on a certain program or at a certain facility, nor need you depend on television commentary either. You can obtain the information readily and consider it yourself, without the heat of polemic. We will discuss many online sources of information that are useful to the student, and the citizen, in the chapters below.

hour, while another takes ten hours to accomplish the same task, after the ten hours, who can tell the difference between the two. Yes, to become a well-educated person does require some endowment of intelligence, and to pretend otherwise seems foolish to us. But you have that endowment, as exemplified by the fact that you already have mastered those preliminary sets of knowledge and skills—through schooling—which gave you the opportunity to be a college student. Now, with enhanced methods to educate yourself—which we offer here—you can become one who synthesizes new knowledge, one who makes a genuine contribution to humanity's knowledge of itself and of the universe around us.

Yes, many of those who have made the discoveries which made it possible for our modern civilization to be had names which are lost in the mists of the past, or are persons found today generally in footnotes rather than as the subjects of monographs. That does not matter. It is that they did contribute to our understanding which made their lives and their inquiries most meaningful. Consider, for example, all those students of optics and light, from the Renaissance to the nineteenth century, who slowly brought us the knowledge that what we see is not an object itself but rather the light that is reflected from that object. Some of them have names that are known to us very well, like Isaac Newton; while others are now forgotten. Without all of them, and the results of their work, Claude Monet could not have acquired the factual knowledge which prepared him for that relevatory insight—that the artist paints light not things—which his searing genius translated into the great Impressionist landscapes that take our breath away. So, perhaps you are not destined to be the new Monet of your profession, or in your time, but you can add to that store of human understanding which, one day, will illuminate the genius of another like Monet, who, in turn, will inspire generations to come. As students and researchers ourselves, we aspire, and have aspired for many years, to be just such people. We hope you will have a similar desire.

We cannot stress too strongly, and we will emphasize, again and again, the importance of using primary sources as the foundation of all of your research and inquiry. Teaching, as we do, in Washington, D. C., we meet many students who come here because of the proximity of the national government combined with their interest in, or even fascination with, political matters. In that context, we often ask students if they have firm, deliberated opinions on the major political questions of the day. Generally, they do. But, when we ask them if they actually have read the primary documents which molded the political discourse on some public question, we find that they have not. For example, almost everyone has some opinion on the decision of the Supreme Court in the matter of *Roe v. Wade.* Yet, we rarely meet anyone who has, in fact, read the opinions of the Court in this case. These opinons delineate in detail the reasoning of the justices in reaching their decision, and the principles of law they adduced, as well. You may disagree strongly with the decision of the Court, but, we insist, you really have no firm idea of what it is that you reject unless you do read the opinions of those justices who wrote them. These documents are never difficult to discover, and are available widely in libraries and online.[5]

If the problem or question before you is important to you, whether it be a matter of choosing an investment or a matter of grave public policy, you will have the means to determine an answer. Of course, there is no "whole truth;" rather there are pieces of that truth which can be unearthed and viewed as contributions to your understanding. And, just as every writer is biased by background, culture, and experience, so, too, will you become biased—but you will be able to discern the nature of your biases and, one hopes, make rational and logical corrections to account for them.

The process of assembling information and analyzing it in a rigorously logical manner will teach you how to think in a systematic and rational way. It is another view of the principle that Thomas Jefferson had in mind when he stated that a democratic society depends upon an informed and educated citizenry.

---

[5] The general lack of understanding about this matter begins with the fact that most people do not know who Roe is, in spite of the fact that her name is no longer a secret and a feature film has been made of the circumstances of her case, nor do they know who Wade is. We, deliberately, are not giving you a citation for the decision of the Supreme Court, or other scholarly and legal writings about the case, in the hope that, if you are interested in this matter, you will use your research skills to find the appropriate material.

The fact that we make this assertion leads us directly to a short explanation of the nature of the college term paper and its origins. You may have been thinking that you have been assigned to write a term paper because millions before you have received such assignments, and that is just the way it is done, like some sort of complex social rite of passage, but that is not the case.

THE TERM PAPER IS A FORMAL ESSAY

At its essence, the term paper is a seamless expository essay on one topic. As such, it is a genre of writing which goes back to the idea of testing a proposition intellectually and documenting that test in writing. The word *essay* comes to us from the Latin word *exigere*, meaning *to ascertain, to inquire into, to examine.*[6] The word *assay*, in the sense of *to test* or *to prove*, is descended from the same Latin origin and has a cognate meaning.[7] We owe the modern use of the word *essay* to the writings of Michel de Montaigne, who published a set of short disquisitions in 1580 with the title *Essais.*[8]

---

[6]The *Oxford English Dictionary* shows as the oldest definition in English: "the action or process of trying or testing," and the earliest usage of the form as: "a trial, testing, proof; experiment" (2d. ed. (1989), *s. v.* "essay," §I, pt. 1). Shakespeare uses the word in just this sense in his Sonnet 110, line 8: "... worse essays proved thee my best of love." Later, it took on the added significance of: "trying to do something" (§II), that is: "an attempt, endeavour" (§II, pt. 5). By the end of the sixteenth century, the word had added the meaning, which we will discuss in greater detail below: "a composition of moderate length on any particular subject, or branch of a subject; originally implying want of finish, 'an irregular undigested piece' [Samuel Johnson, *A Dictionary of the English Language in which the words are deduced from their originals, and illustrated in their different significations by examples from the best writers: to which are prefixed, a history of the language, and an English grammar,* 2 vols. {London: Printed by W. Strahan, for J. and P. Knapton, 1755}, *s. v.* "essay"], but now said of a composition more or less elaborate in style, though limited in range" (§II, pt. 8). The citation for the standard, library version is J[ohn] A[ndrew] Simpson and E[dmund] S. C. Weiner, eds., *The Oxford English Dictionary,* 2d ed., 20 vols. (Oxford: Clarendon Press, 1989). An online version can be found at URL: telnet://bosshog.arts.uwo.ca/oed/.

[7]The oldest and most fundamental meaning of the word in English is: "the action or process of trying, trial generally." (*Oxford English Dictionary,* 2d. ed., (1989), *s. v.* "assay," §I, pt. 1. "The trying (of a person or thing); trial imposed upon or endured by any object, in order to test its virtue, fitness, etc." (*ibid.*)

[8]Michel de Montaigne, *Essais de messire Michel seignevr de Montaigne, chevalier de l'Ordre du roy, & gentil-homme ordinaire de sa chambre,* 2 vols. (Bovrdeavs [Bor-

The nature of inquiry embodied in these short prose works capti-
vated a number of other European intellectuals of the age, notably,
for us, Francis Bacon, who created the first examples of this new
genre in English.[9] While Montaigne's essays were highly personal
expressions of his thinking in a new literary form, Bacon's essays
were more formal intellectual inquiries in which the author's personal experience apparently played no significant rôle. For more
than a century after their time, neither Montaigne nor Bacon had
serious and successful imitators. During the seventeenth century, a
number of writers wrote treatises which they entitled *essays*, even
though they were long expositions of complex ideas and relationships far removed in style and scope from the short essays of Montaigne and Bacon.

In the early eighteenth century, however, both men came to be
admired as much for the careful explication of their ideas in this
form we call the essay as for the broad and ramified curiosity of
their minds.

The English essay in the eighteenth century owed much of its
tone and its structure to the work of Montaigne, as did the great
essays of the Age of Romanticism from the pens of Charles Lamb,
Thomas De Quincey, and William Hazlitt. After this time, however, this type of essay entered into its present construction, a written expression of personal feeling and insight, such as the essays of
Robert Louis Stevenson, Gilbert Keith Chesterton, and E[lwyn]
B[rooks] White. Today, it survives largely in the form of newspaper columns, of which the best American examples perhaps are by
Franklin P[ierce] Adams, James Thurber, and Eleanor Roosevelt.

The Baconian essay had a different fate. It, too, began to attract
notice and imitation in the eighteenth century and, while it was
eclipsed in the Age of Romanticism by the stylistic ideals of Montaigne, it experienced a tremendous revival with the great Victorian
thinkers. The essays of Matthew Arnold, for example, can be seen
in their structure and elaboration to be evolutions and enlarge-
ments of the highest Baconian type, which had, by now, become

---

deaux]: S. Millanges, 1580).
[9]Francis Bacon [later Lord Chancellor of England, Baron Verulam, and Viscount
St. Albans], *Essayes, Religious Meditations, Places of Perswasion and Disswasion,
Seene and Allowed* (London: Printed [by John Windet] for Humfrey Hooper,
1597).

the chief vehicle for the expression of serious thought. This new interest in the presentation of philosophical or critical conclusions became the model for writing at the great English universities at Oxford and Cambridge. Today, the one thing that such an essay, including the term paper, cannot be is an expression of merely personal feeling and interpretation.

Because you must know something of your subject in order to state conclusions about it, the universities added the anterior task of research and learning to the process of writing the essay. Students were assigned readings by their tutors and then, from these readings, they expressed their new learning in the form of well-crafted written expositions. These became the ancestors of the modern term paper.[10]

During the course of its evolution from the mid-Victorian age to our own time, the term paper has become an ideal vehicle for several processes of learning.

First, the student breaks away from the fetters imposed by the authority of the teacher in order to pursue independent study on a topic which has a discrete body of knowledge about it. In the perfected form of this process, the student is encouraged to discover the primary sources which apply to her topic, to retrieve and read them, and to use them as the central elements of her analysis.

Second, the student learns how to use the mechanical techniques and arts of research, from discovering references in scholarly literature to using online databases and catalogues to further the discovery of appropriate materials for study. In this way, the habits which are necessary for writing a good dissertation, a long scholarly article, or a useful and knowledgeable business report begin to form themselves. It is, in effect, the student's introduction to the life of the mind.

---

[10]The phrase "term paper" is American in its origin, and dates probably to the later years of the last century, although the *Oxford English Dictionary* (2d. ed., 1989, *s. v.* "term," §VI, pt. 17: "an essay or dissertation representative of the work done during a single term") gives its first example in print from a publication in 1931: "... a long term paper that will incorporate the results of a semester's reading." (Frances N. Ahl, "The Technique of the Term Paper," *The High School Journal*, XIV:1 [January, 1931], 17). In England, today, such an exercise is still generally called an essay.

Third, by offering to the student the opportunity to practice the analysis of causation from primary materials, the writing of a term paper releases her from dependence on secondary authority as the sole source of "truths" about any topic. The student experiences the priceless freedom of being able to find germane materials and to use them to discover the nearest approach possible to the truth of any matter.

Clearly, the experience of one term paper does not make a finished scholar, or an educated woman or man. It does, however, provide the same introductory guidance as a first piano lesson and the first eighteen holes of a lifetime of golf. The research, analysis, synthesis, and writing of the term paper show the student, by practical means, the methods she can use in every kind of intellectual inquiry to determine concrete answers to questions which may be difficult and complex. Like every other elaborate intellectual technique, the art of the term paper must be perfected through practice and repetition. But it is the first paper, typically written by a freshman in an English, history, or chemistry class, that serves as the foundation for all future intellectual expansion and growth.

Before we begin our journey towards intellectual freedom and independence, it may be worthwhile to consider the relative labels that are attached to the material you will discover in your research.

WHAT WILL YOU DISCOVER?

Consider the following nouns: *data, information, knowledge,* and *wisdom.* The first element, even in the plural, has no intrinsic value at all, because it is not connected in any visible way with any other collection of elements like itself. Let us say that you see the number "7." By itself, it has some value as a numerical indicator, but whatever importance it has lies solely within itself, and not in association with anything else. It is a *datum.* If we add three other numerals, concatenated in a selected way, "1776," we now have some *data* which may prove to be valuable, but we cannot discern whether this is true or not merely from the figures alone. Perhaps you already have begun to associate these figures with other data you have learned earlier. If you have, well and good. But the data "1776" does not signify anything of absolute importance. You may think that it represents a date, but, in itself, it represents nothing except "1776."

You can collect other associated data to complement your original "1776." You may add "July," and "4," and "Thomas," and "Jefferson," to your collection, as well as the preliminary analytical conclusion that the initial set of data represents a year in the Gregorian calendar. Still, what have you now in your possession? A small collection of *information* which, of itself, has little significance. It does allow you to determine how long ago this date was, relative to today's date, if you also use the Gregorian calendar, and the additional data "Thomas Jefferson" seems to be the name of a person who, you may wish to presume, was alive in that year. So, information it is, and it does have weight, because it is related in a logical stream to other data you already possess—today's date, for example, and the recognition that words like "Thomas" and "Jefferson" are most frequently found as the names of persons.

Notice, however, that this small collection of information has no relative importance to anything outside itself. When you group it together with many other items of information, from the smallest collection of data with inherent philosophical importance—"When in the course of human events . . ."— to larger historical issues of the past, the American Revolution and the first efforts by any European colony to become an independent political entity on the same footing in the world as the monarchies of Europe, you begin to have a collection of *knowledge*, not merely information.

One can understand the essential difference between information and knowledge by considering the nature of television quiz shows that are based on a display of the former. The game asks the contestant to recall and display information, not connected in any way to any element outside itself, and does not require the contestant to *know* anything at all. To possess information is not to possess knowledge.

This important distinction must be kept firmly in mind throughout the whole process of researching, analyzing, and synthesizing material for a term paper, since the object of the paper itself is to display a mastery of new knowledge and to use that knowledge to reach new conclusions. These accomplishments will not spring automatically from a vast assembly of information, no matter how difficult it may have been to find and collect.

Finally, the faculty of *wisdom* consists of being able to relate bodies of knowledge to one another, often in appropriate collections of several bodies of knowledge. Largely because we are inundated with huge collections of data and massive arrays of information today, we do not often grasp even the concept of knowledge, let alone the quality of wisdom. How long has it been since anyone was described publicly as a wise woman or a wise man? The word *wise* today is restricted to the epithet "wise guy" and, perhaps, to the story of the "Wise Men" at Epiphany. Yet, the quality of wisdom has not disappeared. It awaits a new generation of students and scholars who understand how to identify and then how to use, with accuracy, *data, information,* and *knowledge*; and, then, to relate bodies of knowledge to one another in such a way as to provide new insights into the human condition and into the universe which surrounds us—actions which become the synthesis of new understandings that will advance human understanding about humanity.

THREE BASIC ASSUMPTIONS FOR RATIONAL THINKING

As you begin to think about any topic, and to plan the methods you will use to collect information about it, there are three fundamental principles of analysis which you need to keep in mind from the very first day of your work. The first of these is Occam's Razor.[11] It has been stated in a number a varying forms through

---

[11]William of Occam or Ockham (c. 1285 – c. 1349) joined the Franciscan order while still very young and then studied at Oxford but never took his degree. He is, pre-eminently, the perpetual student, and is often given the honorific title *Venerabilis Inceptor,* the venerable freshman. Imprisoned for a time in Avignon by Pope John XXII, he fled to the protection of the Emperor Louis [IV] of Bavaria and became a leading defender of imperial claims over papal, which laid much of the foundation for modern theories of government. As a great logician, his fame rests primarily upon his *Summa Logicæ,* which is where his own phrasing of his famous "Razor" is to be found: "Essentia non sunt multiplicanda præter necessitatem" ["Essences are not to be multiplied beyond necessity"]. The first printed edition of this work is: *Tractatus Logicae* (Paris: Johann Higman, 1488); while the principal modern scholarly edition is: *Summa Logicæ,* vol. 1 of *Editiones Instituti Franciscani, Universitatis S. Bonaventurae: Guillelmi de Ockham. Opera Phi-*

the centuries, but its clearest presentation is: *The simplest explanation which accounts for all of the variables is the one explanation which is most likely to be true.* Notice that this rule for examining evidence does not say that the simplest explanation is the true one, nor does it say that true explanations are simple. Rather it asserts that the most straightforward explanation into which all of the data fit sensibly is the explanation which is **most likely** to be the true one. Remember, in this regard, that the *art* in research, as opposed to the *science* or the *technique*, consists, in large measure, in accounting for as many of the variables as you can.

The second principle that you should remember is Sherlock Holmes's rule: *When you have eliminated the impossible, whatever remains, however improbable, must be the truth.*[12] You must employ this maxim carefully, because some things that you will encounter in your first exercise in serious research may appear to be impossible, and yet may be perfectly true.[13] Consequently, you

---

losophica et Theologica: Opera Philosophica (St. Bonaventure, New York: [Institutionum Franciscanum, Universitatis S. Bonaventuræ], 1974). A recent text which includes the original exposition of Occam's Razor is *Philosophical Writings* (Edinburgh: Thomas Nelson and Sons, Ltd., 1957). A recent extensive consideration of his thought is Marilyn McCord Adams, *William Ockham*, 2 vols. (Notre Dame, Indiana: University of Notre Dame Press, 1987).

[12]This famous Holmesian precept is found in chapter six of the second novel about Sherlock Holmes, *The Sign of Four*:

"You [Watson] will not apply my precept," he [Holmes] said, shaking his head. "How often have I said to you that when you have eliminated the impossible, whatever remains, however improbable, must be the truth? We know that he did not come through the door, the window, or the chimney. We also know that he could not have been concealed in the room, as there is no concealment possible. When, then, did he come?"

"He came through the hole in the roof!" I [Watson] cried.

"Of course he did. He must have done so. If you will have the kindness to hold the lamp for me, we shall now extend our researches to the room above—the secret room in which the treasure was found."

See A. Conan Doyle, *The Complete Sherlock Holmes* (Garden City, New York: Garden City Publishing Company, Inc., 1938) 118.

[13] For example, a young student who was researching the battle between H. M. S. *Shannon* and the U. S. S. *Chesapeake*, on June 1, 1813—the occasion on which the *Chesapeake's* commander, James Lawrence, uttered the famous phrase, "Don't give up the ship"—learns that, after the victory of the *Shannon*, the prize was placed under the command of a twenty-two-year old British midshipman, Provo Wallis, to be taken under sail to Halifax, Nova Scotia. Her two modern monographic histories of the battle, Kenneth Poolman, *Guns off Cape Ann: The Story of*

need to understand, from both an historical and a scientific perspective, just what is impossible and what is merely improbable.

---

the Shannon and the Chesapeake (Chicago: Rand McNally, 1961) and H[ugh] F[rancis] Pullen, *The Shannon and the Chesapeake* (Toronto: McClelland and Stewart, 1970), as well as the standard biography of Sir Philip Bowes Vere Broke (1776-1841), the Shannon's commander, Peter Padfield, *Broke and the Shannon* (London: Hodder & Stoughton, 1968), all agree on the identity of the leader of the Cheaspeake's prize crew. When she searches British published records for Provo Wallis, she finds—very readily—Admiral of the Fleet Sir Provo William Parry Wallis, who was a leading figure of naval command in Britain in the later nineteenth century. A standard reference to persons of importance in British military and governmental affairs, Joseph Haydn, *The Book of Dignities*, 3d. ed., continued by Horace Ockerby (London: W. H. Allen, 1894; reprinted Bath: Firecrest Publishing Limited, 1969; reprinted Baltimore: Genealogical Publishing Company, 1970), shows many citations of him. He was appointed Rear Admiral of the Red on August 27, 1851 (p. 829), passed through the other grades of admirals in the Royal Navy in the period before 1864, and became Rear Admiral of the United Kingdom on July 17, 1869, and Vice Admiral of the United Kingdom on February 12, 1870 (p. 822). On May 18, 1860, he was made a knight commander of the Order of the Bath (K. C. B.) (p. 778) and, on May 24, 1873, he became a knight grand cross of the same order (G. C. B.) (p. 770). She learns, further, that the Admiral died in 1892, while still on active duty, technically.

At this point in her research, which after all concerns a naval battle in 1813, and not the history of British law concerning naval officers in the nineteenth century, she does not know that the several reforms of the navy carried out in the middle years of the century placed naval officers from the period of the Napoleonic Wars on a retired list, unless, **specifically**, they had enjoyed an independent command before the close of hostilities—which Provo Wallis had, by virtue of his few days as commander of the prize crew that Broke had transferred from the *Shannon* to the *Chesapeake*. She decides, therefore, that the admiral cannot possibly be the same person as the commander of the prize crew, and that, perhaps, he is the son, or even the grandson, of the earlier figure. On the basis of Sherlock Holmes's rule, she eliminates the admiral from her research consideration. Later, but, fortunately, before she submits the final version of her paper, she discovers two other books, J[ohn] G[eorge] Brighton, *Admiral of the Fleet, Sir Provo W. P. Wallis: A Memoir* (London: Hutchinson, 1892) and William C. Heine, *96 Years in the Royal Navy: The Astonishing Story of Halifax-born Admiral of the Fleet Sir Provo Wallis* (Hantsport, N[ova] S[cotia]: Lancelot Press, 1987), which reveal to her that, incredibly, what she thought to be impossible was only highly improbable—Admiral Sir Provo Wallis was, indeed, the same man who had sailed the *Chesapeake* into Halifax harbor seventy-nine years before his death, and that, through a quirk in legal reform, he had remained on active duty until his end, at the age of one hundred one.

Third, and the most human of all, is to remember that the people of the past, and the things that they created and did, fall inside the same limits of the human condition—precisely the same limits—as the nature of the people living today, including, of course, you yourself. This principle is embodied in Hanlon's Corollary: *Never ascribe to evil or malice those things for which there is an explanation of ignorance or stupidity.*[14]

These three aphorisms will act as a constant corrective to both wild speculation, on the one hand, and illogical and unconnected conclusions, on the other. Later, in this volume, we will discuss more fully the principles of the historical and scientific methods of research, and these maxims will return again.

We began our consideration of the genealogy of the term paper with a discussion of the contribution of Francis Bacon to the genre of the essay, that best form for the expression of human knowledge. It is not without reason that many critics and scholars still regard Bacon's essays, though the earliest in English, as the finest examples of the form that have ever been written. We now end this chapter by quoting one of his shortest essays, yet one of his most important:

> Studies serve for delight, for ornament, and for ability. Their chief use for delight is in privateness and retiring; for ornament, is in discourse; and for ability, is in the judgment and disposition of business. For expert men can execute, and perhaps judge of particulars, one by one; but the general counsels, and the plots and marshaling of affairs, come best from those that are learned. To spend too much time in studies is sloth; to use them too much for ornament is affectation; to make judgment wholly by their rules is the humor of a scholar. They perfect nature, and are perfected by experience; for natural abilities are like natural plants, that need pruning by study; and studies themselves do give forth directions too much at large, except they be bounded in by experience. Crafty men contemn studies, simple men admire them, and wise men use them, for they teach not their own use; but

---

[14]We would like to tell you something about Hanlon, but we cannot. We have tried to identify him for several years, but with no success at all. If you know who he was, please write to us. We will appreciate it very much.

18

that is a wisdom without them, and above them, won by observation. Read not to contradict and confute, nor to believe and take for granted, nor to find talk and discourse, but to weigh and consider. Some books are to be tasted, others to be swallowed, and some few to be chewed and digested; that is, some books are to be read only in parts; others to be read, but not curiously; and some few to be read wholly, and with diligence and attention. Some books also may be read by deputy and extracts made of them by others, but that would be only in the less important arguments and the meaner sort of books; else distilled books are like common distilled waters, flashy things. Reading maketh a full man, conference a ready man, and writing an exact man. And therefore, if a man write little, he had need have a great memory; if he confer little, he had need have a present wit; and if he read little, he had need have more cunning, to seem to know that he doth not. Histories make men wise; poets, witty; the mathematics, subtle; natural philosophy, deep; moral, grave; logic and rhetoric, able to contend. *Abeunt studia in mores.* Nay, there is no stone or impediment in the wit but may be wrought out by fit studies, like as diseases of the body may have appropriate exercises. Bowling is good for the stone and reins, shooting for the lungs and breast, gentle walking for the stomach, riding for the head, and the like. So if a man's wit be wandering, let him study the mathematics; for in demonstrations, if his wit be called away never so little, he must begin again. If his wit be not apt to distinguish or find differences, let him study the schoolmen, for they are *Cymini sectores.* If he be not apt to beat over matters and to call up one thing to prove and illustrate another, let him study the lawyer's cases. So every defect of the mind may have a special receipt.

Choosing Your Topic

Many instructors prefer to assign topics that they have selected themselves. If your instructor has done this, you will need to read this section only to prepare yourself to write papers later on topics you choose yourself.

Most professors, however, do give college students some latitude in selecting their own topics. Often, the instructor will limit your choice to a specific kind of subject, perhaps from her own field of study. This is valid, because your instructor has many students to teach in each semester, and this approach makes it easier for her to know readily whether or not you have done appropriate research, because she knows the sources and the secondary writings on such topics very well. Other instructors will allow you the widest possible latitude in selecting a topic, unlimited by any consideration of academic field.

If you are writing this paper for an English class, you may be asked to write an *explication de texte*. In this type of paper, the student takes a short work of literature, often a poem, essay, or short story, and unearths all of the background to its authorship as well as the critical writings about the work, and then composes an extensive disquisition in which she uses her analysis to come as close as possible to the presumed intention of the work. As its name implies, the *explication de texte*, as a formal essay, began in France, in the last century.[15]

If you are writing this paper for a chemistry course, you may be given the name of a compound and asked to describe in detail, and to document thoroughly, all of the chemical reactions which take place in generating your compound. Such assignments may range

---

[15]For a brief discussion of this form, see J[ohn] A[nthony] Cuddon, *A Dictionary of Literary Terms and Literary Theory*, 3d rev. ed. (Oxford: Blackwell Reference, Basil Blackwell Ltd., 1991) 318; and C. Hugh Holman, *A Handbook to Literature, Based on the Original by William Flint Thrall and Addison Hibbard*, 3d ed. (Indianapolis, Indiana: Odyssey Press, The Bobbs-Merrill Company, Inc., 1972) 214. In its traditional form, the *explication de texte* is a formative exercise in exegesis and leads to longer monographs in which texts, sometimes Biblical, are examined with great thoroughness.

from somewhat simple compounds, like acetylsalicylic acid or Monel metal, to complex atomic structures, like Bucky balls.

We will suppose, however, that you have been given the widest possible latitude in choosing a topic by a generous and understanding professor.

With this in mind, you should select a topic which grows from an interest or enthusiasm that you already have. One student, with a lifelong, passionate interest in poisonous snakes chose to do a study on *Vipera berus*, the common adder, which is not only prolific throughout Eurasia but also is the only venomous creature native to Britain.[16] In his research, he limited himself to the historical placement of *V. berus* in the Linnean classification in the eighteenth century and then to studies of its taxonomic placement thereafter. This made a most suitable topic, because the student could go straight to the work of Karl Linné for his initial discussion,[17] and then follow the taxonomic trail forward to the present day.

Another useful avenue for you to explore while you are deciding on your topic is the primary resources that are available to you in your college or university library or archive and in city or county historical societies. Almost everywhere you look, if you will look, you will find large numbers of diaries, journals, letters, and other papers that survive from the past. Often, they are the only tangible objects which preserve the realities of the lives of many people who have now been forgotten. Every locality in the country has its memories of people of the past who made a significant difference in the lives of their contemporaries, some simply in a local sphere, others, perhaps, on a national or even global stage. Every community has its past artists and soldiers, engineers and politicians, businessmen and activists whose deeds and thoughts were of some substantial significance at one time. Some of these people had original ideas and plans which later stretched far beyond the

---

[16]It appears not to have made it to Ireland. Of course, tradition has it that it did, and that St. Patrick drove it from the island. One Irishman of our acquaintance insists that the English did not invade Ireland in the mid-twelfth century, but that the Irish imported the English to restore ecological balance.

[17]He needed help in translating the original published Latin text into modern English, but that was readily obtainable—for such assistance is to be found easily on most college or university campuses, as we will discuss later in this book.

original intention to have a major effect on the world after their time. You may be surprised at the fascinating body of primary materials about such people that you can find, quite readily, in collections near you.

For example, students at Gettysburg College, in Gettysburg, Pennsylvania, have used the famous battle that was fought there as a point of departure for doing research on both Federal and Confederate soldiers who participated in it. Not the generals, or even the colonels, but rather the lesser ranked, but still important, men who found themselves thrust together on those three famous days.

The principal tenet in choosing a topic is that a very narrowly defined topic, well researched and well analyzed, will be far more likely to reveal new knowledge and fresh insight than a broad topic which has been treated before in many monographs and articles.

Indeed, if you find so much as one book written on the topic you are considering, you will know that your topic is far too broad, and that it needs to be narrowed significantly—although you need not abandon the subject altogether. After all, you are writing a term paper during the course of one semester, in which you will have only a relatively few hours to do all the work that is necessary to produce a good, if miniature, work of scholarship. You are not writing a book, a master's thesis, or a doctoral dissertation, although the same principles that we discuss here will apply to researching and writing them, as well. We do want to mention that several of our students have taken the final texts of their term papers as the foundation for master's theses, and, in one case, of a first-rate doctoral dissertation.

A detailed examination of the tactics of the battle of Waterloo done by a novice in the art of the term paper is far less likely to teach the reader anything new about the battle—which has been analyzed over and over again by the greatest authorities in the history of that period—than a consideration of Napoleon's years-long suffering from hæmorrhoids and how his distress during the opening days of June, 1815, may well have affected the course of European history.[18]

---

[18]See D. R. Welling, B. G. Wolff, and R. R. Dozois, "Piles of Defeat: Napoleon

Novices at the art of the term paper often ask their instructors how many sources or how many references they must use in writing their term papers. The straightforward answer is, of course, *all* of the sources which apply to the topic—whose number is, clearly, unknown when you begin the process of research. Because you will endeavor to locate all of the germane sources, your topic should be quite narrow in scope, so that you can, realistically, gather together all of the relevant material and analyze it during the course of the fourteen or sixteen weeks of your semester.

We recommend strongly to our students that they choose topics which are based on events that happened before the opening of World War I in 1914 or which concern people whose principal activities occurred before that year. Since we emphasize the use of primary materials, topics drawn primarily from the twentieth century often involve materials which still are inaccessible to the student. For example, most military documents from the period of World War I and after, and a considerable volume of other governmental documentation, as well, remain classified—and, hence, unretrievable without a need to know their contents. The private papers of noted persons of this century are often still in the hands of the families or other heirs of those persons and they may be unwilling to make them available, even to established scholars. If they are in libraries or archival collections, their use may be covered by restrictions, often for a fixed number of years after the author's or donor's death. Finally, because a classical analysis of causes and effects can deal only with a process that is closed, no event or person whose effects continue directly today can be the subject of such an analysis. Thus, you should exclude the most modern topics, especially in the case of the first research paper of substance.

One significant example of the problems that arise with serious historical considerations of topics in the twentieth century, and which illustrates both the difficulties in dealing with classified, and formerly-classified, information, on the one hand, and and the inaccessibility of primary materials—in this case the wreck of a ship—on the other, is the case of the circumstances and causes of the sinking of the *Lusitania* on May 7, 1915. From the moment of

at Waterloo," *Diseases of the Colon and Rectum*, vol. 31, no. 4 (April, 1988): 303-305, an article we use an example of bibliographic searching in MEDLINE, below.

the two tandem explosions, the first small and almost insignificant, the second massive and cataclysmic, arguments flew from every quarter about who was to blame and what caused the ship to sink so rapidly, which, in turn, greatly increased the cost in human life. To the Anglo-American claims, that the Germans purposefully sank the vessel as a symbol of their new policy of unrestricted submarine warfare, came the riposte that the second, and more devastating, explosion came as a consequence of the secondary explosion of a shipment of munitions in a civilian passenger liner—thus imputing to the British the use of the passengers as human shields for a part of the British strategic war plans. Literally hundreds of newspaper stories and articles dealt with these issues for more than seventy-five years without shedding any real light on what precisely had happened.[19] Several lengthy monographs in later years attempted to sift through all of the surviving public papers to determine an authoritative answer, but without much success, because the primary evidence, the remains of the ship itself, did not figure in the analysis in these books.[20] In fact, the second, critical explosion was caused by an aerosol suspension of coal dust in the transverse bunkers of the ship, and neither by the destructive power of the German torpedo nor the explosion of munitions stowed on the liner, although there were some. The truth was not glimpsed until the famous undersea pioneer, Robert D. Ballard, undertook a careful exploration of the wreck of the *Lusitania* in 1993. His subsequent articles[21] and his book[22] finally offered a

[19]Three important examples of these are Brenda Ralph Lewis, "Lusitania," *British Heritage* 2:5 (1981): 46-55; E. M. Halliday, "Who Sank the *Lusitania*?," *American Heritage* 27:1 (1975): 33-35, 96, an important book review of *The Lusitania Disaster*, discussed below; and Oscar Handlin, "A Liner, A U-Boat. . . and History," *American Heritage* 6:4 (1955): 40-45, 105.

[20]The two most important of these contributions are Colin Simpson, *Lusitania* (Harlow [London]: Longman, 1972; reprinted Harmondsworth: Penguin, 1974) and Thomas Andrew Bailey and Paul B. Ryan, *The Lusitania Disaster: An Episode in Modern Warfare and Diplomacy* (New York: Free Press, 1975). The later volume was a reply to the thesis offered by Simpson and, in turn, offered substantially different explanations for the event.

[21]Robert D Ballard, "Riddle of the *Lusitania*," *National Geographic* 185 (April, 1994): 68-85 and Robert D. Ballard, Spencer Dunsmore, and John Christie, "Exploring the *Lusitania*," *The American Neptune* 56:1 (1996).

[22]Robert D.Ballard, with Spencer Dunsmore, *Exploring the Lusitania: Probing the Mysteries of the Sinking that Changed History* (London: Weidenfeld & Nicolson,

quite plausible and realistic explanation of what actually happened. Thus, only the readers of the 1990's, and after, really begin to understand the historical reality of an event in 1915. This example shows why students should try, through all possible avenues, to have recourse to primary materials and why they should avoid topics of a more recent date.

Before we proceed to show an example of how you can narrow a topic to an effective length, we should mention that, of course, you should choose a topic in which the largest bulk of the primary source material is in languages you that can read. You may well unearth some materials in unfamiliar languages, as you progress in your research, and, later, we will show you how you can get expert help to determine the value of those materials and to have the relevant portions of them translated. An additional benefit that you will gain when you find some materials in a foreign language that you know is that you will perfect and enhance your knowledge and understanding of that language, through the careful use you will make of it as you examine and translate documents in it. But, it cannot be stressed too strongly that a topic is altogether unsuitable if the principal sources for it are in a language that you do not know.[23]

૎૏ ૎૏ ૎૏

Here is one concrete example of how a general interest can lead you to choose a specific, narrow topic for a term paper.

A student with an interest in the American Civil War stated that she wished to write her freshman term paper on that subject. Once she searched the principal online catalogues, she discovered more than four thousand monographs on the subject and its related

---

1995). See also William H. Garzke Jr, David K. Brown, Arthur D. Sandiford, John Woodward, and Peter K. Hsu, "The *Titanic* and *Lusitania*: A Final Forensic Analysis," *Marine Technology* 33:4 (1996) and Peter Lewis, "Revealed: What Really Sank the *Lusitania*," Toronto *Daily Mail*, 7 October 1995, pp. 40, 42, an excellent synopsis and review of Ballard's discoveries.

[23]This consideration, for example, escaped the young film enthusiast who wished to write a paper on the first films of François Truffault, but could not read French; and the young woman who wished to write, albeit narrowly, about the experience of one person in a German concentration camp, but who read no German.

topics, even without considering the thousands upon thousands of scholarly and general-interest articles that have been published about the War. At first, she thought that narrowing the topic to the Battle of Gettysburg would prove to be sufficient. But, here again, she found hundreds of books and articles on the topic. Remembering the maxim that any topic which already has been, by itself, the subject of a monograph is far too large to be appropriate for a term paper, she gathered a few preliminary items about Gettysburg to seek a smaller and more discrete topic which would be manageable within the constraints of her class schedule, her need to work part-time, and her access to useable primary materials. First, she reviewed one of the standard, traditional histories of the battle, *The Gettysburg Campaign: A Study in Command,* by Edwin B. Coddington.[24] She was struck, in reading Coddington's discussion of the Union Eleventh Corps, with how many foreign and foreign-born officers were in command—the Third Division, in particular, was led by three Germans and a Pole.[25] Later, in reading of the actions on the evening of July 2, 1863, she discovered the critical rôle of the divisions of the Eleventh Corps in protecting the flank of Cemetery Ridge during the Confederate onslaught at that time. The men of the Second Brigade of the Third Division,[26] under the command of Colonel Wladimir KrzyÔanowski, with fixed bayonets, rushed forward to rescue the light artillery batteries which were then suffering the worst Confederate pressure. Their prompt action, without hesitation, saved the Union flank from the possibility of being rolled up and this, in turn, preserved the essential tactical strength of the Union forces during this stage of the battle.

Since she was of Polish ancestry, she decided to learn more about the life and career of Colonel KrzyÔanowski. She soon discovered that he was the highest ranking Pole present on either side of the engagement.

She then turned her attention to a number of published bibliographies solely on the topic of the Battle of Gettysburg. Among

---

[24]Edwin B. Coddington, *The Gettysburg Campaign: A Study in Command* (New York: Charles Scribner's Sons, 1968).

[25]*ibid.*, 306, 583-584.

[26] Including elements of the 58th New York, 119th New York, 82nd Ohio, 75th Pennsylvania, and 26th Wisconsin. See *Coddington*, 584.

them, and, indeed, a valuable resource for anyone interested in this pivotal encounter of the War, is the almost comprehensive work of Richard Sauers.[27]

When she consulted this work, she looked first for references to the units which had been under KrzyÔanowski's command during the battle. She found nothing specific about either the 58th New York or the 82nd Ohio, but she did find a number of entries about the other three regiments, the 119th New York, the 75th Pennsylvania, and the 26th Wisconsin.[28] In addition, she found one listing in the index to Sauers's book which referred directly to material about KrzyÔanowski.[29] When she consulted that citation, she found two other works that also discussed the troops under his command.

Using her original preliminary bibliography, she then turned to a reference work which provides short biographies of all of those men who became general officers during the Civil War, on the chance that KrzyÔanowski had been promoted beyond the rank of colonel at some time after the Battle of Gettysburg.[30] She was

---

[27]Richard Allen Sauers, *The Gettysburg Campaign, June 3 – August 1, 1863: A Comprehensive, Selectively Annotated Bibliography* (Westport, Connecticut: Greenwood Press, 1982).

[28]The material she found on the 119th New York was Theodore A. Dodge, "Left Wounded on the Field," *Putnam's Monthly Magazine* 4 (1869): 317-326; and New York Infantry, 119th Regiment, *Ceremonies and Addresses at the Dedication of a Monument by the 119th Regiment, N. Y. State Volunteers at Gettysburg, July 3, 1888.* (Boston: Wright and Potter Printing Company, 1889). The book on the 75th Pennsylvania was Hermann Nachtigill, *Geschichte des 75sten Regiments, Pa. Vols.* (Philadelphia: C. B. Kretschman, 1886). The 26th Wisconsin was represented by two entries, one of which was a list of casualties of the battle which appeared in the *New York Times* on July 8, 1863. The other was Albert Welber, "From Gettysburg to Libby Prison," in the series *Wisconsin War Papers* of the Military Order of the Loyal Legion of the United States, Wisconsin Commandery, vol. 4 (Milwaukee: Burdick, Amitage & Allen, 1914). This latter essay was reprinted in Ken Bandy and Florence Freeland, comps., *The Gettysburg Papers*, 2 vols. (Dayton, Ohio: Press of Morningside, 1978).

[29]Wladimir KrzyÔanowski, *Wspomnienia z pobytu w Ameryce Gen. W̄odzimierza KrzyÔanowskiego podczas wojny, 1861-1864*, vol. 1 of *Roczniki historyczne Polskiego Muzeum w Ameryce* (Chicago: Polish Museum of America, 1963), translated by James S. Pula as *The Memoirs of Wladimir KrzyÔanowski* (San Francisco: R & E Research Associates, 1978).

[30]Ezra J. Warner, *Generals in Blue: Lives of the Union Commanders* (Baton Rouge, [Louisiana]: Louisiana State University Press, 1964).

fortunate, because Krzyzanowski was raised to the rank of brevet brigadier general of volunteers on March 2, 1865, and thus merited inclusion in Ezra Warner's biographies.[31] From the citation in Warner, she found another source, a comprehensive guide to foreigners who had fought on the Federal side in the War.[32]

From the material in Warner's brief biography, she also learned that it was probable that Wladimir KrzyÔanowski was the highest ranking Pole not only at Gettysburg but, in fact, throughout the War, on either side. A supposition that she was able to verify by examining meticulously the headings in the volume of Warner that she already had, and by examining, in a similar way, Warner's companion volume on Southern generals.[33]

But, as she would soon discover, the General wrote a short memoir of his American career after the War[34] and he was the subject of two lengthy monographs by the same author.[35]

She decided to investigate, with great accuracy and precision, his specific actions at the Battle of Gettysburg, and how his ready response to the emergencies of the evening of July 2 contributed to the Union success at the battle.

In this manner, at the expense of a few hours's review of a few standard sources, which she was able to locate readily, she found a topic that was both manageable and for which she could obtain at least published primary sources. The topic also was a congenial one, because she was sufficiently familiar with both the Polish language and Polish culture to be able to take advantage of sources in Polish, when she found them. Thus, she combined her interest in the American Civil War with her knowledge of her own heritage, a particular asset, to find a very appropriate topic. You, too, should

---

[31] *ibid.*, 273-275.

[32] Ella Lonn, *Foreigners in the Union Army and Navy* (Baton Rouge, Louisiana: Louisiana State University Press, 1951).

[33] Ezra J. Warner, *Generals in Gray: Lives of the Confederate Commanders* (Baton Rouge, [Louisiana]: Louisiana State University Press, 1959).

[34] See note 26, above. This was her principal primary source.

[35] James S. Pula, "Na Polu Chwa⁻y: the Life and Times of W⁻odzimierz KrzyÔanowski (Polish Immigrant, Civil War General, Federal Agent)" Ph. D. diss., Purdue University, 1973; and James S. Pula, *For Liberty and Justice: the Life and Times of Wladimir KrzyÔanowski* (Chicago: Polish American Congress Charitable Foundation, 1978). She later learned that the book was the revised and enlarged text of the dissertation. These became her chief secondary sources.

review your intellectual and existential assets, honestly and carefully, when you choose your topic. Are you interested in metallurgical engineering? If you are, you may wish to consider a paper on the invention and development of Cor-Ten, a once-famous high strength, low-alloy steel. Is music your field? Consider some aspect of the history of the baryton, or the ophecleide. The number of specific, discrete, and narrow topics is greater than the whole number of historically-known people—because each one of them is a topic. And, to that number, you can add all of the devices, artifacts, and processes those people left to posterity, and thus to you. The possibilities are endless.

The archives of your own college or university will contain hundreds of primary documents which are waiting to form the foundation of interesting research papers. In almost every case, you can find the original documentation which tells the story of the foundation and early years of your college, materials which can lead to an article that you may publish in one of your college's journals. Nearby, you will find state, county, city, and other local historical societies, whose collections are rich with materials on the history of the region and on the lives of the men and women who made your community, state, or region what it is today. [36]Almost every professional and special interest society has both a library and an archive in which you can discover fascinating topics that are well within the scope of your project.[37] In addition, you can find special

---

[36]You can discover exhaustive guides to these resources by searching for them in online union catalogues, like OCLC and the Library of Congress catalogue. We will describe how to do this later in this book. One serial you may wish to consult is the *Directory of Genealogical and Historical Society Libraries, Archives, and Collections in the US and Canada* (Niwot, Colorado: Iron Gate Publishing, annually). Are you from the vicinity of Santa Clara, California? Then you may want to consult *The Directory of Heritage Organizations and Resources* (San Jose, California: Heritage Council of Santa Clara County, 1994). How about Ohio? Don't miss the *Directory of Historical Organizations in Ohio*, 4th ed. (Columbus, Ohio: Ohio Historical Society, 1994). It describes itself as "a guide to historical societies, historical museums, historic sites, historic preservation organizations, genealogical societies, historical libraries, and statewide/regional historical associations." There are hundreds of such guides to local or regional resources, and you are sure to find the right one, if you search carefully.

[37]The most valuable aid to discovering these societies and associations is the *Encyclopedia of Associations: A Guide to more than 23,000 National and International Organizations*, 31st ed., 3 vols. (Detroit: Gale Research Company, 1996). The

collections of archival and manuscript materials on many fields of interest and study, including the archives of learned, fraternal, and professional societies; newspaper morgues, and public records of all kinds.[38] In the eastern states of the United States, property records, wills and testaments, and other legal documents that are stored in county courthouses and other public repositories will allow you to explore the lives and deeds of persons who pioneered in the European settlement of your region, and, in addition, you can use these records to trace the history of famous sites and buildings which have been important in the history of your area. And you should not forget museums as places to look for a topic![39]

---

third volume of this work is a keyword index to the first two. Use it to look up subjects that are interesting to you and then use the detailed information under each entry to contact the appropriate organizations. The *Encyclopedia of Associations* also is available online through both the LEXIS/NEXIS service of Mead Data and the DIALOG system of Knight-Ridder. We will discuss both of these, in some detail, below.

[38]There are many sorts of guides to these records which you can find in a careful search of your library's cataloguing resources—online, in microform, and in card form. Two national guides of importance are *The Sourcebook of County Court Records: A National Guide to Civil, Criminal and Probate Records at the County and Municipal Levels within the State Court Systems*, 2nd ed. (Tempe, Arizona: BRB Publications, Inc., 1995) and *The Sourcebook of County Asset/Lien Records: A National Guide to All County/City Government Agencies where Real Estate Transactions, UCC Financing Statements, and Federal/State Tax Liens are Recorded* (Tempe, Arizona: BRB Publications, 1995). Also keep in mind that many local historical societies, genealogical interest groups and clubs, and the court systems themselves frequently have published guides to the public and local records of interest or importance to them. Are you interested in someone who lived and worked in New York City or its vicinity? Do not forget to find and review Fred D. Knapp, *New York Public Records Guide: Southern New York Region*, 5th ed. (New York, New York: REYN Incorporated, 1994).

[39]If you wish to consider this possibility, do not forget to consult *The Official Museum Directory*, 26th ed. (1996) (New Providence, New Jersey: R. R. Bowker, 1995). This massive work is updated frequently. Your college library may well have it in the reference collection. You can find many other specialized directories of archives, museums, and special collections by searching for them in OCLC, or another online union catalogue, with these specific subject terms together with the title "directory" or "guide." For instance, if you are in New Mexico, you will not want to miss the *Directory of Special Libraries and Collections in New Mexico*, 3rd. ed. ([Albuquerque, New Mexico]: S[pecial] L[ibrary] A[ssociation], Rio Grande Chapter, 1995).

In addition, you should search through the older newspapers of your city or region. They often provide good topics themselves, and their stories from the past can guide you to many other topics.

One of our students, a few years ago, chose her topic by taking a short walk through a small local cemetery. She was attracted by the gravemarker for an eighteenth-century burial and decided to try to write a brief biography of the man buried there. Her research in the county courthouse and in the collection of the local historical society led her to a large array of land records, wills, letters, and secondary accounts of a Lutheran preacher who had been close to George Washington at Valley Forge.[40] Her result was a research paper of entirely original content, based almost wholly on primary sources. Needless to say, she deserved the high mark she received for her careful and meticulous labor.

Of course, every field of study or interest has an immense number of research topics waiting to be explored. Ships, chemical processes, musical compositions, electronic devices of all kinds, houses and buildings, and literary remains are but a few of ten thousand subjects for research, just waiting for the interested student to unearth information which will bring the accomplishments of the past to life again.

Before we begin to show you the steps of the process of fundamental research, we wish to return to the prospect that you may desire to publish your work when you are done. Should you wish to do this, you must recall that almost all modern scholarly articles are based entirely, or almost entirely, on primary sources—the actual documents that were produced contemporaneously with your subject, or by persons who were contemporary with your subject and wrote about their experiences later. This should not dismay you. As we have indicated already, every collection of every local organization or library almost certainly contains dozens and dozens of files of primary materials on which you can base a serious paper.

Of course, some major scholarship is done on the basis of materials that have been published previously. In these cases, the writer gathers together a wide variety of disparate sources which bear

---

[40]He was, in fact, the Reverend Mr. Christian Streit, of Winchester, Virginia, whose story we wish we had time to include.

upon the subject, but which have never been gathered together before.

One example of this latter type of paper, which we include in this book as Appendix B, is Johanna C. Cullen's "The Miracle of the Mass of Bolsena" which she wrote for a college composition course in the spring of 1993. She began with two distinct collections of information; one was the body of accumulated knowledge about the appearance of "blood" on a eucharistic host in the thirteenth century, the other was about the discovery and characteristics of the bacteria *Serratia marcescens*. Was it possible that the bleeding communion wafer in medieval Bolsena was, in fact, a remarkable appearance of a colony of *Serratia*, with its distinctive, blood-red pigment, on its favorite medium, a location that was rich in carbohydrates?

She began by using the resources of the interlibrary loan system to identify and retrieve monographs and articles about the history of the Mass of Bolsena, many of which came from Roman Catholic colleges and universities. In the processs, she discovered illustrations of the famous fresco by Raphael, painted early in the sixteenth century, which depicts the moment of the miracle. From the bibliographies in the books she retrieved, she developed another bibliography of scholarly articles and unpublished—but readily available—materials, including theses and dissertations. At the same time, she gathered material on *Serratia marcescens*. She used the MEDLINE database and printed bibliographies on both microbiology and the history of medicine to develop a detailed bibliography of her own. Her collection of materials included references to the original reports and articles from the early nineteenth century which narrated the modern realization that the red-colored patches which appeared on polenta which had been stored after cooking were, indeed, manifestations of microscopic life.

After she completed her collection of information, which took about six weeks, she went on to purchase some wafers of unleavened bread which were made to be used as eucharistic hosts in the Catholic Mass. She then used the laboratory of the department of microbiology at her university, with the permission of one of her former professors, to conduct an experiment to see if she could duplicate the effect which had been described so graphically in medieval accounts of the miracle. She documented thoroughly every stage of her experiment with both notes and photographs. Her results confirmed that it was quite plausible that her original thesis—that the miracle was a microbial event—was true.

The paper she wrote, which presented her research and analysis, and synthesized a new interpretation of the miracle, was the consequence of applying the historical method to materials which had, indeed, been published in the past but which had not been related to one another—since Church history and microbiology are not two subjects which often are connected to one another.

After the semester ended, she consulted with her professor about the possibility of continuing her research to gather together information about minor questions in her study which remained unanswered. It took her about ten more weeks of part-time work to resolve her unanswered questions and to elevate the text to a scholarly level.

At this time, she decided to explore the possibility of publishing her undergraduate term paper in a major scholarly journal. She began by submitting it to the *Journal of Bacteriology*, the leading journal of the American Society for Microbiology. Its editor called her to ask if she would consider allowing him to publish her paper, not in the *Journal of Bacteriology*, but, rather, in the Society's monthly, *ASM News*, in the issue which appeared in conjunction with the Society's annual general meeting in the spring. She accepted this offer and her paper appeared in the April, 1994, issue of *ASM News*.[41] Her work immediately attracted widespread attention for its close reasoning and clear writing. It was reviewed and discussed in the prestigious weekly journal, *Science*,[42] and in the British scientific review, *New Scientist*,[43] within weeks of its publication. She received letters and telephone calls about her work from a number of distinguished and well-established scholars and researchers in the United States, Argentina, and other countries. And, as can be expected, she was misinterpreted by a number of public commentators and essayists, including one well-known essayist for *Scientific*

---

[41]Johanna C. Cullen, "The Miracle of Bolsena," *ASM News* 60:4 (April 1994): 187-191.

[42]"Miracle or Microbe?," *Science* 264 (13 May 1994): 903.

[43]Alexandra Witze, "The Miraculous Microbes of Bolsena," *New Scientist*, no. 1928 (4 June 1994): 14.

American.[44] She responded to this essay with a spirited letter which was duly published by the journal.[45] In the meantime, she has been asked to allow her original article to be reprinted in other countries, including Norway.

Her work is an excellent example of the principles we present in this book. She was thorough and meticulous in her examination of both online and printed bibliographies and she mined the sources she found in them for yet more bibliographical citations. Within weeks, she had accumulated virtually everything that had ever been published on the miracle of Bolsena. She sought help for those aspects of her work which she could not accomplish alone. Her father helped her with translations from Latin, and her mother helped her with texts in German; her former professor of microbiology made it possible for her to conduct independent experiments in the laboratory, which her father documented with photographs to accompany her laboratory notes. She maximized her opportunities by using every notable library and archival collection near her.

In another sense, however, her experience was not unique. Every student can draw upon a special, and uniquely personal, collection of resources and persons to conduct serious intellectual inquiry, as we illustrated with the case of the student who wrote her paper on Colonel Wladimir KrzyÔanowski and his actions at the Battle of Gettysburg. Later, we will present some ideas on what you may wish to do to have your term paper published.

As you explore your options, we do have one final caution. Making new knowledge—and, indeed, that is what you are about to do—is like making a messy porridge, so you must work quickly to decide on, at least, a very close approximation of your final topic, because you do have only one semester in which to research, analyze, synthesize, and write your paper—which cannot be analogous to a messy porridge. And there are many annoying little obstacles which may appear in your path. Many people will have to coöperate with you during the process of research: librarians, archivists, interlibrary loan staff, and photocopier repairmen, among many others. Our experience has been that most professional

---

[44]James Randi, "Investigating Miracles, Italian-Style," *Scientific American* (February 1996): 136.
[45]Johanna C. Cullen, "The Miracle of Microbiology," *Scientific American* (July 1996): 8.

people are eager to support the advancement of learning and will help you all they can. But, you may find some unhelpful people, as well as some unhelpful policies, whose very existence will astound and mystify you. Some collections will be closed to you at first, and you will have to write a letter to the person in charge which explains why you need to have access to the materials in the collection. Sometimes, you will need to have your professor or your advisor write to the controlling functionary to secure permission for you to view the materials you need. Interlibrary loan requests, and much other paperwork as well, are sometimes mishandled, and you will have to submit your requests two or more times.

Remember the inherent truth in Murphy's Law: *Whatever can go wrong, will go wrong.* Because you do not have an endless time to correct what has gone wrong, start early!

In this world, there are no mysteries, only
undiscovered, or unexplained, facts.

Ernest Braund

Getting Started: Part One

Now that you have chosen your topic, there are a few preliminary steps that you need to take to prepare yourself for the research tasks you will do to discover information about it.

Fundamentally, in the first stages of writing the term paper, your function is that of an "information detective." Each topic will require its own pathway to discover information about it. Our book describes some of the more general avenues to information, but there are specialized resources for each type of topic. These resources will require you to use particular research methods that are appropriate to the field. Later, in this chapter, we will discuss some of them briefly, but you should be prepared to discuss your topic extensively with the reference librarians in your own college or university library, as well as with specialists in CD-ROM publishing and online services. Only by consulting those who know the resources that are available to you can you determine which pathways to explore first and which are likely to yield valuable information for your research.

First, you should become thoroughly familiar with your college or university library, and the main sources of general and reference information that it contains. Take a short period of unhurried, private time to explore the library carefully.

One of the things that you will need to know include the location of the desk where interlibrary loan materials are handled and distributed. It may be helpful to you later to get to know some of the staff in that section of the library's services, because you may need to inquire of them often regarding the status of your requests and the procedures for using interlibrary loan materials.

You need to determine whether your library uses the Library of Congress Classification System to organize its collection, or whether it uses the Dewey Decimal Classification System, instead. In either case, you need to locate the place where the *Library of Congress Subject Headings* is made available, because you will need that set of books more than once, as you narrow your searches, in order to determine the correct subject classifications for the material you need. The set usually is located somewhere close by the main card catalogue or near the computer catalogue terminals.

Later, we will describe, in some detail, how you can use this set, and its online version, to the greatest possible advantage.

Mundane as it may seem, you need to identify the sites of the photocopying machines and the cost for using them. Do you need to purchase a cash card to operate the machines? Will you need to insert dimes or other coins into the machine when you use it? One frustrating experience that you want to avoid is to retrieve a number of valuable books and articles and to take them to the photocopying machine only to find that you must have a stack of dimes to operate the machine—and you are standing in front of that cold and unfriendly machine at eleven o'clock on a Friday night.

You need to find the main reference collection of the library and locate several major sources to which you probably will return often. Among these are *The Oxford English Dictionary*, the *Gale Encyclopedia of Associations*, the *American Library Directory*, and, quite probably, the **eleventh edition** of the *Encyclopaedia Britannica*.[46] You also need to determine where reference works which apply to the general subject of your topic are located.

One of your more important early tasks on this visit is to locate the area of the library in which printed bibliographies are shelved.[47] When you find this area of the stacks, browse the shelves which contain bibliographies that are concerned with your general subject of research. Take a few minutes to become familiar with the main bibliographical sources, so that you can return to them, when you need them, quickly and easily. We will discuss some of the more important published bibliographies, and Class Z of the Library of Congress's classification system, below.

You need to discover the locations of the computer terminals which are used for bibliographical searching, either by connection to online facilities or through CD-ROM resources. Note any special limitations of time or date with which you will have to comply in

---

[46]Although you will never use general reference encyclopedias, or even specialized subject dictionaries and encyclopedias, as major sources for your research, they can be used, often with great profit, as places to begin assembling your preliminary bibliography. If you do use them for this last purpose, you need not cite them in your annotated bibliography, because they will not appear among the sources you will use in your actual research.

[47]If your library uses the Library of Congress Classification System, this is Class Z.

order to use these facilities. Some colleges and universities have established special computer searching rooms at their libraries, while others restrict access to these facilities to members of the library's staff, with whom you will have to consult to have your bibliographical and informational searches done.

Once you have become comfortable with the general organization of your library, later visits to do the actual tasks of research become much easier and less confusing.

The next preliminary task is obtain access to the Internet, so that you can take advantage of the tremendous wealth of informational resources it contains. Most colleges and universities offer students free accounts on one or more of the institution's networks. These accounts allow the student to pass from the local network of the college or university outward to the great world of the Internet, through such software as *telnet*, *ftp*, newsreaders, e-mail facilities, and *lynx* and other software to browse the *World Wide Web*. We will discuss how you will use these facilities and this software later, but just one of the thousands of research assets you will acquire through access to the Internet is the ability to search the whole catalogue of the Library of Congress in Washington, D. C.—the world's largest and most comprehensive reference library—right from the keyboard of your own computer.

Perhaps this is the best place to discuss briefly the software that you will use on your own computer to reach the computer system or network of your college or university, whether from your dormitory room, your home, or your office. You need to choose commuications software that is both easy to use and has features which are most helpful to conducting online searches for information. Among the latter, there are two which are mandatory. You must have a **log-to-file** function, so that you can open a file of your own,[48] while your computer is connected to online databases and catalogues, and save what you see on the screen for your later review and consideration; and you must have a **screen-snapshot** function, to allow you, with the stroke of a key, to capture and save to a file, interesting data and information which appears on the screen when your **log-to-file** function is turned off.

---

[48]Typically, with a toggle-keystroke, like a light switch, which often is ALT-L or ALT-FI.

If you have an Intel-based computer whose operating system is DOS or an enhancement that runs on top of DOS, like the *Microsoft Windows* series of software, we recommend *ProComm Plus* for DOS, version 2.01. It is ideal for communicating with the UNIX shell accounts that are provided so frequently to college and university students and faculty. Our students have found it to be very easy to learn; and it has many features which make it an ideal means of communicating on the Internet in a non-graphics mode.[49] Unfortunately, the latest version of the program was released in 1991, which makes it rather elderly today in the world of software, so you may have to seach with some diligence to find it.

There are, certainly, many other programs for communicating with remote sites, and you may well find another that is more modern or one that you like better, or both. If you can, ask others at your college or university, particularly among graduate students who are using online soucres for their research, which software they use, and why. Always be sure, however, that he software that you finally choose has both a **log-to-file** function and a **screen-snapshot** function. A final warning is to note that most colleges and universities still do not permit the users of their systems to employ software that has a graphical user interface (GUI), like *Netscape* and *Microsoft Explorer*. The argument against allowing students and faculty to use such programs, at least not without paying an additional fee, is that they take too many computer resources from limited systems that already are burdened with hundreds, indeed thousands, of users. Remember, you still will be able to reach, and use, most of the sites on the *World Wide Web* with non-graphical software—such as *lynx*, which we will discuss in detail later.

Finally, you need to secure and read carefully one or two manuals on the process of doing effective research in a library. The most important book on this subject to have been published in many years is *A Guide to Library Research Methods* by Thomas Mann.[50]

---

[49]If you use *Windows 3.x*, *Windows NT*, or *Windows 95*, simply click on the icon that takes you to the DOS prompt, go to your root directory, create a new directory, and install *ProComm Plus* there. If this language seems unintelligible to you, ask a friend who is more knowledgeable to help you to get started. The same advice is, of course, true no matter what communications software you use for your research.

This book is so valuable that we recommend, very strongly indeed, that you purchase a copy and learn its methods as thoroughly as you can. Francis Bacon, in his essay "Of Studies," which we reprinted in our introduction, said that some few books are to be "chewed and digested." Dr. Mann's book clearly is one of these.

Another text that you may find very helpful is *The Modern Researcher* by Jacques Barzun and Henry F. Graff. This work is an old standard which has served undergraduate and graduate students well for many years. It has been revised several times and is now in its fifth edition.[51] Part one of this work reviews the fundamental steps for maximizing the use of the library as a research asset. We also recommend that you acquire this text and digest its precepts thoroughly. Both of these volumes should be available in your college or university bookstore; if they are not, the staff of the bookstore can order them for you easily. Both are inexpensive. In addition, your library probably will have a number of copies of both books on the open stacks of the general collection so that you can borrow them.

We hope that you will get and read carefully *A Guide to Library Research Methods* before you begin the actual task of doing your research, because it will make the mechanical tasks of locating appropriate sources and retrieving them much speedier.

During the course of the next pages, we will write extensively about online *services, files* or *databases*, and *software*. At times, the welter of terms we use may seem confusing, but if you keep in mind that we are speaking only of three types of entities, you probably will have little difficulty in understanding the different elements of searching for bibliographic and full-text information. First we will be talking about *systems* or *services*. By this, we mean companies or organizations which offer informational resources to their users. OCLC, which we begin to discuss immediately below, is one of them, as are DIALOG, LEXIS/NEXIS, and WESTLAW, as well as the resources of the Library of Congress.

---

[50]Thomas Mann, *A Guide to Library Research Methods* (New York: Oxford University Press, 1987). The Library of Congress's call number for this book is **Z710.M23 1987.**

[51]Jacques Barzun and Henry F[ranklin] Graff, *The Modern Researcher*, 5th ed.(Boston:Houghton Mifflin Company,1992). **LB2369 .B28 1992.**

Second, we will talk about *databases* or *files* within the framework of these systems. For example, the principal large bibliographic catalogue on OCLC is *WorldCat*, but there are several dozen other databases located there, as well, including both *Pro CD Biz* and *Pro CD Home*, which are two great databases of telephone numbers. DIALOG offers hundreds of files or databases, including many full-text collections of newspapers as well as bibliographic and citational databases on many scientific, technical, and other academic topics. Among them are *ARTbibliographies Modern*, for the fine arts; *America: History and Life*, for students of American history; and *Textile Technology Digest*, for researchers who are interested in the latest information on textiles and their manufacture. These are *databases* or *files*.

Finally, we will discuss some software that these services use to make access to their databases easy and efficient. This software is beyond either the software on your own computer that you use to access your gateway to the Internet through your college, university, or commercial provider,[52] or the software you use at one of the latter locations to manipulate the Internet itself.[53] Such software includes *FirstSearch*, which is the primary interface that OCLC provides to its users to manipulate its databases, and the information that is found on those databases. *DIALOGLink* and *WESTMATE* are other such software interfaces, provided by DIALOG and Westlaw, respectively.

Now that you are ready to begin to explore the wealth of information about your topic that is available to you through the Internet, you first need to become familiar with the resources of OCLC.[54] This valuable academic service, located in Dublin, Ohio, a

---

[52]Such as *ProComm Plus for Windows* and other communication packages for the personal computer.

[53]Of which *telnet* and *ftp* probably are the two most important. If you use *Trumpet Winsock* or another TCP/IP stack to access the Internet, and then inaugurate a set of client software, such as the *Microsoft Internet Explorer* or *Netscape*, or *CuteFTP*, or *Eudora*, you are, in effect, combining the two categories we discuss here. If you have no idea what we are talking about, do not worry. The material inherently is no more difficult to master than driving a car, and when you need to know this, you will learn it.

[54]As the Ohio College Library Center, this system opened in 1967. Early in the next decade, it began its phenomenal growth, as libraries in other states began to add their cataloguing records to the system and to participate in it. Today, there

suburb of Columbus, provides more than sixty bibliographic databases which cover nearly the whole range of scholarship. Of these databases, the first with which you must become familiar is *World-Cat*, a compendium of academic and other library catalogues—in effect, a large union catalogue—which has citations for nearly every published work held in collections in the United States, and in many overseas collections as well.[55]

Colleges and universities offer access to OCLC in several different ways. Some, including most of the major schools of the country, offer access to all students through their campus-wide information systems,[56] either through a choice on a menu which presents a list of information resources that are located off campus or as a direct connection through OCLC's standard log-in procedure. Other schools restrict access to the system to a few terminals in the campus library, in which case you will have to go there and discover the locations of the OCLC terminals. Still other colleges require that students purchase *FirstSearch* access cards from a sales site, often also located in the college library.[57]

Once you have logged into OCLC, almost certainly through its *FirstSearch* service, you should choose *WorldCat* as the first of your voyages of discovery. In Appendix A in this book, we present a brief example of a search through *WorldCat*, but you should get the full suite of documentation for OCLC's databases for yourself. Later

---

are more than five thousand participating institutions, all of which have contributed the catalogues of their own holdings to the system. Its international scope required a change of its name, and it is now called the Online Computer Library Center. *FirstSearch* is only one of the software searching tools for the system, but it is by far both the most popular and the easiest to learn. For a brief discussion of the founding of the system and its earlier history, see Thomas Mann, *A Guide to Library Research Methods* (New York: Oxford University Press, 1987) 81-82.

[55] *WorldCat* is the name that OCLC has assigned to its principal database, the *OCLC Online Union Catalog*, when it is accessed through the *FirstSearch* interface. Now that it is more than a quarter-century old, it contains somewhat more than thirty-five million records in three hundred seventy languages. For details, see the URL: http://www.oclc.org/oclc/promo/9714cols/9714.htm.

[56] Often reduced to the initialism CWIS.

[57] *FirstSeacrh* is a system for accessing the OCLC databases. At this time, if your college uses this method, you can purchase the access cards in denominations of as many as one hundred searches, although cards are available readily in smaller denominations, as well. The current fee is sixty cents per search, so that a card which authorizes one hundred searches is sold for sixty dollars.

in this book, we will show you how to use the *World Wide Web* to get that information, as well as all the other documentation, that OCLC publishes online about its services.[58]

The *FirstSearch* service offers context-sensitive help for each set of choices for each menu, so, at first, you should use this facility frequently—there is no charge for using the help facilities while you are searching. This is true for all of the databases that OCLC offers, including, of course, *WorldCat*.

WorldCat offers many advantages to the researcher which are not to be found anywhere else. But perhaps the two most important of these are the ability to order materials through the interlibrary loan system directly from the display of a bibliographical entry[59] and the ability to locate master's theses and doctoral dissertations on virtually every subject from nearly every American university.[60] This latter advantage will be discussed more fully, below, when we consider how you can obtain the latest, detailed information on a specific narrow topic. One point that perhaps deserves note here is that many students find it both informative and amusing to use *WorldCat* for the first time to discover the academic antecedents of the professors who teach them. Since the degree of doctor of philosophy (PH. D.) is always a research degree, every person who holds the degree will have written a dissertation. If the degree was granted by an American university, the title and subject of the dissertation will appear, almost certainly, in *WorldCat*.[61] It is worth

---

[58]See a full discussion of these, below.

[59]This is available only if your college or university has enabled an interface between *WorldCat* searches and the interlibrary ordering system. Check with your library's interlibrary loan librarian to learn whether or not this interface has been installed at your institution. In 1996, this service filled its sixty-five millionth request for an interlibrary loan.

[60]This very great benefit arises from the fact that universities which participate in the OCLC program furnish copies of their own cataloguing tapes to OCLC, and since every university does catalogue the theses and dissertations of students who have received master's and doctoral degrees from that school. *WorldCat* has become the only national repository of citations to theses. You need to note, as well, that the DISS database, a part of the *FirstSearch* system, is the online version of *Dissertations Abstracts International*, and contains citations for every American doctoral dissertation since 1869.

[61]In addition to this information, the cataloguing entry will indicate the university which granted the degree, and, quite often, the date of birth of the author. Older members of faculties are often bemused by students who offer sympathy

noting here that OCLC's *FirstSearch* system also offers access to DAO, *Dissertations Abstracts Online*. It is a valuable bibliographic compilation which you should search for sources on your topic. Below, in the section on talking to an expert, we give a sample search from DAO and discuss this database more fully.

Once you have become reasonably familiar with *WorldCat*, you will find that you can use OCLC's other databases with a fair degree of ease. You then should begin to explore the other bibliographic databases which are germane to your own research. For example, if your topic is from the realm of language and literature, you will wish to investigate the MLA BIBLIOGRAPHY;[62] if your topic comes from the fields of medicine or genetics, you will wish to explore MEDLINE and BIOSYS thoroughly.[63] In every case, however, you should be aware generally of all the databases and the subjects they cover, because this semester's useless appendage to your searching may become next semester's most valuable asset.

The *FirstSearch* interface to OCLC often is presented to its users in two distinct menus, *FirstSearch Standard*, with about twelve databases, and *FirstSearch Extended*, with about forty others. On the following page, we list these databases—which we will not do with the contents of other services, because OCLC's offerings are so fundamentally important to every beginning researcher, and because most college and university libraries offer access to them.

Early in your research, you should review some of the introductory documentation to OCLC's services. You can find a large collection of documentation—including guides to getting started with OCLC, texts which review all of the commands for searching bibliographic databases with the *FirstSearch* interface, and extensive technical discussions that will help you to become comfortable with the wide range of ways that you can use to manipulate the system's bibliographical data—through the *World Wide Web*.[64] To

when the professor passes her fiftieth or sixtieth birthday, hardly able to fathom how the student discovered the fact.

[62] The *Modern Language Association International Bibliography*.

[63] We discuss MEDLINE more fully, below, in our section on important online resources.

[64] Below, we will show you how to use *lynx* to access the information on the *World Wide Web* directly from your own college internet account, even if you do not have a graphical interface to the internet, such as *Netscape* or *Microsoft Explorer*.

access and retrieve these guides, which we do recommend, use URL:[65] http://www.oclc.org/oclc/menu/t-doc.htm#fs.

THE URL.

The initialism URL stands for *Uniform Resource Locator*. It is a standard way of expressing the location of information on the Internet, in general, and the *World Wide Web*, in particular. [66]Once you understand the basic scheme under which URLs are organized, you will have a useful way to record Internet addresses to which you wish to return, or those which you wish to cite in another document, as we do here. An URL has as many as five parts that tell the Internet where to find the information for which you are looking. The five basic parts are:

(1) the type of software that will deliver the information to you,
(2) the Internet site or server where that information is located,
(3) the directory path to the file where the resource is located,
(4) the file name of the "document" you wish to be delivered to you or the program you wish to be executed, and
(5) optional additional information, called parameters, which a program needs to answer a specific request, such as a submenu at a gopher site.

The first part of the address identifies the type of software that provides the information. For example, addresses beginning with:

http:// uses software that delivers hypertext information to you, usually on the *World Wide Web*.
gopher:// is software that provides you with a menu in a tree-like form from which you can retrieve information in plain text.

---

[65]For the easiest method for using the *World Wide Web*, see our discussion of *lynx*, below.
[66]For the basic material in this section, we are indebted to Sagrelto's Infoworm at the URL: http://www.sagrelto.com/sagrelto/tutorial/snewusr.htm and especially to Infoworm's introduction to urls at
http://www.sagrelto.com/sagrelto/tutorial/urlintro.htm. We recommend the online tutorials that are provided by Sagrelto, they are a helpful way to begin to use the *World Wide Web*.

ftp:// identifies the file transfer protocol, which allows you to retrieve whole files, such as free software that is in the public domain.

telnet:// which we have discussed before, is software that allows you to login to another machine, to use a database or to see other directories and files on the remote machine.

mailto:// allows you to send email from a browser.

file:// delivers a specific file to you.

file:/// allows you to access "local files" that reside on your own computer.

The second part of the address is for the Internet site or "server" where the information resides. It is composed of words separated by periods, which are sometimes followed by a colon (:) and some numbers, or it is composed of four groups of numbers, separated by dots. We will discuss the nature of Internet addresses more fully, below.

The third part of the address provides information about the hierarchical directory path—the location of the specific "file" or document on the server. This part is frequently missing when you are accessing the top level or "home page" of a specific server, because the people who supply that information have a way to direct you to a "default file," which you must access first.

The fourth part, which typically follows the last slash (/), is the name of the file which contains the document you will retrieve, or sometimes a program which will be executed before the information is sent to you. This often is not shown, because the provider of the information you wish already has designated a default top-level document, commonly referred to as a "home page," from which you will follow links to other pages, documents, and programs.

The rest of the address is used only when specific information, called parameters, must be passed to the program. You may see this type of information, for example, when you access a sub-menu at a gopher site. If it is part of the address that you received, use it; otherwise it is of no concern.

Returning now to our earlier discussion about *FirstSearch*, notice that, in the interest of the clarity of the following table, we did not italicize the names of the databases, as we do normally in the text of our book.

FirstSearch Standard Databases

1 WorldCat: Books and other materials in libraries
2 Article1st: Index of articles from 12,500 journals.
3 Contents1st: Table of contents of 12,500 journals.
4 FastDoc: Index of articles with text online or by email.
5 NetFirst: OCLC database of Internet resources.
6 GPO: U.S. government publications.
7 MEDLINE: Abstracted articles from medical journals.
8 MLA : Literature, languages, linguistics, folklore.
9 PapersFirst: An index of papers at conferences.
10 Pro CD Biz: Business telephone listings.
11 Pro CD Home: Home telephone listings.
12 Proceedings: An index of conference publications.

FirstSearch Extended Databases

1 A&H Search: Arts & Humanities Search: citation index.
2 AGRICOLA: Materials relating to agriculture.
3 AIDS/Cancer: AIDS and Cancer Research.
4 ArtAbstracts: Leading publications in arts.
5 BasicBIOSIS: A wide range of bioscience topics.
6 BioDigest: Digests in biology, ecology & health.
7 BooksInPrint: R. R. Bowker's Books In Print.
8 Bus Dateline: Citations on regional business articles.
9 BusinessNews: Daily news and info. from 350 sources.
10 BusinessOrgs: Organizations for business and industry.
11 BusPerInd: Popular business magazines.
12 CINAHL: Cumulative Index to Nursing
13 ConsumerIndx: Index of articles of consumer info.
14 DataTimes: An index of regional newspapers.
15 Disclosure: Reports on publicly owned companies.
16 Diss: Dissertation Abstracts Online.
17 EBSCO: The EBSCO MasterFILE. 2,400 magazines.
18 EconLit: An index of economic literature.
19 Environment: Key aspects of environmental science.
20 EventLine: Scheduled conventions, exhibits, etc..
21 FactSearch: Facts and statistics on current topics.
22 GenSciAbstracts: Leading general science periodicals.

23 GEOBASE: Literature on geography and geology.
24 GeoRef: Guide to geology and earth sciences.
25 HumanitiesAbs: Abstracts of articles in the humanities.
26 INSPEC: For physics, electronics and computing.
27 MDX Health: Digest of medical and health info.
28 MicrocompAbs: Microcomputer Abstracts.
29 ReadersGuide: Readers'Guide to Periodical Literature.
30 ReadGuideAbs: Abstracts from popular magazines.
31 RILM Abs: RILM Abstracts of Music Literature.
32 SocioAbs: Abstracts to articles on sociology.
33 SocSciAbs: Guide to the literature in social sciences.
34 WilBusAbs: English-language business periodicals.
35 Worldscope: Financial reports on companies.

Further along in this book, we show an example of a bibliographic display from *WorldCat*, and dissect it, so that you can see the full range of information it contains. In addition, in Appendix A, we show the process of doing one search of this database

The next source of bibliographic information with which you need to become familiar is the collection of databases that are available on the Internet from the Library of Congress in Washington. This collection includes not only the Library's gigantic book and serials catalogues, but also the online version of the *Library of Congress Subject Headings* and information about the Congress's legislative activities, among others.

Before we describe how to get there from your own computer, through your Internet account, we need to explain a bit about how your college's computer communicates with other computers around the 'net. You probably already use a computerized word-processor or, perhaps, you play a variety of games on your computer. You know that, if you have a DOS-based machine, or one with DOS and Microsoft *Windows*, you have a system prompt which looks something like this:

C:\>

Your college's computer has a similar system prompt, although it may not be displayed as the same group of characters that you find familiar.

If you use a wordprocessor on your own computer, you know that you type a character or a small group of characters and press [ENTER] to begin to operate that software. Perhaps you enter the following:

wp

The wordprocesing software is not the same as the operating system, and you readily perceive the difference. In the world of Internet communications, there are three software programs that you need to master swiftly, even when you are a novice at surfing the 'net. They are *telnet*, *lynx*, and *ftp*.

Telnet, in effect, dials your college's computer communications line outward to another address, quite like the way you reach another person by dialing a telephone number. When you dial a long distance number, you already are familiar with the grouping of four collections of digits that identify the unique location you are trying to reach. For example:

1-301-555-1212

In the same way, the *telnet* software is associated with a look-up table which translates a letter-based address into the Internet's *dotted quad* address, which may actually look something like:

198.93.93.103

In fact, however, most Internet addresses regularly are indexed as groups of letters which seem to be rather spurious words. As you become used to these, you will notice that the last group of letters indicates the kind of organization or institution that you are calling. For example, *.edu* indicates an educational institution, *.org* indicates a publicly-accessible organization, *.com* indicates a commercial firm, and *.gov* indicates a computer host within the United States Government. Your look-up table, in effect, takes an entry which you type, such as:

gwis2.circ.gwu.edu

and converts it to:

128.164.168.248

to which it then connects.

Now, use your communications software to log on to your institution's computer system or network with your user identification and password and, if you are not taken directly to a system prompt, find that option on the menu and select it. To use *telnet*, type the word "telnet," followed by a space, followed by the letter-based address of the remote computer you wish to reach.

With this little introduction, you now are ready to reach the databases of the Library of Congress. Enter the following at the system prompt of your computer account:

telnet locis.loc.gov

Almost instantly, you will see a screen with a menu which welcomes you to the Library of Congress Information System (LOCIS). Take some time to become familiar with the resources that are available to you at this location. You should be concerned particularly with the main resources of the Library, its book catalogues, SCORPIO and MUMS, and other bibliographic aids, such as LCXR.[67] Take some time to become comfortable with this system, and just enter h for help when you think that you are lost. Please note that LOCIS now is available on the Internet twenty-four hours a day on weekdays, with additional daylight hours on weekends. The catalogue also is available on the *World Wide Web* with several different options for searching it. This service is available, however, mainly during the hours when the Library is open to the public.[68] Further

---

[67]Documentation for these is available to you at no charge by *ftp*. Later, we will describe in detail how you can retrieve and use this material to further your knowledge and understanding of these valuable resources.

[68]The URL for the Library of Congress's new Web-based catalogue is: http://lcweb.loc.gov/catalog. The Library's hours of public operation are Mondays, Wednesdays, and Thursdays, from 9:00 A. M. to 9:30 P. M.; and Tuesdays and Fridays from 9:00 A. M. to 5:30 P. M.; and Saturdays, from 9:00 A. M. to 5:00 P. M., all Eastern Standard Time or Eastern Daylight Time, as appropriate.

along, we give a sample of a machine-readable card from the computerized catalogue of the Library of Congress, and we describe how to read that computerized record to extract the essential information from it to determine whether or not it may be germane to your research. In addition, in Appendix A, we show one example of how to use the online version of the *Library of Congress Subject Headings* and how you can use the results of that search to find specific materials in the Library's catalogues.

OTHER LIBRARY RESOURCES ON THE INTERNET

In addition to the databases of the Library of Congress, several thousand other library catalogues are available to you by using *telnet*. To find them, you can use a nearly complete, and regularly updated, catalogue of all the Internet addresses for library catalogues. This index, called HYTELNET, can be reached, and searched, at the URL: **http://library.usask.ca/hytelnet**.

Some other locations on the *World Wide Web* that you should check when you are searching for libraries and library resources include the web page for *Bibliophile Research Tools*, which you can find at: **http://www.clark.net/pub/rmharris/research.html**[69] and the web page of the *ARL Member Libraries' Information Servers* at the URL: **http://arl.cni.org/members.html**.

Before you continue onward with your preliminary searches for information about your topic, you really do need to take the time to become comfortable with these two great repositories of bibliographic information, OCLC and the Library of Congress, because you do not want to be so inundated with data that you are bewildered by the task of narrowing the number of citations to a quantity which is both specifically germane and manageable.

When you examine the cataloguing record for a possible source for your research, you need to take the time to read the whole entry carefully. The data that are included in the cataloguing record, whether it is an online record or one on a catalogue card in your library, will help you to determine whether or not the work is worth consulting.

[69]You can connect directly to a comprehensive index of English-language library catalogues by pointing your browser to *Accesses to Major English-Language Online Libraries* at: **http://www.clark.net/pub/rmharris/research/librar.html**.

First, you need to remember that, while some general or popular books do have bibliographic materials, all scholarly books have them. You need the bibliographies from your sources to continue your pursuit of both important secondary scholarship and primary sources.[70] Consequently, if the entry does not show that a book or article has a bibliography or bibliographical notes, you may want to skip the work entirely, or to consider it only after you have examined work that potentially are more valuable to you.

You should also take note of the age of the work at whose cataloguing entry you are looking, as well as the subject cataloguing for the work. The latter often will provide you with a group of terms which you can analyze with simple Boolean algebra to determine whether or not the work seems likely to be of value.[71]

This stage of your research probably is a good time for you to become familiar with the most important of all guides to assigning subject terms to materials in a library catalogue. The *Library of Congress Subject Headings* (LCSH)[72] is the master list of subject

---

[70]Remember, **the concept of the primary source is the most important single element in your understanding of how to do serious research on any topic.** See the discussion of this most important point, above.

[71]The principles of Boolean algebra, stated in the simplest terms, consist of grouping two or more sets with the connectors AND, OR, AND NOT. Let us say that you have two terms, "Lincoln" and "Presidency." If you group the two as "Lincoln OR Presidency," you will retrieve all the citations that include the term "Lincoln" together with all the citations that include the term "Presidency." Your combined set will, doubtless, be immense. The connector OR should be used only to gather together sets which include like terms which may have been used variably to catalogue the same information, such as "Motion Picture OR Film," so that you will retrieve all the entries for both, since either term may have been used at some time by a cataloguer. If you group together the term as "Lincoln AND Presidency," you will create a set which includes both "Lincoln" and "Presidency." Thus, your set will show materials about President Lincoln, but not about Lincoln's life outside his term in the presidential office. If you group the two terms as "Lincoln NOT Presidency," you will create a set which contains all the available materials about Lincoln other than his presidential service.

Do remember that, in *WorldCat* and other *FirstSearch* databases, you must use AND NOT for those refinements of searches which, in other databases, you would use NOT by itself.

[72]*Library of Congress Subject Headings*, 19th ed., 4 vols. (Washington, D. C.: Cataloging Distribution Service, Library of Congress, 1996) The 5,979 pages of LCSH 19, as the nineteenth edition is known familiarly, contains all the headings that were established by the Library of Congress through December, 1995.

headings that are assigned to the books in most library systems in the United States, as well as many others throughout the world.[73] The nineteenth edition of this monumental guide to library cataloguing, published in 1996 in four volumes, is, like its predecessors for many decades, bound in bright red covers. Nearly every library in the United States has at least one copy, which is often found on tables near the terminals for the online catalogue or near the card catalogue, or both. If you do not see it at once—and its binding was chosen specifically to make it easy to locate—check the shelves in the immediate area of the terminals or the card catalogue. If you still do not see it, ask a librarian where to find it. **You need this book!**

Every library uses standardized subject headings, in order to reduce, if not eliminate, confusion about how books are catalogued from library to library, from place to place, and from time to time. However, these terms often are not the same as those that you expected to find. For example, you might expect that the word "films" was a legitimate subject heading, but, in fact, the proper term is "motion pictures." Similarly, books and other materials that you might think were catalogued under the headings of "sororities" and "fraternities" are, in fact, to be found under the heading of "Greek letter societies." And, in a famous instance of an older term being retained in modern cataloguing for the sake of uniformity and coherence, "cookbooks" is not used as a subject heading, but "cookery" is.

You need to know, from the beginning, some of the conventions and abbreviations that are used in the LCSH. Below we list a few of them that are essential:

```
Bold type = use this term—it is the accepted
            subject heading.
```

---

[73]For part of the material we use here, we are indebted to the staff of the Undergraduate Library of the University of Illinois at Urbana-Champaign, and to the text of their presentation on the LCSH that can be found on the *World Wide Web* at the URL: http://www.grainger.uiuc.edu/ugl/howlcsh.htm.

```
NT = "narrower terms." Search with these terms to
     narrow your search and make it more specific.
BT = "broader terms." Search with these terms to
     broaden your search and make it more general.
RT = "related terms."; These are other headings
     which may be useful. Related terms do not
     necessarily broaden or narrow your search,
     rather they are simply other terms that are re
     lated to your subject in some way.
UF = "used for." These terms are cross references
     only and are not used as subject headings
     at all.
USE = informs you that the term you found is NOT
     a legitimate subject heading, and that you
     should look under the term indicated by USE.
```

For example, suppose your topic is how William Alexander Hammond (1828-1900) became one of the first modern investigators to study derangements of sleep. As a part of your research, you decide to survey briefly some modern works on the subject, to see what has changed, and what has not changed, in our understanding of the subject since Hammond's time. You consult LCSH 19 to see if the subject term "Disorders of sleep" is the correct one with which to search catalogues. You find, under that heading, a USE reference that takes you to the proper term, which you find to be "Sleep disorders." Under that heading, in turn, you find:

> Sleep disorders
>   (RC547)
> uf Disorders of sleep
> bt Nervous system—Diseases
> nt Dreams
>   Hypersomnia
>   Insomnia
>   Narcolepsy

"Sleep disorders" is the main subject heading. UF [*used for*] tells you that the subject heading "Sleep disorders" is used for the phrase "Disorders of sleep." BT [*broader term*] tells you that "Nervous system—Diseases" is a more general, broader term for the main subject heading; while NT tells you that the terms listed are narrower, more specific, than the main subject heading. Now you can turn confidently to either *WorldCat* or the Library of Congress's catalogues online with the correct subject term.

Other things you need to know about the organization of material in "the big red books" are that the subdivisions of the main headings are preceded by a dash. They will appear after the main headings and may be useful to you, if you wish to narrow your search. Also, the names of many cities and persons do not appear in the *Library of Congress Subject Headings* as proper nouns, even though they are used as subject headings in library catalogues.

You also can reach LCSH 19 online. *Telnet* to **locis.loc.gov** and, from the menu which appears, select the first entry, LIBRARY OF CONGRESS CATALOG. Once the secondary menu appears, choose the seventh item, LIBRARY OF CONGRESS CROSS REFERENCES — LCXR. You are now connected to the online version of the *Library of Congress Subject Headings*. Later, we will present a full searching exercise in which this online version will be essential.

It is quite often useful to note, as well, the name of the publisher of a monograph, simply because the famous academic and trade publishers have reputations to protect. This causes them to have the manuscripts that are submitted to them for possible publication to be reviewed carefully by recognized authorities in the field before they will commit themselves to publishing the work.

Please remember to save, with your software's **log-to-file** function, the detailed presentation of cataloguing entries from *World-Cat* and SCORPIO, because the various items of data which appear in the cataloguing records will be of use to you in evaluating a work as a possible source for your research.

Now that you have learned something about *telnet*, we want you to know about *lynx*, and how you can use it to retrieve information from the *World Wide Web*, before we continue our discussion of places to search for information.

From the system prompt at your college account, type the word *lynx*, and press ENTER. You will be taken automagically to whatever homepage your college has set up for its own interface to the *World Wide Web*. Take a few minutes to become familiar with how to operate *lynx*, especially by noting the short help guide at the bottom of the opening screen, and by pressing H to read the help files. *Lynx* is very versatile, indeed, once you become comfortable with it. On the following page, we show a table of the keystrokes that you can use to manipulate the software. Of these, we wish to draw your attention to G [GO], which opens a highlighted line on which you can type the URL you wish to reach; and P [PRINT], which opens a window entitled "Printing Options," one of which is "Mail the file." If you use the down arrow on your keyboard to highlight this option, and then press ENTER, you can type in your e-mail address and the entire contents of the document you chose will be sent directly to you.

In our opinion, *lynx* is the best software to use to explore the *World Wide Web* in text, rather than in graphics, mode. If your aim in exploring the *Web* is to find and retrieve information, then *lynx* will help you to do it faster and with less wasted time than any other program. Of course, it does not offer you, as browsers like *Netscape* and *Microsoft Explorer* do, the visual attractiveness of graphics, but it is faster than the more popular and famous browsers, simply because it does not load graphic images. In addition, most colleges and universities have *lynx* already loaded on their student networks, so you do not need to install and configure any software to use the *Web* immediately. And, since that is the case, the cost to you for exploring the *Web* is nothing!

In Appendix E, we present a short guide to determining the value of the data and information that you find on the Internet, in general, and the *World Wide Web*, in particular. Please review it carefully, before you spend time collecting vast amounts of non-bioliographical data from the *Web*, especially. The critical faculties that you bring to evaluating a book or article for its trustworthiness and appropriateness to your research must be heightened even more when you evaluate material on the Internet, because it is so easy for anyone who is familiar enough with the procedures and techniques for creating *web* pages, and similar documents, to put anything at all into cyberspace.

Lynx's Keystroke Commands

MOVEMENT:
Down arrow - Highlight next topic
Up arrow - Highlight previous topic
Right arrow - Jump to highlighted topic
Return, Enter, or Left arrow - Return to
previous topic

SCROLLING:
+ (or space) - Scroll down to next page
- (or b)   - Scroll up to previous page

ORGANIZATIONAL CHANGES:
c - Create a new file
d - Download selected file
e - Edit selected file
f - Show a full menu of options for
current file
m - Modify the name or location of
selected file
r - Remove selected file
t - Tag highlighted file
u - Upload a file into the current
directory

OTHER OPTIONS:
? (or h) - Help (this screen)
a - Add the current link to your
      bookmark file
c - Send a comment to the document owner
d - Download the current link
e - Edit the current file
g - Goto a user specified URL or file
i - Show an index of documents
j - Execute a jump operation
k - Show a list of key mappings
m - Return to main screen

```
o  - Set your options
p  - Print to a file, mail, printers, or
     other
q  - Quit (Capital 'Q' for quick quit)
/  - Search for a string within the
current document
s  - Enter a search string for an
     external search
n  - Go to the next search string
v  - View your bookmark file
z  - Cancel transfer in progress
[backspace] - Go to the history page
=  - Show file and link info
\  - Toggle document source/rendered view
!  - Spawn your default shell
CTRL-R  - Reload current file and refresh
the screen
CTRL-W  - Refresh the screen
CTRL-U  - Erase input line
CTRL-G  - Cancel input or transfer
```

Now you can try a brief exercise which will show you a small sample of the wealth of useful information that you can reach through using *lynx* to access the materials on the *World Wide Web*. At your system prompt, on your college account, type **lynx** and press ENTER. When the first screen appears, type G [GO]. When the highlighted line for entering an URL appears, type:

http://uts.cc.utexas.edu/~churchh/janeinfo.html#janetoc.

After a few moments, to load the first page, you will see the table of contents for a vast array of texts, criticism, and miscellanea about the great English novelist, Jane Austen. You can discover still more about *lynx*, its capabilities, and plans for its future, by reading the *Lynx Information* page on the *World Wide Web*. You can reach this page at the URL: **http://lynx.browser.org**.

When you remember that there are now millions of pages on the *World Wide Web*, the Jane Austen home page will suggest to you how much of value can be found on the *Web*, even though you must take care to weigh carefully the value of the information you retrieve in this way—since there is no hierarchy of value to the information that people put on their pages. Some academic and scholarly organizations are making efforts to categorize the sources on the *Web* in terms of their accuracy and value to research. One of these listings is *NetFirst*, another service of OCLC. This service, which is updated weekly, is a searchable index that is arranged in the form of bibliographic citations that include abstracts, subject headings, and classification codes. The citations point the user to a wide variety of resources that can be reached on the Internet, including *World Wide Web* pages and LISTSERVERS, as well as USENET newsgroups, *FTP* sites, *Gopher* servers, and electronic publications in many formats. OCLC has tried to index only those resources which have some value, and they have had some real success. It still remains true, however, that you must mistrust all the information that you find on the Internet, in whatever form, until you can verify its accuracy.

Thus far, we have described, in some detail, two of the major repositories of bibliographic information, and two major types of software that you can use to access information on the Internet.

The bibliographical resources, however, are general, not specialized; that is, you will use them to locate a first collection of sources which are germane to your topic. You need to be aware that there are a vast number of specialized collections of data and information, some of them online, some on CD-ROM, and some still exist only in the form of published books.

In order to ensure that you do not miss any of the bibliographic resources which may be of value to you, take the time to become familiar with the specialized collection of information in your field. Consult with the reference librarians in your college or university library, as with the librarians who maintain the CD-ROM and other electronic collections, as well. Explore the volumes in Class Z of your library's collection to determine if there are any published bibliographies which will be useful to you.[74]

BIBLIOGRAPHIES OF BIBLIOGRAPHIES AND RESEARCH GUIDES.

The most efficient and useful way to discover what published bibliographies are available for you to use in your research is to consult several of the great bibliographies of bibliographies. Perhaps the best-known, and most frequently used, of these is Theodore Besterman's renowned *World Bibliography of Bibliographies*, of which the fourth and last edition is the most valuable.[75] Since Besterman's cumulation stops with the year 1964, you also should not omit looking at its supplement by Alice F. Toomey.[76] Her

[74]Class Z, Bibliography, identifies these books in the Library of Congress Classification System, which now is used widely throughout the world. If your library still uses the Dewey Decimal System to classify its collection, you will wish to explore the works that are applicable to your topic in Class 016.. Before you begin this exploration, you should review chapter 8, "Published Bibliographies," in Thomas Mann's *A Guide to Library Research Methods* (pp. 72-79).

[75]Theodore Besterman, *A World Bibliography of Bibliographies and of Bibliographical Catalogues, Calendars, Abstracts, Digests, Indexes, and the Like*, 5 vols., 4th ed. rev. (Totowa, New Jersey: Rowman and Littlefield, 1965; Geneve: Societas Bibliographica, 1965-1966). The Library of Congress's call number for this set is Z1002.B5685, and your own library's call number probably is the same, or very close to the same. The fifth volume is a master index to the other four.

[76]Alice F. Toomey, *A World Bibliography of Bibliographies, 1964-1974: A List of Works Represented by Library of Congress Printed Catalog Cards, a Decennial Supplement to Theodore Besterman, A World Bibliography of Bibliographies*, 2 vols. (Totowa, New Jersey: Rowman and Littlefield, 1977). The Library of Congress's call

massive work brings the master cumulation up to the year 1974. You also should consult the volumes in the most important serial cumulation of bibliographies, *Bibliographic Index*. The *Index* is cumulated from quarterly numbers and annual cumulations, the annual being the last quarterly issue.[77]

With so many library catalogues available to you on the Internet, it may, at first glance, seem unnecessary for you to review which institutions have published their catalogues in book form. Although we wax very enthusiastic, indeed, about the wealth of resources that are available for use on the Internet, you must recall that this new digital institution is still in its infancy. Generally, any new technology evolves its fundamental form over the space of about thirty years. If you consider the automobile, for example, and mark the date at which it first began to be sold to the public as 1890, then you will realize that the evolutionary phase came to its end about 1920. By that time, automobiles took on the fundamental appearance that most of them have today—an engine in the front, a steering wheel, some means of shifting a set of gears, headlights, a closed body, and so forth. With the steam engine we see a similar evolution in the period between 1810 and 1840. The technology of digital information really began about 1980, although a few databases and services were available before that time. If we expect that this technology, too, will undergo its fundamental development over the space of thirty years, then we realize that we are still in the stage of experiment and flux, with large amounts of critical information still accessible only in printed form. So, even though there are now thousands of library catalogues online, you should not forget to look at Bonnie R. Nelson's *Guide to Published Library Catalogs*.[78] Nelson's book, since it was published in 1982, probably never will be augmented or superseded, because of the digital revolution. Few libraries today will be willing to incur the

---

number for this set is Z1002.T67.

[77] *Bibliographic Index: A Cumulative Bibliography of Bibliographies* (New York: H. W. Wilson Company, quarterly). The series began with volume 1, number 1, in 1937. Volume 1 continued until 1942, and annual volumes followed thereafter. The Library of Congress's call number is Z1002.B595.

[78] Bonnie R. Nelson, *A Guide to Published Library Catalogs* (Metuchen, New Jersey: Scarecrow Press, 1982). The Library of Congress's call number is Z710.N44.

great expense of publishing their catalogues, since an online digital cumulation is both cheaper and more current than any published version.

Finally, you should look at the most recent of master cumulations, Gary C. Tarbert's *Periodical Directories and Bibliographies*.[79] Tarbert's work is very important for its retrospective consideration of later nineteenth-century items, but it is limited to sources that were published in the English language.

In addition to these works, you will want to look at the specialized bibliographies of bibliographies and the published research guides that cover the general field of your research—and there are many of these. For example, Rowman and Littlefield, Theodore Besterman's American publisher, brought out a series of such bibliographies, after his death in 1976, which they called *The Besterman World Bibliographies*. They are selective reprints of sections of Besterman's great work. Among the best-known of the separate works are William A. Wortman's on modern literatures,[80] which, together with John H. Fisher's work on serial bibliographies in modern languages and literatures,[81] is absolutely essential for work in their fields. Similarly, students doing research in the humanities and social sciences will want to see Richard A. Gray's work,[82] while young historians should not miss David P. Henige's book.[83] Medievalists will need the great cumulation by Richard H. Rouse and

---

[79]Gary C. Tarbert, ed., *Periodical Directories and Bibliographies: An Annotated Guide to Approximately 350 Directories, Bibliographies, and Other Sources of Information about English-language Periodicals, from 1850 to the Present, Including Newspapers, Journals, Magazines, Newsletters, Yearbooks, and Other Serial Publications* (Detroit, Michigan: Gale Research Company, 1987). The Library of Congress's call number is Z6741.P47 1987.

[80]William A. Wortman, *A Guide to Serial Bibliographies for Modern Literatures*, 2d ed. (New York: Modern Language Association of America, 1995). Z6519.W67 1995.

[81]John H. Fisher, "Serial Bibliographies in the Modern Languages and Literatures," *Publications of the Modern Language Association of America [PMLA]* LXVI:3 (April 1951): 138-156. Reprinted: New York: Modern Language Association of America, 1951. The Library of Congress's call number for *PMLA* is PB6.M6.

[82]Richard A. Gray, *Serial Bibliographies in the Humanities and Social Sciences*. (Ann Arbor, Michigan: Pierian Press, 1969). Z1002.G814.

[83]David P. Henige, *Serial Bibliographies and Abstracts in History: An Annotated Guide* (Westport, Connecticut: Greenwood Press, 1986). Z6201.A1H45 1986.

his colleagues.[84] Researchers in religious studies will not want to miss Michael J. Walsh's work.[85]

Every field, and nearly every sub-specialty, has been the subject of at least one master cumulation of bibliographic sources, as well as valuable research guides: music,[86] philosophy,[87] the biological sciences,[88] chemistry,[89] American literature,[90] geography,[91] and on and on.[92]

---

[84]Richard H. Rouse, J. H. Claxton, and M. D. Metzger, *Serial Bibliographies for Medieval Studies,* vol. 3 of the *Publications of the Center for Medieval and Renaissance Studies* (Berkeley, California: University of California Press, 1969). Z6203.R66.

[85]Michael J. Walsh, *Religious Bibliographies in Serial Literature: A Guide* (London: Mansell, 1981; Westport, Connecticut: Greenwood Press, 1981). Z7753.W34 1981.

[86]James W. Pruett and Thomas P. Slavens, *Research Guide to Musicology,* a part of the series *Sources of Information in the Humanities,* no. 4 (Chicago: American Library Association, 1985). ML3797.P78 1985; and James Coover, *Antiquarian Catalogues of Musical Interest* (London: Mansell Publications, 1988). ML152 .C65 1988.

[87]Terrence N. Tice and Thomas P. Slavens, *Research Guide to Philosophy,* a part of the series *Sources of Information in the Humanities,* no. 3 (Chicago: American Library Association, 1983). B52.T5 1983; and Charles J. List and Stephen H. Plum, *Library Research Guide to Philosophy,* a part of the *Library Research Guides Series* (Ann Arbor, Michigan: Pierian Press, 1990). B52.L57 1990.

[88]Roger Cletus Smith, W. Malcolm Reid, and Arlene E. Luchsinger, *Smith's Guide to the Literature of the Life Sciences,* 9th ed. (Minneapolis, Minnesota: Burgess Publishing Company, 1980). QH303.S6 1980.

[89]R. T. Bottle and J. F. B. Rowland, eds., *Information Sources in Chemistry,* 4th ed. (London: Bowker-Saur, 1993). QD8.5.I47 1993.

[90]Charles H. Nilon, *Bibliography of Bibliographies in American Literature* (New York, R. R. Bowker Company, 1970). Z1225.A1N5.

[91]Takashi Okuno, *A World Bibliography of Geographical Bibliographies,* 4 vols., *Tsukuba Studies in Human Geography* [*Tsukuba Daigaku jimbun chirigaku kenkyu*], Special publication, nos. 1-2, 6-7 (Tsukuba, Japan: Institute of Geoscience, University of Tsukuba, 1992-1994). Z6001.A1O38 1992.

[92]And, if you are interested in what bibliographic services can be obtained through the various libraries of the parliaments of European countries, perhaps for research in diplomacy or European politcal affairs, you will not want to miss Ernst Kohl, *Bibliography of Bibliographic Services of European Parliamentary Libraries* [*Bibliographie der bibliographischen Dienste europäischer Parlamentsbibliotheken*], a publication of the European Centre for Parliamentary Research and Documentation (Bonn: Deutscher Bundestag, Wissenschaftliche Dienste, 1990). Z675.G7K64 1990.

Be sure to look carefully for such valuable references in your own field of research. You can find them by seaching the subject cataloguing, either online or in the card catalogue, under the headings: YOURFIELD — BIBLIOGRAPHY and YOURFIELD — CATALOGS. You also should review carefully chapter eight, "Published Bibliographies," in Thomas Mann's *A Guide to Library Research Methods.*[93]

For many other pathways to accuate information, you need to explore what is available to you in microform sets, government documents, and special collections. For more about these important resources, see chapter twelve, "Hidden Treasures," in Thomas Mann's *Guide.*[94]

If your topic is a person or an event from the past two centuries, you should not omit a careful search of contemporary newspapers. While they are not scholarly sources, and almost never are complete or unbiassed, they are always correct as to the time of events. The most important of these sources is, undoubtedly, *The Times* of London; while, among American dailies, it also is useful to check *The New York Times* and, for the period after World War II, *The Washington Post.* You can find microform collections of these and other important papers in almost every college and university library, and in many larger public collections, as well.

Of course, newspapers once played a much larger rôle in disseminating news and information to the population at large than they do today. Often even small communities had two or three daily papers in the early years of this century, not only in Europe and the United States but also in many less-developed parts of the world.[95]

---

[93]Mann, *Guide,* pp. 72-79. We gave you a citation to Mann's book earlier, but we will repeat it here, because the work is so valuable. Thomas Mann, *A Guide to Library Research Methods* (New York: Oxford University Press, 1987). The Library of Congress's call number for this book is Z710.M23 1987.

[94] Mann, *Guide,* pp. 133-153.

[95]Consider, for example, Evansville, Indiana, which, in the last century and in the earlier years of this, never had a population of more than one hundred thousand. The city had not only its present daily, the *Evansville Courier,* but also the *Daily Dispatch,* the *Enterprise,* the *Daily Journal,* and, to meet the needs of the large German immigrant population of a former time, the *Taglicher Evansville Demokrat,* which ran continuously from 1864 to 1918. In addition to these dailies, the town had an assortment of weeklies, as well, including the earliest paper, the *Evansville Gazette* (1821-1825) and the *Wochentliche Evansville Union* (1863-1885); and monthlies, including *Der Armen Seelen Freund.* Of course, not all of these papers were contemporary with one another, but, generally, Evans-

Local libraries and archives frequently have the morgues[96] of local newspapers that disappeared from the stands long ago. Check to see what holdings your local collections have of these.

Of course, you must discover and use the digital resources that apply specifically to research in your field. Every major area of study today is buttressed by a wealth of specialized bibliographic information to help researchers locate germane information for their work. Some of these already are well known generally, such as MEDLINE, the comprehensive medical bibliographic database, and ERIC, the bibliographic database for materials in education. But others, equally as valuable, often are little known. For example, the *Eagle Eye* database of government contracts and procurements is a primary source of information about which companies do work for the United States government and what work they do. Yet, this asset is little known outside the community of marketers for government contractors. Likewise, a vast number of important materials on almost every subject can be found by using the *MLA International Bibliography* online, because so much writing from the past, in every field of study, is treated today as literature, rather than as writing within an intellectual or academic discipline. Consider, for example, that the writings of Thomas Carlyle, so important for the study of historiography, political economy, and social criticism, are now not to be found in bibliographies that are concerned with these fields, but rather in bibliographical materials for the study of Victorian literature.

---

ville had at least two dailies from the 1880's to the 1920's—the noonday of American journalism.

[96]The word *morgue* began its career as the name of a building in Paris in which the bodies of persons found dead were exposed for the purpose of identification. From this, especially in the United States, it became any building or room used for the same purpose. Later, in newspaper offices, the word was used as the name for the collection of material which the paper had assembled for the future obituaries of persons still living. And, from this, in turn, came to identify the paper's collection of cuttings, photographs, and information, as well as the holdings of past issues of the paper itself, for the purpose of providing research materials to reporters and feature writers. The oldest use of the word in this last sense to have been documented in print was in 1918. See *Oxford English Dictionary*, 2d. ed. (1989), *s. v.* "morgue".

Before leaving this brief introduction to the importance of using online sources of information well, we must sound several important warnings about them.

First, the information that you see is only as good as the conscientiousness of the person who entered the data, and the person who proofread the entry, if the latter was done at all. Because of this, be prepared to notice many incongruous typographical errors, such as "Detroit, N. Y." for Detroit, Michigan.[97] These errors that you *do* notice represent only a small part of the problem, because there are many more which you will *not* notice, when you begin to collect information on a topic for the first time. These errors are much more frequent in online cataloguing than they are in well-maintained library card catalogues, because cards, even in the largest catalogues, are seen often by a widely diverse audience of researchers, who then draw the attention of the library's staff to errors in filing or misprinted information. With an online catalogue, whose maintainers often are hundreds, and even thousands, of miles away from the person who notices an error, the specific record must be recalled to a maintainer's workstation and the error corrected. The person who does this task is seldom the person who took the report of an error, and miscommunication, as well as lack of education, training, and dedication, often leave many errors permanently uncorrected.[98]

One senior colleague of ours likes to envision the users of online information as persons seated at the top of an inverted triangle, which tapers downward to a single worker embedded below the boiler room of a great library. Here the lonely information specialist feeds data, item by item, into the great mouth of the machine. On days when he is out of sorts, or has had a little more alcohol

---

[97]On October 11, 1995, *WorldCat* exhibited seven such specific examples: accession numbers 32899534, 32898338, 32898336, 32898334, 16962131, 13717781, and 13717768.

[98]For this reason, when you encounter the name of an author or title with unusual spellings, or spellings that can have many variants (such as Peterson, Petersen, and Pedersen) it is wise to check all of the possible variants that come to your imagination as well as all the misspellings you can contrive. One common error to notice is the reversal of two letters, where "Nelson," for example, become "Neslon." You can see one example of this type of error in WorldCat, accession number 5300907, where a work about the American painter, Maxfield Parrish, has the subject cataloguing "Maxwell Parrish."

than he can stomach well, the data become more and more confused, but the flow never stops.

Remember also that little data are available for material created before the mid-1960's, when machine-readable library cards and other bibliographic data forms were invented. It still is necessary for every researcher to return to printed bibliographies and to other printed sources to find older, but perhaps still very valuable, citations and other information. This is most important, because, all too often today, younger students and scholars believe that they can find "everything that is needed" on the Internet, or its subset, the *World Wide Web*. This is far from the case. By the close of 1996, we estimate that there were bibliographical references in some digital form to about forty percent of materials of some intellectual importance, and that only about two percent of such material actually was available online.

Finally, no online catalogue or database is all-inclusive. It represents only the data, and information, that the creator of the database thought to be worthy of inclusion; and, in any case, all such large repositories of data are more general in scope than specific. For this reason, we recommend strongly that you use these important resources as you first place to search for a preliminary bibliography, but that you develop and enlarge your bibliographical sources, in order to continue your research, from the materials you find in the bibliographies and bibliographical notes in the sources you discover through online catalogues. It has been observed by one notable scholar on the life and writings of Thomas Carlyle that the most exhaustive catalogues he has examined have included no more than sixty percent of the known publications by and about the great English sage.[99]

These three conditions should persuade you to rely on the various electronic facilities no more than is necessary to get you firmly started on your research. After all, the bibliographic material in scholarly books and articles about your topic was created by men and women who were devoted professionally to the increase and diffusion of knowledge about that topic, while the data in the great electronic databases were entered into them largely by employees of commercial and governmental entities who were not motivated

---

[99]Conversation with George Allan Cate, October 5, 1995.

by any great love for, or devotion to, the information they were conveying to you, the final user of their efforts.

Getting Started: Part II
Mining, Not Surfing, the 'Net

In addition to the fundamental bibliographic catalogues we have discussed, the Internet also offers you access to more worlds of information, some of which may be quite valuable to you in your research.

First, we wish to introduce you to a few of the commercial online database services which are accessible both through their own proprietary software and through the Internet. In the latter case, you can use the standard terminal emulation that you use for your e-mail, typically vt-100, to search and display records from these commercial services.

In general, your college or university library will have an account with at least some of these services, or some parts of them. In many cases, you will not be allowed to do the searching yourself, but rather will have to submit a request to have a librarian do the searches for you. In the more technologically-advanced schools, access to these services is available widely to students, often through a choice on the menu for the main library catalogue. Check with the reference desk of your library to see how you can have access to the DIALOG system, to the LEXIS/NEXIS service, and to other similar repositories of sound bibliographical information. Remember, most of these services began in the 1970's and did not do retrospective cataloguing of materials in the fields they cover. Consequently, you will have to resort to earlier published bibliographies to find appropriate citations to articles and other material that was published before the digital version of the index or catalogue began.

Before we begin to talk about the value of various database systems and their products, we must say something about the need for current information and how that need varies from field to field. If your research lies in one of the physical or biological sciences, or in engineering or medicine, the results of the latest research are of great significance to you. A report on the gene structure of human chromosome 11 that was published in 1988 probably will be of little value to you, in comparison to a similar report that was published in a major scholarly journal only four months ago. On the other hand, if you are in any of the historically-based disciplines—philosophy, history, English, music, art history, foreign languages and literatures, archæology, or Classics—then an article published a century ago may contain information just as relevant, and essential for your research, as it was when it was published originally. This is a sound principle to keep in mind, especially when using online databases of all kinds. Again, we wish to emphasize that most of these databases contain materials, and references to materials, which are, at best, only a few decades old. Only a small number of major systems—the Library of Congress catalogue, the online version of *Dissertations Abstracts International*, and a few others—have incorporated retrospective cataloguing in their online services. Most other databases, however, have printed catalogues, indexes, and abstracts, which will allow you to search for information that predates the establishment of the online service. You should not forget to do this searching, too.

I. DIALOG

The DIALOG Information Service collects together more than four hundred databases that were created, and are maintained, by many different organizations and vendors. DIALOG, in effect, is a second-party reseller of information that has been collected and digitized by others. With its vast array of resources, the system has bibliographic and full-text material of value to every researcher. To find out what is available today for you, consult the most recent edition of their the annual *Database Catalogue*, which you should find among the reference materials for online searching in your library.[100] In the same collection, you should find four looseleaf binders that contain the complete guide to the system, as well as the "blue sheets," which are guides to searching the individual "files" or databases that DIALOG offers.[101] If you can do the searching yourself, you may wish to learn the contents of the brief *Pocket Guide to DIALOG*, which is available on the World Wide Web as

---

[100][DIALOG] *Database Catalogue* (Mountain View, California: Knight-Ridder Information, Inc., annual).

[101] *Searching DIALOG: The Complete Guide* (Palo Alto, California: Dialog Information Retrieval Services, constantly updated). The four binders are: [1] *Text*; [2 and 3] *Blue Sheets*; and [4] *Yellowsheets and Dialorder Information*.

well as in printed form.[102] You also should review the short pamphlet *Getting Started on DIALOG: A Guide to Searching.*[103]

Since so many different organizations and companies create the databases on DIALOG, and their files appear in so many distinct formats—full-text, citations, and abstracts, among others—it is difficult to choose one sample entry from one database to illustrate DIALOG's presentation. We chose File 56, the online version of *ARTbibliographies Modern,*[104] as the location for a brief search for recent materials on the nineteenth-century court painter, Franz Xaver Winterhalter. Our search, under his name alone, produced nine citations. The last of them is:

---

[102]*Pocket Guide to DIALOG* ([Palo Alto, California]: Dialog Information Services, frequently updated). See also the URL: http://www.dialog.com, the homepage for the system, from which you can retrieve the full text of the *Pocket Guide.*

[103]*Getting Started on DIALOG: A Guide to Searching* ([Palo Alto, California]: Dialog Information Services, Inc., 1994). This publication also is available in an online version from the URL listed above.

[104]The online version of *ARTbibliographies Modern* covers materials in the fine arts from 1974 to the present. It was created and is produced by ABC-CLIO, Inc. For its contents before 1974, you must check the printed version, under the same title.

1/5/9
DIALOG(R)FIle 56: ARTBIBLIOGRAPHIES Modern
(c) 1996 ABC-CLIO.

076254 076254

PORTRAITS OF FREDERICK CHOPIN
PORTRET FRYDERYKA CHOPINA
WARSAW, POLAND: TOWARZYSTWO IM. FRYDERYKA
CHOPINA (7-29 OCT. 1975). H. WROBLEWSKA. 84PP. IN
POLISH AND FRENCH. 46 ILLUS.
Document Type: EXHIBITION CATALOG

THE EXHIBITION INCLUDED OIL PAINTINGS AND WATERCOL-
OURS, DRAWINGS, PRINTS, SCULPTURES, MEDALLIONS AND
PLAQUES DONE IN POLAND AND ABROAD FROM
1826-1975. IT WAS ARRANGED CHRONOLOGICALLY, SO
THAT THE APPEARANCE OF THE COMPOSER MIGHT BE SEEN
IN RELATION TO HIS COMPOSITIONS. THE FIRST AVAILABLE
PORTRAIT WAS OF CHOPIN AT THE AGE OF 16. THE ARTISTS
WHO DID PORTRAITS AND WHOSE WORK WAS HERE PRE-
SENTED INCLUDE ELISA RADZIWI, ARY SCHEFFER, CHARLES-
HENRI LEHMANN, FRANZ-XAVER WINTERHALTER, JEAN-
FRANCOIS-ANTOINE BOVY AND THEOPHILE KWIATKOWSKI.

Descriptors: PORTRAITS; ART AND MUSIC; RADZIWI (ELISA);
SCHEFFER (ARY); LEHMANN (CHARLES HENRI); WINTERHAL-
TER (FRANZ XAVER); BOVY (JEAN FRANCOIS ANTOINE);
KWIATKOWSKI (THEOPHILE)

Notice, especially, that entries in online catalogues generally do
not reproduce the special characters of the original, even when the
language is written in Latin letters. For example, in the entry
above, the name "H. WROBLEWSKA" will, in the actual publication, be "H. Wrุblewska." Similarly, the titles of journals and
other words that usually are italicized will appear in plain Roman
type. Notice, also, that the terms listed in the "Descriptors" field

are equivalent to those which appear in the "Subjects" field of an online library catalogue.

We already have mentioned a number of the important reference works that are published by Gale Research Company in Detroit, Michigan. DIALOG offers several of them in digital form, including not only the *Encyclopedia of Associations* (File 114), which we discussed earlier, but also the valuable *Gale Database of Publications and Broadcast Media*, which is File 469.[105] The firm publishes many other reference books and series which may be of help to you. You can browse their catalogue and get more information about them from their home page on the *World Wide Web*. You can reach it at the URL:

http://www.thomson.com/gale/default.htm.

II. LEXIS/NEXIS

The online services of the Mead Corporation began in 1973 with the founding of the LEXIS system as a resource for those doing legal research. Soon afterward, the company added the companion NEXIS service, which covered newspapers and other news media as well as subjects in business, finanace, and other areas of inquiry that were related to law. Today, nearly a quarter century later, the combined LEXIS/NEXIS service still maintains this orientation, although it has expanded manyfold in its range of coverage.

Most people who use the service for non-legal research do so for access to the full-text of many newspapers and news magazines and for access to the online versions of major reference works that are useful in business and finance, including the online edition of the *Encyclopedia of Associations*.[106] In December, 1994, LEXIS/NEXIS was purchased by Knight-Ridder, the newspaper publishing conglomerate.

While most law students, and virtually all law schools, have LEXIS/NEXIS accounts, you also may be able to do searches on the system at terminals in your library, or by requesting a librarian to do the search for you, if you are not permitted to have access to a

---

[105]This is the online version of Gale Reasearch's annual publication, *Gale Directory of Publications and Broadcast Media* [129th ed., 3 vols., 1997] (Detroit, Michigan: Gale Research Incorporated, 1997).
[106]File ENASSC in the BUSREF "library."

terminal yourself. If you do have the ability to do your own searches on this system, we recommend that you review some published guides to the system before you begin. These guides usually are to be found in that part of your library's reference collection that covers online searching in general.

The *LEXIS/NEXIS Product Guide: Alphabetical List* is a looseleaf publication of a bit more than fifty pages. It is a list of contributors to the LEXIS/NEXIS system, together with the extent of coverage and routes to their information.[107] There are two large guides to searching the system effectively: Jean Sinclair McKnight, *The LEXIS Companion: A Complete Guide to Effective Searching*[108] and Christopher G. Wren and Jill Robinson Wren, *Using Computers in Legal Research: A Guide to LEXIS and WESTLAW.*[109] The latter, while oriented primarily to people who do legal research, is valuable for others, as well, because of its extensive coverage of the organization and manipulation of the system. Whether you use one of these guides or not, you should master the essential points in *Learning LEXIS: A Handbook for Modern Legal Research*, the system's own manual for training.[110] In addition, you may find, near the terminal you will use for your searching, a small pamplet entitled *Search Tips: LEXIS-NEXIS.*[111] If you cannot find it, ask your librarian if a copy is available for you to use. If your topic is one about law or things legal, you may wish to consult Gary Watson, *Online Legal Research for College Students*, for its useful suggestions.[112]

III. WESTLAW.

Soon after the Mead Corporation established the LEXIS service, the West Publishing Company, of St. Paul, Minnesota, established a rival service for legal research, WESTLAW. Though its legal resources are nearly as exhaustive as those on LEXIS, its usefulness

---

[107] *LEXIS/NEXIS Product Guide: Alphabetical List* (Dayton, Ohio: Mead Data Central, Incorporated, 1995), frequently updated.
[108] Reading, Massachusetts: Addison-Wesley Publishing Company, 1995.
[109] Madison, Wisconsin: Adams & Ambrose Publishing, 1994.
[110] Dayton, Ohio: Mead Data Central, Incorporated, annual.
[111] [Dayton, Ohio]: Mead Data Central, Incorporated, 1992.
[112] [Los Angeles], California: California State University, 1995.

for non-legal research lies primarily in a cooperative relationship with DIALOG, by which many of the latter's databases are available through WESTLAW under the heading, DIALOG ON WESTLAW. If you already have access to the DIALOG system, and you are doing non-legal research, you probably do not need WESTLAW for your work. If your college, university, or law school library has WEST-LAW but not DIALOG, you may be able to locate many of your research materials through DIALOG ON WESTLAW.

The West Publishing Company provides a number of valuable reference books and charts to the WESTLAW system, but, unfortunately these texts are not available online at the present time, as are the reference materials for DIALOG and LEXIS/NEXIS. Two works that are valuable, if you are going to make extensive use of WEST-LAW, are *Discovering WESTLAW: The Essential Guide*[113] and the *WESTLAW Reference Manual*.[114] Near the terminals you will use to search WESTLAW, you should find copies of three aids, the *WESTLAW User Guide*,[115] the *WESTLAW Desktop Command Reference*,[116] and the *WESTLAW Database List* .[117] If you cannot find them, ask your librarian where they are shelved. As with all references that are published by the providers of these commercial systems, these publications are updated frequently, so there may be newer editions of them than those cited below.

If you use the DIALOG ON WESTLAW service, you should consult Rosalie Massery Sanderson's *Beyond Legal Information: Searching DIALOG on WESTLAW: A Guide for Law Students*.[118] If you intend to make extensive use of the service, you should consider the latest version of Nancy P. Johnson's *Winning Research Skills*.[119]

---

[113]*Discovering WESTLAW: The Essential Guide*, 6th ed. (St. Paul, Minnesota: West Publishing Company, 1996).

[114]Nancy Johnson-Maloney, *WESTLAW Reference Manual*, 5th ed. (St. Paul, Minnesota: West Publishing Company, 1993).

[115]*WESTLAW User Guide* (Eagan, Minnesota: West Publishing Company, 1995).

[116]*WESTLAW Desktop Command Reference* ([Eagan, Minnesota]: West Publishing Company, 1994).

[117]*WESTLAW Database List* (Eagan, Minnesota: West Publishing Company, serial). This publication is updated or reissued several times each year.

[118]Minneapolis/St. Paul, Minnesota: West Publishing Company, 1993.

[119]Nancy P. Johnson, *Winning Research Skills*, 2nd ed. (Minneapolis, Minnesota: West Publishing Company, 1993).

Finally, for users of both LEXIS/NEXIS and WESTLAW, we recommend an article by Eleanor DeLashmitt, "LEXIS and WESTLAW: Searching for Hamlet on a Dark and Stormy Night."[120]

IV. OTHER LARGE COMMERCIAL SERVICES.

There are a number of other large commercial services to which some colleges and universities give access. Perhaps the best-known of these is the collection of Bibliographic Retrieval Services, better known as BRS. In 1994, Ovid Technologies, Incorporated, purchased this system, which now offers about eighty databases to its users, most of which are now more readily found on DIALOG or LEXIS/NEXIS. For more details on BRS, see the file descriptions and the documentation, called "field guides," at http://www.ovid.com.

Another commercial service, with a heavy emphasis on the fulltext presentation of business and business-related information, is the DOW JONES NEWS RETRIEVAL SERVICE. Though it offers almost fourteen hundred files, many of them are the same sources that are offered through DIALOG, particularly in the case of newspapers and magazines. If your library offers access to this service, you may wish to look at the information about it that is available at the URL: http://www.bis.dowjones.com. A list of the databases and files that are offered by the service can be seen at the URL: http://www.bis.dowjones.com/clipping/custom-clips /publications/publications.html.

V. RLIN [RESEARCH LIBRARIES' INFORMATION NETWORK]

The Research Libraries Group has a significant set of catalogues that includes the holdings of more than thirty of the major universities in the United States as well as specialized resources for students of anthropology, architecture, literature, and the history of science and technology. The principal interface to this collection is *Eureka*, which many colleges and universities make available to their students. The files that are available on RLIN are:

---

[120]*Legal Reference Services Quarterly*, vol. 12, no. 4 (1993): 43-74; reprinted ([New York, New York]: The Haworth Press, Incorporated, 1993).

BIB: Records for books, serials, sound recordings, and other materials.
ANL: Anthropological Literature
AVE: Avery Index to Architectural Periodicals
EST: English Short Title Catalogue (ESTC)
HST: History of Science and Technology
IIN: Inside Information

The bibliographic file (BIB), for example, contains information about more than twenty-two million books, periodicals, recordings, scores, archival collections, and other kinds of material held in major research institutions.

Use Eureka also to discover and locate books, journals, maps, sound recordings, musical scores, films, archive collections, and computer files that are held by research, corporate, and public libraries, as well as museums, archives and historical societies. You can print, download, or e-mail to yourself, the results of your searches easily.

VI. MELVYL.

MELVYL is the online union catalogue of the libraries of the University of California system. It also serves as a gateway to other databases and files and to a large periodical index. The CAT database lists more than eight million items, including books, archives, audio-visual materials, computer files, dissertations, government documents, maps, musical scores, sound recordings and video recordings. It is also possible to search CAT by title for periodicals held by the various branches of the University of California and by other libraries in the state. MELVYL's PE database now lists more than 798,000 periodical titles.

The great advantage of MELVYL for the student is that it operates twenty-four hours a day, every day of the year, unlike OCLC, which is closed for a few hours each night, and the Library of Congress's catalogues, which frequently are closed when the Library itself is closed. When it is three o'clock in the morning and you need to expand a bibliographical citation that you have just found in a footnote, so that you can search more effectively for the work later, then MELVYL is your friend. You can reach MELVYL by *telnet* at the

URL: telnet://melvyl.ucop.edu. Enter VT100, when you are asked for the type of terminal that is emulated by your communications software. Help is available on MELVYL to guide you through almost every type of search, but you can find documentation on the system at URL: http://www.dla.ucop.edu/welcome.html.

VII. MEDLINE.

Of the hundreds of specialized databases and bibliographic catalogues that are available through the Internet, we think that MEDLINE provides a fine example of the best type. MEDLINE is the National Library of Medicine's bibliographic database. It includes such topics as microbiology, the delivery of health care, nutrition, pharmacology, and environmental health. The categories covered in the database include anatomy, organisms, diseases, chemicals and drugs, and many other topics connected to the world of medicine. When the database began, in 1966, it was simply a digitized collection of bibliographical citations. Later, in 1975, abstracts and a greater depth of subject cataloguing were added, and MEDLINE became the chief source of citations for the whole world of medicine. It is available widely through almost every commercial database service, including DIALOG and OCLC.[121]

Below, we show a citation, with abstract, to an article which considers the possibility that an acute and painful attack of hemorrhoids may have struck Napoleon just before the battle of Waterloo, thus preventing him from functioning at his strategic best.

---

[121] If you wish to learn more about MEDLINE and the ways to use the information it contains, we recommend three good articles: Michael E. DeBakey, "The National Library of Medicine: Evolution of a Premier Information Center," *JAMA: The Journal of the American Medical Association* 266:9 (4 Sepetmber 1991) 1252-1258; D[avis] B. McCarn, "National Library of Medicine—MEDLARS and MEDLINE," in Jack Belzer, Albert George Holzman, and Allen Kent, eds., *Encyclopedia of Computer Science and Technology* (New York: Marcel Dekker, Inc., 1978) 11:116-151; and Donald A. B. Lindberg, Elliot R. Siegel, Barbara A. Rapp, Karen T. Wallingford, and Sandra R. Wilson, "Use of MEDLINE by Physicians for Clinical Problem Solving," *JAMA: The Journal of the American Medical Association* 269:24 (23-30 June 1993) 3124-3129.

MEDLINE EXPRESS (R) 1983-1989
TITLE: Piles of Defeat: Napoleon at Waterloo.
AUTHOR(S): Welling-DR; Wolff-BG; Dozois-RR
ADDRESS OF AUTHOR:
Section of Colon and Rectal Surgery, Mayo Clinic, Rochester,
Minnesota 55905.
SOURCE (BIBLIOGRAPHIC CITATION): Dis-Colon-Rectum.[122]
1988 Apr; 31(4): 303-5
INTERNATIONAL STANDARD SERIAL NUMBER: 0012-3706
PUBLICATION YEAR: 1988
LANGUAGE OF ARTICLE: ENGLISH
COUNTRY OF PUBLICATION: UNITED-STATES

ABSTRACT: Major events of history have frequently turned on seemingly
trivial matters. One such situation involves Napoleon Bonaparte at Waterloo. Napoleon was not feeling well on the day of the battle of Waterloo,
despite fighting well at Ligny, a few   days before the last, dramatic
June 18 battle. There is considerable indication that Napoleon was both-
ered by very painful thrombosed hemorrhoids. Did this affect his general-
ship that day? What is the evidence that Napoleon was afflicted with
thrombosed hemorrhoids? What contribution could this factor have made
to the French defeat at Waterloo?
MEDICAL SUBJECT HEADINGS:
France-; History-of-Medicine,-18th-Cent.;
History-of-Medicine,-19th-Cent.
MEDICAL SUBJECT HEADINGS:
*Famous-Persons; *Hemorrhoids-history;
*War-history
CHECKTAGS: Human; Male
PUBLICATION TYPE: HISTORICAL-ARTICLE; HISTORICAL-BIOGRAPHY;
JOURNAL-ARTICLE
PERSONAL NAME AS SUBJECT: Bonaparte-N
MEDLINE ACCESSION NUMBER: 88195741
UPDATE CODE: 8808

---

[122]This type of shortened bibliographical citation for the title of a journal is quite
common, especially in scientific and technical bibliographies, databases, and
notes. Most online services and published bibliographies have tables which translate these abbreviated titles into the full citation for the journal. In this case, the
journal is *Diseases of the Colon & Rectum*, published in Philadelphia by J. B. Lip-
pincott in cooperation with the American Society of Colon and Rectal Surgeons
and the American Proctologic Society. It is published in eight numbers a year,
beginning with volume 1 (January/February 1958).

VIII. THE ARGUS CLEARINGHOUSE.

The Argus Clearinghouse, which began at University of Michigan at Ann Arbor and has since become an important Internet entity of its own, provides indexes and links to many topical guides to the resources on the Internet. These guides, which are reviewed by the Clearinghouse for their value, identify, describe, and evaluate Internet-based information resources. All of the guides that are listed, and linked, in the Clearinghouse are available in electronic format—either in HTML, or plain text, or both—and are accessible through the Internet. Each guide, in turn, provides links to other information resources on the Internet, including *Web* pages, *Gopher* and FTP sites, USENET newsgroups, and electronic mailing lists. Each guide concerns one specific topic, or more than one if they are connected closely to one another. The primary purpose of each guide is to help users to access the topical information that is available on the Internet. The use of all the guides is entirely free of charge.

Created by a group of dedicated librarians, the Argus Clearinghouse is one of the major sources you should search in your quest for bibliographies and other reference materials which are germane to your topic. To reach this site, open *lynx*, *Netscape*, or another browser for the *Web* and go to: http://www.clearinghouse.net.

IX. THE DECEMBER LIST.

More officially known as the home of *CMC Information Sources*, this site is the home of a massive directory of sources of information about online communication and the Internet. Founded in 1992, it has become widely known as "The December List," from the name of
its founder, John December. You can learn more about this valuable asset at John December's home page, at the URL: http://www.december.com. You also can go immediately to it by choosing the URL: http://www.december.com/cmc/info.

The same site has a comprehensive index of tools for you to use in exploring the Internet. You can reach this index either from the home page that is listed above or by going directly to the main query page at the URL: **http://www.december.com/net/tools.**

X. ALTAVISTA.

With so many resources on the Internet, and, more especially, on the World Wide Web, you may well think it impossible that you will find specific locations which will have information to help you in your research. You need not rely on luck to find sites of potential importance to you, however, thanks to another triumph of the digital age, the search engine. This software array goes out onto the Internet, much like a well-trained bloodhound, to discover and index, in a fully-searchable way, as many *Web* pages and archives of USENET newsgroups as it can find. While there are a number of sites with important search engines—LYCOS,[123] INKTOMI,[124] and EXCITE,[125] to mention three—the most comprehensive in content and versatile in responding to searches by users is ALTAVISTA.

ALTAVISTA began in the summer of 1995 at the Research Laboratories of the Digital Equipment Corporation in Palo Alto, California. On December 15, 1995, the system went online with a full-text index of more than sixteen million pages that were then available on the Web and in the USENET archives. By May, 1996, the index had exceeded thirty million pages, and, by late 1996, ALTAVISTA was responding to more than twenty-two million queries of its index every day.

Take the time to learn at least the rudiments of searching this comprehensive resource. You can begin at the home page for the system, URL: **http://www.altavista.digital.com.** Once you have mastered some of the nuances you can learn for getting to the information you wish as quickly as possible, you probably will wish to go immediately to the advanced query page. You can do this by entering the URL:

http://altavista.digital.com/cgi-bin/query?pg=aq&what=web&text=yes

---

[123] Its home page can be found at the URL: **http://www.lycos.com.**

[124] URL: **http://inktomi.berkeley.edu.**

[125] URL: **http://www.excite.com.** Excite is particularly useful because of its additional finding aids and links, including databases for addresses and telephone numbers and for email addresses.

or by choosing it from the main menu and then bookmarking it with your browser so that you can return to it swiftly.

XI. YAHOO.

YAHOO is a hierarchically-organized subject-oriented guide for the World Wide Web and other sources of information on the Internet. Like a number of important resources on the Internet, it began under the sponsorship of a major university—Stanford University in Palo Alto, California, in this case. Today, YAHOO is an independent institution of great importance to all researchers on the Internet.

The system lists sites by categories according to subject and then arranges those categories in a logical tree. It has its own search engine, which makes finding the material you wish quite easy, but the arrangement of links in branches according to subject also makes it easy to find other sites which have material that is related closely to the subject matter of the site you found first.

For example, if you are searching for sites on the Internet to help you with your writing, you will find a substantial number of them indexed at YAHOO under:

Social Science:
   Linguistics and Human Languages:
     Languages:
       English:
         Grammar, Usage, and Style.

The currency of information on YAHOO—it is updated on every day of the year—and its interface, which is very easy to use, makes this site one which is visited frequently by almost every serious user of the Internet. Most *Web* browsers allow you to select a specific *Web* page at which your browser will start each time you use it. Many users have chosen to make the home page at YAHOO their default *Web* page when they use their browsers. Like ALTAVISTA, YAHOO responds to millions of queries of its database every day.

To reach YAHOO, use the URL: **http://www.yahoo.com**. If you are using *lynx*, or another non-graphical browser for the *World Wide*

Web, you should use the URL for the text-only home page at: http://www.yahoo.com/text.

There are, quite literally, millions of pathways to valuable information, both bibliographical and textual, on the Internet, of which we have mentioned only a few. You must remember that your purpose in using the Internet for serious research lies not in recovering the full texts of either primary or secondary sources—we probably are at least one generation away from that—but rather in using modern bibliographic techniques, which are, themselves, merely digital versions of traditional cataloguing and indexing, to locate the places where you can find your sources. Here is an appropriate place to remind you, once again, that published bibliographies and finding-aids are just as important as online resources—and, in many cases with research in the arts and humanities, much more important than they are at the present time.

XII. WILSON INDEXES AND ABSTRACTS

Another useful collection of resources which you should not omit from your consideration is the collection of abstracts and indexes that are issued by the H. W. Wilson Company.

Their most well-known product, the *Readers' Guide to Periodical Literature*, now is available in two online versions on OCLC.. More importantly, for the purposes of serious research, are the company's two dozen other indexes and abstracts, for *Applied Science & Technology, Art, Biology and Agriculture, Business, Education, General Science, Humanities, Legal Periodicals & Books, Library Literature, Social Sciences*, as well as *Book Review Digest* and the *Vertical File Index*. Most of these are available on CD-ROM and online, as well as in print. Many are a part of the *FirstSearch Extended* service on OCLC; while many college and university networks have mounted the CD-ROM versions on their local networks so that students and faculty can have access to them readily. All of the Wilson products are updated frequently. Other Wilson indexes include *Bibliographic Index, Biography Index, Cumulative Book Index, Essay and General Literature Index, Play Index*, and *Short Story Index*.

Your First Sources

At this stage of your work, you should have gathered together the first works you found in searching online catalogues and the catalogue of your own college or university library. Probably you will have found several books which have sections that include discussions of your topic, and you may have found several scholarly articles, as well.

Of course, the books almost certainly will not provide you with very much information about your topic. A modern monograph is, almost by definition, a synopsis or epitome of a broad topic; and the much narrower topic you chose will, therefore, be only a small part of the larger narrative of the monograph.[126] The books that you found are, however, very important to your work, because of the bibliographic citations you can glean from them. As we mentioned before, do remember that, while some general or popular books have bibliographies, all scholarly books have them; and these bibliographical materials are the most important items you will find in your first stages of collecting information.

You now should begin to think of the research process as analogous to peeling back the layers of an onion, one by one.[127] The works that you found in the first searches that you made for information are, in effect, the outermost layer of the research onion. They are often quite far removed from the valuable material you will discover as you trace carefully the genealogy of information backward through the sources that you discover, which you do by tracing citations to new sources. You must remember always that successful research is a matter of serious **sitzfleisch**,[128] and your

---

[126]There are some monographs which deal extensively with the most minute aspects of research, but these are only a small percentage of the total number of scholarly books that have been published.

[127]And, like the layers of an onion, you will find nothing at the core, by which we mean to say again that there is no whole truth, only a portion of past reality which illuminates a tiny part of the truth. It also is useful to remember that when you have completed your research, if you have done your work carefully, you will have exhausted all the accessible materials which apply to your topic.

[128]From the German *sitzen* "to sit" and *fleisch* "flesh." It is the ability to endure or persist in some activity. The word was transferred in exactly its German, and present, meaning into English, apparently by D. H. Lawrence in his novella *The*

failure to be both patient and persistent will be visible in any short-comings in your final paper. This quality of sitzfleisch also is the perfect solution to one of the most common complaints of beginning researchers: "There is so much to learn that I can't possibly do it." Of course, as in every aspect of knowledge, one student will master the requisite information on a subject very quickly, perhaps in a few days only, while another may take several weeks to gain the same mastery of the same information. So what! After the second student has mastered the subject, who can tell the difference between the two?

This moment probably is an opportune one to alert you to the fact that you will, almost certainly, discover a number of contradictions in your secondary sources. Do not be alarmed by conflicting dates of birth or death, or by conflicting accounts of when and where a person performed certain deeds—or by variations in the spelling of names and titles! We all make errors, no matter how meticulous we may be. Few of the erroneous statements you find will have been made through a deliberate effort to deceive or misdirect. Rather, you simply are finding the lapses of concentration or effort that bedeviled earlier writers on your topic. Even the greatest scholars inadvertently have contradicted themselves from one part of their writing to another and have created fresh errors by momentary lapses of scholarship.[129]

Lovely Lady (D[avid] H[erbert] Lawrence, The Lovely Lady [London: Martin Secker, 1932] 165: "They simply hadn't enough Sitzfleisch to squat under a bho-tree."). For additional illustrative quotations, see the Oxford English Dictionary, 2d ed., s. v. "sitzfleisch."

[129]Even so great an historian as Ludwig von Pastor, the author of the monumental History of the Popes in forty volumes, has created confusion, simply because of the vastness of his own scholarship—so great that we are amazed at his exhaustive understanding of the materials which underlie his books. In volume six of the English translation of his great work [The History of the Popes, 2nd ed., ed. by Frederick Ignatius Antrobus (St. Louis, Missouri: B. Herder, 1902)] he narrates the dramatic scene in which Francesco Maria della Rovere, nephew of Pope Julius II and Duke of Urbino, stabbed Cardinal Francesco Alidosi to death on a public street in Ravenna, crying out, as he did so, "Traitor, art thou here at last! Receive thy reward!" (p. 350). In the next volume of his history, volume seven [The History of the Popes, 2nd. ed., ed. by Ralph Francis Kerr (St. Louis, Missouri: B. Herder Book Company, 1923)], Pastor recounts how Julius II's successor, Leo X, summoned della Rovere to Rome to account for many of his actions,

This is a good time to draw your attention to the great importance of correctness in your own transcriptions and quotations as well as in your citations, especially those which have many numerals in them. As a single writer, you do not have the power to reduce the rate of error in such matters, but you do have the power to prevent the rate from increasing. In verifying the accuracy of your own work, you probably will have the great advantage of having the original text in front of your eyes, for you probably will not take notes from your sources but rather gather together photocopied materials, which you will have beside you as you write.[130] The transmissions of information from one locus to another will, therefore, be reduced by one. In taking great pains to avoid propagating errors in your own texts, always remember the famous phrase in medical ethics that is paraphrased from the Hippocratic Oath,

---

both in Julius's time and in Leo's. One of them was "his participation in the murder of Cardinal Alidosi." Pastor leaves us uncertain, now, whether della Rovere, in fact, did stab the cardinal to death (he did, indeed!) or whether he "participated" in some less dramatic way.

Another example of an author who lapsed in concentration from one part of a book to another can be seen in the novel *Washington Square* by Henry James. In the first paragraph of chapter two of that work, James wrote: "The Slopers had been but two in number, and both of them had married early in life. The *younger, Mrs. Almond* by name, was the wife of a prosperous merchant... He [Dr. Austin Sloper] preferred Mrs. Almond to his sister Lavinia, who had married a poor clergyman,... Mr. Penniman...." Later, in paragraph twenty-seven of chapter six, James wrote: "He addressed himself to the *elder of his sisters, Mrs. Almond*—...." (bold italics, ours). Thus, in the space of a very few thousand words, James has reversed the relationships of the three siblings. Where once Mrs. Elizabeth Sloper Almond had been his younger sister and Mrs. Lavinia Sloper Penniman had been the elder, now Mrs. Almond becomes the elder of the two and Mrs. Penniman, the younger . This lapse appeared in the first book edition of the work (New York: Harper & Brothers, 1881) and remained uncorrected by James through the remaining thirty-five years of his life.

[130]When you find materials that cannot be photocopied, because of their delicate physical condition or their rarity, or because of policies which forbid photocopying, you must make careful transcriptions of the passages you will need later in your work. If it is posssible, use a laptop computer and transcribe the text directly into your wordprocessor, in a separate file for each work you consult. Verify carefully that your transcription is comlpetely accurate, including punctuation and any typographical peculiarities, like misspelled or missing words. Once you have done this, not only will you have confidence in the accuracy of your notes, but you also can transfer any text you wish to quote directly from your own transcript into your manuscript.

"First, do no harm."[131] It is for this reason that the photocopier has become a good friend to all serious researchers. If properly and clearly made, a photocopy eliminates the possibility that the researcher has made an error in her transcription of materials. Below, in the section entitled "Preserving Your Paper Trail," we discuss the value and use of the photocopying machine more extensively.

In the process of analysis, which we will describe later in this book, you will learn how to compare various elements of conflicting data in such a way as to try to determine which of two or three contradictory statements is the true one. When you have documented the first occurrence of an error in a narrative, you can discern how that error was transmitted from one published source to a later published source, and so forth to the present time. This establishment of a chain of repetitions of errors is known as a "genealogy of error," and your work may well serve to relegate myth to its proper place and to establish the factual materials on their proper footing.[132]

---

[131] In the famous Oath, the traditional text of Hippocrates states "Into whatsoever houses I enter, I enter to help the sick, and I will abstain from all intentional wrong-doing and harm, especially from abusing the bodies of man or woman, bond or free." On the next line of the text rests the age-old absolute confidentiality of discussions between doctor and patient: "And whatsoever I shall see or hear in the course of my profession, as well as outside my profession in my intercourse with men, if it be what should not be published abroad, I will never divulge, holding such things to be holy secrets." See W[illiam] H[enry] S[amuel] Jones, *Hippocrates, with an English Translation*, 4 vols. (London: William Heinemann, 1923) I:299-300. For a fascinating discussion of the Oath through history, see also W[illiam] H[enry] S[amuel] Jones, *The Doctor's Oath: An Essay in the History of Medicine* (Cambridge: The University Press, 1924), with texts of the oath in Greek, Arabic, Latin, and English, and a bibliography on page 62.

[132] You should note that some errors are committed by the principal persons in your topic, the very creators of the primary source material, and that your corrections will be based on other primary sources which were not available, or not consulted, by the principal persons in your research. One example of this, which is a salutary example, is the birthday of Chester Alan Arthur, the twenty-first president of the United States. He, himself, thought that he was born on October 5, 1830, and so stated this "fact" during all of his adult life. He apparently never bothered actually to look at the entry in his mother's family bible which noted his birth. Had he done so, he would have discovered that he was, in fact, born in 1829—and was, thus, a year older than he thought he was. Before you yield to the impulse to smile, you should reflect that you probably do not remember your own birth and that you rely on the testimony of others for the facts sur-

Another experience you almost certainly will have, if not for this first research paper, then later in other professional work, is a phenomenon which we can call the "circularity of sources." This occurs when you discover a wide array of secondary material on your subject, and all, or nearly all, of it was based on one or two texts. If you do encounter this, you will recognize immediately that all of this pile of secondary material is, fundamentally, useless to you, and you must—as the earlier authors did themselves—go to the sources on which they all relied. In such a case, you need to concentrate strongly on identifying those sources that underlie those secondary sources upon which everyone else relies. This makes your detective work more difficult, because, we may charitably presume, some of the authors who have relied on the earlier published material did make an attempt in good faith to do the same thing—that is, to discover the antecedent primary material—but with no success.

Finally, we need to say a word here about the differences between **subject bibliographies** and **descriptive bibliographies**, because you may well encounter some of the latter in your own searching. All of the published bibliographies, and many of the online sources, we have discussed thus far fall into the category of subject bibliography. They are compilations of books, articles, manuscripts, and other items of scholarly value about the subject of your inquiry. Descriptive bibliographies, on the other hand, contain detailed descriptions of books and other published materials when they are considered as objects in their own right. Often limited in scope to the works of one author, works published by one press, or works published in one place or during a specific period, they represent one of the achievements of technical scholarship in the life of the book from the fifteenth century to the present time. When you hear of the sale or discovery of a rare first edition, for example, it is the work of the descriptive bibliographer which allows us to know just what the characteristics of that first edition are, and how to identify them. While you may have no need for

---

rounding your entrance into the world. In this regard, the testimony of a written record, perhaps a birth or baptismal certificate, may well be more reliable than the verbal testimony of relatives—although one presumes that your mother does remember the occasion of your birth and does, therefore, make an excellent witness.

such bibliographies now, in your first researching effort, unless you are writing the history of one book itself, you should know about the field of descriptive bibliography. It is a fascinating one.[133]

BROWSING THE SHELVES—PHYSICALLY AND DIGITALLY

Another method that you can use to find information about your topic is a very commonsensical one, but one which many people never even consider—that of browsing or reading shelves. Many people who are not conducting research use this technique quite frequently, and with happy results, to find books for their reading pleasure. We ourselves, and many of our friends, pass hours in libraries simply browsing. This technique, however, can be put to use for scholarly research, if performed in a systematic way. We discussed earlier the importance of becoming familiar, yourself, with the cataloguing system that your library uses, which probably is either the Library of Congress Classification System or the Dewey Decimal System. Once you have discovered the books, and the bound volumes of serials, that are about the general area of your topic, you can browse through the bookstacks where they are shelved. Reading the shelves is possible in those libraries which have open stacks, which probably is the case with your college or

---

[133]The modern scholarly study of descriptive bibliography really begins with Ronald [Brunlees] McKerrow, *An Introduction to Bibliography for Literary Students* (Oxford: At the Clarendon Press, 1927; 2d impression with corrections, 1928; reprinted, Winchester [England]: St. Paul's Bibliographies, 1994). This famous manual began as a revision and enlargement of McKerrow's "Notes on Bibliographical Evidence for Literary Students and Editors of English Works of the Sixteenth and Seventeenth Centuries," *Transactions of the Bibliographical Society*, XII (1914). Almost contemporary with McKerrow, and often revised since, is Arundell James Kennedy Esdaile, *A Student's Manual of Bibliography* (London: George Allen & Unwin Ltd., The Library Association, 1931), now in its fifth edition as: *Esdaile's Manual of Bibliography*, revised by Roy Bishop Stokes, 5th rev. ed. (Metuchen, New Jersey: Scarecrow Press, 1981). The great American contribution to the field remains Fredson Thayer Bowers, *Principles of Bibliographical Description* (Princeton, New Jersey: Princeton University Press, 1949; reprinted, New York: Russell & Russell, 1962; reprinted, Winchester [England]: St. Paul's Bibliographies, 1986 and 1994), St. Paul's Bibliographies, 15. The modern standard introduction is Philip Gaskell, *A New Introduction to Bibliography* (Oxford: Clarendon Press, 1972; 2d. impression, corrected, 1974; reprinted Winchester [England]: St. Paul's Bibliographies, 1995).

university library, and certainly is the case in almost all public libraries. Some large collections, however, such as the Library of Congress, have closed stacks, so you cannot simply walk in to look at the items on the shelves. If that is the case, do not despair!

Thanks to the organization of the online catalogues of the Library of Congress, you can carry out this process in a digital way, as well. See Appendix A for a short tutorial on how to use the **brws call** command to "browse" the collection of the Library of Congress according to the order in which the books are placed on the shelves.

CITATION SEARCHING

Citation references began with the study of law in the later years of the nineteenth century. After the Second World War, a scholar from Philadelphia, Eugene Garfield, realized that the same principles of bibliographic reference which allowed a lawyer to trace the evolution of some aspect of case law or some specific decision by a judge forward in time would be equally worthwhile to researchers and scholars in other fields.[134] In 1958, he founded the Institute for Scientific Information to provide researchers with access to current research information. Today, the Institute maintains a comprehensive, multidisciplinary, bibliographic database of research information that embraces more than sixteen thousand international journals, books, and proceedings in the sciences, social sciences, and arts and humanitites. The Institute indexes the complete bibliographic data on each of the articles in these journals together with all of the references that were cited by an author and the abstracts for every item it includes.

Of all of the many varieties of information which can be retrieved through this monumental database, the citation indexes are the most important. A citation search leads you to new material about your topic, because it gives you references to scholarly publications whose authors have cited the same article or book which you found in your earlier searching.[135]

---

[134]For much of this introductory information, we are indebted to the pages of the Institute on the *World Wide Web*. This material can be found at URL: http://www.isinet.com.

[135]Please read the excellent discussion of citation sources in Mann, *Guide*, 61-65.

The indexes allow you to uncover both current research and retrospective information, because they are generated by capturing and indexing all of the bibliographical references that were cited in the scholarly books and journals that the database stores. Through them, you turn your place in the stream of scholarly research and writing from a position at the point or vertex of a cone—from which vantage point you look backward at what has been done on your topic, and related topics, before—to the position of standing at the waist of an hourglass—from which vantage you see not only what has been done before but also how the material you already have discovered has, itself, been used after its original publication, based upon the number of times a book or article has been cited in bibliographical notes by other scholars in the field.

When you perform a citation search, you are, in effect, asking the authors of scholarly articles themselves to lead you to further information. Thus, citation searches produce additional bibliographical references for you to use that you might otherwise miss.

For example, let us suppose that you have found one book and three scholarly articles which discuss your primary source material in considerable scholarly and critical detail. The book was published in 1968, and the three articles appeared in 1976, 1981, and 1986, respectively. In spite of your careful use of *WorldCat* and the Library of Congress's databases, and searches in published bibliographies and catalogues, you have not found anything more recent than the last article. By conducting a citation search with the authors and titles of the four works you have in hand, you will discover which other authors have cited them in references in which other books and articles. Perhaps you will discover references to the article published in 1981 in other articles published in 1989, 1991, and 1995. Yes, you missed these in your original search, because they were not indexed or catalogued under the same subject headings that were used for your original discoveries, but now you have found them.

Once you retrieve and examine the new material, you may experience what one freshman writer called the "boomerang effect." That is, the new articles will have still other bibliographic references, other than those for which you searched originally, which may be older still and contain valuable information about your topic. Thus, you have swept forward in time in your search for material and, by doing so, you found other valuable references which "boomeranged" you backward to material which antedates the books and articles with which you started.

Of course, citation searching is a favorite bibliographical technique of many members of college faculties and other authors who publish frequently, because it reveals to an author just who is using her past publications as sources. Thus, the greater number of citations of an author's work, the more flattered and encouraged the author is.[136]

The three files which cover the range of the Insitute's database are:

> *Science Citation Index*
> *Social Sciences Citation Index*
> *Arts and Humanities Citation Index.*

Science Citation Index is the oldest of the three. It began in 1955 and has been published continuously since that time. [137]An online version, called *SciSearch*, began in 1972,[138] and there is a CD-ROM edition as well,[139] which most college and university libraries have in their digital reference collection. In addition, the Institute has published one massive retrospective cumulation, which covers the period from 1945 to 1954,[140] and several master cumulations.[141]

---

[136]Of course, reputations in a community of peers, and promotions and funding for continued research, now often depend of how well one does in other people's searches through citation indexes. For a discussion of this new importance, see "Citation Data is Subtle Stuff—A Primer on Evaluating a Scientist's Performance" *Scientist* 1(10):9 (6 April 1987).

[137]*Science Citation Index.: An International Interdisciplinary Index to the Literature of Science* (Philadelphia: Institute for Scientific Information, 1955; quarterly, then bimonthly; with annual and quinquennial cumulations)

[138]It is available on DIALOG in two forms. The index from 1974 to the present is *File 434*, while a restricted cumulation from 1988 forward is *File 34*. The files are updated weekly.

[139]The CD-ROM edition is produced quarterly, with each issue being cumulative for the year. This edition also contains full abstracts.

[140]*SCI, Science Citation Index, 1945-1954, Ten Year Cumulation: An International Interdisciplinary Index to the Literature of Science, Medicine, Agriculture, Technology, and the Behavioral Sciences*, 10 vols. (Philadelphia: Institute for Scientific Information, 1988).

When you use *Science Citation Index*, you will want to know just which publications are included in the Institute's database and for which years they are covered. This information can be found in a small publication entitled *Source Publications for the Science Citation Index* which is published regularly by the Institute. Every library which has at least one version of the *Index* should have the list of sources, as well.

Social Sciences Citation Index began in 1966. The earlier years of its publication had annual cumulations, while later years have quinquennial cumulations.[142] The online version, called *Social SciSearch*, began in 1972 and is available on DIALOG as *File 7*. Its contents are updated weekly. The CD-ROM version, with abstracts, began in the summer of 1989 with the simultaneous release of annual cumulations for the years 1986 through 1988 and the second-quarter cumulation for January through June, 1989.[143] Of course, there also is a list of the journals that are covered in the Index which the Institute publishes regularly.[144]

Arts & Humanities Citation Index began in 1975 and has published, in three quarterly issues with annual and quinquennial cumulations, since then.[145] The online version began in 1980 and is available, as *Arts & Humanities Search*, on OCLC, as a part of the

[141]A particularly valuable one is *SCI, Science Citation Index, 1955-1964, Ten Year Cumulation: An International Interdisciplinary Index to the Literature of Science, Medicine, Agriculture, Technology, and the Behavioral Sciences*, 12 vols. (Philadelphia: Institute for Scientific Information, 1984). The increasing depth of coverage in the *Index*, as well as the increase in scientific and technical publication, is shown by the fact that the five-year cumulation that covered the period from 1970 to 1974 was published in fifteen volumes in 1976.

[142]For an appraisal of just how important the citation indexes have become in the conduct of American academic life, see Mary Alice O'Connor, "Dissemination and Use of Library Science Dissertations in the Periodicals Indexed in the Social Sciences Citation Index," unpublished dissertation, Florida State University, 1979.

[143]The quarterly issues thereafter are cumulative, with the fourth issue each year comprising the final archival cumulation for that year.

[144]*Source Publications for the Social Sciences Citation Index; Social Sciences Citation Index, Compact Disc Edition; Social Sciences Citation Index, Compact Disc Edition with Abstracts; Social SciSearch; and Social SciSearch on Magnetic Tape* (Philadelphia: Institute for Scientific Information, serially).

[145]The first five-year cumulation covered the period 1975 through 1979, inclusive. Beginning in 1989, the Institute has published a semi-annual cumulation, as well.

FirstSearch Extended service, and on DIALOG, where it is *File 439*. Its contents are updated weekly. The CD-ROM edition, with abstracts, began in 1989 with the issue of one retrospective disc that covered the period from1980 to 1989, followed by annual cumulations thereafter. Of course, there also is a list of the journals which are sources for the *Index*.[146]

In Appendix A, we give an example of a successful search in the *Arts & Humanities Citation Index*.

---

[146]Search under the title *Arts & Humanities Citation Index: Guide & Lists of Source Publications* or for the title *Arts & Humanities Citation Index: Guide & Journal Lists*.

The Annotated Bibliography

Before the arrival of the digital age, students were taught to make a bibliographic card, typically a five-by-eight or four-by-six index card, for each source they found. On that card, they placed the full citation of the work together with specific comments about the contents of the work and the general value of the material to the research process at hand. Often, college students would accumulate a shoebox full of cards, all alphabetically arranged, which disclosed the full scope of the works they had examined on their way to writing the term paper. Today, we have automated that process completely, but its fundamental importance remains the same. You begin each bibliographical entry with the details of a work you have found in an online catalogue, a printed bibliography, or a footnote or bibliographical citation in another work. If you need to order the work from another location through interlibrary loan, or perhaps through a consortium of libraries to which your college belongs, you will note the date on which you placed the order, so that you can check back with the staff of your library, if it fails to come in a timely fashion or if the lending institution sends the wrong volume.

When you actually read each item, you add comments to your entry which describe the contents of the work, in sufficient detail for you to make use of the comments later, together with some notes on the utility of the work to your research.

Sometimes, as you carry out the preliminary stages of your research, you will find a master's thesis or a doctoral dissertation that is close to your precise topic.[147] If you do, as with the germane entries in the bibliographies in books or the bibliographical notes in articles, you should consider starting an entry in your annotated bibliography for each cited work that you believe you must examine. As you retrieve and review each one, you can add appropriate comments, together with a cross-reference to the source from which you got the citation in the first place.

Remember that you do need to have a complete record of all the paths you have followed in your searches and what you found there. Perhaps, later, you will write another paper on a similar or

---

[147]If it exactly covers your topic, you will need to choose another.

tangential topic. If you do, your original annotated bibliography from the first research paper will allow to review what you have done in the past to determine what aspects of your earlier research efforts will help you in your later one. If you have not maintained a good record, you will find yourself looking at sources which you already had consulted in the past. There is nothing, just nothing, so annoying as finding yourself doing the same job twice!

If you choose to carry forward your research beyond the end of the semester, perhaps with a view to publishing you work, you almost certainly will need to add some material which you could not include in the original academic exercise because of a constraint of time or of access to sources that you needed. After even a few weeks, you will start to forget the fine details of the research process, and you will need your annotated bibliography to remind you not only of what you reviewed or read but also of what value each item was to you in your work.

As you review your first group of sources, you should begin your annotated bibliography. Do not omit this step. You need to know, at every stage of your research, just what works you have seen already, and how those works fit into the whole journey of your research. Below, we offer two sample entries from a very well-annotated compilation, one of a book and one of an article:

Rosenberg, John D. *The Darkening Glass: A Portrait of Ruskin's Genius.* New York and London: Columbia University Press; London: Routledge & Kegan Paul, 1963. 287 pp. Reprint: New York and London: Columbia University Press, 1986.

A signal and influential study of Ruskin's mind and art which serves at once as a valuable introduction to Ruskin and a telling synthesis of previous Ruskin scholarship. The book's eleven chapters are divided into five sections: Art, Architecture, Society, Wilderness, and Peace. Includes bibliography, pp. 253-261.

Arthos, John. "Ruskin and Tolstoy: 'The Dignity of Man'." Dalhousie Review 43:5-15.

Estimates both Tolstoy's allegiances to, and his misunderstanding of, Ruskin, and concludes by examining both men's similarity of dispositions as defenders of humane values in the late nineteenth-century world of mechanism, both Marxist and capitalist.[148]

As you can see from these examples, the researcher has created a complete bibliographical citation for each work that he examined and, beneath each entry, he has described succinctly, but carefully, the appropriateness and value of that work to his own research. Remember, when your paper is complete and you are ready to append your bibliography to it, you can take a copy of the computer file which contains your annotated bibliography, strip out the annotations,[149] and print what remains as the last part of the final form of your term paper.

How should you arrange the citations in your annotated bibliography? There are several methods that are of equal intellectual and categorical validity, but one which seems to serve the organizational needs of almost every researcher very well is to place your primary sources first, arranged alphabetically by author; followed by monographs,[150] again arranged alphabetically by author; then scholarly articles, with the same interior arrangement; and, finally, ephemeral and non-print materials, including prints, photographs, films, recordings, and other such material, arranged alphabetically according to the surnames of the principal figures associated with each work.[151] See the end of the sample term paper we include, "The Miracle of Bolsena," for a good bibliography that was prepared according to this method.

---

[148]Slightly adapted in bibliographical format from George Allan Cate, *John Ruskin: A Reference Guide, A Selective Guide to Significant and Representative Works about Him* (Boston, Massachusetts: G. K. Hall & Co., 1988), pp. 75-76.

[149]Which is the reason that you should use a copy of the original file, and not the file itself.

[150]A monograph is a treatise on one subject, usually bound as a book or a group of books, with numbered volumes. Many books, by which we mean texts bound within one cover, contain articles, excerpts, or selections from a number of texts. Among such books are commemorative volumes and *festschriften*.

[151]A photograph will be listed under the surname of the photographer, a print will be listed under the surname of the engraver, but a film may well be listed by title, followed, first, by the name of the director. The type of material will dictate the way the alphabetization will unfold in this part of your bibliography.

Preserving Your Paper Trail

Thus far, in the course of this book, you may have thought that we proclaim the computer to be the best friend of the researcher and writer. In fact, however, it is your second best friend, for your greatest immediate technological asset is the photocopying machine.

From the very beginning of your research, you will need to keep a meticulous record of all of the materials that you examine in your work. From the first book that includes some discussion of your research topic to the final letters and diaries that you unearth, you must be able to look at the paths you have traversed and to understand how each source is connected to your other sources.

For each work you view, you can make a complete bibliographical and contextual record with a photocopying machine. You should copy, at a minimum, the following information—title page, verso and recto;[152] bibliographical information, whether in the form of a gathered bibliography at the end of the book or article or in the form of bibliographical footnotes or endnotes; the information in each source which applies directly to the subject of your own research; and, last but very importantly, the foreword or preface that contains your source's acknowledgments of help and guidance. This last information needs to be emphasized especially, because it is too often overlooked by the novice researcher. Remember that the bibliographical materials show you the documentary sources that the author of the source at which you are now looking used to research and write her text, but the acknowledgments reveal to you the names of the persons who provided direct help to her in researching and writing the text at which you are now looking. Just as you will mine the bibliographical citations carefully to discover other sources of information about your topic, so, too, you should be prepared to mine the acknowledgments to discover the names and locations of persons you can contact to learn more about your subject, and special collections and archives which contain materials about it.

---

[152]*Verso* refers to the right-hand pages of an open book—those with odd numbered pages—while *recto* refers to the left-hand pages, those with even numbers.

Sometimes, of course, you will wish to copy the complete text of an article, or a suite of documents, that are interesting in themselves or crucial to your research, or both. The copyright laws permit you to make one photocopy of any printed material, as long as it is for the purpose of study or research, and will never be sold to someone else.[153]

After your computer and your modem, the photocopier is your greatest asset as a researcher, because, with it, you can preserve all of the significant documents and texts that you find in your research easily and accurately—and, if you will be meticulous in copying the title page verso and recto, you will have, ready to hand, all of the necessary documentation to annotate your own writing with the full story of your discoveries.[154]

Before you commit yourself to spending money in operating a photocopier, take a few minutes to learn the way in which the particular machine you are using is to be operated. Find out if it has any custom features which will make the copying of your materials both easier and less expensive. For example, if your printed text has margins on every *pair* of pages that enclose a text that is smaller than eight and a half by eleven inches, you probably can copy two pages of your printed source onto one page of photocopied

---

[153]So that you will feel comfortable with this assertion, below you will find the precise text which applies to this sort of use of copyrighted material:

107. Limitations on exclusive rights: Fair use

Notwithstanding the provisions of sections 106 and 106A, the fair use of a copyrighted work, including such use by reproduction in copies or phonorecords or by any other means specified by that section, for purposes such as criticism, comment, news reporting, teaching (including multiple copies for classroom use), **scholarship, or research**, is not an infringement of copyright. In determining whether the use made of a work in any particular case is a fair use the factors to be considered shall include—

(1) the purpose and character of the use, including whether such use is of a commercial nature or is **for nonprofit educational purposes**;

(2) the nature of the copyrighted work;

(3) the amount and substantiality of the portion used in relation to the copyrighted work as a whole; and

(4) the effect of the use upon the potential market for or value of the copyrighted work. The fact that   a work is unpublished shall not itself bar a finding of fair use if such finding is made upon   consideration of all the above factors. (17 USC §107)

[154]Similarly, you should photocopy the cover and the table-of-contents page of each issue of each journal from which you take information.

material. If the machine has the facility of reducing the size of the image, you may be able to copy even quite large quarto texts as two pages on one. If you do this, be sure to leave the widest margin on the photocopy at the top of the copied material, so that you can place your copies in a prong or three-ring binder, which will make consulting your ever-growing collection of sources easier.

It is very important that you preserve carefully the original borders of the pages that you photocopy, because there you will find the page numbers of the text. You will need these when you prepare your citations. Nothing is more frustrating, when you sit at the keyboard, typing your final draft, than to notice that you have all the materials you need to cite at hand but that the page numbers have been chopped off in the process of photocopying. You know, of course, that you must show these in your citation and, therefore, you must retrieve these items once again, just to get those page numbers. Make certain that this does not happen to you!

As you progress with your research, you will notice your cardboard box or drawer of materials grow and grow. In order to keep an accurate, but brief, account of all the materials—a running inventory, if you will—you should start to prepare an annotated bibliography at the time you begin to collect your materials. In a well-preserved wordprocessing file, you should type up a full bibliographic citation for each item you review and add a few brief comments of your own in which you describe how useful, or how unhelpful, each source is to your own project, and note carefully how the bibliographic information this source contains helps you to progress onward with the task of locating primary, or published primary, source material.[155]

---

[155]This task introduces you to an academic process which is often called a "literature review" or "literature survey." Almost every college student today envisions some active professional career in modern society. Yes, some may work a lifetime in serving fast food, but most probably do not aspire to a career in this occupation. Since that is the case, and since it is the case that almost every profession today demands at least one graduate degree for acceptance into full membership in the profession, it is worth knowing now that your master's thesis director, or similar faculty advisor, will almost certainly demand a full review of the current state of scholarship in your chosen field as a prerequisite to accepting a specific topic as appropriate for a master's thesis, or, indeed, a large seminar paper, which may lead onward to a doctoral dissertation or scholarly publication. After all, your

Your annotated bibliography will help you to remember which materials you have seen, when you saw them, and of what importance they were to you in your own research. One of the more frightening experiences that can occur to a novice researcher comes near the end of the whole process of research, analysis, and writing, when she discovers a reference to an article that seems, on the surface, to have great import, and yet the time for retrieving and digesting new information is past, and the final deadline approaches. She rushes to open the computer file that contains her annotated bibliography and she discovers that she already reviewed that very article two months before and found it to be both superficial and unhelpful. She breathes a sigh of relief, certain, now, that she has covered this point and that her ship of knowledge has not sprung a leak. On the other hand, if she did not maintain a meticulous annotated bibliography, she must rush, in her doubt and uncertainty, to obtain this article, about which she has forgotten completely. A day later, she unearths it in a bound volume of the serial, only to find that, at first glance, she recognizes it as something with which she dealt before, and which she discarded as inappropriate to her work—in spite of its apparently germane and attractive title—and for which she made no note. Her reproaches of herself for this panicky waste of several precious hours may excite comment in the bookstacks of the library. If she found that she had to order this item from another institution, she may well prolong her sense of doubt and incompleteness for many days.[156] Just to escape from

thesis or disserttaion director does not want you to embark on a long, time-consuming, and perhaps costly program of research on a specific topic only to have you discover, six months later, that another thesis was done on exactly the same topic two years before at another university. At the same time, if you are working in the biological sciences, or another field which is experiencing a tremendous increase in the volume of knowledge at the present time, your advisor will want you to know about work that is similar to yours that others are doing in your professional community.

The annotated bibliography, therefore, will return, again and again, as a major part of the preliminary work of scholarship, no matter how many times you carry out the act of research and writing.

[156]The annotated bibliographic computer file will save you more labor at the end of your writing. If you have organized and maintained your citations well, you can make a copy of this file. Open this copy, block and remove the annotations you have written. The citations will now collapse together to form, automatically, the full bibliography that you need to place at the end of your term paper.

this type of fright alone is a good reason to regard the annotated bibliography as a great asset to your process of research.

At this point, we would like to review two concepts which provide the intellectual foundation and rationale for these tasks.

In your past schooling, your teachers may have mentioned or discussed the scientific method of research or the historical method of research. Fundamentally, both of these are the same, with only a minor difference with regard to the concluding purpose of such research. In the application of the scientific method, which can be stated in a number of ways, you carry out an experiment by carefully noting all of the variables which apply to the time, place, and condition of the experiment; then you document the process of the experiment with great precision and completeness. With this documentation in hand, your reader can, with due consideration for the variables involved, repeat your experiment and achieve the same, or nearly the same, result. What you have done is to provide your reader with a well-marked trail which discloses, without confusion or ambiguity, exactly what you did, so that the stream of cause and effect that you show in the experiment can be duplicated, almost at will, by anyone else who cares to do so.

In the historical method of research, you document the full extent of your own searches for information, the relationships among those sources, and the complete analytical process which those sources suggested as appropriate for the topic in hand. In this way, your reader can, if she wishes, follow your footprints in the sands of research—placing her foot exactly in the pattern left by your own. The difference in concept between the scientific and historical methods lies in the nature of the conclusion. In the scientific method, complete repeatability is the goal. In this way, the conclusion of each repetition is identical, presumably, to that of every other repetition. All those elements of knowledge which we regard as scientific fact are held to be so because of this Aristotelian

---

Some students prefer to enter their bibliographic data and associated comments into a database, rather than a wordprocessing file. There are several software products which have been designed with just such a purpose in mind. Perhaps the best of these is *ProCite*, which comes in DOS, Windows, and MacIntosh versions. If you do use a database program to create and update your annotated bibliography, you will need to format the information properly, delete the comments, and then print the file and append it to the back of your term paper.

model of repeatability. That is, if a phenomenon occurs in the same way in every case, we may assume, however tentatively, that it will always occur in this way. Through these acts of repetition, for example, we persuade ourselves that the spermatozoön and the ovum are the antecedent elements of reproduction in most natural creatures among the higher orders of the Linnæan classification, and not the phenomenon of spontaneous generation of creatures which was held to be true for so long by so many people. Likewise, we are convinced that the Moon has geological antecedents that are not distantly removed from those of the Earth, and that it is, after all, not made of green cheese.

In the historical method, by contrast, your reader must understand, through your clear and careful exposition of your sources and your precise documentation of your process of reasoning, exactly how you came to your conclusion. Your reader, however, is under no obligation, other than the bounds of logical reasoning, to agree with your conclusion.

Because the documented events of the past cannot change, in our quite non-Einsteinian view of human time, that which is preserved from the past is as static in its individual reality as a geological or physical artifact. We can assume, however tentatively, that the American Declaration of Independence really was a text which was presented to, debated by, and approved by the members of the Second Continental Congress in the early days of July, 1776.

In both cases, you should note carefully, that meticulous documentation is the key to a clear and unambiguous presentation of the fruits of your research.[157] As we did in the case of Thomas Mann's very valuable *Guide to Library Research Methods*, we often will draw your attention to sources that we have found to be partcularly important for the woman or man who wishes to become educated. One such book is Gilbert Joseph Garraghan's *A Guide to Historical Method*.[158] It an exposition that covers more than four hundred pages, he traces carefully and precisely all of the pathways,

---

[157]Of course, your conclusions may well, in the case of either method of research, provide the point of departure for another researcher to continue where you stopped.
[158] Gilbert J[oseph] Garraghan, [S. J.], *A Guide to Historical Method* (New York: Fordham University Press, Declan X. McMullen, distributors, 1946; reissued, 1951; reprinted Westport, Connecticut: Greenwood Press, 1974).

both in research and in logic, which the researcher must traverse in order to be sure of having done a thorough job. Garraghan's book is not so readily available as it once was, but copies of it can be found on the shelves of many libraries and, of course, you can order it through the interlibrary loan system if you cannot find it locally.

Before we press onward to discuss other mechanical techniques of research with which you should be familiar, we need to take a few moments to place this particular aspect, that of complete and thorough documentation, into its broad historical context, as a way of emphasizing its great importance.

Let us suppose for a moment that you take as a representative sample of humanity a man or woman who died one hundred thousand years ago; and you, through the agility of human imagination in language, transport that person, resurrected, to another human community that existed eight thousand years ago. Even though we have only a limited understanding of what both periods were like for their human inhabitants, we can assume that after a period of acclimatization, the person from one hundred thousand years ago would come to understand and cope with the society of eight thousand years ago. Of course, the Paleolithic person would observe many more kinds of stone tools, almost all of which would be manufactured with greater complexity and sophistication than those with which she had been accustomed, ninety two thousand years before, because Neolithic society was somewhat more technologically, and societally, developed. Now let us imagine that we have the power to revive both a person who lived one hundred thousand years ago and a person alive eight thousand years ago and bring them, side by side, to the main concourse area of Kennedy International Airport in New York. May we believe that both would enter a state of profound shock? Would either survive more than a few minutes of this extreme anxiety and emotional, as well as intellectual, trauma? Would these people see in us their descendants? Would they even recognize us as fellow human beings like themselves?

The human condition, as a purely biological entity, has undergone little, if any, Darwinian or Huxleyan evolution in the whole span of time we discuss here—your DNA is their DNA. So, if that is the case, what makes the period from one hundred thousand years ago to eight thousand years ago one of gradual, in some cases almost imperceptible, change, and the period from eight thousand years ago to our own time one of profound and accelerating change in the nature of the way we live our lives? The answer, of course, is an increase in the volume of stored information we have available to us.

And that great volume of stored information rests upon the discovery of literacy, in the ancient Near East, about seven thousand years ago.[159] Indeed, the only human difference between a Greek of the Golden Age in Athens, in the fifth century B. C., and ourselves is two thousand five hundred years of additional information; and the only difference between ourselves and a Roman of the zenith of the Empire, in the second century A. D., is eighteen hundred years of additional information.

The accumulation of this information, and the knowledge which has stemmed from it, occurred and was maintained by the clear relationship of an earlier element of it to a later one, which was discovered only because of the antecedent presence of the earlier element of information. Thus, we can see that the development of the steam turbine, by Sir Charles Algernon Parsons (1854-1931), as an industrial effect which made possible, for example, the modern age of rapid transatlantic ship crossings, was a consequence of the perfection of steam power itself during the course of the nineteenth century. James Watt (1736-1819) is antecedent, and necessary, to Sir Charles Parsons, in the same way that volcanism is antecedent to, and necessary for, metamorphic rock.

Only the documentation, not merely of fact, but also of speculation and error, has made possible the continuing expansion of

---

[159]We are not sure whether this marvelous concept originated with the Sumerians and was passed swiftly, probably through trade, to the Egyptians, or whether the pathway was the other way around. What seems to be clear is that the representation of ideas, either in the form of symbolic pictures of the ideas themselves or symbolic pictures of the words which identified the idea, was invented only once and spread throughout the Old World from its original seed. We are not talking here about arithmetical notation or labels for persons or places, for those developments occurred to the Mayans, and to a lesser extent to the Incas, as well. We are, specifically, talking about the ability to place and elaborate train of thought into one coherent and connected whole.

human knowledge about humanity itself and the universe which surrounds it.

External change, while of little importance to the fundamental nature of the human condition, is of great importance to the circumstances in which each of us leads our lives. Preliterate societies offered each new generation of people a period for learning which lasted only so long as parents and other elders of the extended family remained alive to pass on the existential wisdom of their own experience, including, of course, the learning they had from their parents. Literacy offers each new generation the ability to review swiftly not only the activities and learning of the immediately-past generation but of a hundred generations. That is the whole foundation of modern human society.

By documenting your own research, meticulously and carefully, you add to the whole foundation of human knowledge, because you provide to the people who learn from you—your readers—the whole of the physical and intellectual process which you experience, that which is a part of your existential life, and you make it unnecessary for someone else to recapitulate exactly the precise mental road you followed, although, of course, your reader may well choose to do exactly that, if she wishes to continue forward where you stopped.

HOW TO READ *Worldcat* DISPLAY SCREENS

Below, you will see a sample entry from the *WorldCat* database of OCLC. Reading a catalogue entry, such as this one, will provide you with a large volume of preliminary information to allow you to decide whether or not this work is likely to be one that is germane to your research. After looking at the entire entry, we can break down the information in the various fields in the cataloguing to determine some essential characteristics of this book. Each portion of the entry that has a fully-capitalized term as its identifier is called a *field*; the whole of a single entry is called a *record*. This *record* contains eleven *fields*, but many records contains two dozen or more fields, each of which has information to help you evaluate the item that has been catalogued.

ACCESSION: 23950795
AUTHOR: Peterson, William S.
TITLE: The Kelmscott Press: a history of William Morris's typographical adventure.
PLACE: Berkeley, Calif.:
PUBLISHER: University of California Press,
YEAR: 1991
PUB TYPE: Book
FORMAT: xiv, 371 p.: ill.; 28 cm.
NOTES: Includes bibliographical references (p. 355-357) and index.
ISBN: 0520061381
SUBJECT: Morris, William, — 1834-1896 — Knowledge — Book
 arts and sciences.
Kelmscott Press.
Private presses — England — Hammersmith (London) — History
 — 19th century.
Book design — England — Hammersmith (London) — History —
 19th century.
Printing — England — Hammersmith (London) — History — 19th
 century.
Hammersmith (London, England) — Imprints — History — 19th
 century.
London (England) — Imprints — History — 19th century.

ACCESSION: 23950795

The accession number is OCLC's unique identifier for this volume and for this cataloguing record. It is the reference number for ordering the book through the interlibrary loan program. If your college or university library does not yet have online ordering for interlibrary loans, you will need this number to order this particular copy from another collection.

AUTHOR: Peterson, William S.

Obviously, you say, this field merely contains the author's name. But there is much more than that hidden in this simple collection of data. With the name at your hand, you can use *WorldCat*, the

Library of Congress's online catalogue, and other easily-reachable online sources, to discover a great amount of information about the author's background, his scholarly accomplishments, and his record of published scholarship. Quite often, this field also will include the author's date of birth and, if dead, the date of death.

TITLE: The Kelmscott Press: a history of William Morris's typographical adventure.

PLACE: Berkeley, Calif.:

PUBLISHER: University of California Press,

The firm or institution which published the book is an important datum in your preliminary evaluation of the work as a possible source. Since it is the case that all scholarly manuscripts undergo a scrupulous review of their content and accuracy before a major press will undertake the considerable financial and reputational risk involved in publishing the book, the name of a significant scholarly press is some indication of the work's value to the scholarly community. A work published by the University of California Press, for example, is likely to be of greater value than one published by, shall we say, Magnet Books. Even within the academic community there is a well-established hierarchy of reputation. The major English university presses, Oxford and Cambridge, stand in a select community that also includes the presses of the most distinguished American universities, including Harvard, Yale, Chicago, Stanford, and Princeton. Of course, this is not an invariable index of the importance and quality of any specific text, and major works have been published frequently by smaller university presses and even by small trade presses, such as the Edwin Mellen Press and Greenwood Press. Nevertheless, if your preliminary bibliography has many dozens of citations for you to consider, the publishers may well prove to indicate which of these many works you will want to review first.

YEAR: 1991

The year of publication is another valuable datum. In the humanities and the arts, the relative age of a work is not of particular significance. Indeed, works published in the last century are often the most valuable ones today. The present passion for modernity leaves many students with the impression that a work diminishes in value with age, but this is certainly not the case in many fields. The excavation reports of William Matthew Flinders Petrie, done late in the last century for the Egypt Exploration Fund, remain masterpieces of their kind, and often are the only reasonable sources for learning about early dynastic royal tombs in Egypt. The fact that these books are now more than a century old does not in any way lessen their value for the student and the scholar.

On the other hand, in the various fields of the sciences and technologies, the age of the text often does play a significant role in evaluating worth. A book on plant genetics that was published in 1980 is likely to be of much less value to the modern researcher than one published last year, simply because of the additions to our store of knowledge about plant genetics during the intervening period. So, the date of publication of a work has a variable importance which depends on the subject of the work, and its purpose.

PUB TYPE: Book

The great online catalogues, and database systems, now available to students and scholars, have records for many types of non-monographic and non-book material that are held by libraries, archives, and special collections. These include films, videotapes, recordings of all kinds, prints, photographs, manuscripts, and many other varieties of research materials. It is important for you to notice what type of work is represented by the cataloguing record at which you are looking.

FORMAT: xiv, 371 p.: ill.; 28 cm.

The *format field* also contains information of value. While the length of a work does not, by itself, give any indication of its value, it often does show the relative depth of treatment that the subject received at the hands of the author. A biography of a major figure of the past in one hundred fifty pages is likely, but not certainly, to be less significant than another of seven hundred pages. The information in this field also will show you whether or not the work has illustrations, as this particular book in our example does; and it will show other types of included material besides text, such as portraits, examples or diagrams, drawings, and frontispieces.

The vertical height of the work is shown as the last datum in this field. At first glance, this may seem of small importance. However, if you are using an open-stack collection, in which you go to retrieve the book yourself, rather than having an attendant do this for you, the height of the book often indicates where in the collection it is shelved. Most bookstacks have "folio" or "oversize" shelves that are located separately from the main collection. If a book is more than thirty-two or thirty-four centimeters high, it probably is shelved there rather than in the normal sequence in the general shelving.

NOTES: Includes bibliographical references (p. 355-357) and index.

The information in this field is particularly valuable for both the student and the scholar. As we have mentioned before, while it is the case that some non-scholarly works have notes and bibliographies, all scholarly works have them. So, a work which is not shown to have bibliographical material—information which appears in this field—probably is of lesser value than one which does. Remember, you will have to be able to document the primary sources of the information that you use in your term paper or article, and a source which gives no indication of where the author acquired her information will prove, automatically, to be a dead end. Of course, this maxim does not apply to works which are themselves published primary sources, such as autobiographies and memoirs, but it does apply in nearly every other instance.

We do not need to preach the value of a book with an index over a book which does not have one. While indices vary in quality greatly, in general, any index is a useful addition to the work, because it enables the reader to find the information for which she is searching without the necessity of scanning the whole work.

ISBN: 0520061381

The initialism ISBN stands for *International Standard Book Number*. This is a unique identifier for each book published since 1967.[160] It does not represent just the *title*, but also designates the *edition* and the *format* of that edition. For example, a hard-cover edition and a paperback edition of the same work, published at the same time, will have different International Standard Book Numbers. There is also a series called ISSN, which stands for International Standard Serial Number. It identifies uniquely each separate serial title.

Today, these numbers often are used as part of the ordering and accounting systems for interlibrary loan, as well as by commercial book dealers to place their special orders for customers. For the latter reason, the ISBN also is convenient for the student or scholar who wishes to purchase a copy of the book, because most bookstores have databases which have this number in a searchable field. If you wished to purchase a copy of Professor Peterson's book, for example, you need only supply your bookstore with the ISBN and your order should be handled smoothly and expeditiously.

SUBJECT: Morris, William, — 1834-1896 —
Knowledge — Book arts and sciences.
Kelmscott Press.
Private presses — England — Hammersmith (London)
        — History — 19th century.
Book design — England — Hammersmith (London) —
        History — 19th century.
Printing — England — Hammersmith (London) — History — 19th century.

---

[160]In the United Kingdom; it was introduced in the United States in the following year. For additional technical details on the ISBN, see *The Bowker Annual Library and Book Trade Almanac, 40th Edition, 1995*, ed. by Catherine Barr (New Providence, New Jersey: R. R. Bowker, Reed Reference Publishing Company, 1995) 564-568.

Hammersmith (London, England) — Imprints — History — 19th   century.
London (England) — Imprints — History — 19th century.

The terms that the cataloguer used to indicate the subjects encompassed by the work are especially important to you. They provide you with a group of terms which you can analyze with simple Boolean algebra to determine whether or not the work seems likely to be of value.[161] In addition to this great asset to your evaluation of a work, the subject cataloguing terms point you to specific groups of term which you can search, either online or in your library's printed or card catalogue, to find other works on the same general subject. For example, if you wish to find more about William Morris's education and state of knowledge, you can return to *WorldCat* to search again with the qualifier:

su:Morris, William, — 1834-1896 — Knowledge

and, if you wish to know more about the history of the community in which Morris established the Kelmscott Press, you can search with the following term:

su:Hammersmith (London, England)

---

[161]The principles of Boolean algebra, stated in the simplest terms, consist of grouping two or more sets with the connectors AND, OR, AND NOT. Let us say that you have two terms, "Lincoln" and "Presidency." If you group the two as "Lincoln OR Presidency," you will retrieve all the citations that include the term "Lincoln" together with all the citations that include the term "Presidency." Your combined set will, doubtless, be immense. The connector OR should be used only to gather together sets which include like terms which may have been used variably to catalogue the same information, such as "Motion Picture OR Film," so that you will retrieve all the entries for both, since either term may have been used at some time by a cataloguer. If you group together the term as "Lincoln AND Presidency," you will create a set which includes both "Lincoln" and "Presidency." Thus, your set will show materials about President Lincoln, but not about Lincoln's life outside his term in the presidential office. If you group the two terms as "Lincoln NOT Presidency," you will create a set which contains all the available materials about Lincoln other than his presidential service. Do remember that, in *WorldCat* and other *FirstSearch* databases, you must use AND NOT for those refinements of searches which, in other databases, you would use NOT by itself.

Notice that the fewer parts of the subject cataloguing term you include in your search, the broader your searching will be. If you wish to find materials that deal not with the history and geography of Hammersmith but rather only with the books that were published there, you would annex the term — Imprints to the elements you typed in for your search. The importance of the subject cataloguing cannot be overemphasized. It is your clearest guide to where this work lies in the taxonomy of all of humanity's knowledge. It performs the same role as the complete Linnæan classification does when you are identifying a living creature precisely—kingdom, phylum, subphylum, class, order, family, genus, species, and variety.

Labels for *WorldCat*

A '+' following the name of a Kind of Search means you can   search
for simple plurals.

KIND OF SEARCH	LABEL	REMARKS
Subject+	su:	Includes subject headings, titles, and contents notes. The label is not required. EXAMPLES: su:criticism
Author	au:	au:saul bellow
Title+	ti:	ti:gone with the wind
Subject Headings+	sh:	
Notes+	nt:	
Publisher	pb:	
Publication Place	pl:	
Series	se:	
Accession Number	an:	Use this label for searching only. There is no wordlist.
Gov Doc Number	gn:	
Report Number	rn:	
Standard Number	sn:	ISBNs, ISSNs, LCCNs.
Uniform Title	ut:	

BOUND-PHRASE SEARCHES	LABEL	REMARKS
Author	au=	A bound-phrase search looks for
Title	ti=	the FULL title, author, etc.,
Subject Heading	sh=	to appear EXACTLY as you type
Conference Name	cn=	it. We recommend that you find your term in the Wordlist first. Then follow the HINTS on that
Corporate Name	co=	screen to search it.
Music Number	mu=	

Beyond all the other advantages of using *WorldCat* to locate resources for research, it has one asset that can be found no where else—the ability to locate master's theses. Because OCLC receives cataloguing tapes from all of its participating libraries, including all the institutions in the United States and Canada which grant advanced degrees, *WorldCat* embodies the collective union cataloguing of all the holdings of these universities. Unlike doctoral dissertations, which are indexed in *Dissertations Abstracts*

International, and its online version, *Dissertations Abstracts Online* (DAO), there is no printed or CD-ROM catalogue of master's theses. Consequently, only an inclusive, online service can catalogue all of them successfully. An even greater advantage lies in the fact that a thesis note appears in a field of its own, making it possible for the researcher to identify all of the relevant master's theses in a search easily and surely.

It is important to emphasize the value of master's theses in searching secondary sources. They often are among the most valuable texts for beginning new pathways of inquiry. There are a number of cogent reasons for this. First, a thesis almost always is on a narrow and well-defined topic, and, consequently, its bibliography frequently is nearly all inclusive on the subject of the thesis. When the thesis is on a scientific or technological subject, and is quite recent, it often will embody knowledge that has not yet been published in monographic form, or even in a scholarly article.[162] And, even when a thesis is quite old, it may contain documentation or an exposition of materials to be found nowhere else.[163] Thus, the beginning researcher is always wise to look carefully for master's theses on the topic at hand and on intellectually-adjacent topics, as well.

HOW TO READ LIBRARY OF CONGRESS LOCIS SCREENS

Below, you will see a sample entry taken from the SCORPIO system of the Library of Congress—now a part of LOCIS, the Library

---

[162]Many scholarly articles from newly-fledged authors are, in fact, condensations or elaborations of sections of their master's theses.

[163]For example, several editions of the financial accounts of the constables of Bordeaux, which contain to most complete analysis of the financial aspects of English administration in the Bordelais during the High and Later Middle Ages, are to be found in master's theses. See John Robert Wright, "The Accounts of John de Stratton, Constable of Bordeaux (1381-1387) and John Gedeney, Constable of Bordeaux (1387-1390)" (M. A. thesis, Emory University, 1959); Joseph Righton Robertson, "The Accounts of Richard Rotour, Constable of Bordeaux (1375-1379) and William Loryng, Constable of Bordeaux (1379-1381) (M. A. thesis, Emory University, 1960); Francis Albert Young, "The Account of John Radecliffe, Constable of Bordeaux (1419-1423) (M. A. thesis, University of Maryland, College Park, 1972); Richard Paul O'Connor, "The Account of William Faryngton, Constable of Bordeaux (1401-1413) (M. A. thesis, University of Maryland, College Park, 1975).

of Congress Information System. It also shows another cataloguing of William S. Peterson's book, *The Kelmscott Press: A History of William Morris's Typographical Adventure*:

89-3351
Peterson, William S.
The Kelmscott Press: a history of William Morris's
  typographical adventure by William S. Peterson.
Oxford (England): Clarendon Press; New York: Oxford University
Press, c1991. xiv, 371 p.: ill. (some col.); 28 cm.

LC CALL NUMBER: Z232.M87 P45 1991

SUBJECTS:
  Morris, William, 1834-1896—Knowledge—Printing.
  Kelmscott Press.
  Private presses—England—Hammersmith
  (London)—History—19th   century.
  Book design—England—Hammersmith
  (London)—History—19th   century.
    Printing—England—Hammersmith (London)—History—19th
      century.
    Hammersmith (London, England)—Imprints—History—19th
      century.
    London (England)—Imprints—History—19th century.

DEWEY DEC: 070.5/09426/5 dc20
NOTES:
  "Published in the United States by University of California
    Press"—T.p. verso.
  Includes bibliographical references (p. 355-357) and index.

ISBN: 0198128878 : $52.00
LCCN: 89-3351

Notice that this record has some different information from the comparable entry from *WorldCat*. For example, you will see, annexed to the field which shows the International Standard Book Number, an entry which gives the original list price of the book. In addition, the field that is headed LCCN shows the Library of

Congress card number, which is the actual serial number of the cataloguing itself—originally on cards, hence a card number. This number, of which the first two digits are the year in which the cataloguing was done and the remaining digits are the serial number of the process, is the other important number, together with OCLC's accession number, which is used almost universally by librarians to refer to an item.

Most importantly, for your work as a researcher, the entry shows both the Library of Congress's call number and the corresponding number in the Dewey Decimal System. One of these two systems—probably that of the Library of Congress, if your college or university has modernized its own cataloguing in the past few decades—almost certainly will be the number under which your own library will have catalogued and shelved the book, or will be very close to it. It is an important reference. In Appendix A, we have an example of seaching this database as a part of a larger presentation which also shows you how to use the online version of the *Library of Congress Subject Headings*.

Finding The Right People

Very often in your research, you will want to know about the latest scholarship in your field and who is working in that field today.

Your bibliographic citations, which you got through both your online searches and your searches through published bibliographies, will, of course, show you the dates of publication. Especially in the sciences and technologies, you will be very concerned with discovering the latest information to have been published about your topic. As you review these recent books and articles, you will notice that some names will appear more frequently than others. It is not at all uncommon for one scholar to publish two books and five articles on the subject of her research within the space of five or seven years. The names that crop up again and again in your bibliographic searches are, almost certainly, the names of the recognized experts in your field. When these publications are recent, you have some reason to assume that the author is alive and still active in research. Whether the work at whose citation you are looking is new or old, you must now pay some attention to the affiliation note on the title page of a book or article, the line of text beneath an author's name which discloses the institution with which she is associated. This is your primary guide to how to reach that author for more information. Of course, if the text is an older one, the author may no longer be at the institution or organization that is cited in the affiliation note.

TALK TO AN EXPERT

Of course, as we already have hinted in the text above, printed materials and manuscripts are not your only source of valuable information about a topic. The most detailed information about many topics comes from the contacts you make with persons who are recognized already as experts in the field. You will have identified some of them, at least, by the time you have worked on your study for about two weeks—as we have said, they will be the people whose names appear again and again in the bibliographical material you discover and who are thanked frequently in the acknowledgments of the books and articles you have read.

Before you begin your quest to discover the locations of these experts and to talk to them about your own research, it is valuable to recall that they will be eager, in almost every case, to talk to you. Your problem is not getting your expert to speak with you and to help you in your research; rather your problem is getting them to stop giving you more and more information. This is true of scholars in every field, without exception. The reasons are clear. To "profess" a subject is to commit yourself to the knowledge of that field above any self-interestedness.[164] The love of learning does not spring from a desire to gain wealth or fame from it. Because every profession will die if older professionals cannot recruit younger students to follow them and advance the knowledge of the subject, every professional hopes that a student who avows an interest in some subject of which the expert has knowledge may become a successor in that profession.[165]

If your expert happens to be associated with a major corporation or an agency of the government, she may be willing to make the knowledge base of her organization available to you, as well.

The types of information you will learn from experts in your field are many and wide-ranging, far beyond merely a larger collection

[164]From the Late Middle English word *professe*, a profession of faith. Originally it was the formal declaration made by one entering a religious order or the document containing this profession. Before 1500, the word had no other meaning. In the early sixteenth century, it also came to mean "to declare openly, announce, affirm; to avow, acknowledge, confess, oneself to be (or do) something." Later, in the same century, profess came mean "to affirm or declare one's faith in or allegiance to; to acknowledge or formally recognize as an object of faith or belief." Later still, it came to mean a recognition of a claim to some knowledge of, or skill in, some art or science. In these senses—the final loss of which would be a major loss of meaning in the English language—any occupation which rewards its participants with wealth and fame is not a profession. A professional, one who professes, holds the object of his or her profession to be higher than any worldly consideration or gain. It is for this reason that people who aspire to become college or university professors should expect to be poor. In a world in which the word *professional* is used for every sort of person, from the golf player to the successful businessman—"he's a real pro"—it may be useful to recall the meaning of the verb *to profess*. See the electronic version of the second edition of *The Oxford English Dictionary* at URL: telnet://bosshog.arts.uwo.ca/oed/profess.

[165]The failure of experts in Classical languages and literatures to recruit successors successfully has led, in our own day, to a major crisis in Classical studies in many colleges and universities. Participants in other fields of study have this example before them as they face a younger generation of students.

of bibliographical citations. Your expert will tell you about what others are doing in the field, and often will provide you with names and telephone numbers so that you can reach still more experts. Notice that you are, in this way, taking the first steps to being enfolded into the professional network of scholars and students in the field, so that, if you do become fascinated by the subject, you will have a point from which to begin to learn more and more about what your future colleagues are doing today.[166]

Another point that we can discuss conveniently here is the question of the aging of information and the consequence of that process for your research. In general, the significance of information aging to your process of research is proportion to the degree to which information is increasing in the field. For example, nearly all of the seminal work on classical literature was done in the nineteenth and early twentieth centuries, so that only a small percentage of knowledge about the subject has changed significantly in the past few decades. By contrast, knowledge in genetics is increasing almost daily, altering in every way the intellectual lens with which we look at every living cell. Before 1960, the chromosome itself was a somewhat mysterious and arcane entity. The discoveries of Watson and Crick made all past observations of chromosomal phenomena obsolete. Consequently, the past three and a half decades have seen an explosion of new information about cellular life which has changed our intellectual view of genes and genetics completely. If you are studying the implications of Agricola's activities in Britain, in the first century, A. D., a book or article printed in, shall we say, 1884, may be very important to your understanding of the subject. By contrast, an article on the markers on a certain chromosome that was published in 1991 may be no longer of great intellectual importance, and also may, in fact, embody information that is no longer thought to be factual by scholars working in genetics today.

Once again, therefore, we need to emphasize that the currency of information is proportional to the speed with which fundamental information in a certain field is changing and expanding. Do not

---

[166]Remember to cite all the conversations and interviews you have had that produced information, or led to information, that you use in your paper. Every major style manual has a section which shows you just how to cite interviews, both those you do in person and those which you conduct on the telephone.

omit the great value of older materials simply because their date suggests obsolescence. Older materials may be the most valuable sources you can find for information in many fields.

With these salient points in mind, we now are ready to consider the question of how you can identify, locate, and speak with these experts.

As we mentioned earlier, your first clue to the identities of such persons is from the bibliographical materials in the books and articles you find first in your preliminary searching. Certain names will crop up again and again as authors. Many of these same names also will appear in the acknowledgments that other authors of books and articles make in the front matter of their writings. Let us say that you discover, through your online searching and through browsing carefully through published bibliographies, that one woman finished a doctoral dissertation in a certain field in 1977; then you find that the revised and expanded text of that dissertation was published as a book in 1979—with the same title, which tells you that the second text is the successor of the first; then you find three articles in scholarly journals in the field, one published in 1981, one in 1987, and one in 1991. In addition, you discover he name on the acknowledgments page of two other books and you find her name in the bibliographical citations in four other books and four other articles. You can begin to have confidence in the regard with which she held by her professional colleagues; and you can note her name on your list of experts to be consulted. But how will you find her?

One the title page of her books, and on the first page of the articles she wrote—either directly under her name or in an included note at the bottom of the page—you probably will find an affiliation note. This is a short notice, often in italic type, which names the institution with which she is affiliated, hence the name.[167]

Your first step is to call, write, or—most importantly—send email to the expert at the institution that was named in the affiliation note—including the name of the academic department or the section or division of a non-academic entity—to ask for help. At the

---

[167]Do not make the mistake of assuming that this notice applies only to books and articles that were written by people in academic life. Such notes appear frequently for authors who are associated professional with government agencies, commercial laboratories, corporate entities, and learned societies, as well.

same time, if you write or email, rather then telephone, you also should write to the department or other division named in the note and direct your letter to the head secretary or to the administrative assistant, in order to verify that your expert still is with that institution.[168]

Let us suppose, for a moment, that this attempt fails, and that you are not successful in reaching the author. Perhaps she has moved on in her career to another institution or perhaps she is doing an extensive program of research in another library, laboratory, or research institution. In such cases, you may be able to get a forwarding address and telephone number, or the name of a colleague to contact, to speed you in your search. But, again, perhaps you will find only a dead end, with, apparently, no easy way to continue. Do not become frustrated. If you do receive an address without a telephone number, or if you receive the name of another person to contact for more recent information, you often can discover a telephone number or an email address, as well, by using the collections of digital white pages, either on CD-ROM or online. Two of the more useful compendia of telephone number are *Pro-Phone* and *SelectPhone*. The latter also is available online as a part of OCLC's *FirstSearch* system.[169] Remember to try these resources whenever you have a name that is not attached to an address or a telephone number. Of course, if you know the address, these digital white pages almost certainly will yield a telephone number to you. Scholars, as a rule, do not fancy unlisted numbers.

---

[168]The old scholar's advice that the secretary is the real embodiment of knowledge about an institution holds especially true here. She, almost certainly, will know more about the people there, past and present, than will the present departmental chair or the divisional head. If, for example, the person for whom you are searching is retired, the secretary often will tell you how to contact the retired scholar. Perhaps only she will know a current address and telephone number.

[169] A quite comprehensive listing of directories, both national and international is available for students to use freely at the URL: http://www.contractjobs.com/tel. For the United States, an extremely useful resource, which can be searched in many different ways, is at the URL: http://www.switchboard.com. Also of note is the Yahoo People Search at http://www.yahoo.com/search/people. Here you often can locate e-mail addresses as well as geographical addresses and telephone numbers.

ENCYCLOPEDIA OF ASSOCIATIONS

Every profession has, in almost every country, an association that is devoted to the population of student, scholars, and practitioners in the field. In the United States, for medicine, it the American Medical Association; for microbiology, it is the American Society for Microbiology; for history, it is the American Historical Association; and for scholars in language and literature, it is the Modern Language Association. There is a national club for everybody. You can find them readily in the *Encyclopedia of Associations*, either in book form or online.[170] Simply use the name of the subject in which your expert is to be found as the keyword for the index to the *Encyclopedia*. Under that keyword you certainly will find a number of numerical indicators for professional and academic societies, but the one which has a conspicuously large membership will be the national association for that particular field. Once you have determined the correct name of the organization for professionals in the field, call them and ask to speak with the membership office or to the membership secretary. In most cases, professional organizations will provide you with both a contact address and telephone number for a member. [171]So be sure to check the *Encyclopedia of Associations* for the address and telephone number of the national organization which covers the work of your author. She, almost certainly, will be a member; and the membership secretary may be willing to give you a current point of contact.

As we mentioned before, the *Encyclopedia* is a very valuable asset for researchers on any topic. No matter how minute or arcane you may think a subject to be, it will lead you to one or more organizations that are concerned specifically with that topic. Perhaps the subject of your research is some aspect of the history of coleopterology, or some famous coleopterologist of the past. If you search

---

[170]*Encyclopedia of Associations*, 30th ed., 3 vols. (Detroit, Michigan: Gale Research, Inc., 1995).

[171]In recent years, many of these organizations have offered their members the opportunity to withhold personal information from persons who inquire for them, in order to comply with the requirements of the Privacy Act. Most members of these associations do not avail themselves of this option, however, because they do wish to make themselves available to former colleagues who may have lost touch over the passage of time.

the *Encyclopedia of Associations* with under the keyword **beetle**, you will find an organization through which you should be able to locate a large number of American experts on beetles, and a good many more in other lands, as well. On the following page, you will see the results of just such a search as a sample of the wealth of information you can find in this source.

For example, if your study is about the first scientific inquiry into the life of the salt-marsh beetle, *Bledius spectabilis*, and you soon discover a recent article on this curious submarine creature, "Submarine Beetles: *Bledius spectabilis*, the Salt-marsh Beetle, Defends Its Young from Parasitoid Wasps and the Tide,"[172] you almost certainly can locate its author, Tristram Wyatt, through the organization listed in the entry below. He is, if not a member himself, almost certainly known to members to whom the staff of the organization can guide you.

---

[172] *Natural History* 102 (July, 1993), 6ff.

ASSOCIATION NAME: Coleopterists' Society
ADDRESS: c/o Ed Zuccaro
    PO Box 767
CITY: Natchez, MS 39121
STATE: (MS) Mississippi
ZIPCODE: 39121
COUNTRY: United-States
SUBFILE: U.S.
PHONE NUMBER: (601) 442-2824
FAX NUMBER: (601) 442-2866
OFFICER NAME: Ed Zuccaro, Treasurer.
YEAR FOUNDED: 1969
NUMBER OF MEMBERS: 600
ABSTRACT: MULTINATIONAL. DESCRIPTION: Professionals and ama-
teurs with an interest in Coleoptera (beetles). Promotes the ad-
vancement of the science of coleopterology. Conducts field
expeditions.
PUBLICATIONS: *Coleopterists Bulletin: An International Journal De-
voted to the Study of Beetles,* quarterly. Provides annual indexes of
authors, article titles, and new taxa- or taxonomic names; contains
book reviews and literature notices. PRICE: $30.00/year for mem-
bers; $50.00/year for institutions. ISSN: 0010-065X.
ADVERTISING: not accepted.
PUBLICATION DETAILS: *Coleopterists Bulletin: An International Jour-
nal Devoted to the Study of Beetles.* FREQUENCY: quarterly. TYPE:
Journal.
ADVERTISING ACCEPTED: No.
CONVENTIONS & MEETINGS: Seminar, Workshop.
KEYWORDS: Entomology; Beetles
SUBJECT CATEGORY:
Engineering-Technological-and-Natural-and-Social-Sciences-
    Organizations
GALE SOURCE BOOK: (N) *National-Organizations-of-the-US*
SECTION NUMBER: 04

Remember also that, if an academic institution is mentioned in the affiliation note, you should consider contacting the graduate secretary in the academic department which covers the author's field of expertise. She may be able to tell you where the author is now. Similarly, if the author received a degree from the college or university that is mentioned in the note, the secretary of the alumnæ association may be able to help you locate her.

You also can find experts by reading, and carefully considering, the acknowledgements that appear in the front-matter of most scholarly books, and some articles, as well. Again, those names which appear in the acknowledgements of two or more books on the same general subject are testimony to the fact that the authors of those books regard these persons as experts, for they have consulted them with sufficient intensity as to make it important to acknowledge their contributions to their books. Most persons who have some academic or scholarly standing will be identified with their institutions in the acknowledgements, just as in the case of the affliation note, discussed above. In this way, you have a starting point in your search for them.

Should these efforts to make contact with the expert with whom you wish to speak also fail, there are yet other avenues to explore which may yield rapid results.

DISSERTATIONS ABSTRACTS ONLINE [DAO]

Does your expert hold the degree of doctor of philosophy? If so, she will have written a doctoral dissertation, because the Ph. D. is exclusively a research degree, which demands a dissertation of its recipients. You can discover whether or not your expert holds a research doctorate by checking the indices in *Dissertations Abstracts International*, again in either print or online form.[173] Should you find your expert's name, you also will find the name of the university from which she received her degree, the subject of her dissertation, the year in which the degree was granted, and, quite often, the name of her dissertation advisor. In addition, in the entries from more recent years, you will find the abstract of the

[173]The online version, called DAO, is available through OCLC's *FirstSearch* system, where it is listed under the filename DISS. It also is available through DIALOG, where it is File 35.

dissertation, just as it appears in the front matter of the original manuscript.

Below is the result of a search of *Dissertations Abstracts Online* for information on Pope Eugene III, done by a student who was writing about the origins of the Second Crusade. Of course, she already had found three citations to this work in WorldCat, but now she has an abstract as well as the standard bibliographical data. Since she is searching, first of all, for the most scholarly and inclusive works on her subject, with the most extensive bibliographies that will support her further searching, she is delighted to find that this is not a dissertation of only some two hundred or two hundred fifty pages but rather an extensive study of more than six hundred pages.

ACCESSION NO.: AAG8813744
TITLE: THE LIFE AND REIGN OF POPE EUGENE III (1145-1153)
AUTHOR: SPORNICK, CHARLES D. G.
DEGREE: PH.D.
YEAR: 1988
INSTITUTION: UNIVERSITY OF NOTRE DAME; 0165
SOURCE: DAI, VOL. 49-06A, Page 1550, 00604 Pages
DESCRIPTORS: HISTORY, MEDIEVAL; RELIGION, HISTORY OF; BIOGRAPHY

ABSTRACT: This work concerns the life and career of Bernard of Pisa, elected to the papal throne on February 15, 1145 as Pope Eugene III. The first part of this study considers Bernard's early life, his ecclesiastical career, his conversion to the White Cowl of the Cistercians, and his brief tenure as abbot. Also treated are his selection into the college of cardinals and the rationale for his successful candidacy as Lucius II's successor.

My aim is to demonstrate the continuity of the objectives, policies and accomplishments of Eugene's reign with those of his reformed predecessors. Such continuity is clear in Pope Eugene's call to take up the cross for the second crusade, his convocation of councils, his adjudication of cases involving disputed episcopal elections, and his commitment to promote and protect monastic reform. In each of these areas the pope sought to further the central platform of the reformed papacy: *libertas ecclesiae*—the church's freedom from lay control, the promotion of the moral reform of priest, prelate, and monk, and the primacy of the bishop of Rome over all churches. Eugene also sought, as Paschal II and Honorius II, a moderate course in "church-state" relations with the German emperor and the kings of Western Europe.

This study considers not only Eugene's continuation of reformed polity but also his contribution to the reformed papacy of the twelfth century. Eugene kept the crusade a papal enterprise through his issuance of the first crusade bull, outlining in juridical categories the purpose, obligations, and benefits of taking up the cross to liberate the church, his preaching of the crusade, and his appointment of crusade legates. Eugene's reign represented a watershed in the development of the papal judicial system, hearing an unprecedented number of cases at Rome, convening two papal consistories, and developing a system of papal "judges-delegate." Finally, Eugene is to be credited for his unparalleled gains in the recovery of lands for the patrimony of St. Peter and for his efforts to insure the defeat of Arnold of Brescia and those who opposed papal temporal rule over Rome.

With this full and complete information in hand, you can write or telephone to the academic department at the university whose name you found. When you reach the department, you should speak with the graduate secretary. If your expert received her doctorate within the past few decades, the graduate secretary may well know where she is, or where a colleague can be found who can help you locate her. In addition, the graduate secretary may put you in contact with your expert's dissertation advisor, if she is still active, either in teaching or as a professor emerita.

Should this avenue prove to be fruitless, you may try to locate your expert through the alumnae office of the same university. If that, too, does not provide you with a point of contact for your expert, you are now reduced to the last, but nearly always successful, method. You can write to her, as the author of a particular book or article, in care of the publisher of the book or in care of the editorial office of the journal in which the article was published. In virtually every instance, these publishers or editors will forward your letter on to the author very speedily. This is your last method for locating your expert, simply because the time involved in an exchange of correspondence in this way may preclude your getting information to help you in the brief semester's time you have to complete your study.

No matter what means proves to be successful for you in locating the scholar or expert with whom you need to speak, always be sure to ask each contact on your quest if your expert has an email address. More and more frequently, scholars and researchers, as well as the general public, include email addresses with their geographical addresses and telephone numbers in the data they furnish to associations, alumni offices, publishers, conferences, and academic institutions. You should recall that it was academics in the physical sciences and engineering who pioneered the use of email for the rapid exchange of information and ideas, when networking first emerged in the early 1980's, with a government-sponsored system called ARPAnet.

Of course, whether you speak with your expert by telephone as your first contact with her, or whether you write to her, be sure to ask the same informational question—may I have your e-mail address? With digital communication, you can exchange a number of informative messages in the same time that it would take you to exchange one letter, and you can develop a serious dialogue which still allows you, and the person with whom you communicate, to have time for some reflection on important questions, an ability which is not given to you in a telephone conversation which does not encourage minutes-long periods of silence.

Our final, and most important, admonition about contacting experts is that you should be well familiar with both the general subject at hand and with your expert's writings on the subject. Nothing is more flattering and soothing to the ego than to have the disembodied voice of a student on the telephone begin a conversation by saying, "I have read all four of your articles on this subject, as well as your dissertation!" By contrast, nothing is more likely to produce irritation in your expert than a conversation which begins, "I am just getting started and do not really know much. Can you help me?"

TEXTS IN FOREIGN LANGUAGES.

Another occasion on which you may need to consult heavily with others may arise when you locate materials that are appropriate and germane to your subject—or, at least, you think that they are—which are in languages or scripts that you do not know. Do not despair.

Does your college or university have a department in which the language is taught? If so, consider making an appointment with a member of the faculty in that department. Take your materials with you. Perhaps the professor will not have the time, or the willingness, to make extensive translations for you, but she may well take the time to give a cursory review to your materials and describe broadly to you their contents. In this way, especially if you know rather precisely the information for which you are searching, she may help you to determine whether or not the materials you have found are, in fact, helpful to your research.

If you cannot find a department whose faculty can help you, consider your fellow classmates, and the membership of local churches, temples, and synagogues whose members may know the language of your text. One student who found a number of titles in

Chinese characters in a published bibliography, but whose college did not have a faculty which taught Chinese, canvassed local Chinese restaurants until she found someone who would translate the titles for her.[174] Another student found that the USENET newsgroups that were available on her campus's internet server included a large group under the heading soc.culture. She had a text in Ukrainian which was unfathomable to her, but she posted a message on the newsgroup soc.culture.ukrainian with happy results. Though she was in Gettysburg, Pennsylvania, she received an e-mail response from another user of the newsgroup who lived in Detroit. She did have to transcribe her four-page passage as best she could, using Latin letters for Cyrillic ones, and then e-mail the transcription to the woman who had offered to help. The translation came back to her, by e-mail, within three days. She thankfully acknowledged the help she had received in a footnote.

From this kind of preliminary exploration of the texts you discover, you may find that there are extensive passages whose contents you need to know quite fully and accurately. Realizing that your time for the paper is limited, you may choose to try to find another student, graduate or undergraduate, who will be willing to undertake the translation for a small fee. If your funds are very limited, you may wish to set the text aside, commenting in a footnote that the text exists, and explaining that you cannot obtain a translation in time to use the text in your paper. If you do contemplate continuing your research, you may well have to get that translation before you can consider preparing a manuscript for publication.

Several of our students have asked us not to close this section of the book without saying how valuable they have found the process of looking up their professors and instructors on the databases which are likely to contain records of their theses, dissertations, books, and articles. In this way, any student can view the academic and scholarly contributions and credentials of those who teach her, and often gain insight into the particular areas of expertise of each professor, as well. One clever student we know regularly uses the interlibrary loan system to order copies of the theses, dissertations and publications of each of her professors, at the beginning of each

---

[174] From that first, rather frantic, encounter, she became a regular and faithful customer of that restaurant for the remaining three years of her life on campus.

semester. She looks through them to determine if any of the material pertains to the course she is taking. If she finds germane material, she reads it and notes it carefully. Later, in class, she does not miss the opportunity, at the appropriate moment, of getting the professor's attention to say, "What you have just said fits nicely with the complementary argument you presented in chapter four of your dissertation, when you said . . ." or "How does this relate to the point you made in your 1976 article, when you said that . . . ." She claims that, on one occasion, she stunned her instructor into goggle-eyed silence for a full ten seconds! So uncommon is the independent undergraduate researcher and informed thinker today, that many members of the faculty cannot imagine a sophomore who has found the professor's dissertation or one of her more important articles. But, as we have said, research will set you free—to be the discoverer of all the information you need for your own purposes and to be the sole judge of what is valuable and worth learning and what is not.

Actually, without altogether realizing it, this student had returned, in part, to an old academic standard which maintained itself for a century and a half before the Second World War—that undergraduate students regularly read the works of their professors so that they would have a deeper background in the material of the courses from which vantage they could **learn more**.

See Appexdix A for one student's approach to choosing a topic through the use of DAO and *WorldCat*.

Analysis

Before we begin to discuss some methods of analysis, it is important to take notice of exactly what analysis itself is. The word comes to us from Greek, where its principal meaning is to "loosen into parts" or to "break up."[175] It is in this sense that it has the absolute significance of "breaking (things) up into their constituent parts." The second edition of the *Oxford English Dictionary* defines the word as "the resolution or breaking up of anything complex into its various simple elements, the opposite process to synthesis; the exact determination of the elements or components of anything complex (with or without their physical separation)."[176] In the practical way in which you will analyze the data and information you will have collected about your topic, the process of analysis means two things.

First, you will determine the proper order of causes and effects among the items of information you have. Wordsworth did say "the Child is father of the Man" but this is, of course, strictly untrue.[177] Your principal task is to determine specific causes and their relation to specific effects. Let us take, for example, the placement of the letters on the keys of your computer's keyboard, called a

---

[175] analysis, *loosing, releasing*, hence a resolution of a problem by the analysis of its conditions, the opposite of synthesis (Aristotle, *Nichomachean Ethics*, 1112b23); and, in the *Logic* of Aristotle, a reduction of the imperfect figures into the perfect one (Aristotle. *Prior Analytics*, 51a18). See the Liddell-Scott-Jones Greek lexicon at URL: http://www.perseus.tufts.edu/cgi-bin/lexindex. Emendations from its definitions and examples are ours.

[176] The electronic version of the second edition of *The Oxford English Dictionary* at URL: telnet://bosshog.arts.uwo.ca/oed/analysis. *Cf.* the use of the stem *lys* in the sense of breaking up in the microbiological phrase "to lyse a cell wall (as by a bacteriophage)," in commercial products which purport to perform this action to kill bacteria, like *Lysol*; and, of course, in the name of the title character in Aristophanes's play, *Lysistrata*, "the woman who breaks armies."

[177] "My Heart Leaps Up," l. 7. The poet is, however, using a distinctive rhetorical figure, or trope, called *hysteron proteron*, in which the logical order of cause and effect or former and latter is reversed for effect. In fact, the old expression about "putting the cart before the horse" is taken directly from George Puttenham's translation of the Greek rhetorical term *hysteron proteron*. See also George Puttenham, *The Arte of English Poesie* [1589], ed. Gladys Doidge Willcock and Alice Walker (Cambridge: Cambridge University Press, 1936). Of course, this also is an example of a paradox.

QWERTY keyboard, from the order of the letters in the top letter-row. You probably already have noticed that the relationship between the frequency with which letters are used in English [ETAOINSHRDLU] and the placement of the keyboard's letters on the home row [ASDFGHJKL] have nothing to do with each other. When Christopher Latham Sholes (1819-1890) perfected the first practical typewriter, in 1867, he spent considerable time in laying out the keyboard so that the letters would be in the most efficient places for the typist's fingers. Unfortunately, for him, people became rapid typists very quickly, indeed their typing speed was greater than the typewriter's mechanism could respond to it. Consequently, his invention was soon rejected, because the keys were constantly jamming in bunches at the letter guide. To save his invention, and his reputation, he redesigned the placement of the letters on the keyboard to position them in the most *inefficient* places, in order to slow the speed of the typist's fingers, and thereby to minimize the chances for bunching the keys. In spite of the fact that the manual typewriter has disappeared, we are left with the effect it caused, the poorest possible placement of the letters on the keyboard.[178] In doing your analysis, you must not fall into the logical fallacy called *post hoc, ergo propter hoc*, that is "after this, therefore because of this." After all, some event that takes place earlier in time does not necessarily have as an effect some other event that is later in time.

Second, but no less important, you analyze items of information to determine the relative importance of those items, both with regard to one another and with regard to the thesis of your term paper. There is a tendency today to regard all items of information as of uniform importance—that the fact that George Washington wore false teeth is as important as his leadership in the Revolutionary War, for example. Of course, a moment's reflection reveals that this is not the case. Often, however, students will discover a vast array of facts about the subject of their papers and then will recite those facts serially in the subsequent texts, without any regard for the relative importance of these facts to one another—George Washington's career during the Revolution may be the subject of a

---

[178]For a more detailed history of Sholes's typewriter and its problems, see Arthur Toye Foulke, *Mr. Typewriter: A Biography of Christopher Latham Sholes* (Boston: Christopher Publishing House, 1961).

very long monograph while the false teeth can be relegated to a one-line footnote.

In determining the relative importance of items of information, it is well to remember the maxim that the future validates the past. All the materials you will have as the consequence of your labors of research are, in fact, historical materials, whether they come to you as a matter of pure historical research or not, because they were written or created at some time earlier than the moments in which you do your work. But the relative importance of those historical materials will vary widely with the passage of time. A primary source may tell you how important some event of its time was, and yet you will see the same event as of little consequence. Some other item of information from the same time may be very difficult to locate because it describes or identifies an event which was re-garded as of little, if any, importance at that time. You, however, will regard that same event as of very great importance, indeed, be-cause of the consequence it had for the future, which persons of the time could not recognize. One clear example of this shift in relative importance can be seen in the birth and childhood of every subsequently famous person. In England, in 1732, the greatest public attention was taken up with the revelation that more than a third of all the excise revenues on tobacco were being lost because of smuggling and collusion. Since every government of the time depended on tariffs and excises almost exclusively as the source of general revenue, such a discovery was of great importance indeed. The government's response was swift and comprehensive. On March 14, 1733, Robert Walpole, then the prime minister, intro-duced a wide-ranging Excise Bill into the House of Commons, to correct the abuses that had been discovered in the preceding year and to place England's public revenue on a more stable footing. Of course, in this uproar, no one, outside of the immediate family, took notice of the birth of George Washington, on February 11, 1732.[179] This is not to say that the excise scandal of 1732 is not im-portant to us, for the reforms begun at that time led to the fiscal and revenue policies which so angered the American colonists forty years later that a revolution against England's government seemed,

[179]Not February 22. England and her colonies were still observing the Julian cal-endar in 1732, and changed to the Gregorian calendar in September, 1752, at which time most anterior dates of record were shifted by eleven days.

in the end, to be the only practical solution to the Americans' perception of their tax problems. But, at the same time, we recognize also that the birth of Washington is of equal importance to our general understanding of the later eighteenth century in America. Of course, we can make similar observations about the births of all other famous persons—little regarded events of the time—except, perhaps, in the cases of the births of heirs to great thrones.

Thus, the births and childhoods of the great provide an easy way to identify the changes in relative historical importance of different items of information from one time to another, later, time. But there are many, many other examples that you can draw which illustrate the same principle. The whole period from 1789 to 1815 was filled with the romance, glory, horror, and tragedy of the Revolutionary and Napoleonic Wars in Europe, and the documents of the time almost all reflect the chaos of the age in both mind and spirit. There are only a few examples, buried in the welter of documents of the time, which describe the invention of the process of preserving foods *in vacuo*, which led to all modern canned foods, or to the application of steam power to greater varieties of work, which led to the Industrial Revolution.

Analysis, then, is concerned primarily with determining the causes of things by a careful and rational examination of the discoverable effects of those things. When you do research, you unearth a wide variety of effects, in much the same sense that a dead person has left behind her effects. These effects, or consequences of causes, can be found in secondary writings about a subject, in the primary documentation about a subject, and in other forms, including pictures, recordings, and objects which are a consequence of some human action of the past. Once you have gathered together all of the effects you can, you begin to break apart your collection of data and information into its constituent parts, based upon their relative importance to the subject you are studying. Here, you may well devise charts which trace secondary, or intermediate, effects to their secondary, or intermediate, causes. You may create chronological charts or tables which relate items of information to one another in terms of time. You may trace changes in a design, pattern, or idea in an evolutionary way, showing the simpler and more primitive expression of some idea and then showing, elaboration by elaboration, the growth of that idea or design into something more complex and sophisticated. Consider the case of the archeologist who discovers thousands of fragments of broken pottery on a site. By collecting all of them, she can find, no matter how minute or disconnected they are, that she has the ability, once she returns to her laboratory, to assemble these fragments back into whole pots, some of which may have physical features—from which their purpose may be discerned—that were hitherto unknown. The action of reassembling the pots from the apparently-unrelated myriads of fragments is the process of **analysis**. The process of determining the purpose of the newly-reassembled pot from its shape, thickness, size, and workmanship is **synthesis**, which we will discuss more fully below.

This process of analysis is one which requires you to control your speculation and to deal with only the actual evidence you have before you. You must be logical, in a quite formal sense, and rational, restraining your own creativity and imagination—that persistent desire of human beings to create a whole explanation for an event as quickly as possible—in the interest of seeking as much of the documentable truth as you can find. This is the reward for the endless hours you have spent in bibliographical and archival searching, peeling back the layers of the onion, one by one, to reveal the essential information about some effects in order to expose the causes of those effects to light.

Of course, in honest analysis, there are certain things which you may not do under any circumstances. You may not, for example, omit from your consideration essential documents and texts which you have discovered but which present unhappy or unpleasant things about your subject with which you would rather not deal. You may not make capricious choices from the information you have discovered in order to support a predetermined set of conclusions about it. And, of course, you will not lie to your readers by misrepresenting any of the sources your have discovered or by passing off as your own any texts or ideas which were created by others.[180]

---

[180]A complete discussion of annotating your own texts to show the paths you have taken in your research and to point your reader to places to begin new inquiries is Francis A. Burkle-Young and Saundra Rose Maley, *The Art of the Footnote: The Intelligent Student's Guide to the Art and Science of Annotating Texts*

You must be confident about the accuracy of the data and information you discover before you include it in your materials for analysis. If you are not, you must either discard it altogether, or weight your analysis in proportion to your belief in the unreliability of the data you use. In addition, you must explain your conclusions about some data's unreliability in the text of your research paper. You must consider all of the past conclusions by others about your subject, and you must present opposing or contrasting views completely. Elsewhere we have said:

> Suppose that you consult twenty sources to gather together as many views as possible about a person or event or thing, for your own learning. Nineteen of those earlier scholars present a view with which you agree, and that is the view you adopt in your paper. Yet, the twentieth, who disagrees entirely with the others, also is a respected scholar with a substantial reputation in the field. Your reader must have the confidence in your work to know that you will not have omitted this twentieth view, even though it conflicts substantially with your own and the views of many others in the field. Of course, you need not search assiduously for comments and opinions by those who are on the "intellectual fringe," but you must not omit the opinions and conclusions of men and women who have reached them only after great study and analysis.[181]

A fair, honest, and inclusive analysis of your materials, followed by an honest and thoughtful consideration of each of the conclusions of your analysis, will help you to create a valuable new appraisal of your subject which will illuminate the ideas and conceptions others have about your subject and an appraisal which will be different from anyone else's.

As we have done elsewhere in this book, we wish to draw your attention to a major work which considers the various kinds of logical errors into which students and scholars often fall when they

---

(Lanham, Maryland: University Press of America, 1996). You may expect us to like this book, since we wrote it. It is, indeed, the only book of its kind, and shows clearly, in its short one hundred fifty pages, just how to document honest research honestly. We hope you will read it.

[181]Burkle-Young and Maley, *Art of the Footnote*, 73.

analyze the information they have collected and begin to write about their subjects. David Hackett Fischer's *Historian's Fallacies* is a work of such great importance that every student who would become educated, and many scholars whose lapses have accumulated over time, should read it and digest it thoroughly.[182] Fischer's work is available readily in nearly every college and university library, and you should make a strong effort to read it soon.

Do remember that, in this stage of your work, what you are doing now is inherently different from synthesis, which will follow later, when your analysis is as complete as it can be.

Now is an appropriate time to discuss briefly the principle that classical analysis, the method you will employ to examine the information you have collected, is a process of **induction** rather than **deduction**. The latter process, which likewise is important, will come later when you synthesize new knowledge from your analysis. **Induction** is the process of proceding from specific examples or elements of evidence — in this case, your collection of information — to general principles or conclusions about them. You induce, in the logical sense of the word, by examining effects in order to establish the causes of those effects.[183] Thus, you induce, from contemporary documentary evidence, that George Washington was the son of Colonel Augustine Washington by his second wife, Mary Ball Washington.

By contrast, **deduction** is the logical process by which you reason from general conditions or principles to specifics that are based on

---

[182]David Hackett Fischer, *Historian's Fallacies: Toward a Logic of Historical Thought* (New York: Harper & Row, Publishers, 1970).

[183] Again, a clear, short definition of this is to be found in the *Oxford English Dictionary*, 2d. ed, *s. v.* "induction," §7a, together with two important illustrative quotations, one from the work of Henry Thomas Buckle, a great synthesizing historian of the nineteenth century whose most important work remains *The History of Civilization in England*, and the other from the famous textbook on logic by Thomas Fowler: "Logic, considered as a science, is solely concerned with induction; and the business of induction is to arrive at causes." [Henry Thomas Buckle, *Miscellaneous and Posthumous Works of Henry Thomas Buckle*, 3 vols. (London: Longmans, Green, and Co., 1872) I:41]; and "Induction. . .may or may not employ hypothesis, but what is essential to it is the inference from the particular to the general, from the known to the unknown" [Thomas Fowler, *The Elements of Inductive Logic: Designed Mainly for the Use of Students in the Universities*, 3d ed., corrected and revised (Oxford: at the Clarendon Press, 1876), preface].

them. You deduce, in the logical sense, when you proceed from causes to effects, from generals to particulars.[184] Thus, we deduce from the fact that Washington's decision to limit himself to two four-year terms in the presidency became a powerful precedent for his successors, because only one of them chose to exceed Washington's self-imposed limit, and, afterwards, this limit was incorporated, by amendment, in the *Constitution of the United States*.

You must make a careful distinction between induction and deduction, without becoming confused yourself. Remember, Sir Arthur Conan Doyle did become confused when he identified the logical aspect of Sherlock Holmes's work as "**deduction**" when, in fact, it was **induction**.[185] Detectives induce, and you are a detective in the analytical aspect of your work.

Remember that, in deductive reasoning, you draw inferences from general statements or generalize from what is true in one case to what you suspect is true in another related case. Since your analysis is inductive, your examination of the information at hand

---

[184] *Oxford English Dictionary*, 2d ed., *s. v.* "deduction," §6a, together with good illustrative quotations: "Deduction is the process of deriving facts from laws, and effects from their causes" [William Thomson, *An Outline of the Necessary Laws of Thought: A Treatise on Pure and Applied Logic*, 5th ed. (London: Longman, Green, Longman, and Roberts, 1860) #113]; "By deduction we descend from the abstract to the concrete" Henry Thomas Buckle, *History of Civilization in England*, new ed., 3 vols. (London: Longmans, Green and Co., 1867) III:v, 91. This leads, in mathematics, to "the rule or metatheorem that if within a system a formula B is derivable from a formula A, then `If A then B' is a theorem of the system; the principle of conditionalization;" (*OED*, 2d ed., *s. v.* "deduction," §8), illustrated by the quotation: "The principle of conditionalization (or `deduction theorem'). . .was taken for granted by Aristotle" [W[illiam] C[alvert] Kneale and Martha Kneale, *The Development of Logic* (Oxford: Clarendon Press, 1962) v, 320].

William Thomson (1819–1890), now sadly forgotten by most, was an Oxford divine who established his popular reputation with the work from which the quotation above is taken. He was bishop of Gloucester, 1861–1863, and archbishop of York, 1863–1890.

[185] Doyle entitled chapter 2 of his first Sherlock Holmes story, *A Study in Scarlet*, "The Science of Deduction. Later, in chapter 4 (¶ 8), he has Holmes say: "I am simply applying to ordinary life a few of those precepts of observation and deduction which I advocated in that article." [Samuel Orchart Beeton, *Beeton's Christmas Annual, 1888* (London: Ward, Lock, and Tyler, 1887)]. Of course, Holmes is inducing here, not deducing.

will not involve generalization at all. We will return to the use of deductive reasoning in our discussion of synthesis, below.

Before we begin to discuss the formal principles of logical analysis that you will use to reach conclusions about the topic you are studying, we wish to talk briefly about five essential modes of thinking that you need to keep in the front of your consciousness as you begin to arrange, classify, and assess the value of the information you have collected. These five principles are generic to the whole process of right thinking, in the strictest Victorian sense of that expression.[186]

The first of these is **Occam's Razor**, which we mentioned earlier. Let us state it once again:

The simplest explanation which accounts for all of the variables is the one explanation which is most likely to be true.

Once again, we need to emphasize strongly that this principle does *not* mean that the simplest explanation *is* the correct one; nor does it mean that an explanation which satisfies all of the variables is the correct one; nor does it mean that the correct explanation is a simple one. It does mean exactly what it says, and what it says has been the foundation of a considerable body of scientific, technical, and historical analysis for the past several hundred years.

William of Occam[187] did not, of course, create the logic embodied within the aphorism that is named for him—its principles are entirely Aristotelian. He did, however, make a succinct statement of the principle and stated it so well that his essential wording is the form in which it comes to us today.

Let us take a famous example of how Aristotle's logic corrected a fundamental scientific error that Aristotle himself made—the master correcting the master, as it were—as a good demonstration of the working of Occam's Razor.

Aristotle held that the local planetary system was geocentric in nature, that is, that the Sun, the Moon, and the five planets that are visible to the eye all revolve around the Earth. Superficially, that is precisely what appears to be true to the earth-bound

---

[186]For a clear exposition of this principle, see the chapter on "Hebraism and Hellenism" in Matthew Arnold's brilliant treatise, *Culture and Anarchy*.
[187]See note 11, above.

observer as she looks upwards at the heavens. And this concept is with us still in some essential forms of applied mathematics, including, most importantly, navigation. If the geocentric model of the planetary system is correct, however, there are elements of planetary motion which appear to be highly irregular. The three outer, naked-eye planets—Mars, Jupiter, and Saturn—all exhibit periodic anomalies of motion in which they appear to slow gradually in their progress through their orbits, then stop briefly, then appear to take on a momentary retrograde motion, and then, finally, to resume their proper motions through the heavens.[188] In order to account for these anomalies, Classical mathematicians developed a series of geometric addenda to the orbital pattern called epicycles.[189] As astronomical observation increased in accuracy through the Middle Ages, the variations between the orbital motions of these planets grew more complex, and the epicycles began to have smaller epicycles within them, and so forth to an ever increasing degree of complexity.

When Copernicus took up the problem in the sixteenth century, entirely from an academic rather than an observational perspective,[190] he used Occam's razor to attack the wide range of variables for which some account had to be made in explaining planetary motion—the epicycles within epicycles. He realized that in a model of the planetary system in which Mercury and Venus were within the Earth's orbit, relative to the Sun, and in which Mars,

---

[188]This phenomenon is caused by the Earth overtaking each of the outer planets into terms of orbital alignment, and then passing forward beyond the position of the observed planet, over the space of a few nights. You can experience the same phenomenon in your car when, as you travel at a significantly higher rate of speed than another car, you overtake the slower vehicle to your right. As you approach the other car, it seems to slow appreciably in its forward motion; as you pass beside it, it seems virtually to stop for a fraction of a second; and as you sweep forward of its position, relative to your own car, it seems momentarily to travel backward; and, then, as you pass significantly beyond it, it seems to resume its normal motion of travel, in the same direction in which you are going.

[189]For a discussion of epicycles and Copernicus's realization of their futility, see *Astronomy of Copernicus and Its Background*, volume 3 of *Colloquia Copernicana* and volume 13 of *Studia Copernicana* (Wroclaw: Ossolineum Wydawnictwo Polskiej Akademii Nauk, 1975).

[190]The greatest regret of his very active intellectual life was that he never even saw the planet Mercury, which generally was too low on the horizon, and for too short a period, to be observed from his latitude in Poland.

Jupiter, and Saturn lay in orbits outside that of the Earth, again relative to the Sun, all of the complex explanations that were necessary to account for the irregularities of planetary orbital motion went away—the need for any epicycles at all just disappeared. Of course, he was now left with a smaller, but still important, series of new variables, those which would account for the motion of the Moon. If the Aristotelian model were kept for this body alone, then the new set of apparent anomalies also went away. Even though Copernicus believed that planetary orbital motion was circular and not elliptical, he had solved the major errors in Aristotle's concept of the motion of heavenly bodies, *and* he had used Aristotle's own logic to demonstrate the error!

This wonderful example shows Occam's Razor at work in a straightforward and unambiguous way.

In your own research, you will have many chances in your analysis of your array of information to use this principle to form an explanation which accounts for all of the many, and often apparently conflicting, elements of information that bear upon one central point of your thesis.

The second principle that is of great value to you, not only in preparing your term paper but also in applying the force
of reason to many other problems, is often called **Sherlock Holmes's Rule:**

When you have eliminated the impossible, whatever remains, however improbable, must be the truth.[191]

Again, when you apply this principle to your own thinking, you must be sure that those things which you eliminate as impossibilities *are*, in fact, truly impossssible—not merely improbable. For example, an event, *A*, which occurs in time before some other event, *B*, cannot have been caused by event *B*, because effects cannot lie in time before their causes.

One of the great historical stories which illustrates perfectly the operation of Sherlock Holmes's rule is Doctor Edward Jenner's discovery of that the disease cowpox, a rather innocuous affliction

[191]See note 12, above. Of course, Sir Arthur did not invent this maxim. But his version of this logical element became the best known statement of it because of the widespread popularity of the adventures of Sherlock Holmes.

which had no lasting consequences for either the cows or the people who came in contact with those cows, was intimately related to the much more dangerous disease smallpox, which had grave consequences for the human beings who contracted it. Small pox had been a scourge of human populations for centuries throughout the Old World. Countless investigations by well-educated and rational people had been devoted to determining what caused it and how it could be cured or prevented. Doctor Jenner's thinking first turned to the problem when he was told, while a young medical student, that milkmaids in Gloucestershire proverbially were immune from smallpox, while all around them contracted the disease with the same regularity as other populations elsewhere, and died in about the same numbers.

The speculations on the cause of smallpox were as wide and varied as there were investigators, past and present, and theories on how to prevent or ameliorate the disease were nearly as many.

Jenner began, systematically, to eliminate all of those factors of life which the milkmaids shared in common with their contemporaries in time and geography. Eventually, over some years of time, he swept away possibility after possibility until he was left with only one phenomenon, namely that the milkmaids never contracted smallpox *because* they already had been infected with cowpox. The result was startling. However improbable it might have seemed, the only explanation, since Jenner had eliminated all of the impossible things, was that having cowpox conferred immunity to smallpox. Twenty-seven years after he had first heard the folk wisdom that milkmaids in Gloucestershire never were infected with smallpox, he carried out his first test with cowpox. On May 14, 1796, he punctured cowpox lesions on the hand of a milkmaid named Sarah Nelmes and then inoculated an eight-year-old boy named James Phipps with the effluent from the girl's pustules. On the following July 1 came the life-threatening, light-giving moment, when he again inoculated Phipps, this time with matter from a smallpox lesion. Within a few days, Jenner's years of exercising Sherlock Holmes's rule was rewarded. The boy was immune to smallpox.[192] After other similar experiments over the following

---

[192]This explains why the immunization against smallpox is called vaccination, from the Latin word vacca, a cow. Other forms of immunization against other diseases are, therefore, not properly vaccinations, but rather immunizations.

two years—stretched out in time because cases of cowpox were rather rare, and he needed a living source for his inflected fluid—Jenner wrote the first of his treatises on his discovery. Its title is significant, because it identifies precisely what he had done in his logical analysis, *Inquiry into the Cause and Effects of the Variolæ Vaccinæ.*[193]

Jenner had eliminated systematically the impossible causes of the immunity of his population of milkmaids until he reached the one improbable condition that all the immune girls shared in common, the condition of having had the disease cowpox. Consequently, since all immune milkmaids had had cowpox, and no persons who had not had cowpox were immune, it was, therefore, cowpox that made human beings immune to smallpox.[194]

Of course, Jenner had worked meticulously through the lives and work of his milkmaids until he had truly identified what was impossible and what was merely improbable. This is the key to the proper application of Sherlock Holmes's rule. Its principles, however, are even more frequently misapplied, because investigators eliminate, as a clear impossibility, agents or events which are really not impossible at all.

A clear illustration of this error also can be found in the history of medicine. More than smallpox, malaria is the great devastator of human health and life. And, like smallpox, serious, intelligent, and committed investigators searched for centuries to explain its causes, and to find cures and ameliorations. Their observations, that persons contracted malaria when in a swampy or marshy environment, and did not contract the disease when in a dry locality, were true and reasonable. It also was clear that people acquired the disease in warmer rather than colder seasons of the year. Taking

---

[193]Edward Jenner, *An Inquiry into the Causes and Effects of the Variolæ Vaccinæ, a Disease Discovered in some of the Western Counties of England, particularly Gloucestershire, and Known by the Name of the Cow Pox* (London: Printed for the author by S[ampson] Low, and sold by Law, 1798).

[194]The rest of Jenner's labors to overcome public skepticism about his work are too complex and involved for our little guide, but are covered fully in a number of reliable sources. For a modern, scholarly biography of Jenner, see Richard B. Fisher, *Edward Jenner, 1749-1823* (London: André Deutsch, Ltd., 1991). The traditional life of Jenner, which still has value, is John Baron, *The Life of Edward Jenner, with Illustrations of His Doctrines, and Selections from His Correspondence,* 2 vols. (London: H. Colburn, 1827).

these two conditions as true, over generations of time investigators eliminated as impossible every condition which did not fall fully within the conditions of the disease which they observed. When they were done, they were left with one common characteristic, namely that swampy or marshy land in warm temperatures exudes the smell of decaying vegetation, a smell which most people find unpleasant, and even noxious. Indeed, some people are nauseated by an intense exposure to the smell of rot of any kind. Therefore, the fetid, decaying smells were identified as the cause of the disease, and, in fact, the name of the bad air, the *mal'aria* in one variety of colloquial Italian, was transferred to become the name of the disease itself. But all these generations of investigators had eliminated one condition which was within their observational capability, this is that those who contracted the disease were those who were bitten by mosquitoes, and that those not bitten did not contract the disease. In fact, one of the four organisms which cause the disease, all of which are varieties of the genus *Plasmodium*, was seen in the microscope and identified as the cause of malaria in 1880, while the connection to the vector of the disease, the *Anopheles* mosquito, was not identified until a decade later. Thus, the faulty application of Sherlock Holmes's rule not only eliminated the bite of a mosquito as a possible cause of the disease but actually retarded the identification of the rôle of the mosquito for many years.[195]

The failure of the most advanced European investigators lay in their eliminating the connection that all persons who contract malaria have been bitten by a mosquito, and their failure to note that no persons not bitten by a mosquito contracted malaria, so, through a faulty application of the rule, they failed to note that the bite of the mosquito *may* be connected with contracting malaria. This was an observation that might have been made by an

[195]For one of many texts which shows the faulty reasoning in the investigation of the cause of malaria, see Benedictus Muhlius, *De Febrium Intermittentium Theoria et Therapia* (Helmstadtii: Typis H. D. Hammii, 1721). For a more accessible text of the same general nature, see James Lind, *An Essay on Diseases incidental to Europeans in Hot Climates, with the Method of Preventing their Fatal Consequence*, 5th ed. (London: John Murray, 1792). For a general treatment of the whole mess, see Robert S. Desowitz, *The Malaria Capers: More Tales of Parasites and People, Research and Reality* (New York: W. W. Norton & Company, 1991), 123-276.

investigator as careful and as meticulous as Jenner was in the case of cowpox. And, of course, it had been. When German colonists began to populate the mainland areas of Tanzania in the later nineteenth century, they were told politely by the natives that malaria was caused by the bite of the *mbu*.[196] This indicates clearly that some East African Jenner of long ago did make a correct application of Sherlock Holmes's rule to the case of malaria. The Germans, who knew better, ignored the information and went on dying.

A third maxim to which we need to draw you attention is called **Hanlon's Corollary**.[197] Its text is often stated:

> **Never ascribe to evil or malice those things whose cause you can explain entirely by ignorance or stupidity.**

This admonition is somewhat less of an appeal to the rules of logic than those we have mentioned before, but it serves to remind us all that most people's motives in doing the actions they do arise from no particular desire to harm others, even though such motives may be entirely self-serving.

One large historical example serves very well to illustrate the principle of Hanlon's Corollary. It has become fashionable in recent years to condemn some of the political heroes of the later eighteenth century in America, like George Washington and Thomas Jefferson, on the moral grounds that they owned slaves, which, today, we hold to be a supreme social evil. But their morality was not our morality, and, indeed, they contributed specifically to the change in moral opinion that led to the views which the great majority of people hold to be true in our time.

Slavery was a human social institution which was prehistoric in its origins; that is, when the earliest civilizations which left us written records, Mesopotamia and Egypt, began to do that, their people left documents that discuss the slaves in their societies. Men like Washington and Jefferson, and the writers who influenced them, Voltaire, Rousseau, Montesquieu, and Locke, were the first

---

[196]The Swahili word for mosquito. See Desowitz, 175.
[197]We cannot tell you who Hanlon was, nor can we tell you to what this maxim is corollary. We wish we could. If you can tell us, please write, and we will acknowledge you gratefully in the second edition of this book.

modern thinkers to raise the question of whether or not this ancient and accepted institution was, indeed, a moral evil. So, if you wish to hold, as a personal philosophical position, that men like these were ignorant of their violation of absolute moral principle, you may do that. But you cannot hold them to be evil or malicious persons because they failed to perceive what everyone else failed to perceive—including, it must be said, the slaves themselves with regard to the institution itself. You will, we think, owe them some admiration for being among the first to turn moral eyes to look at the institution of slavery.

LOGIC FOR ANALYSIS

Of course, every successful analysis depends completely on a sound use of logic. If you have not studied the subject or if you have not had a course in logic, you should now take the time to become familiar with the fundamentals of logic, so that you will avoid the sorts of logical errors which will cause your final paper to be of little value. There are three noted textbooks on logic which are available widely and which provide sound and cogent introductions to the subject: *The Elements of Logic* by Stephen F. Barker[198], *Introduction to Logic* by Irving M. Copi and Carl Cohen[199], and *Critical Reasoning* by J. B. Cederblom and David W. Paulsen.[200] Any one of them can be read in one long day of concentrated effort and care. And, if you do this, you will have, as a body of knowledge in your mind, a guide to good reasoning which will help you, over and over again, throughout your life.

In addition, there are a number of sources on the *World Wide Web* which can help to to master the essentials. Among them, we recommend the *Logic and Argument* page at the Department of English of the University of Victoria,[201] the three-page linked

[198]Stephen F[rancis] Barker, *The Elements of Logic*, 5th ed. (New York: McGraw-Hill, 1989).
[199]Irving M. Copi and Carl Cohen, *Introduction to Logic*, 9th ed. (Englewood Cliffs, New Jersey: Prentice Hall, 1994).
[200]J[erry] B[ruce] Cederblom and David W[arren] Paulsen, *Critical Reasoning: Understanding and Criticizing Arguments and Theories*, 4th ed. (Belmont, California: Wadsworth Publishing Company, 1995).
[201]URL:
http://webserver.maclab.comp.uvic.ca/writersguide/Logic/logicToc.html. We

discussion on *Argumentation* at Orbit,[202] and Brian Yoder's *Fallacy Zoo*.[203]

From this last source, we have excerpted for you his categorical table of contents, with some modification, so that you can see at once some of the pitfalls which you *must* avoid in your analysis. You will find this table at the end of this discussion on logic. You also can find longer discussions of the logical fallacies at the URL: http://www.nizkor.org.

CONSTRUCTING A LOGICAL ARGUMENT[204]

Logic is the science of reasoning, proof, thinking, or inference. Logic lets you analyze an argument or a piece of reasoning, and then determine whether or not it is correct. To put this assertion in its precise technical terms, logic allows you to determine whether or not the reasoning in an argument is valid or invalid. Of course, there is no requirement that you must study logic in order to reason correctly; but a fundamental knowledge of logic is helpful when you construct or analyze an argument.

This discussion is concerned only with simple Boölean logic, which is, fundamentally, Classical logic as it has developed formally from Aristotle's time to our own. There are other types of mathematical logic, such as fuzzy logic, which obey different rules; but, when people talk about logical arguments, they usually mean the types that we will discuss here.. One problem with Boölean logic is that people need not be consistent in their goals and desires. There are some elements of the human condition that are too individual to be the subject of analysis with Boölean logic, and other rules, such as those in fuzzy logic, apply to them. For example:

---

are indebted to this site for some of the material on this page and for some of the logical precepts we discuss below.

[202]URL: **http://www.tcp.com/~prime8/Orbit/MOCR/argument1.html**.

[203]An exceptionally valuable resource, at the URL:

http://www.primenet.com/~byoder/fallazoo.htm.

[204]We are indebted for the arragement of this material and for some of the examples to part 3 of the text of frequently-asked-questions [FAQ] for the **alt.atheism** USENET newsgroup.

"Mary wishes to speak to the person in charge.
The person in charge is Elizabeth.
Therefore, Mary wishes to speak to Elizabeth."

Logically, that argument is valid. But Mary also may have another goal which is in direct conflict with his desire "to speak to the person in charge"—to avoid talking to Elizabeth—which makes the answer that you obtain by logical reasoning inapplicable to real life. Garlic may taste good to you, and strawberry ice cream also may taste good to you, but you are justified in thinking that strawberry garlic ice cream is a good idea only in Boölean logic. Sometimes, principles of valid reasoning which people once thought were universal have turned out to be false. For example, for almost two thousand years, people thought that the principles of Euclidean geometry were universal laws. However, the principles of analysis which you will use to test the validity of the arguments that you advance in your term paper will follow the rules of Boölean logic.

An **argument** is, at essence, **a statement or fact that you advance for the purpose of influencing the mind or the thinking of your reader.** It is a reason that you offer in support of a proposition, and, in formal logical constructions, it is the middle term in a syllogism. You also can define an argument as **a connected series of statements or reasons by which you intend to establish a rational position, and, in so doing, to refute the opposite.**[205]

The fundamental elements of every logical argument are **statements** or **propositions.**[206] Each of these is a single claim which is either true or false. You may **assert** your statement by claiming that it is true, or **deny** your statement, by claiming that it is false. When you assert a proposition based on some antecedent argument, you **affirm** it.

---

[205]Cf. the *Oxford English Dictionary*, 2d. ed., *s. v.* "argument" §§ 3.a and 4.

[206]For the outline of this small presentation on Classical logic, and for some phrasing of terms, as well, we are indebted to material in part 3 of the text on frequently-asked-questions [FAQ] of the alt.atheism USENET newsgroup. This text can be found readily at many sites on the *World Wide Web*, and it is posted regularly on the newsgroup.

Some logical propositions:

> Moscow is the capital city of Russia (assertion).
> Venus is closer to the Sun than the Earth (assertion).
> Polar regions of the Earth are warmer than equitorial regions (assertion).
> Dogs are more able in their use of language than human beings (assertion).
> Rome is not the capital city of Italy (denial).
> Mercury is not closer to the Sun than the Earth (denial).
> Polar regions of the Earth are not warmer than equitorial regions (denial).
> Wildebeest are not more intelligent than human beings (denial).

You are to construct and consider each proposition in terms of its meaning, and not necessarily on your choice or arrangement of particular words. Thus, the two propositions: *The equitorial regions of the Earth are warmer than the polar regions of the Earth are* and *The equitorial regions of the Earth are not colder than the polar regions of the Earth are* both are statements of the same proposition. It is better, however, to word your propositions carefully, and to maintain a consistent word order throughout your statements.

There are three parts to every argument, the premise or premises, the inference or inferences, and the conclusion.

Every argument must have at least one initial proposition, although there may be more than one. Each one of the initial statements is called a **premise** of the argument, and you must state each one explicitly. The premises are the reasons you offer for having your reader accept the argument as being true, or the evidence on which your claim that the argument is true is based. You often will indicate your premises with words or phrases such as "because," "since," "so," and "let us assume."

You build your argument in a step-by-step process of **inference**. In the process of inference, you state one or more propositions which you have accepted, and which you expect your rational reader to accept. You then use those propositions to reach a new proposition. You can use each new proposition in still later parts of the process of inference. There is more than one type of valid inference as well as some types which are invalid. You probably will identify your inferences with words or phrases like "therefore," "hence," and "thus."

Finally, there is the conclusion of the argument, which is, itself, another proposition. The conclusion can be stated to be the final stage of inference. You affirm your conclusion based upon your original premises, and upon the inferences you drew from them. You probably will indicate your conclusions with words or phrases such as "I conclude that," or "it must follow that." Please look again carefully at the three stages of a logical argument:

STAGE ONE: PREMISES

For the argument to function at all, you need one or more initial propositions. These initial statements are called the premises of the argument, and must be stated explicitly. You can think of the premises as the reasons for accepting the argument, or the evidence upon which the argument is based. People often indicate premises with phrases such as "because," "since," "obviously," "let us assume," and so on.

Note carefully that many people view the phrase "obviously" with suspicion, because it is used frequently to intimidate people into accepting things which are not true at all. If something does not seem obvious to you, do not be afraid to question it. You can always say "Oh, yes, you are right, it is obvious" after you have heard the explanation.

STAGE TWO: INFERENCE

Next the argument continues, step by step, in a process called inference. In inference, you start with one or more propositions which have been accepted. You then use those propositions to arrive at a new proposition. The new proposition can, of course, be used in later stages of inference. There are various kinds of valid inference—and also some invalid kinds. Often, you will denote an inference with phrases such as "implies that" or "therefore."

STAGE THREE: CONCLUSION

Finally, you arrive at the conclusion of the argument, which is another proposition. It frequently is true that you will state your conclusion as the final stage of inference. You affirm your conclusion based entirely on your original premises, and the inferences you drew from them. People often indicate their conclusions with phrases such as "therefore," "it follows that," "we conclude," and so on.

TYPES OF LOGICAL ARGUMENT

There are two Classical types of logical argument, **deductive** and **inductive**, which mirror the two essential patterns of reasoning in the human mind. A valid **deductive argument** is one which provides its own absolute proof of its conclusions—if all of the premises are true, then the conclusion also must be true. An **inductive argument** is one in which the premises provide some evidence for the truth of the conclusion. You do not label it as valid or invalid, but rather you discuss it in terms of whether or not it is stronger or weaker than another argument. In inductive arguments, you also may discuss how likely it is that the premises are, in fact, true.

Classical deductive arguments are the most rigorous forms, and are, therefore, those which you, and your reader, may regard as the most convincing.

A **deductive** argument:

> Premise I: *Every event has a cause.*
> Premise II: *The universe has a beginning.*
> Premise III: *All beginnings involve an event.*
> Inference I: *This implies that the beginning of the universe involved an event.*
> Inference II: *Therefore, the beginning of the universe had a cause.*
> Conclusion: *The universe had a cause.*

Remember that the conclusion of one argument may become the premise, or one of the premises, in another argument. Any proposition can be a premise or a conclusion of one particular argument only.

Sometimes, when you construct your arguments, you will not follow the order we have just described. For example, you may state your conclusions first, and then state the premises which support that conclusion. This is valid, although it may tend to confuse some of your readers. Most people find that arguments are harder for them to recognize than are premises or conclusions. Indeed, some writers load their texts with assertions, and never produce an argument. What is worse for any rational reader is that some statements that resemble arguments are not arguments. Consider the statement:

"If Gibbon is correct, the Roman Empire fell either because of the rise of Christianity or because of a collapsing economy."

This statement is not an argument, but rather is a conditional statement, as indicated by the introductory preposition *if.* And, it does not present the premises which are needed for a valid logical conclusion. Similarly:

"Your parents created you, therefore honor them."

In this example, the phrase "honor them" is neither true nor false. Therefore, it is not a logical proposition, so the sentence is not an argument.

Remember that one of the major purposes of an argument is to establish a true reltionship between a cause (**A**) and an effect of that cause (**B**). Let us suppose that you wish to present an argument that there is something wrong with the engine of your car? Let us examine two statements of the form **A because B**. First:

"My car will not start, because there is something wrong with its engine."

155

Here, you have not presented an argument for there being something wrong with the engine, but rather you have offered an explanation for the fact that your car will not start. You have explained the condition of **A** (*"My car will not start. . ."*) by using **B** (*". . .because there is something wrong with its engine."*) as the explanation. Now consider a second statement:

> *"There must be something wrong with the engine of my car, because it will not start."*

Here, you argue that the condition **A** (*"There must be something wrong with the engine of my car. . ."*) is true and you offer **B** (*". . .because it will not start."*) as evidence for the truth of **A**. The statement **A because B** is a valid logical argument. At first glance, you may not see the fundamental difference between the two cases, but, if you recall that **A because B** is exactly equal to **B therefore A**, we can restructure the two statements to become:

> *"There's something wrong with the engine, therefore the car won't start."*

And:

> *"The car won't start, therefore there's something wrong with the engine."*

Since the argument is supposed to be about whether or not there is something wrong with the engine, but now it is plain that the first statement has nothing to do with that at all. Only the second statement actually argues that there is something wrong with the engine.

IMPLICATION IN DETAIL

There is one very important thing that you must remember: The fact that a deductive argument is valid does not mean necessarily that its conclusion is true. If this seems confusing to you, it is because of the slightly counter-intuitive nature of how implication works.

Obviously, you can build a valid argument out of true propositions. But you can also build a completely valid argument by using only false propositions. For example:

All insects have wings (premise)
Woodlice are insects (premise)
Therefore woodlice have wings (conclusion)

The conclusion is not true, because the premises of the argument are false. If the premises were true, however, the conclusion must be true. So the argument is entirely valid. More subtly, you can reach a true conclusion from false premises—even ludicrously false ones:

All fish live in the ocean (premise)
Sea otters are fish (premise)
Therefore sea otters live in the ocean (conclusion)

However, there is one thing no one can do: start with true premises, progress with them through a valid deductive argument, and then arrive at a false conclusion—because of the precise definition of a valid deductive argument. Here is a **truth table** for implication. The symbol "=>" denotes an implication; "A" is the premise, and "B" the conclusion.

Truth Table for Implication

Premise	Conclusion	Inference
A	B	A => B
false	false	true
false	true	true
true	false	false
true	true	true

The table reveals the three following logical conditions:

(1) If the premises are false and the inference is valid, then the conclusion can be true or false— as shown in **1** and **2**.

(2) If the premises are true and the conclusion is false, the inference must be invalid—as shown in line **3**.

(3) If the premises are true and the inference is valid, the conclusion must be true—as shown in line **4**.

A sound argument is a valid argument whose premises are true. A sound argument always arrives at a true conclusion. You must take great care **NOT** to confuse sound arguments with arguments that are merely valid.

Ultimately, the conclusion of a valid logical argument is only as compelling as the basic premises it is derived from. Logic, in itself, does not verify for you the basic assertions which support arguments. To do that, we must have some other method. In fact, the principal means that rational human beings use to verify their basic assertions is enquiry that is based upon the scientific or historical methods of research. In other words, you own research with appropriate material, preferably primary sources, like your proper conduct of experiments in the laboratory, provides you with the means to verify your basic assertions about the subject of your work.

In order to ensure that your arguments are sound, you must avoid logical fallacies. Below is a short table of some of the principal fallacies, taken from Brian Yoder's *Fallacy Zoo* on the *World Wide Web*. In Appendix C, we include a longer and more detailed examination of logical fallacies, which you should review carefully before you place the finishing touches on your paper.

FALLACIES

FALLACIES OF DISTRACTION:

> **False Dilemma**: you give two choices when, in fact, there are three or more options.
> **From Ignorance**: because something is not known to be true, you assume it to be false.

Slippery Slope: you draw a series of increasingly unacceptable consequences.

Complex Question: you cojoin two unrelated points as a single proposition.

APPEALS TO MOTIVES IN PLACE OF SUPPORT:

Appeal to Force: you persude your reader to agree by an appeal to force.

Appeal to Pity: you persude your reader to agree with you by appealing to her sympathy.

Consequences: you warn your reader of unacceptable consequences if she does not accept your argument..

Prejudicial Language: you attach value or moral goodness to the act of believing you.

Popularity: you argue that a proposition is true because it is widely held to be true.

CHANGING THE SUBJECT:

Attacking the Person:
(1) you attack a person's character.
(2) you take special note of a person's circumstances.
(3) you argue that a person did not practise what she preached.

Appeal to Authority:
(1) you argue that the authority whom you wish to refute is not an expert in the field.
(2) you state that the experts in the field whom you wish to refute disagree with one another.
(3) you argue that the authority with whom you disagree was not serious in advancing her own argument..

Anonymous Authority: you do not name the authority whose prior arguments you support.

Style Over Substance: you present an argument with   rhetorical devices that you hope will affect your reader's grasp of the truth of the conclusion.

INDUCTIVE FALLACIES:

Hasty Generalization: your sample of the whole condition or population is too small to support an inductive generalization about the whole condition or population

Unrepresentative Sample: your sample is unrepresentative of the whole.

False Analogy: you compare two objects or events which are relevantly dissimilar.

Slothful Induction: you deny the conclusion of a strong inductive argument despite the evidence you have to the contrary.

Fallacy of Exclusion: you exclude from your consideration some evidence which would change the outcome of an inductive argument.

FALLACIES INVOLVING STATISTICAL SYLLOGISMS:

Accident: you apply a generalization when circumstances suggest that there should be an exception.

Converse Accident : you apply an exception in circumstances where a generalization should apply.

CAUSAL FALLACIES:

Post Hoc, Ergo Propter Hoc:[207] you argue that, just because one thing (**A**) came after another thing (**B**) in time, and only for that reason, **A** was the cause of **B**.

Joint Effect: You argue that one thing caused another when, in fact, they were both the joint effects of an another underlying cause.

---

[207] *Post hoc, ergo propter hoc*, Latin, "after this, therefore because of this."

Insignificant Cause: you argue that one thing caused another, which it did, but you do not note that this cause was insignificant when it is compared to other causes of the effect.

Wrong Direction: you reverse the direction between cause and effect.

Complex Cause: the cause you identify is only a part of the entire cause of the effect.

MISSING THE POINT:

Begging the Question: the truth of the conclusion is assumed by the premises.

Irrelevant Conclusion: your argument in defense of one conclusion instead proves a different conclusion.

Straw Man: you attack an argument that is different from, and weaker than, the best argument for another conclusion.

FALLACIES OF AMBIGUITY:

Amphiboly: you structure a sentence in such a way as to give your reader two different interpretations of what you men by what you say.

Accent: you suggest, by placing special emphasis on a word or phrase, often with italics in a quotation, that there is a meaning in the sentence that is contrary to what the sentence actually says.

CATEGORICAL ERRORS:

Composition: you argue that, because the attributes of the parts of a whole have a certain property, therefore the whole has that same property.

Division: you argue that, because the whole has a certain property, therefore the parts have that same property.

NON SEQUITURS:[208]

Affirming the Consequent: you argue that if there was an **A** then there was a **B**; and, because there was a **B**, therefore there must have been an **A**.

Denying the Antecedent: you argue that if **A** happened then **B** happened; but, because **A** did not happen, therefore **B** did not happen.

Inconsistency: you assert that contrary or contradictory statements are both true.

Stolen Concept: you use one concept while attacking another concept on which it logically depends.

---

[208] *Non sequitur*, Latin, "it does not follow."

Synthesis

You are now about to begin the most important, and the most intellectually difficult, part of the serial tasks that are involved in serious research and writing. In the act of synthesis, you will take the fruits of your analysis of the information you have unearthed and, from them, create new ideas and understandings. While it is true that almost all research is inductive in nature, the most important consequence of writing the research paper is the synthesis, which often is deductive in nature.

We should begin with a clear understanding of just what synthesis is. The *Oxford English Dictionary* offers the following definition of the word:

> **The action of proceeding in thought from causes to effects,** or from laws or principles to their consequences. . . . In wider philosophical use and gen[erally,] the putting together of parts or elements so as to make up a complex whole; the combination of immaterial or abstract things, or of elements into an ideal or abstract whole. . . . Also, the state of being put so together. . . . A body of things put together; a complex whole made up of a number of parts or elements united.[209]

Synthesis is a part of the deductive process which proceeds from the generalized whole of the information you have collected and analyzed to specific conclusions about the significance of what you have found in your information and analysis. As analysis is like induction, so synthesis is like deduction. The two processes are, of course, inextricably united to one another, but, in the process of synthesis from research you reveal your understanding of the consequences of the actions you have studied, whether the actions of a person, or the changes wrought by some human or natural process.

Thomas Case, a distinguished logician of the later nineteenth century, and once the president of Corpus Christi College at Oxford, used a geometrical example to illustrate the whole deductive process in relation to both analysis and synthesis:

---

[209] *Oxford English Dictionary*, 2d ed. (1989), CD-ROM edition, *s. v.* "synthesis."

Deduction is analysis when it is regressive from consequence to real ground, as when we start from the proposition that the angles of a triangle are equal to two right angles and deduce analytically that therefore (1) they are equal to equal angles made by a straight line standing on another straight line, and (2) such equal angles are two right angles. Deduction is synthesis when it is progressive from real ground to consequence, as when we start from these two results of analysis as principles and deduce synthetically the proposition that therefore the angles of a triangle are equal to two right angles, in the order familiar to the student of Euclid.[210]

In a more particular sense, and one that applies directly to you, we may say that, in scholarship, synthesis is your creation of rational new ideas which arise from your analysis of the information you have at hand, as you see it.

Remember that, when you synthesize new knowledge from the consequence of your analysis, you may well draw upon deductive reasoning to help you see parallels and relationships that are common to both the consequence of your own analysis and to larger elements of the human experience. But you must be careful never to assume that what applied to one situation, or was an essential characteristic of it, will ever apply to any other situation, or be a characteristic of it. Hasty generalization often leads to conclusions that are based on insufficient information. It is for this reason that polls, in spite of the best efforts of statisticians and demographers to qualify them properly, often predict results which are at considerable variance with the actual outcomes of human processes, like elections and economies.

For example, a survey of adults in a socially-sophisticated metropolis, like New York or Washington, may reveal that a large percentage of people know little about the Internet and never use it. Since the process of the use and expansion of the Internet is an open one, it cannot be the subject of a classical analysis of a closed process. Consequently, the synthesis of knowledge from the data will be deductive in nature. But a hasty generalization from the

---

[210]Thomas Case, "Logic," in *Encyclopædia Britannica*, 11th ed., 29 vols. (New York: The Encyclopædia Britannica Company, 1911) XVI:892, col. 1.

data may lead to the conclusion that a large number of people are ill-informed about the Internet because of their choice to ignore the wide-spread discussions about it or their lack of interest in, or even fear of, the technology which created it and supports it, or both. The synthesizer— rather than the analyst, in this case—may, however, fail to consider dozens, if not hundreds, of other factors which bear upon the question. Just one of these, for example, may be that the widespread adult illiteracy of our times precludes the use of the Internet by a very large percentage of our adult population. The number of variables in the human condition is so vast that any generalization about specific persons or incidents is dangerous, and hasty generalizations almost always lead to false conclusions. So, if your generalization cannot be proved by a combination of primary evidence and sound, logical analysis of that evidence, do not advance it!

Each experience of synthesis is as unique as you are, yourself. If all "truth" already had been revealed, there would be no need for any more research and writing on any subject, and certainly no need to reconsider past actions and events at all. Of course, when you consider things that we believe to be matters of existential fact, the whole of past human synthesis about it is not recapitulated—as when you describe water as having the atomic constituency H_2O, you do not describe the whole analytical and synthetic process by which this was discovered to be "true." On the other hand, when you consider any aspect of the human condition, past or present; gather all of the data and information you can find about it; and you analyze that data, your synthesis will be somewhat different from anyone else's. This is the case because you will bring to your synthesis the sum total of your own experiences in life, your emotions and ethics about the subject, your particular assembly of sources, and your own process of insight and understanding, in a special way that no one else can.

Consider the case of the American Revolution, for example. If all of the data and information about it had been gathered together and analyzed by one person, who then wrote one grand volume about it, would you think that there would be no further need for any more books or articles about the subject? Surely not! Because the synthesis of that person, arising from her own time, life, and experience, could not reveal anything like "the whole truth" about the Revolution. Hence, libraries have dozens of shelves filled with monographs and serials about the American events between 1775 and 1783. And, moreover, her synthesis would fail to present more than just a few of the myriad consequences of that historical event on the millions of people who came afterwards in time.

Let us consider, for a moment, that one of the consequences of the Revolution was the emergence of a society many of whose memebers believed that any central government should have as little power over the daily lives of its citizens as possible. One reflection of this was the absence of military conscription from American life for many decades. With the exception of brief exercises of it in the Civil War and in World War I, the nation essentially was free of the institution until just before our entrance into World War II—a century and a half into American national history. Because this was the case, a middle-aged Swedish peasant woman of strong religious convictions, including pacifism, decided, in 1880, to abandon her homeland, which did have a compulsory conscription which surely would enmesh her sons if she stayed, and emigrate to America. Because she brought her children with her, of course, her daughter rose to adulthood, married, and had her children, in turn, in the United States. Her son, the grandson of the pacifist Swede, became a metallurgical engineer and invented an important number of the armor-plating steels that the United States used in World War II. The lives saved by his work may well be reflected in the lives of children, grandchildren, and still later descendants who contribute, in turn, their lives, works, and ideas to modern American society. This is just one of millions of unintended consequences of the fact that the American Revolution happened when it did, where it did, and with the immediate political results it had. Yet, even the greatest historian of the Revolution would be very unlikely to consider this particular consequence of the eighteenth-century event, unless it was an immediate part of her own history. On the other hand, a descendant of that Swedish peasant woman may well bring her experience to bear in synthesizing an explanation of the consequences of the Revolution.

For millions of reasons, such as the one adduced above, every synthesis is unique. Its value for others, however, lies in a combination of the worth of the information that was analyzed to develop it, the principles of sound reasoning that were brought to bear on it, and the clarity—both logical and linguistic—that is used to explain it.

Consequently, we cannot provide you with a set of rules by which you will synthesize new knowledge from your research. Rather, we offer some general guidance and some helpful techniques which will, we hope, help you to determine for yourself if your conclusions about your material are likely to be valid.

In many academic fields, there has been an increasing tendency to reduce elements of the human experience to fit some preconceived model or models of human behavior and thinking. Inherently, this approach to synthesizing new knowledge is flawed, because no two human beings ever can be expected to react in the same predictable way when faced with the same challenge, if, indeed, any two challenges themselves are ever the same. And it is the very unpredictable natural freedom of man's thinking and action which generates the specific effects, from day to day, which become the causes of quite different effects in the next link in the endless chain of causes and effects. For this reason, predictions about anything—the future activity of a nation's economy, the weather, elections, what your best friend will do tomorrow—are likely to be wrong; and, if they are right, the outcome is more likely to be the result of luck rather than genuine synthesis.

Of course, it would be easy for us to prescribe rules for you—and many people, students and others, wish very much to have them. The list of people who have developed them is endless. Just a few of the names are Karl Marx, Georg Wilhelm Friedrich Hegel, John Maynard Keynes, Sigmund Freud, and Burrhus Frederic Skinner. In every case, the models developed by these men, and many other men and women, have proven not to be the reliable predictors that their creators hoped. Yes, it is true: there are no "isms" which are of any lasting value as syntheses of human action. Each of us is too separate and particular, as a human being, to be reduced into a generalized model of the human condition. The great nineteenth-century æsthete, critic, and historian, Walter Pater, perhaps gave the clearest of all observations of this reality when he warned his readers, in the "Conclusion" to his most important work, *The Renaissance: Studies in Art and Poetry*:

> What we have to do is to be for ever curiously testing new opinions and courting new impressions, never acquiescing in a facile orthodoxy, of Comte, or of Hegel, or of our own. Philosophical theories or ideas, as points of view, instruments of criticism, may help us to gather up what might otherwise pass unregarded by us. "Philosophy is the microscope of thought."[211] The theory or idea or system which requires of us the sacrifice of any part of this experience, in consideration of some interest into which we cannot enter, or some abstract theory we have not identified with ourselves, or of what is only conventional, has no real claim upon us.[212]

More recently, David Hackett Fischer, whose *Historian's Fallacies* is the leading book on the logical fallacies into which analysts who use historical materials often fall, stated the same principle in a more acerbic and less elevated tone:

> A historian who swears to tell nothing but the whole truth, would thereby take a vow of eternal silence. A researcher who promises to find the whole secret for himself condemns himself to perpetual failure. The whole truth, at any stage of an inquiry, is an ideal that ought to be abolished from historiography, for it cannot ever be attained. Historians are bound to tell the best and biggest truths they can discover, but these truths are very different from the whole truth, which does not and cannot exist. A scholar who seeks the whole truth is on

[211]Victor Hugo, *Les Misérables*, part 5 ("Jean Valjean"), vol. 1, book 2, chapter 2 (Paris: J. Hetzel et A. Lacroix, 1862; trans. by Isabel F. Hapgood, 5 vols., New York: Thomas Y. Crowell and Company, 1887). This good translation is now available in electronic form from Project Gutenberg: ftp://uiarchive.cso.uiuc.edu/pub/etext/gutenberg/etext94/lesms10.txt.
[212]Walter Pater, *The Renaissance: Studies in Art and Poetry*, 4th ed. (London: Macmillan, 1893); reprinted and edited with textual and explanatory notes by Donald L. Hill (Berkeley, [California]: University of California Press, 1980) 189.

a road which can only end in the intellectual side of relativism, or else in that condition of methodological anomie which characterizes so many of my colleagues.

Georg Wilhelm Friedrich Hegel, poor twisted Teutonic soul that he was, is an easy mark for a methodologist. Most of the fallacies in this book [*Historian's Fallacies*] could be illustrated by his arguments. But there are many other examples of the holist fallacy, which is an exceedingly common form of error. All metahistorians, by definition, are guilty of this mistake—Toynbee, Spengler, Sorokin, Marx, Comte, Kant, Condorcet, Vico—and others who have tried to discover *the* "meaning" of *the* whole past.[213]

There are no hard rules after analysis, which does, most emphatically, have a set of rules—logic. Synthesis has no rules! Synthesis, to be successful, requires that the thinker—you—explain the significance for your reader of the data and information that you have collected and analyzed. This significance almost always will show how the effects or remains of some action by a person, or some persons, or some natural events, in the past produced consequences which affect, clearly and unambiguously, the lives of people today, and which may be expected to continue in some way to have an effect on the lives of people to come.

Synthesizing an explanation of how the invention of the carburetor, from an observation of a perfume atomizer, changed forever the way people in developed nations live their lives is easy. Almost as easy is an explanation of what effects the life and career of Abraham Lincoln had on the American people's perception of themselves. But to determine, with intellectual reliability and demonstrable evidence, *why* Abraham Lincoln thought and behaved in the way that he did is very difficult. If you do attempt such an explanation, after appropriate research and analysis, you will conceive it out of your own human understanding of yourself,

---

[213]David Hackett Fischer, *Historian's Fallacies: Toward a Logic of Historical Thought* (New York: Harper & Row, Publishers, 1970) 66.

combined with the knowledge of Lincoln that you have acquired. And, while you may agree on nearly every point with great scholars who have preceded you in this work, you will not agree in every respect and on every point.

John Henry Muirhead, a teacher of philosophy and the author of a once-well-known text, *The Elements of Ethics: An Introduction to Moral Philosophy*,[214] put the problem of synthesis for every researcher in a clear, but carefully worded, passage in a once very accessible place:

> There is no logical principle which requires that we should derive qualitative change by logical analysis from quantitative difference. Everywhere experience is synthetic: it gives us multiplicity in unity. Explanation of it does not require the annihilation of all differences but the apprehension of them in organic relation to one another and to the whole to which they belong.[215]

Now that we have concluded the troubling process of trying to explain carefully just what synthesis is, we do think you should have some guidance on how to carry out this most difficult of intellectual acts.

Above, we wrote briefly about the work of the archeologist who tries to determine the purpose and use of a certain kind of pot, once she has reconstructed it from the thousands of fragments she found on her dig. In order to make this determination, she must consider how physical factors are related to functions. For example, a thicker and heavier pot is more likely to have been used as a storage vessel for some heavy material, whether liquid or solid, than is a thinner and lighter vessel.

Let us consider what aids you can develop for your own material that will help you to discern this kind of relationship. For the second time, but this time with conclusions of analysis rather than with assemblies of evidence, you should consider making a series of charts or tables which will allow you to

---

[214]New York: Charles Scribner's Sons, 1892.
[215]"Idealism," *The Encyclopædia Britannica*, 11th ed. (New York: The Encyclopædia Britannica Company, 1910) XIV:286.

relate consequences to one another. For example, three tables which show three elementary analytical conclusions about men who have become presidents of the United States are:

1. All these men, with one exception, have names which reveal that their patronymic ancestries were northern European: English, German, and Dutch.

2. All of them, again with one exception, were raised in religious beliefs which were in the general mainstream of northern European Protestantism.

3. All of them, with only two exceptions, were married or were widowers when they were elected.

From these three tables, it is easy to conclude that the overwhelming majority of American presidents have been Anglo-German Protestants in background and have been family men to one degree or another. That is clear. What is not so clear is *why* the American people, at many different stages of their national history, have preferred specifically such men to hold the highest national political office. Perhaps you will conclude that it is because, throughout American national history, the majority of the country's voting citizens have come from similar backgrounds and experiences themselves. But this is not true, at least certainly not since a time early in this century. Perhaps you will conclude that the long force of tradition itself reinforces the desire of Americans to perpetuate the sort of "presidential personality" that seems to be represented by these earlier men. With that conclusion, some analysts of the presidential office certainly would agree. But can that be altogether true when you add other variables, such as economic and social class—the differences in background between a George Washington and a Theodore Roosevelt, on the one hand, and an Andrew Jackson and an Abraham Lincoln, on the other?

So, just why *do* Americans perpetuate the tradition of electing men of quite similar ethnic, religious, and family backgrounds to the presidency? We have no predetermined answer for you! An answer to the question, one that is at least partially true, will have to come from your own synthesis. Your charts and tables of interrelated parts of your analysis, however, may make a collection of relationships clear when they may otherwise not be so.

How can you best arrange your own time and effort to obtain a successful synthesis? Some researchers find that the very act of beginning to write up their analysis will cause them to begin to synthesize final conclusions that represent new knowledge about their subjects. Others find that rearranging—either mentally or by a physical manipulation of charts, tables, and other paperwork—their analytical conclusions—much like rotating a kaleidoscope—will reveal new shapes that become the synthesis. Still others find that the process of synthesis begins when they prepare an outline of the way in which they will present their information and analysis in the final written paper. Which physical actions you will take to carry out your synthesis are impossible for us to determine, but you must remember that these actions are simply an aid to thinking carefully about the *meaning* of what you have discovered. The important act *is* the thinking—and thinking is hard to do.

Your synthesis is the product of a carefully controlled creativity—carefully controlled because you cannot deviate from the actual evidence you have unearthed, you cannot ignore evidence selectively to "make your thesis work," and you cannot violate the logical principles you used in performing your analysis. Yet, you must bring yourself, as you are, into the process, to join your own humanity with the lives, ideas, and imaginations of these other people whose lives, actions, or products you have studied. Based upon your past work, you do have the means and the power to make this leap towards revealing the significance of your work for others.

You must not forget that the power of synthesis is the greatest intellectual force humanity has created to develop new ideas. The most important philosophical understandings and factual explanations have arisen from this faculty. Before we conclude this section, we want you to see one example of how this process can have the most profound effect on our lives and our understanding of ourselves.

Charles Darwin spent almost five years[216] as a naturalist on board H. M. S. *Beagle*. As other naturalists did who served aboard British naval vessels, both before and after his time, he spent his days and hours *collecting data* from the remote corners of the globe to which his ship sailed. Today, we remember, most of all, the data he collected on five of the Galapagos Islands in the eastern Pacific, and we remember his memoir of his great adventure, *The Voyage of the Beagle*.[217] Later, at home in England, he *analyzed* the data he had assembled by using an Aristotelean technique—that of classifying the various items into categories that were based upon morphology. That is, he arranged his data according to the shapes, sizes, and colors of each of the examples of each species that he had observed, and then he placed these arrangements side-by-side with the geographical locations where he had made these various observations. This logical principle allowed him to see that one example of a species of creature most resembled another of the same species when the two examples he observed were close to one another geographically. The farther away the two examples were from one another, the greater the differences in gross morphology. From this analysis, and other similar analyses of related data, he *synthesized* the theory of natural selection, which, in turn, became the fundamental principle that underlies our understanding of biological evolution.

Darwin's analytical care was meticulous and exhaustive. He did not omit from his consideration any data that he had collected on the voyage of the *Beagle*. His logical principles of analysis, likewise, were careful and rational. When he finally

[216]December 27, 1831, to October 2, 1836.

[217]Charles Darwin, *Journal of Researches into the Geology and Natural History of the Various Countries Visited by*

H. M. S. Beagle under the Command of Captain FitzRoy, R. N., from 1832 to 1836 (London: H. Colburn, 1839); many times reprinted, usually with the title *The Voyage of the Beagle*. One edition that is accessible easily is the Everyman edition, published in both London and New York by J. M. Dent and E. P. Dutton, respectively. The text of the work which is volume 29 of *The Harvard Classics* (New York: P. F. Collier, 1909) is now available in digital form by ftp. The URL is: ftp://wiretap.spies.com/Library/Classic/beagle.txt.

presented—with the greatest reluctance and only after twenty years of considering and reconsidering his methods and logic—his synthesis to the reading public, in *The Origin of Species*,[218] his intellectual solidity was so great and so clear that he revolutionized the life sciences immediately.

Of course, your professor will not ask of you that you synthesize new knowledge that is equal in importance to the idea of biological evolution. She *will* ask that you take the whole range of conclusions that you reached in your analysis of the sources you collected and then to use them to try to determine if there are new ideas about your subject—ideas that you can perceive and describe clearly.

---

[218]Charles Darwin, *On the Origin of Species by Means of Natural Selection, or Preservation of Favoured Races in the Struggle for Life* (London: John Murray, 1859). This work has been reprinted many times, and has been translated and reprinted in dozens of foreign languages. The text of the first edition is available in digital form through the Internet from the notable resource of the *Oxford Text Archive*. The URL for it is: ftp://ota.ox.ac.uk/pub/ota/public/english/Darwin/origin.1783.

Writing

The word **thesis** comes to us directly from the Greek, and means *putting or placing a proposition or affirmation*, from a root in the Greek verb *to put or to place*. In the sense that it is used in the phrase **thesis statement** it means a proposition that you establish or state as a theme to be discussed and proved, or one which you will maintain against some attack. Ephraim Chambers, in his famous *Cyclopædia*, provided a solid illustration of the meaning of the term:

> Every proposition may be divided into thesis and hypothesis, thesis contains the thing affirmed or denied, and hypothesis the conditions of the affirmation or negation.[219]

In precisely the modern sense of a thesis statement, Thomas Jefferson wrote to one interlocutor, who had advanced an idea with which he thought Jefferson would agree, "On such a thesis, I never think the theme long."[220]

Your thesis statement for your first research paper probably will be quite straightforward and direct, perhaps no more than a sentence or two. Later, you may well have a thesis statement as the defining term for a longer and much more complex paper, such as a master's thesis[221] or a doctoral dissertation. If you do, you will simply

[219]Ephraim Chambers, *Cyclopædia, or, An Universal Dictionary of Arts and Sciences Containing an Explication of the Terms, and an Account of the Things Signified thereby, in the Several Arts both Liberal and Mechanical, and the Several Sciences, Human and Divine: The Whole Intended as a Course of Antient and Modern Learning, Extracted from the Best Authors, Dictionaries, Journals, Memoirs, Transactions, Ephemerides, &c. in Several Languages*, 4th ed. corr. and amended, with some additions, 2 vols. (London: Printed for D. Midwinter, 1741), *s. v.* "thesis."

[220]Thomas Jefferson, *The Writings of Thomas Jefferson: Being his Autobiography, Correspondence, Reports, Messages, Addresses, and Other Writings, Official and Private*, ed. by H[enry] A[ugustine] Washington, 9 vols. (Published by the order of the Joint Committee of Congress on the Library [of Congress], from the Original Manuscripts, Deposited in the Department of State; New York: Derby & Jackson, 1859) II:42.

[221]Which is why the term **thesis** is attached to this type of longer paper that students submit as part of the requiremetns of the university for granting a higher

elaborate the same method of evidence, exposition, and logical analysis that you have used here to maintain and prove that thesis.

The single most catastrophic mistake that students make in determining what they will write as their final research paper is a failure to develop and write a clear thesis statement, which should be placed prominently near the beginning of the text. Without such a clear thesis statement, your paper will lack focus and direction. It will look as if you have written your paper without having taken the time to determine just exactly what it is that you are writing about. Of course, you may have been thinking about your thesis statement extensively as your volume of information increased and you began to realize just what sorts of materials you had in hand with which to work. As you did your synthesis, you probably began to have an even clearer idea about what you would be able to say about your topic. Now is the time to make concrete these earlier random thoughts and to choose, finally, just what you will say about your topic. So, at the very beginning of the process of writing, make sure that you develop a clear thesis statement. Put yourself in the place of your reader to ask yourself if the thesis statement is clear, if it indicates the precise direction where your seamless, expository essay will go, and if it is interesting enough intrinsically to make your reader wish to continue to read what you have written. By the time you reach the end of your writing, you may have to change your thesis statement somewhat, to reflect the actual organic evolution of your paper. But the first concrete thesis statement will give you, yourself, a definite direction for your writing and will draw your attention to what you believe will be the major point that you will explore in your paper. With it as a central focus, you can make preliminary choices about what you will include from the large array of evidence that you have unearthed and what pieces of information are not directly germane to your thesis—information that you will relegate to footnotes.

OUTLINE

One well-regarded method for preparing yourself to write your final paper is to make an outline. If you decide to do this, and we

degree.

recommend it, remember that the one rule you must observe in the organization of your outline is consistency. [222]

In your outline, you can use either a topical or a sentence structure. In a **topical outline**, you will use words or phrases for all of your entries, and use no punctuation after each of your entries. The advantages of a topical outline are that it shows a brief, general view of your thinking and generally is easier and faster for you to write than a sentence outline. The disadvantage of this form is that your structure is briefly written and you must keep in mind the elements of information that you will use to expand the structure when you write your text.

In a **sentence outline**, you will use complete sentences for all of your entries, and use correct and complete punctuation in each of them. The advantages of this form are that it shows a more detailed view of your thinking, including, possibly, topic sentences for your paragraphs, and you will find it easier and faster to use a sentence outline when you write your text.

If you construct your outline properly, it will be **a logical, generalized description** of your research, analysis, and synthesis; **a schematic summary** of your whole work; **an organizational pattern** that you can use to elaborate your points, and the evidence which supports those points, in your paper; and **a visual and conceptual design or model** for your writing.

If you are careful and meticulous in creating a good outline, it will exhibit clearly both your logical thinking and your rational grouping of information and ideas into proper categories.

The purpose of writing an outline is to help you to visualize the process of writing an essay that is often complex and elaborate. The outline serves several distinct parts of the writing process at once. It helps you to organize both your information and your ideas. It reveals your material in a logical form. It shows the relationships of ideas to one another in your writing. It presents an orderly, general view of your whole essay. And, finally, it helps you to define categories of information and ideas, related groups of data and information, and the boundaries or limits of your final paper.

[222]We are indebted for the general scheme of this section to the useful digital handout from Purdue University's Online Writing Laboratory. The good aid for writers can be found at url: **http://owl.english.purdue.edu.**

Before you begin to prepare the outline, you must determine three essential characteristics of your final manuscript: its **purpose**, its **thesis**, and its **audience**. Once you have decided these three points, you are ready to begin to construct the outline itself.

Review your synthesis and list all of the ideas about your topic that you wish to include in your paper. Then associate all of the evidence—the relevant information and data—and your analysis of that evidence which prompted you to the specific ideas you will include in the essay.

Now, organize your ideas by gathering them in groups according to the relationships among them. Perhaps this will be a chronological arrangement of causes and effects, which often is the case when you write a short biography of someone—that is, you are unlikely to discuss your subject's birth in the same part of your paper as that where you discuss her research accomplishments or her political triumphs. Perhaps it will be a list of subtopics, each on the same general chronological plane as the others, as might be the case if you are writing about Albert Einstein's specific loves for, and contributions to, mathematics, physics, and music. In this case, place all of the ideas about each subtopic in a separate group. With these separated groups before you, arrange the synthesis, analysis, and evidence in each group according to a descending, or deductive, pattern—from the general to the specific, or from the abstract to the concrete. Finally, write down the main and subtopic headings for your outline, and then write the coordinate levels of your outline in a parallel form that is strictly logical.

A correct outline has a balanced structure which keeps to the logical requirements of parallelism, coordination, subordination, and division.

Parallelism:

In writing your outline, coordinate headings should be expressed in parallel form.[223] Nouns should be made parallel to nouns, verb forms to verb forms, adjectives to adjectives, and so forth. (Nouns—*monarchs, presidents, dictators*; Verbs—*to rule, to delegate, to command*; Adjectives—*divine-right monarch, benevolent despot, elective*

---

[223]If this sentence is unclear, please refer to the section on coordination, which follows this one; and then return to this discussion.

king.) Although you do need to keep as much of a parallel structure as you can, you should not sacrifice logical and clear writing simply to maintain parallelism. There may be some structures, for example, when you will use nouns and gerunds—nouns which have been constructed from verbs—at the same level of your outline. You should prefer a flexible form to a rigid one, as long as you do not violate the rules of logic.

Coordination:

In your outline, those items which you think are of equal significance should have comparable levels of numerals or letters; that is, an **A** is equal to a **B**, a **1** to a **2**, and an **a** to a **b**. You should make the ideas or information which have the same value to your analysis also have the same level of coordinate. Coordination is that principle of organization which enables you to maintain a coherent and consistent essay.

Correct coordination:

> A. Presidents
> B. Senators
> C. Representatives

Incorrect coordination:

> A. Presidents
> B. Martin Van Buren
> C. Roscoe Conkling

In the incorrect coordination that is shown above, Martin Van Buren was a president—or, rather, in this case, an example or a type of a president—and his name should be placed in a subdivision of **A.** Roscoe Conkling, though he tried more than once to get his party's nomination for the presidency, was never a president, and his name should be placed, as a subdivision, in some other category, perhaps—in the case of the correct coordination, above, under **B. Senators**. One way to correct the faulty coordination in the incorrect example may be to revise your main headings, or categories, to reflect topics that are common to them:

> A. Types of politicians
> 1. Martin Van Buren
> 2. Roscoe Conkling
> B. Evaluations of political success
> 1. Martin Van Buren
> 2. Roscoe Conkling

Subordination:

In order for you to indicate the relevance of each of your ideas, and the associated analysis and information, to your topic as a whole—that is the varying levels of significance of your ideas, you will contruct your outline with major headings with various minor headings under them. In ordering your ideas, you should organize your material from the general to the specific, or from the abstract to the concrete. The more general or abstract your idea or concept, the higher the level or rank in the outline. This principle allows you to order your material in terms of strict deductive logic and requires you to articulate clearly the relationships among the components you use in the outline. So each subdivision of each major division should always have the same relationship to the whole. Here is an example of a correct subordination in an outline:

> **A. Pre-Civil-War Presidents**
> **1. Millard Fillmore**
> **2. Franklin Pierce**
> **B. Post-Civil-War Presidents**
> **1. Ulysses Simpson Grant**
> **2. Rutherford Birchard Hayes**

By contrast, here is an example of faulty subordination:

> A. Pre-Civil-War Presidents
>   1. Franklin Pierce
>   2. Successes as president
>   3. Failures as president

There are two problems here. First, there is an A without a B; and, second, terms 1, 2, and 3 are not logically equal—Franklin Pierce was, indeed, a president of the United States before the Civil War, but the concepts of "success" and "failure" are qualities, and, therefore, not in logical equality with "Franklin Pierce," a person, not a quality. One way to correct this faulty subordination is:

> **A. Pre-Civil-War Presidents**
>   **1. Millard Fillmore**
>   **a. Successes as president**
>   **b. Failures as president**
>   **2. Franklin Pierce**
>   **a. Successes as president**
>   **b. Failures as president**
> **B. Post-Civil-War Presidents**
>   **1. Ulysses Simpson Grant**
>   **a. Successes as president**
>   **b. Failures as president**
>   **2. Rutherford Birchard Hayes**
>   **a. Successes as president**
>   **b. Failures as president**

Division:

When you divide something, your result will always consist of at least two parts;[224] so, therefore, there can never be an A without a

---

[224]"The association of the word "divide" with the concept of "two" is very old, coming to us from Greek, through Latin. The word element "di" is the same as that found in every other word where the prefix "di" indicates the concept of "two," from "dimidiate" (*Heraldry*) to "dichroic" (*Geology*). This was clear in its earliest uses in English, as shown in John Wycliffe's great translation of the Bible, completed in the 1380's, when he translates the famous judgement of Solomon in I Kings iii:25: "**Deuydith**, he seith, the quyk child in two parties."

B, or a **1** without a **2**, or an **a** without a **b**. Usually, you can find more than one way to divide the parts of your topics and subtopics logically. However, when you do divide, use only one basis of division at each level of your logical hierarchy, and also make the basis for your division as sharp and clear as possible—for you, as you construct the outline; and for your reader, as she reads the seamless and logical flow of your text. For example:

> A. Edward I's Castles in Wales [Physical aspects]
>   1. Types
>   2. Locations
>   3. Costs
> B. Personnel in Edward I's Castles [Human aspects]
>   1. Military personnel
>   2. Bureaucrats
>   3. Craftsmen
>   4. Laborers and servants

or:

> A. Galleys
>   1. Roman
>   2. Byzantine
>   a. Size
>   b. Cost
>
> B. Uses for galleys
>   1. Strategic warfare
>   2. Commerce protection

Of course, you can use any form of logical labelling for your headings. Two of the more common and reasonable are Roman numerals and letters, and the decimal form, in which lower levels of categories have longer labels, based on their logical distance

[Authorized Version (1611): "And the king said, **Divide** the living child in two, and give half to the one, and half to the other."]. See the *Oxford English Dictionary*, 2d. ed., *ss. vv.* the words quoted above.

from the main heading. The former is the older, academic preference, while the latter has become very common in scientific and technical outlines, and in government documents.

Roman Numeral	*Decimal*
I.	1.0
A.	1.1
1.	1.2
a.	1.2.1
b.	1.2.2
2.	1.2.2.1
a.	1.2.2.2
b.	
B.	
1.	
a.	
b.	
2.	
a.	
b.	
II.	2.0
A.	2.1
B.	2.2
C.	2.3

NINE PRINCIPLES OF GOOD WRITING

Now that you have completed your analysis of the information that you discovered, your synthesis of new information, and your logical outline, you are ready to begin to write your paper—in which you will set forth the questions you will attempt to answer, offer a full exposition of your research and document it, present your analysis of the materials you discovered, and delineate your synthesis of conclusions about your topic. And you will do all of this in one, seamless, expository essay. If you are to accomplish this successfully, in such a way as to get and hold your reader's attention until your writing is done, the chief attribute of your writing must be its clarity—a characteristic upon which we will devote many words, below.

Before you type your first characters into your word processor, however, we have a few tips which may make your task much easier and much more successful. This section does not review the whole of English mechanics, or even the fundamental rules of grammar. We hope that you have mastered these things during the course of your primary education. It may be the case, however, that you, yourself, see the need to refresh your memory on some fundamental principles of grammar. Should you wish to do that, we recommend strongly *Harper's English Grammar* by John B. Opdycke. A short and inexpensive work, it covers all of the elements of grammar in a concise, straightforward fashion, without ambiguity.[225]

The text in the following section also is not concerned with your writing style. We offer you some general tips to improve the clarity of your writing. To the extent that this may influence your own style, we are guilty of of the sin of prescribing a mode of writing. But our only real concern is clarity. Remember that a letter that you write involves both you and your reader in a rather complex series of actions which draw your reader into some tangible, physical relationship to your writing. You type or wordprocess your

[225]John B[aker] Opdycke, *Harper's English Grammar*, rev. and ed. by Stewart H. Benedict (New York: Harper & Row, Publishers, 1965; reprinted New York: Warner Books, 1983). The present paperback edition by Warner Books is priced at $4.50, perhaps the greatest bargain in books for students today.

letter, fold it, put it in an envelope, add a stamp, and drop it in the post. Your reader must retrieve your letter, open it, unfold it, and then begin to read your text. All of this effort involves your reader with your writing in a direct, physical way. Perhaps, then, your reader will not cast aside your prose quickly and cavalierly—after all, this involves yet another physical process, that of rising to drop your letter into the waste basket and, later, emptying it, in turn, into the daily trash. By contrast, your reader can dispense with your e-mail letter, if it is annoying or unclear, simply by pressing her mail program's DELETE key. Consequently, since the reader's physical involvement with your writing is minimal, it is only the writing itself that will attract enough attention from your reader to keep her reading on through your text. The only general principle of writing which will elicit that favorable attitude is clarity. Your reader wants to know exactly what is going on in your prose, what persons or things are involved and what specific actions are taking place with regard to those persons or things. Any cloudiness in your expression of ideas and description of actions is quite likely to move your reader's finger directly to the dreaded DELETE key. And the busier and more active your reader is in her life, the more swiftly this will happen. You must command attention for your own writing and, again, clarity is the principal method by which you can do this.

Perhaps it seems somewhat strange to you that we should discuss an effective letter at this time, since you are about to start writing a term paper. We do this because every piece of non-fictional writing is, or should be, a seamless example of expository prose. Whether you write a letter of complaint or a doctoral dissertation, you begin by explaining the essential point of your writing. You follow this with an exposition, usually chronological, of the actions which took place, and then you offer your conclusions, in which you express your ideas about the consequence of those actions. So, we think that the principles which apply to an effective and arresting letter do apply equally well to a term paper, a master's thesis, a doctoral dissertation, or a major and lengthy monograph.

Since you have gotten this far in our little book, we hope that you have **NOT** noticed that it was written with the principle of clarity above all other considerations. We do, however, hope that you have understood what we have had to say with the least amount of difficulty. We hope that you have not had to read and reread portions of our text in order to discern what we meant by what we said. If this is, in fact, the case, then the following material will explain precisely the techniques that we have used to achieve this clarity of expression.

As we said, in the paragraph above, the primary goal of every serious writer is clarity. Clarity above all. Every example of your writing, whether it is a letter, an essay, or a long monograph, needs to explain its ideas to its readers with the least amount of strain on their part. After all, you cannot persuade or inform anyone about anything, if your readers must struggle, again and again, to understand what you actually mean by what you have said.

Remember, also, that most of the people who learn about your ideas in your lifetime will come to do so by reading them, not by hearing you expound them in oral form. The rise of electronic communications of all sorts — telefacsimiles, e-mail, and digital text — when added to traditional forms of written communication — typewritten and handwritten documents of all kinds — means that most of the people who know you will know you through your writing, and may never meet you in person. The office memorandum that you write in New York today may be read by people in your firm's branch offices throughout the world on the next day; and then may be circulated to others, outside your firm, in those countries on the day after that. Your note to your boss, if it includes ideas of real merit, may be read by a client in Singapore or Sidney within hours of your submitting it—thanks to the miracle of electronic communication. In this regard, you need to have in your thoughts, as you write, the fact that fewer than three hundred million people speak and write American English as a native language. Another two hundred million people have other varieties of English as their primary language, principally Britons and descendants of Britons in former British colonies. But more than one and a half billion other people speak or write some form of the English language as a second or third tongue every day, because English has become the *lingua franca* of international business, diplomacy, and scholarship, as well as the language of computers and the Internet. These one and a half billion people will not recognize readily odd idioms from any local or national experience; and, even less, they may find your writing unintelligible, if you stray very far from the logical constructions of accepted grammar, punctuation, and syntax. In order for them to be successful, your ideas must be expressed in such a way that almost everyone can understand them. Reading is a hard task, and it is a new one in our natural life. The human eye was not designed by nature to scan rapidly over as many as several thousand characters in a minute and then to translate those characters into mental images of spoken words, which then become ideas inside the brain of another person—all within the space of a fraction of a single second. Because this is true, you must make the act of reading as effortless as possible for your readers. It is a human obligation![226]

The art in art lies in concealing the art. Clarity is not noticed by your readers, but your ideas are. Clarity in expository writing achieves several things for you at once:

ᕙ Your reader is impressed immediately by your knowledge of your subject, because you waste no time in presenting extraneous or unconnected material, and your narrative unfolds in a logical and coherent way.

ᕙ Your discussion is persuasive, because your forthrightness and directness of speech show that you have given great attention and thought to arriving at your conclusions.

ᕙ Your reader imagines you to be rational and mature—a person whose research, conclusions, opinions, and suggestions are worthy of serious consideration, because your use of language presents a seamless discussion, without disorder and confusion.

---

[226]Richard Lederer, in his remarkable book, *The Miracle of Language,* offers some cogent numbers on the use of English in world communication: "The majority of the world's books, newspapers, and magazines are written in English. Most international telephone calls are made in English. Sxity percent of the world's radio programs are beamed in English, and more than seventy percent of international mail and seventy-five percent of cable messages and telexes are written and addressed in English." Richard Lederer, *The Miracle of Language* (New York: Pocket Books, Simon & Schuster, Inc., 1991) 19-20.

And, in addition to all of this, writing, rather than speaking in person, presents your mind as it really is—it is your true humanity, with no consideration of age, gender, race, or anything else which causes some to mask from themselves the quality of your ideas and opinions. In this way, no cultural or national affinity distracts your reader from an honest appraisal of your work.

Below, you will find twelve keys which you can use to achive the maximun degree of clarity in your writing. All of these helpful methods rest upon the quality of preciseness—in choosing nouns, verbs, adjectives, and adverbs—as the necessary handmaiden to reaching clarity.

I. Avoid, whenever possible, the use of the passive voice.

Your fellow humans, like you yourself, are curious creatures. When a writer or speaker describes or identifies some action, readers or hearers, like you, yourself, want to know who did the action. In a news story about a murder, most people are more interested in the murderer than in the victim. Even an unpleasant order sounds more humane in the active, rather than the passive, voice. "The president requires you to inform him of your decision" sounds much better than "You are required to inform the president of your decision." Who requires you to inform? You wish to know who has done the action!

Here is the magic bullet which will kill any meaningless use of the passive voice forever. If you can append the phrase, "by my grandmother" to any verb in any sentence, and the sentence still makes sense, then it is in the passive voice. Notice, for example, in the sentence above, how you can use the bullet: "You are required [by my grandmother] to inform the president of your decision."

We owe you a strict technical definition of the construction of sentences in the passive voice. In them, the normal direct object of the sentence becomes the subject instead; the verb is reduced to being an auxiliary of the verb *to be*; and the normal subject becomes an object of the preposition *by*. In most cases, people who write in the passive voice habitually will omit the actual object of the preposition *by*, and thus believe that the real doer of the action is concealed from the reader or hearer. But people are not stupid.

They can determine, with some effort, who the doer of the action is, and they will believe that the speaker or writer who tried to conceal this fact from them is intellectually dishonest, at best, and a dissembling hypocrite, at worst. They are unlikely to vest much faith in the words of such persons, hence people's dislike of bureaucratese and other similar discourse.[227]

Now, of course, we think you are entitled to know when you should use the passive voice. You should use it only when you speak in general historical terms, where you need not identify specific doers of specific actions. "George Washington is considered [by my grandmother] to have been a great man" generally is true, and it is not necessary to try to narrow that opinion to some expression like "Twenty-three and nine tenths of the adult male population in Bennington, Vermont, in September, 1923, considered George Washington to have been a great man."!

II. Gerunds, and gerundives, are NOT verbs.

Gerunds are the majority of those words in English which end in *ing*. All of them are nouns which were created from antecedent verbs. *Sewing is a useful passtime,* for example, depends for its meaning on the earlier verb *to sew.* Similarly, *reading* is based upon *to read,* and *writing* is based upon *to write.* These words are necessary, because you must be able to describe the absolute quality of some action in general with a noun. When you do use a gerund to describe part of the action in a sentence, the gerund **always** appears as an auxiliary word of some part of the verb *to be,* and **always** describes some secondary action in the sentence. A gerund **cannot**

---

[227]No one has put the prescription for avoiding the passive voice better than H[enry] W[atson] Fowler, in his great work, *A Dictionary of Modern English Usage*:

> [The use of the passive voice] in addressing another... often amounts to a pusillanimous shrinking from responsibility *(It is felt that your complaint arises from a misunderstanding. / It is thought that ample provision has been made against this contingency).* The person addressed has a right to know who it is that entertains a feeling he may not share or a thought he may consider mistaken, and is justly resentful of the suggestion that it exists in the void.

> H. W. Fowler, *A Dictionary of Modern English Usage*, 2d ed., rev. by Sir Ernest Gowers (New York: Oxford University Press, 1965) 440.

function as the main verb in any sentence. Consider the following four sentences:

a. She continued with her sewing while her house was burning.
b. She sewed while her house was burning.
c. She continued with her sewing while her house burned.
d. She sewed while her house burned.

In sentence (a), the principal verb is *continue*, and the actions of *sewing* and *burning* are of secondary importance, which they should not be, given her predicament, because the grammar—which is simply a word to describe the logic of language, and which grows from the language and is not imposed down upon it—is constructed to show this. *Sewing* is a gerund in this example precisely in the sense that it is in the sentence, "I must do my *sewing* on Tuesday." In sentence (b), the verb is *sew*, and is the principal action in the sentence, while the *burning* is secondary. In sentence (c), *burn* is the principal verb, while *sewing* is secondary. In sentence (d), however, the verbs *sew* and *burn*, together, describe the amazing quality of the woman's actions, and thus is the best phrased of the four examples.

You can remember that gerunds are nouns by recalling such little aphorisms as: *Swimming is a good exercise* and *Reading is fun*. Notice that the word *is* in both sentences is a part of the verb *to be*, and is necessary if you use a gerund in a verbal phrase.

You should **not** try to make gerunds be the principal verbs in a sentence, simply because they cannot function in that way. If you do, you will have made some part of the verb *to be* the real principal verb in your sentence.

In this same general class of words, English also has a vast array of nouns which were originally Latin nouns derived from Latin verbs. These are the words that have the endings *tion* and *sion*. Unfortunately, modern writers of American English have resorted to the custom of placing these nouns in verb phrases which point to the preposition *of*. You can recognize these lapses whenever you see the phrase "in the ......tion of." Consider the following example as a representative of this usage: "She will help in the implementation of our new plan." Since the verb *to implement* is derived from Latin, as is the noun *implementation*, it seems illogical, indeed silly, to bring the expression full circle from verb to noun to verb, changing the inflection with each change, thus creating a long, unwieldy phrase to describe a direct, and often simple, action. A better expression of the thought in the example, above, may be: "She will help to implement our new plan."

It is worth recalling that verbs usually are the most important words in English sentences. A successful writer, who achieves the greatest degree of clarity in her expression, is one who chooses carefully the appropriate active verb—one which describes, as precisely as possible, just what action is taking place in the sentence. A series of sentences with clear, precise verbs in them seems to have an energy and liveliness which other sentences, without these clear and unambiguous verbs, lack.

III. Use precise nouns.

The English language today has a greater wealth of nouns to describe specific things than any other language in the history of humanity. This abundance is a major reason that English has become the world's language for business, politics, and scholarship. Because English is so rich, every writer of it has the chance to make her writing stronger and more precise by choosing carefully the nouns which label the persons, things, and ideas about which she is writing. For example, let us suppose you wish to discuss the serious implications for our present environment of the deforestation of large parts of North America in the nineteenth and early twentieth centuries. A sentence which states that this topic is worthy of a reader's attention could be phrased in the general way we have just stated it, of course. But a much stronger expression of this idea may be: "Modern America's environmental problems may well have begun in the last century with the final destruction of the continent's primeval forests of hardwood; the great expanses of oak, maple, elm, and ash which the earliest settlers found here when they arrived." The preciseness of words like *primeval, hardwood, oak, maple, elm,* and *ash* add a degree of clarity and sharpness which is lacking in a blander, more general statement about the

192

problem. All of your writing should reflect your own thoughtfulness about the phrasing of your ideas, so that your reader senses, at once, that you have not tossed off your prose in an apparently rapid and ill-considered way. After all, why should your reader invest her time and interest in reading your prose if she she senses that you did not invest your time and interest in writing it?

Your precise use of appropriate nouns displays your care in choosing just the right word to identify the things which are the subject of your discourse. Trees? What kinds of trees? *The small grove of old elms to your right* is a much more captivating phrase than *Those trees over there.*

Your precision in choosing your nouns adds to the strength of your conclusions automatically. You must strive to say precisely what you mean so that your reader will believe in the value of your ideas. You must avoid the reader's condemnation in the language of the old English aphorism: "How can I possibly believe that you mean what you say when you apparently cannot say what you mean."

IV. Keep the whole form of the verbs in your sentences together.

When you were in primary school, if you had a rather old-fashioned teacher, you were admonished not to "split the infinitive" of a verb. You were taught to write "to go faithfully to the gymnasium" rather than "to faithfully go to the gymnasium." Of course, if your primary education took place in more recent years, you probably were not taught this at all. What the admonition means is simply that English has split the construction of verbs into a collection of words, rather than relying on a series of written inflections, as do most of the other Indo-European languages. Consider the Spanish infinitive "hablar." In English, this must be represented by two words, "to" and "speak," in order to form the same infinitive. Thus, in Spanish, as in French, Italian, German, and the other Indo-European tongues, there is no opportunity to "split the infinitive," because the infinitive is just one word.

Similarly, Spanish, and the other tongues we have mentioned, construct whole verb forms in single, inflected words. The Spanish word "hablábamos," for example, may be translated into English as "we were speaking." Thus, in Spanish, you have no chance to mangle understanding with an expression like "we were recently speaking," because the verb form simply does not let you do that. Because verbs describe precise actions or states of being, the whole form of any verb should be kept together, whenever possible, in order to make clear precisely what the action or state of being is. For non-native speakers and writers, who may be conditioned by their own tongues to expect intact verb forms, a fragmented verb may not be merely confusing but, in fact, unintelligible. And when you recall that the majority of the readers of your writing may be just such non-native speakers, the intact verb becomes a distinct contributor to the clarity of your writing.

Consider the following common expression in American idiomatic English: "She could also readily have gone to the bookstore when she went to see her mother." This sentence, while quite satisfactory in daily informal speech, will be clearer in a written form if it appears as "Also, she could have gone to the bookstore readily when she went to see her mother." By uniting the whole of the principal verb, **could have gone**, the writer has made the expression both clearer and tighter. This care to maintain the integrity of the verb will promote a greater understanding by your readers of what you have written.

V. Punctuate your sentences according to their internal logic, not according to patterns of speech—although your own patterns generally do, in fact, follow the logic of your expression. Remember that inside every compund, complex, or compound-complex sentence is a simple sentence screaming to get out. Consider the following example: "President Eisenhower, even though he had had no earlier political experience, *per se*, was, in spite of this perceived shortcoming, a good chief executive." The simple sentence is, of course, "President Eisenhower was a good chief exectutive." All of the other elements in the sentence serve only to modify or qualify some part of the simple sentnce. These are the elements that you should mark off with commas, in order to promote your reader's ability to isolate the main point you state.

For those of you who find the art of correct punctuation to be an arcane mystery whose secrets are opened only to the elect, we recommend Karen Elizabeth Gordon's delighful little treatise, *The New Well-Tempered Sentence: A Punctuation Handbook for the Innocent, the Eager, and the Doomed.*[228] Her exposition of the topic is clear and unabiguous, and her comments and examples are pithy and clever—designed to bring a smile to the lips of even the most tired and frustrated writer during an all-nighter. Most importantly, she observes that:

> every word carries a pack of punctuation marks in its pocket to attach wherever and whenever needed in its exciting, unpredictable life. Virtuoso use of this motley collection is as enhancing to your writing as a full-spectrum vocabulary and a snazzy grammar to keep it in.[229]

VI. Avoid noun-noun-noun constructions.

Recently, American English has been characterized, more and more, by the use of strings of nouns to act as modifiers to some other noun, a usage quite reminiscent of the German style of creating compund nouns to meet new demands for labels. Originally, this custom started with military texts from the beginning of the twentieth century, when most major treatises on such matters were, indeed, written in German. Young American officers and cadets, eager to impress their superiors with their understanding of the latest military theories, began to adopt a style of German phrasing in English. By the later years of this century, this practice had evolved into such ugly phrases as the *Integrated Logistic Support Plan Problem Resolution Conference.* Of course, such a thing is, in fact, a conference to resolve problems that have arisen with plans to provide integrated logistic support—a concept that can be understood quite readily, when it is written in English.[230]

---

[228]Revised and expanded edition, NewYork: Ticknor & Fields, 1993.

[229]Gordon, p. viii.

[230]Not too long ago, the United States Navy established teams of men, based on aircraft carriers, who swept out to rescue pilots whose planes plunged into the sea, either when they took off or when they tried to land. The work of the men on these teams is valuable and important, but you can imagine their chagrin when the Navy called them Fleet Air Recovery Teams, which was converted to a new initialism immediately. The Navy now calls them Carrier Air Recovery Teams.

From its pompous military and naval beginnings, the habit of using strings of nouns to modify another noun spread outward through other government bureaus, then to business and commerce, and now, at last, into general usage among many parts of American society. Of course, the English language is in a constant state of change, since people's speech in daily life really does determine how the language is structured; and it may well come to pass that such noun-noun-noun constructions will become elements of standard American English some day. But that day is not here. The great majority of people who use English as a medium of thought and communication throughout the world do not yet subscribe to this convention, and may not understand the subject of your discourse, if you employ elaborate noun phrases to describe it. Indeed, past experience in English shows us that, like German, we create compound nouns as independent words when we have nouns that regularly modify other nouns—a briefcase, for example, originally identified a case in which lawyers carried their briefs. We do not, however, usually join a series of nouns together to create one single compund noun, as German does. You should avoid noun-noun-noun constructions if only because your reliance on them eventually may lead to a condition in which we English speakers will have an organization called *Unternehmensbeteiligungsgesellschaft Baden-Württemberg Aktiengesellschaft*, which we will have to reduce to an initialism, UBW, as the Germans have, just to prevent our tongues from becoming crippled.

Again we say, because your writing should reflect the greatest possible degree of clarity for all of your present and potential readers, you should avoid, wherever possible, the use of these noun-noun-noun constructions. Use a few more words, if necessary, to clarify for your readers just exactly what it is about which you are speaking.[231]

For the sake of your reader's sanity, it is better to take the time to indicate clearly that you are discussing a curriculum that you designed to help to rehabilitate young criminals than it is to say

---

[231]Imagine our surprise, the other day, to hear a recorded voice tell us to remain on the line while "cutomer service representatives" were serving other "Lucid Technologies customers." We like to think of ourselves as lucid, but we are not sure of the technology part!

that you are discussing your youth offender rehabilitation curriculum.[232]

Before we close this brief discussion, it is worth mentioning that almost every noun in English has its complementary adjectival form. You may have to resort to a dictionary to find it, but it is there. For your discussion of an historical figure who was born in Glasgow, you can avoid calling her a *Glasgow native* in favor of calling her a *native of Glasgow*—or, if you wish to be as precise as possible, even at the sacrifice of some immediate clarity, you can call her, most properly, a *Glaswegian*.

VII. *Because* and *so*, two valuable words for writers.

We already have discussed, in our section on verbs, how every reader wishes to know who the doer of the action in every sentence really is. A complement to this truth is that every reader also wishes to know the chain of cause and effect which explains why something has happened in the way that it has. This was a relationship which you worked hard to establish in your analysis. The English language has, from ages past, two important words which indicate just that: *because* and *so*.

Because always links some effect to some specific cause, while *so* links some specific cause to some effect of it: an effect *because* of some cause; a cause *so* some effect. "I was late to work today [*effect*], **because** the rain held up the traffic [*cause*]." "The rain held up the traffic [*cause*], **so** (that) I was late to work [*effect*]." Recently, many writers have weakened the link between cause and effect by using the conjunction *and* to join together, often with no specific relationships at all, causes and effects: "John was born into a very poor family **and** he had to become clever and crafty just to survive." This last sentence can be made much clearer simply by showing poverty as the *cause* and the development of craftiness as its *effect*. "**Because** John was born into a very poor family, he had to become clever and crafty just to survive."

That the word because always identifies the cause of some effect is embodied in the origins of the word itself. It really is a

---

[232]You can imagine how depressed we were, the other month, to learn that one of us was assigned to teach a "19th Century Literature Survey Course."

portmanteau word which unites the preposition *by* with the substantive word *cause*—by cause. The phrase or clause which follows the word *because* identifies the cause of the effect that you describe.[233]

The word so, in contrast to the word because, has many uses in the English language. The *Oxford English Dictionary*, for example, discusses our particular use of the word in only two small sections of a very large entry.[234] The American use of the word *so* to act as a pointer from some *cause* to some *effect* is a shortened form of the expression *so that*, in the sense of: "Nerissa went to college *so that* she could have the career she wanted." Other words which can serve the same purpose—that of showing the relationship of some *cause* to some *effect*—include *therefore* and *consequently*, as well as the phrase *for that reason*. But the value of *so* above these other words is that it is short and to the point—there is no need to use a four-syllable word (*consequently*) when a one-syllable word (*so*) will do. Consider how the following sentence: "Jessica finally went to the Library of Congress in Washington **and** she found the book for which she had been searchng all semester" is improved by the clearly-defined relationship of cause to effect: "Jessica finally went to the Library of Congress in Washington **so** she found the book for which she had been searching all semester."

VIII. Complete the full grammatical construction of all of your sentences in your formal writing.

The use of the rheorical figure *ellipsis*[235] has been a part of human speech since prehistoric times. All of us, in our daily conversation, regularly omit words from our sentences which really are necessary to complete the whole logical construction. Again, however, when you recall that the vast majority of readers of English do not use the language as their primary means of thinking and expression, you certainly will wish to enhance your own clarity by including in

---

[233] *Oxford English Dictionary*, 2d. ed, *s. v.* "because".

[234] *ibid., s. v.* "so," §§ II:10:a and V:23.

[235] The *Oxford English Dictionary* offers the following definition of the rhetorical term: "The omission of one or more words in a sentence, which would be needed to complete the grammatical construction or fully to express the sense" (2d. ed., *s. v.* "ellipsis," §2).

your sentences all of those elements which are necessary to give a full, logical exposition of your thought.[236]

Consider the following example: "Portia established new rules enabling workers to have longer vacations." The full grammatical construction of this sentence, which eliminates the use of a gerund as a verb, and which clarifies the whole expression, is: "Portia established new rules to enable those who worked for her to have longer vacations." Similarly, the fragment: "Mail me your response," which is perfectly clear in idiomatic American English, may well be interpreted by your reader in Indonesia as an instruction to have her stuff *you* in an envelope. It becomes much clearer, when you complete the whole grammatical construction: "Mail your response to me." Finally, consider the following sentence: "The names listed in this brochure, while significant, represent only a few of the persons buried in this cemetery." How much clearer the thought becomes in the expression: "The persons whose names are listed in this brochure are those who were significant in their time, but they are only a few of the many people who are buried in this cemetery." Yes, the second example contains almost twice as many words as the first one does, and it also uses several forms of the verb "to be," yet it is a clearer sentence, because it delineates, carefully and precisely, the factual statement that the writer wishes to make.

IX. Always use standard diction and usage.

Ben Jonson's observation:

> *Language* most shewes a man: speake that I may see thee. It springs out of the most retired, and inmost parts of us, and is the Image of the Parent of it, the mind. No glasse renders a mans forme, or likenesse, so true as his speech. Nay, it is likened to a man; and as we consider feature, and composition in

---

[236]If you have any lingering doubt that this is the right thing to do for your readers, consider the comment of Alexander Pope, the Wasp of Twickenham: "The ellipsis, or speech by half-words [is the peculiar talent] of ministers and politicians." [bracketed material, *Oxford English Dictionary*] (Alexander Pope (supposed author), *PERI BAUYS: or, Martinus Scriblerus, his Treatise of The Art of Sinking in Poetry* [London: Printed for B. Motte, 1727] 115).

a man; so words in Language: in the greatnesse, aptnesse, sound, structure, and harmony of it.[237]

though written in the early seventeenth century, remains as true today as it was in his time, and was as true centuries before him as it is true today. Whether we like it or not, almost all people make personal and societal, as well as intellectual, judgements about others based upon the way that any speaker uses the language she is speaking or writing. Two members of an appreciative audience who approach the performer after the event will be estimated quite differently if one says: "Yo, that was really kewl," while the other says: "That truly was an outstanding performance." Which one of them, do you suppose, is identified by the performer as the better educated, as the more informed listener, as the member of a higher social class? You may not like this sort of judgement, but, we suggest, almost everyone does it, including, perhaps, you yourself. Indeed, George Bernard Shaw crafted his best-known play, *Pygmalion*—and from it, in turn, came *My Fair Lady*—exactly to illustrate this fact.

When you remember that the majority of the people who will read your texts throughout your life are persons who will never see your physical self, it becomes even clearer that, for most people, your writing *is* you. All of the mental images your readers will create of you are based solely on the nature and appearance of your writing. With this in mind, you need to choose your words carefully, concisely, and appropriately.

If you think that your ability to be precise in your language is not what it should be, we can direct you, enthusiastically, to the handbook which has stood on the desks and writing-tables of almost every serious writer of English for almost three quarters of a century; *A Dictionary of Modern English Usage* by H. W. Fowler.[238]

[237]Ben Jonson, *Timber: or, Discoveries*, in W[hitney] F[rench] Bolton, *The English Language: Essays by English and American Men of Letters 1490-1839* (Cambridge: at the University Press, 1966) 42. Its first appearance in print, as *Timber: or, Discoveries Made upon Men and Matter: as they have flow'd out of his daily readings; or had their refluxe to this peculiar notion of the times* was in the 1640 folio of Jonson's complete works, *The Workes of Benjamin Jonson* (London: printed for Richard Meighen, 1640). The contents of the folio are separately paginated and bear different imprints. *Timber* is gathered with *Horace* and the *English Grammar*, and is in signatures M-R6, with the date of imprint as 1641.

This remarkable book, by an acerbic, but clear, compiler, is quite prescriptive in its approach to written English. And while its orientation is to British English, nearly every admonition can be used with benefit by American writers, as well.

Remember, in all your writing, the great aphorism of Jonathan Swift: "Proper words in proper places, make the true definition of a style."[239]

Before we leave this section, we would like to say a few words about citations and bibliographical style. The most important single attribute of a well-annotated paper is consistency. Whatever style guide or style sheet you adopt for your citations, be sure to follow its precepts carefully and consistently. Of course, you will use the style manual which is prescribed by your publisher, university, college, department, or professor. If no one prescribes or recommends a manual to you, then perhaps your best choice is the standard manual by Kate L. Turabian, *A Manual for Writers of Term Papers, Theses, and Dissertations*.[240] Portions of the current edition of *Turabian*, as the work generally is known, are based upon the fourteenth edition of an even more impressive and famous standard, *The Chicago Manual of Style*, published in 1993.[241] This edition is significant, because it offers, for the first time, the formats for citing various forms of information that are stored on electronic media.[242]

---

[238]H[enry] W[atson] Fowler, *A Dictionary of Modern English Usage*, 2d. ed., rev. by Sir Ernest Gowers (New York and Oxford: Oxford University Press, 1965), many times reprinted and now available in an inexpensive paperback edition. We ourselves just corrected our incorrect use of the word *precision* based on our discovery in Fowler's entry, "preciseness, precision." It is a book of daily value to us, and we hope it will be so for you, too.

[239]Jonathan Swift, *A Letter to a Young Gentleman, lately enter'd into Holy Orders* (London: Printed for J. Roberts, 1721). This is the first London edition. The text was first published in Dublin, 1720, with the title: *A Letter from a Lay-patron to a Gentleman, designing for Holy Orders*, and signed *A. B.*, a pseudonym used by Swift. The letter is dated "January the 9th, 1719-20."

[240]Kate L. Turabian, *A Manual for Writers of Term Papers, Theses, and Dissertations*, 6th ed., revised by John Grossman and Alice Bennett (Chicago: The University of Chicago Press, 1996).

[241]*The Chicago Manual of Style*, 14th ed. (Chicago: The University of Chicago Press, 1993).

[242]Until a new edition of a major manual of style addresses the issue of citing information that is stored and retrieved electronically, the *de facto* standard is Xia Li

Keep in mind that all of your citations must contain the complete collection of information which allows your reader to go directly to your source with the least trouble. Do not force your reader to guess at the full title of a work, or which edition you have used; do not force her to labor to determine the date of a radio or television interview, or which version of a film you have seen.

---

and Nancy B. Crane, *Electronic Style: A Guide to Citing Electronic Information* (Westport, Connecticut: Meckler Publishing, 1993). Several guides to citing electronic information are avaialable on the Internet. On the World Wide Web, you will find *Bibliographic Formats for Citing Electronic Information.* URL: http://www.uvm.edu/~xli/reference/estyles.html. The *MLA Style Citations of Electronic Sources,* by Janice R. Walker, is based upon the Modern Language Association's bibliographical principles. URL: http://www.cas.usf.edu/english/walker/mla.html.

Mining the Internet—Again.

Earlier, we described to you a very small number of the vast array of informational sources that are available to you through the Internet. In this brief section, we wish to point you towards a number of additional locations on the 'net which are designed to help writers to do their tasks well. Recently, a number of universities and scholarly institutions have created services called online writing laboratories, or OWLs. Some of the hypertext links, below, will guide you to the better OWLs. If you have specific questions about English mechanics, these services may be able to help you.

First, we recommend the *World Wide Web Resources for Rhetoric and Composition*, which can be found at the URL: http://www.ind.net/Internet/comp.html. This page contains a large number of links to many resources, including pages that offer online help for writers, as well as informational pages on style, grammar, and usage.

Another valuable site is *Resources for Rhetoric and Composition: Other Sites and Resources* at the URL:
http://www.dla.utexas.edu/depts/drc/othersites.html. Here, you will find another large collection of useful links for writers, many of which are to OWLs. You also may wish to look at the helpful guides and links at *The Rhetoric Page at the South Dakota School of Mines and Technology*:
http://www.sdsmt.edu/www/rhetoric/rhetoric.html. You also can connect directly to the best-known OWL, at Purdue University.
You can find this resource at URL: http://www.english.purdue.edu.

If you are interested in learning more about the ornaments of the language and how to use them, the resources on Classical schemes and tropes at the Georgia Institute of Technology is a useful place to start. You can find this page, which is called *Rhetoric Resources at Tech*, at: http://www.gatech.edu/lcc/lcc1001/rhetoric.html.

Finally, you can find a large collection of useful links to all sorts of resources about the English language at Yahoo, the extensive web indexing service we mentioned earlier. You can see the valuable resources there by going to the URL:

http://www.yahoo.com/Social_Science/Linguistics_and_Human_Languages/L anguages/English.

A SUMMING UP

We think that our few suggestions, if taken together, especially, will enhance the clarity of your writing significantly. At the same time, we also think that you should make every effort to adhere, as strictly as possible, to the general conventions of "good" grammar, punctuation, syntax, diction, and usage. Many students have asked us why it is necessary to be so formal in writing, when ordinary conversational idiom serves just as well. The answer is, of course, the expectations of your readers. Reading itself is a formal act, and persons who read expect that someone who writes for them will present that writing in an expected, conventional form. Some readers, with some justice, regard a writer's failure to observe the standard conventions of written English as something of an affront to the reader. Why not, then, make every effort to put your reader in a receptive frame of mind, open enough, at least, to consider your writing and the ideas it contains?

Once the paper is complete, the are a number of actions that you can take to verify, for yourself, that your ideas are sound and that your writing is clear.

For example, you can put your paper aside for some period of time, perhaps as much as five days or a week, and then read it again with what some old-fashioned editors once called a "cold eye." You will almost certainly see some mechanical errors, some places which deserve less wordiness, and some infelicities of expression which you can correct with relative ease.

You may choose to read the whole text of your paper aloud, to yourself, or perhaps have a friend read it aloud to you. The sounds of your words, as they flow into your own ears, will reveal some of the same easily-correctable errors that the approach with a "cold eye" does.

Finally, one step that you can take to ensure that your prose does achieve the degree of clarity that is necessary to convey your ideas successfully is to have your paper read by a friend, roommate, or relative, who knows nothing about the subject at hand, and who will read your work only out of personal regard for the author—you. The one question you wish to pose to this friendly reader is whether or not the material in the paper is explained clearly and effectively. If that reader agrees that it is an effective exposition of your research, analysis, and conclusions, then you probably are on your way to a successful paper, and a high mark for it. If not, well, we hope there is still time for one more revision. Here are two final thoughts for this section which we think to be very important:

REMEMBER THE PRINCIPLE OF SELF-EDITING:

One of the most important fundamental skills that every good writer must have is the ability to edit a text before its first reader sees it. It is not enough to write an essay or paper and then turn it over to someone else for appraisal or critique. One method which works well for many students and professionals is to write a draft of the text and then put it away for two or three days. When that time has passed, the author returns to the text with a "cold eye." This detachment in time allows the writer to see more dispassionately the logical, grammatical, syntactical, and punctuational errors that she has written. For very important papers, often three or four such iterations are necessary before the text begins to assume its final appearance. When this is done with a good command of the rules of standard written English, the final paper often is quite good and requires no further emendation. We hope that you will try this technique with all the texts that you write.

CLARITY ABOVE ALL

Again and again, we say the most important criterion in judging any paper is clarity. The simple, logical, and coherent presentation of ideas and facts is the one characteristic that distinguishes good writing from bad. Since the most important task any reader has is to understand clearly exactly what you mean, it should be your principal task to work to make the reader's job as easy as possible. The reader already is committed to working hard to understand your ideas, so why burden her with the additional strain of laboring to discover what you mean by the language that you use. Plain English, well-organized and well-presented, is the strongest step you can take to winning the sympathy and understanding of your reader.

Annotating Your Own Text:
Footnotes, and How to Use Them

The purpose of this section is to acquaint you with the footnote as the most effective method for presenting all of the information that is necessary to make every manuscript lucid for every potential reader.[243] Remember that your paper is, or ought to be, an immediate personal communication from you to each of your readers. As we have said, when your writing is most effective, it is a clear, seamless expository essay, with no digressions to distract the attention of your reader from the essential points of your discourse. It does not matter, inherently, whether your work is a ten-page undergraduate term paper or a major exposition of a weighty topic in a monograph of six hundred pages or more, the principle remains the same. Because this is the case, all those complementary elements, the interruptions or parenthetical expressions of thought, should be removed from the main text and placed in some convenient location to which the reader can refer, if she wishes to do so; or ignored altogether, if the reader wishes only to come to a swift understanding of the author's main points. Only in this way can the seamless quality of the expression be preserved.

Footnotes are, in a sense, your footprints in the sands of research, analysis, and writing. They make it possible for each reader to follow your physical steps in research as well as the progress of your analysis. Each new element of complementary information, which you thought was necessary to your own understanding of your topic, can be found by the reader, as well.

Footnotes are meant to be ignored by the reader who has only a casual interest in the topic or a limited time for its consideration. That is precisely why they are indicated by small superscripted numbers in the text. They need not even break the flow of the eye across the page. Often, in former times, it was common for a serious reader to give a work a first perusal in which she ignored the footnotes altogether. Later, she would revisit the text for a second reading, with a full consideration of those notes she found to be

---

[243]For a full discussion of the range of scholarly documentation, with examples, see Francis A. Burkle-Young and Saundra Rose Maley, *The Art of the Footnote: the Intelligent Student's Guide to the Art and Science of Annotating Texts* (Lanham, Maryland: University Press of America, 1996).

useful for her own understanding. Of course, as you would, your-self, she was likely to do this only if she found the material valuable or exciting, or both. With this approach, the uninterrupted flow of the main text becomes a type of epitome or synopsis of the author's research and analysis and the footnotes complete the whole exposi-tion of the writer's work and thought. If the reader wishes to elaborate her understanding of the topic and the author's consid-eration of it, she has the footnotes at her disposal to ease her labors.

In a world of increasingly large volumes of information, no one reader, however well educated, can be expected to know the back-ground of any particular paper or essay; so that you may think that you have a scholarly need to elucidate every point you can in the text. At the same time, you have the obligation to present your writing in a readily-accessible way. It is the inherent conflict be-tween these desires that has led to the war between the writers for a select, informed audience, on the one hand, and those writers who claim that a work is successful only if every reader understands the material easily and fully, on the other. In this section, we show how these positions, which appear to conflict with one another, can be reconciled, so that you can be successful in documenting your work to the satisfaction of even your most meticulous reader, and every reader can extract all of the information she desires from your text.

Today, many writers omit those details of research and investiga-tion which allow a reader to retrace, with ease and exactitude, the precise steps that a writer has taken in her research, yet this is the fundamental purpose of scholarly notation.

We should say a word or two here about the materials of re-search and experiment which do not go in footnotes. You should place in an appendix, or appendices, an extensive table or a series of tables, transcripts of documents, secondary or tertiary texts which only are tangential to your thesis, and any other matter which will take more than a single-spaced page for its presentation or explanation.

We also need to indicate the place where you should place the sign for a footnote. The number, or symbol, for the note is inserted either immediately after the mark of punctuation which follows the word or phrase which you are noting—typically this is at the end of the sentence which contains the item to be noted—or immediately after the word or term which you wishe to note. The latter placement always is the case when you provide a definition for an unusual word or when you provide a translation of a word to or from a foreign language.

Footnotes, properly conceived and properly placed, provide the one means by which you can document thoroughly the methods and directions of your research, so that each reader can follow your work and thought precisely. In this way, footnotes serve as a guarantee of intellectual honesty; because they promote a spirit of openness and fairness in the scholarly community for the spread and consideration of research and ideas; and they provide a full and thorough documentation for later investigations, experiments, and study.

Please remember that footnotes actually are notes to the reader. They are your way of addressing your audience directly, quite like an actor who makes an aside in a play—a monologue, not a soliloquy. Footnotes include all of those sorts of asides and comments which would take place normally in a discursive conversation, but which generally should not appear in the main body of a formal essay. One surviving sign of the fact that the footnote really is a personal note to the reader is that bibliographical citations in notes are full sentences, and have a very different appearance from their form in bibliographies or lists of works cited. The bibliographical footnote has one period only, at the end of the "sentence" that is the complete citation.

Footnotes are not difficult to incorporate into your text, your wordprocessor has automated this task for you. Check your manual, or the online context-sensitive help files, for how to use this function.

We think that the best general observation about footnotes can be found in the great vademecum[244] of every graduate student in English literature, Richard D. Altick's *The Art of Literary*

---

[244] *Vademecum*, from the Latin *vade*, the singular imperative of *vadere* ("to go") and *me-cum* ("with me"). A manual of ready reference that is often carried about by the reader. For an elaboration of this definition together with illustrative quotations, see *The Oxford English Dictionary*, 2nd ed., 20 vols. (Oxford Clarendon Press, 1989), s. v. "vade-mecum."

Research.[245] Here is a portion of his discussion on the appropriate use of footnotes in a scholarly paper:

> Now a word about documentation. A superstition akin to the one about avoiding the first person singular holds that the scholarly quality of a paper is directly proportional to the number of footnotes, as if the heavy ballast at the bottom of each page insures against the balloon's soaring errantly into Cloud-Cuckoo-Land. No such thing. Footnotes, it is said, are for use, not ostentation.[246] They have two purposes. "Documentary" footnotes provide the reader with the sources of all the facts, as well as the opinions that are not original with the writer, so that if he is at all skeptical, he can check for himself. Moreover, they are an indispensable courtesy to later scholars who may wish to utilize some of the material and need clear directions as to where to find it. "Substantive" footnotes allow the writer a place to put incidental but relevant comment which would interrupt the flow of discourse in the text proper.

Finally, we need to add a small discussion of the use of footnotes in a paper that you may wish to submit for publication in a journal or magazine. No editor of any journal, no matter how narrow the topic or specialization of that publication, can be expected to know everything about the subject covered by the journal. Consequently, when an editor receives you article, she will make only a preliminary decision about whether or not your writing is suitable for publication. If she decides that it is, she then will send a copy of your article to a reader, or sometimes two readers, whose area of expertise is close to the subject of your paper. The fullest possible documentation and commentary in your notes will allow that reader to see, at once, just

---

[245]Richard D. Altick, *The Art of Literary Research*, rev. ed. (New York: W. W. Norton & Company, Inc., 1975) 219 and n. 20.

[246]*Cf.* the Roman emperor in Gibbon's *Decline and Fall of the Roman Empire* (Chapter 7): "Twenty-two acknowledged concubines, and a library of sixty-two thousand volumes, attested the variety of his inclinations; and from the productions which he left behind him, it appears that the former as well as the latter were designed for use rather than ostentation." [*Altick's note*]

what you have done, and what you have not done, in your work. In this way, the reader can make her recommendation to the editor quickly, because she can see the whole range of the sources you have consulted, the background you have brought to your writing, and the depth of your exploration in yuor research. With little or no documentation, she will need to take much more time to review your material—time which may not be available. If you have not taken your own time to open the whole path of your inquiries to an easy view, your efforts to publish may well come to nothing.

Of course, when your article is published, you may find that the editor, because of constraints of time and space, has stripped many of your original notes from the published version of your paper. This is quite common today. Usually, when an editor does this, a small note will appear at the end of the article which advises readers to write to you for a full bibliography, or, indeed, a copy of the original manuscript.

To see an example of this process, compare Johanna Cullen's original paper on the Mass of Bolsena, in Appendix B, with the published version.[247] If you do, you will see that only a few of Ms. Cullen's original notes have been retained in the published text. Nevertheless, had she not included all the documentation and commentary she did, it is unlikely that either the editor or the reader would have decided to publish her work, because the process of determining whether or not her paper had scholarly merit would have required too much time. Remember that, when you send a manuscript to a journal, you are competing for space in the publication with many others. The editor's job is to present the best material as quickly as possible and, generally, at the lowest cost. If you also remember the old adage that time is money, you can see readily that a full documentation and annotation, which demands the least effort and strain for checking sources and verifying background, helps you to success in your efforts to appear in print.

---

[247]Johanna C. Cullen, "The Miracle of Bolsena," *ASM News* 60:4 (April 1994): 187-191.

BIBLIOGRAPHICAL FOOTNOTES

Bibliographical notes include, of course, references to more than just secondary matter that has been printed in books. These notes are your opportunity to point your reader to articles in journals and newspapers, interviews, speeches, lectures, film, telephone conversations; letters, diaries, and manuscripts; sources in literature, including the Bible; and, increasingly, online data and information.

All of these citations must contain the complete col- lection of information which allows your reader to go directly to your source with the least trouble. Do not force your reader to guess at the full title of a work, or which edition you have used; do not force her to labor to determine the date of a radio or television interview, or which version of a film you have seen.

To reduce the possibility that your reader may become confused about the information you have included, all of your bibliographical citations should be uniform in the way you present them. This you can do by adhering strictly to one style of presentation, *i. e.* to the format shown in one particular style manual.

Use the style manual which is prescribed by your publisher, university, college, department, or professor. If no one prescribes or recommends a manual to you, then perhaps your best choice is the standard manual by Kate L. Turabian, *A Manual for Writers of Term Papers, Theses, and Dissertations.*[248] Portions of the current edition of *Turabian*, as the work generally is known, are based upon the fourteenth edition of an even more impressive and famous standard, *The Chicago Manual of Style*, published in 1993.[249] This edition is significant, because it offers, for the first time, the formats for citing various forms of information that are stored on electronic media.[250]

---

[248]Kate L. Turabian, *A Manual for Writers of Term Papers, Theses, and Dissertations*, 6th ed., revised by John Grossman and Alice Bennett (Chicago: The University of Chicago Press, 1996).

[249]*The Chicago Manual of Style*, 14th ed. (Chicago: The University of Chicago Press, 1993).

[250]Until a new edition of a major manual of style addresses the issue of citing information that is stored and retrieved electronically, the *de facto* standard is Xia Li and Nancy B. Crane, *Electronic Style: A Guide to Citing Electronic Information* (Westport, Connecticut: Meckler Publishing, 1993). Unfortunately, this volume chiefly is characterized by its slim contents and its high price.

Whatever manual you choose, or your instructor directs you to use, do adhere strictly to its requirements for all of your citations.

In general, the horizontal hierarchy of your biblio- graphical information should progress from the most significant elements to the least significant, in terms of your reader's physical search for the work you have cited. Thus, the author's name and the title of the work come first; followed by information on the edition, the editor, or the reviser, if any; then the publication information, which includes the place of publication, the publisher, and the date of publication. Last, you indicate the volume number, if appropriate, and the page number or numbers. These last elements are valuable only after your reader has secured the item to which you refer. The logic is precise. And, of course, a single bibliographic citation is a single, complete sentence. It opens with a capitalized word—generally the first name of the author—and closes with a period, just as every other complete sentence does. This form is quite different from the way in which you list works in a bibliography, or a list of works cited, at the end of your paper, thesis, or dissertation.

In preparing bibliographical citations, there are a number of conventional abbreviations which are used regularly. You should become familiar with them, and employ them properly. Take note that, in all those abbreviations which are derived from Latin or Italian, the plural form of the abbreviation doubles the primary letter used for it. Thus, *p* for *page* and *pp* for *pages*, *v* for *verse* and *vv* for *verses*, *MS* for *manuscript* and *MSS* for *manuscripts*.

BRIEF BIOGRAPHICAL NOTES

It is not at all uncommon, of course, when you write a paper about some well-known figure of the past to have many references to other persons of the time in your work. Sometimes, it almost seems as if your litany of names is like the cast of a long-forgotten play or an old dusty novel. If this is the impression your whole text leaves with your reader, you have deadened your writing so much that even the most interested reader will lay aside your work with a yawn. One notable scholar has likened the pleasure he derived from reading such papers to the pleasure he derived from reading the telephone book. You must avoid the phenomenon of "telephone-book writing" at all costs. One way to do this, and, at the same time, preserve your reader's interest in the secondary people in your paper, is to place brief biographies of them in footnotes, when you mention them for the first time. More than one student has become fascinated with a historical figure or enthralled by a time in the past, not by reading a text about a major figure but by reading a footnote about a fascinating minor personage.

This principle is equally true for papers that are not, in the slightest degree, historical in their subjects or outlooks. In a paper on the evolution of chemical or physical processes or discoveries, when you may mention the names of persons living and working in their fields today, it is helpful to provide your reader with a brief note on the person's background and accomplishments, as well as a mention of where the person is working today. This last particular element often is called an "affiliation note," because you mention the organization with which the subject of your note is affiliated.

So, briefly identify persons of importance in your narrative who might be unknown to your reader. Indicate the time they lived and something of their accomplishments to set them into your narrative, without detracting from the main line of your discourse. Sometimes, of course, there really is nothing to discover about the people you encounter in your research. No matter how hard you search, you cannot find any significant biographical details about them. Nevertheless, you should make some attempt to place them in the context of your writing. Perhaps the only material that you can find is from public or church records, or from a mention in someone else's letters or papers. Indeed, the latter case is quite often the way that these phantom persons of the past enter the writing of a modern student or scholar. If this is all that you have, by all means tell your reader that this is the case. If you can find more, perhaps in the same general source in which you found the person in the first place, then include that material to give some idea of flesh, blood, and time to the name you have just typed.

GEOGRAPHICAL IDENTIFICATION

The world is filled with hundreds of thousands of named locations—cities, towns, rivers, mountains, deserts, gardens, palaces, office buildings, and cemeteries, to mention only a few. Not even the best educated reader will be familiar with more than a small percentage of them.

You should add a note to describe and locate places that are strange or unfamiliar to your reader, so that she may follow your writing with a heightened understanding of the geography in which your text moves.

Of special importance are those cases where the names of towns, cities, and natural features have been changed, which obliges you to make your reader fully aware of these changes. If you do not take the time to identify the names of unfamiliar places for your reader, she simply will be looking at a list of words—devoid of a sense of place, color, time, and human association.

This type of footnote also is valuable for providing detailed descriptions of small geographical entities to help your reader to understand not only the size and placement of a site in relation to its surroundings but also something of its detailed appearance and use, past or present.

DESCRIPTIONS OF OBJECTS

Use a footnote to describe physically any object which your reader must be able to visualize. Even if you provide an illustration in the text or in an appendix, your reader may not really comprehend the size or scope of the object.[251] You may, for example, have an occasion to mention some device from the past and note its purpose, yet your reader may not be able to visualize with clarity the object you describe—not just the physical dimensions but also the placement of the object in its surroundings, especially with regard to its use. For example, almost everyone, at least in film, has seen hames.

---

[251]This is the principal reason that archeological photographs, and some others, as well, always have a scale or rule placed within the image itself. Earlier, photographers would place people in the photograph just for the purpose of showing a relative scale, as is the case with so many illustrative photographs of monuments in Egypt that were taken in the last century.

Yet how many people can be expected to know, with any real precision, what the device was or how it was used.[252] Likewise, you can use this kind of footnote to identify esoteric occupations and the devices or mechanisms associated with them.

The descriptive footnote can be concerned with function as well as form. Indeed, many readers may be able to visualize an object or mechanism without having a clear idea of how that entity functions. Yet, in a closely reasoned essay, you may need to ensure that your reader does understand the operative nature of something, before she can proceed to a consideration of its general effect.

EXPAND INFORMATION ON A SECONDARY TOPIC

Use a footnote to refer your reader to more detailed sources of information about an important, but secondary, topic in your essay, especially when that topic is not central to the main thesis of your paper but may be of considerable interest in its own right.

GLOSS UNUSUAL WORDS OR EXPRESSIONS

Use a footnote to define, and perhaps to illustrate with examples, words, phrases, or expressions with which you are quite certain that your reader is unfamiliar. This note is not just for jargon, but also for words that you use in unusual ways or terms which may be confusing to your reader, because they have several different, but quite close, meanings.

You must remember that the English language today has a vocabulary of nearly seven hundred thousand words. No reader, no matter how well-educated or informed, can know more than a fraction of the words that are available to you, the writer. Because this is true, any word that you expect to be beyond the knowledge

[252]The hame was the collar placed over the neck of a draught animal. Since daught animals often worked in teams, hames, in the form of a cojoined pair, also were common. The devices frequently were gilded or ornamented elaborately —often to a degree that they could be called works of art. Generally, hames were secured to the animal with leather straps, which were, in some cases, passed back through the upper part of the collar and backward to the driver's hands, thus forming reins. The American surname "Haymaker" derives not from someone who made hay but, rather, from the German word "hammacher," one who made hames.

of the generally well-informed reader deserves a footnote, to ensure that your reader grasps fully your intention in choosing the word.

You can use this type of footnote to comment on common words or expressions which you find particularly interesting, perhaps in a special context, and which you think your reader will, too. This type of note is quite separate from the notes that you use to gloss or translate words or expressions from foreign languages. These are discussed below.

Sometimes it is not a word but a term or expression, often from the past, that needs a gloss. In the biological sciences this is especially true, because the taxonomy of both living and extinct creatures has undergone several changes, and many elaborations, in this century. Your reader may not know that the particular name of an organism might have been changed several times, even in the past few decades, so that two or more references to the same creature, but under different names, need to be explained carefully in your notes. Much the same thing is true of the names of chemical compounds, mathematical expressions, and other scientific terminology. Only in this way can you maintain the continuity of your discussion without modifying the actually texts of the earlier sources that you quote or to which you refer.

DOCUMENT CONTRASTING VIEWS

The footnotes in which you point your reader to opinions other than your own, or those which are at odds with the prevailing or majority view of some person, event, or idea, are among the most important parts of any paper or book. This is the case because your reader is entitled to know the whole range of legitimate speculation which you have encountered in your own work.

Suppose that you consult twenty sources to gather together as many views as possible about a person or event or thing, for your own learning. Nineteen of those earlier scholars present a view with which you agree, and that is the view you adopt in your paper. Yet, the twentieth, who disagrees entirely with the others, also is a respected scholar with a substantial reputation in the field. Your reader must have the confidence in your work to know that you will not have omitted this twentieth view, even though it conflicts substantially with your own and the views of many others in the field. Of course, you need not search assiduously for comments and opinions by those who are on the "intellectual fringe," but you must not omit the opinions and conclusions of men and women who have reached them only after great study and analysis. You must remember, as you incorporate these notes into your text, that there was a time when Galileo's view of planetary motion was only the opinion of one scholar and was in conflict with the whole accepted view of the universe in his time. Had his ideas not been spread by others who read his work and quoted his views, his intellectual triumph might be lost today. Of course, eventually, the facts he unearthed would have come to light as a product of someone else's work; but there was not need for that, because his own accomplishments were the subject of many discussions in the schools and universities of Europe, in spite of ecclesiastical opposition. That they were discussed, and written about, so extensively is testimony to the willingness of scholars and students, both, to quote and cite opinions that are at variance, often very much at variance, with the accepted "facts" of any time. Much the same can be said about the work of Vesalius or Darwin or Goddard.

Centuries of scholarship rest on the free and open discussion of a wide-ranging collection of views and opinions on nearly every subject, and the reputation of most of the great men and women who have lived the "life of the mind" rests not only on their own discoveries—often quite startling, or even objectionable, to their contemporaries—but also to the vigor and honesty with which their work was discussed by others. The citation, and even extensive discussion, of contrasting views in footnotes is one of the principal ways in which each writer can preserve and protect the atmosphere of intellectual honesty.

We cannot let this opportunity go by without mentioning that works about difficult questions, be they political, philosophical, social, or scientific, which omit notes that discuss conflicting views, or even citations to works where such views can be found, are, in our opinion, intellectually suspect—as is so often the case with books and articles on modern political and social problems in America.

So, do use a footnote to mention, or even to discuss, views that are different from, or even conflict with, your own and those of other scholars whose views you have adopted. In this way, you preserve for your reader the opportunity to learn about varying opinions and intellectual debate, so that she can read further on the topic. This kind of note is perhaps the principal example of how footnotes work to preserve intellectual honesty.

Often, in this type of footnote, you will see the abbreviation *cf,* which means *confer,* the Latin equivalent of the English word *compare.* Much of the time, a reference that is introduced with this abbreviation merely points the reader to a text which confirms or elaborates the material that is being discussed. But it also does frequently point the reader to other material which presents a contrasting, or even contradictory, opinion or interpretation—which allows the reader to "compare" the two.

One use for this type of footnote that can be especially valuable is a discussion of some point of reasoning or explanation which is different from the one you have adopted in your paper, yet one which reaches the same conclusion—getting to the station by a different route. By offering your reader other rational pathways to the same conclusion, you enhance greatly the probability that your own reasoning will be understood. Indeed, however correct your principles of reasoning may be, the trail of your explanation may be as impenetrable to one reader as it is transparent and perfectly orderly to another. If you can show another method by which the same conclusion, or at least the same progress of reasoning, can be attained, your reader may well grasp the point you wish to make more readily, and will thank you for it heartily.

We must not fail to mention that one special variety of this type of note is used to correct the errors in published materials that you found in your own research—and you will find many of them, because all of us are fallible, even the most renowned scholars. You can use this footnote to document facts which have become garbled, such as discrepancies in dates of birth or death which appear in your sources. Sometimes, you will find errors of larger importance, such as the misattribution of a published work to the wrong author or errors in detailing the family background or ancestry of a person. Such mistakes, by the way, often are repeated, again and again, through a genealogy of errors. This happens when a writer misquotes or mis-notes factual matters from a primary source, and, later, other writers copy the original errors by relying on the scholarship of the first researcher, without checking the primary sources themselves. The effect of this shoddy method by later writers is to proliferate the error from one article or book to many articles and many books.

YOUR OWN ASIDES AND COMMENTARIES

The aside or commentary is the place where you can address your reader personally on some point which you would like to add, but which is really an addendum to the discussion or entirely divorced from it. With this kind of note, you can make direct, conversational connections to your reader without disrupting the flow of your essay.

In such a note, it is common to change the tone of the discourse, which can be an opportunity for the author to add whimsicality or amusement to material which might otherwise be dry. This type of note also allows you to add facts or commentary which you think the reader might like to know, just for the sake of intellectual curiosity.

While creating this note may be tricky, and can be overdone, it is, at its best, one that will bring a decided reaction from the reader, from a smile to an audible expression of discovery.

One of the great benefits of having the footnote available as a place to make an aside is that you can inject a note of humor into a discussion which may, by necessity, be somewhat dense or complex. Your direct speech to the reader may well be on a topic which is related only tangentially to the subject of your paper, but it can reinforce an important point which you wish your reader both to understand and to remember.

FOOTNOTE RELATIONSHIPS AND ASSOCIATIONS

You should use a footnote to identify and make clear the relationships between or among people, especially—but also between persons and things that are associated with them.

Footnotes which describe relationships offer your reader the chance to understand the material in your text more completely.

Of course, the types of relationships that you document in footnotes can be more than just those between or among people and the things associated with them. Scientific and mathematical relationships, too, can be the subjects of such notes. Because it is so important, in scientific and technical writing, to keep the central point of your discussion before your reader's eye, no extraneous material must be allowed to interrupt the flow of your text or to disturb the concentration of your reader. So, even the most important secondary materials must be relegated to a footnote. Often, great expositions of scientific principles are marred by an author's tendency to ramble from the subject at hand to lengthy explanations and proofs which are not germane directly to the topic. The great *Principia Mathematica* of Bertrand Russell and Alfred North Whitehead is a masterpiece of dense, but entirely appropriate, rational exposition.[253] As they move from one category of idea to another in their fulsome notation, they restrict all of their asides to small sentences or short paragraphs that are interspersed in the notation—forming a rather different kind of annotation than the one with which most readers are familiar. Nevertheless, Russell and Whitehead provided all subsequent writers in mathematics and the sciences with a lesson in precision and rational order which can be followed, with great profit, by any writer on these subjects.

TRANSLATIONS TO OR FROM ANOTHER LANGUAGE

We all know the adage that a translation can never fully approach the meaning or the intention of the original. Because that is true, your own translations may well miss a shade of meaning or an image which is perfectly clear in the original, but which is lost in the translation. And translations done by others, no matter how scholarly, are prone to the same errors as your own. How, then, are you going to be sure that your reader understands the material you have quoted with the same fullness as you do, yourself?

---

[253]Bertrand Russell and Alfred North Whitehead, *Principia Mathematica*, 3 vols. (Cambridge: Cambridge University Press, 1910-1913).

Since your reader may know the language from which you got the passage, she may well appreciate the opportunity to read it in its original form, so the best response is to provide her with the text in the original language—and in the script, character, or alphabet of that of language—in a footnote. With a modern wordprocessor, and easy access to so many fonts of so many languages, this is a simple task, although it does require care and meticulous attention to detail.

Perhaps you will prefer to insert the original text in your paper, for the sake of exactness and accuracy. Then what is to become of your reader's search for understanding, if she does not read the language of your passage? The answer, again, is a simple one. You must provide your reader, in such a case, with a translation of the text into the language in which you have written your paper, again, in a footnote.

In either case, a footnote of this type will serve to increase your reader's understanding of the material that you wish to use from a foreign language. Use footnotes to give either:

a. The original text of a passage you have translated in
the main body of your writing

OR

b. The translation of a passage that you have used in the main
body of your text.

This type of footnote is useful also as a place to put the definition of a word or phrase from a foreign language that you have used in your text in the sense or meaning that it has in that other language. How useful is it for your reader to surmise that YOU seem to know the meaning of the word *Weltanschauung*,[254] because you have used it in your writing, if she has no idea of the meaning of the word in German and no idea, therefore, of your reason for including it in your text.

---

[254] *View of the world* or *world view.*

CROSS-REFERENCES

One of the most useful kinds of footnotes is a cross-reference to another part of your own
paper, where your reader may find more detail about the subject under discussion than she will at the place where you insert the note. The purpose of this type of note, as with all footnotes, is to help your reader to understand your research, analysis, and writing with as little difficulty or inconvenience as possible. This note always should be used sparingly, but it may be necessary on those occasions when you return to a point of discussion at some distance from your original presentation of it, or when you wish to indicate to your reader that some element of your discourse, to which you now make a passing allusion, will be considered in greater detail later in your text. Certainly, you should not need such notes in a short paper of ten, or fifteen, or even twenty pages, but you may well need such notes in a longer presentation, especially one in which you elaborate several points that are closely interwoven with one another.

In these cross-references, there are a few conventional abbreviations which have long been standard and which you should use. More modern writers tend to use the English forms, "see above" and "see below"; while more traditional annotators will use *"vide supra"* and *"vide infra."* If you use the latter, italicize them. Whenever you use a cross-reference note, always be sure to indicate the page number of your own text where the other material can be found—"see above" or "see below" by themselves are not enough.

Because you do need to insert the page number in such notes, they will, of necessity, be the last notes that you will enter in your paper. You may choose to insert the numbers during your original typing, as reminders to fill in the full cross-reference later. Or, you may choose to simply go through the final draft of your paper and insert them just before you print your text. Most wordprocessors show the number of the page on the screen in the lower right corner of your display.

One easy method for constructing your cross-references is to go to the page, or pages, that have the main body of the discussion to which you want to *refer*. Note the number of the page, and then go to that place, or those places, in your text at which you wish to insert references to the main discussion and enter your cross-references. In this way, if you wish to make more than one reference to some part of your discussion, perhaps before the main element of the discourse, perhaps after it, you will place the same numbers in two or more cross-references without any possibility of confusion.

Remember to use cross-references sparingly. If your text is the straightforward, seamless expository writing it should be, you will need to use such a device only rarely, and only when the paper is a longer one with several paths of elaboration.

EXPRESS ACKNOWLEDGMENTS AND THANKS

A footnote is an ideal place to express your thanks to someone else who may have rescued you from an impasse in your research or who merely volunteered an interesting fact or opinion which you would otherwise have missed. At the same time as it gives you the chance to display courtesy, if offers your reader the name, and, often, the position of a person whom you have found to be well informed on the subject of your paper. As we already have discussed at length, in serious research, a student or scholar should speak with the recognized authorities on the subject of that research well before she believes her task is done—always call an expert.[255] By thanking the people with whom you speak, you also inform your reader of your attention to this technique of scholarship and you provide her with the name of someone she can talk to, if she wishes to learn even more about the state of scholarly work in a field today; or, perhaps, if she just wishes to explore the subject for the sake of curiosity. After all, most people, no matter how high

---

[255]A good exposition of this technique is in chapter eleven, "Talking to People," in Thomas Mann, *A Guide to Library Research Methods* (New York: Oxford University Press, 1987) 119-132. Most researchers have found that the problem with calling an expert is not getting the person to speak with you but, rather, getting them to stop talking about the subject which commands so much interest in their lives. In former times, of course, such inquiries were by letter, rather than telephone, and we suspect that, in the future, such inquiries, more and more, will be done through electronic mail.

their academic or professional position, are eager to speak with anyone who evinces a strong interest in their work.

Of course, the benefits that will accrue to you, if you sincerely acknowledge those who help you, may be incalculable. An old friend of the subject of your biographical paper, herself not a scholar, may be delighted to find her name in print in your writing. Such attention is not flattery, but merely the due of the person who helped you. And you may be rewarded later by further bits of knowledge or further access to unpublished papers and documents, or both.

This particular kind of note also represents the tradition of collegiality in academic and professional life. The freshman, as well as the full professor, by her research, enters into the community in which ideas and opinions are exchanged freely. By citing the sources of these facts and opinions, just as the writer does in the bibliographic citation, you acknowledge your debt to this longstanding openness. Of course, this tradition survives in many places outside of academia. In journalism, for example, when a source provides information, she often is mentioned by name in the ensuing article, sometimes with an apposite quotation. The candidness with which information is shared openly is, itself, one of the foundations upon which the whole work of the intellectual life rests. Your footnote, even if it is only one line, plays its part in maintaining this spirit.

Sometimes, in your research, you will discover an avenue to unpublished, and undocumented, sources that are central to your own work.[256] These new sources may, however, be entirely within the province and custody of an institution which is not one primarily devoted to scholarship and research, like a library or an archive, and, of course, they will not be in the hands of a private person whose aid you would otherwise solicit. In such cases, you must depend on the goodwill and assistance of the staff of the institution for any access you get, and any copying of material you may do. In such a case, it is almost mandatory to thank the people who made your research possible. While you may acknowledge the institution formally as well as the specific persons who helped you on your acknowledgments page, if you use one, you should recognize these

---

[256]When you recognize these sources for what they are, when others have overlooked them, you will have experienced the gift of serendipity.

persons again at the point in your narrative where you make use of the information that they supplied to you.

Now that you have come to the end of this section, we hope that you have a clear idea of what a good footnote is and how to create it. There is no a mystery about them, they are simply a narrative extension, in many forms and styles, of the pathways you took in doing your own research and analysis. By revealing completely the whole of your work, you, the author, contribute, directly and personally, to the expansion of knowledge. While we will never know "the whole truth," it is the case that, through these techniques and procedures, we can come just a little bit closer to a true understanding of each problem we, as humanity, tackle.

The most complete source of information about abbreviations and acronyms of all kinds, including the recognized forms for abbreviating the titles of scholarly journals, is the *Acronyms, Initialisms, & Abbreviations Dictionary* published by Gale Research in Detroint, Michigan.[257] It is an annual. See also Appendix D for the abbreviations that you will find most frequently in footnotes.

---

[257]*Acronyms, Initialisms, & Abbreviations Dictionary*, 20th ed. (Detroit, Michigan: Gale Research, Inc., 1995).

Assembling the Final Paper

Now you have typed the last word of your conclusion and you are ready to assemble the whole of your manuscript to submit to your professor. Here is a checklist which we hope will be helpful to you as you hasten to conclude the experience which, we also hope, will have revolutionized your understanding of research, writing, and freedom.

Review your whole text with the following principles in mind:

A. Evidence:

1. You have documented thoroughly **every assertion of fact** and **every opinion that is not your own** in a full and complete note, from which your reader can retrieve all of your sources straightforwardly and without doubt or confusion.

2. You have provided a note which explains and clarifies:

a. The identity and some detail about every person whom your reader is unlikely to know.

b. The location and some pertinent details about every place that is likely to be beyond your reader's knowledge.

c. A clear description and brief discussion of every object with which you think your reader is unfamiliar.

d. A brief discussion of each secondary topic which, if you had discussed it in the body of your paper, would have detracted from the flow of your essay.

e. A brief gloss which defines and illustrates every word or term which your reader probably does not know.

f. A full reference to, and brief discussion of, each contrasting view or opinion about a point in your paper.

g. A full and accurate translation of each quotation you have made in the body of your text from a foreign language or the full text in the original language of each passage you have quoted in translation in the body of your text.

h. Full cross references to different elements of the same topics or subtopics which you present in different parts of your text.

i. A full acknowledgement and expression of thanks to each person who helped you or guided you to information which you used in your text.

B. Analysis:

1. Thesis statement: You have made the subject of your paper clear, and your thesis statement tells your reader just what you are going to reveal and discuss.

2. Logic. You have reviewed your paper one last time to verify that **you have made no logical errors.** Remember, even one error in logic can weaken seriously a paper which would otherwise have great merit.

C. Writing:

1. Grammar: **Your paper is free from errors in formal grammar, syntax, and punctuation.** The diction conforms in every way to standard American usage. **Your presentation is clear,** moving smoothly and seamlessly from one part of your exposition to the next, without jumping suddenly from random point to random point.

2. Spelling: You not only have used the spelling checker in your wordprocessing program, but you have taken the time to proofread your paper carefully. You must remember that **your wordprocessor's spelling checker does not substitute for a proofreader,** because it will not flag misspelled words that are, in fact, other words—it will pass a "he" when you mean "she," and a "the" when you mean

"there." If you present a paper that is replete with misspelled words, your instructor will think, pardonably, that you have not taken enough time to warrant your instructor's time to consider your paper carefully.

D. Bibliography:

1. You have provided a citation in your bibliography for each work you discovered and consulted in the course of your research.

2. You have placed all examples of full, or extensive, documentation in appendices, together with illustrations, charts, graphs, and other supplementary materials.

E. Other back matter, including appendices and an index, if one is warranted.

A SAMPLE FORMATING FOR YOUR PAPER:

We recommend that you do not use a cover sheet, binder, or other embellishment of any kind for your paper. Your professor probably has many final papers to grade within a few days at the end of the semester,[258] and probably wishes to minimize the number of pages she has to handle. Consequently, extra bulk of any kind may detract from a speedy and favorable reading of your work.

You should use a one-inch margin for all four sides of your pages, which is the default setting for most wordprocessors.

It is standard academic practice to place, in a header, your name, the section number and time of your course, and your student identification number in the upper right-hand corner of each page.

---

[258]Many undergraduates never know that a standard practice in American colleges and universities is to require the instructor of each course to submit the final grades for the students in that course within forty-eight hours of the time that was set for the final examination in that course. Consequently, instructors in courses that require considerable writing by the students—including essay examinations as well as other written submissions, such as term papers and out-of-class themes—often are pressed to read many pages of new text at the end of each semester. With hundreds of pages to read, binders and extra sheets of paper that you incude for any purpose, just add to the necessary pile.

In a footer, in the lower right corner, number each page consecutively. Do not use running titles or any other material other than page numbers and personal identification in headers or footers.

Double-space all of your text, and use a 12-point type, which is the standard for wordprocessed manuscripts. Avoid sizes of type that are smaller, because they are too difficult to read, or larger, because they present an unprofessional appearance. Set your footnotes or endnotes in 10-point type, in the same font that you used for your text. Be sure to choose a font that is clear and whose letters are formed for ease of reading. See what fonts are available with your wordprocessor and, if you can, choose a standard book font with serifs, such as Caslon,[259] Baskerville, Century Schoolbook, or Garamond. If possible, try to avoid fonts which were designed for other purposes and then digitized for use with wordprocessors, such as `Courier and its various derivatives` which was created as a monospaced font for typewriters, and Times Roman, and its digital successors, like Times New Roman, which are based on a famous design by Stanley Morison for the London *Times* and seek to alleviate the strain of reading a large amount of text in the narrow vertical columns of a newspaper. Your paper is not a newspaper article. In any case, be consistent in your choice of fonts. Choose one that is easy to read and then use it for both your text and your footnotes. Do not mix fonts, because your paper is not supposed to be an object of typographical display, but rather one which is easy on your reader's eye.

At your instructor's wish, staple your paper together once in the upper left-hand corner, or use a paperclip in the upper left-hand corner to fasten the pages together. Make sure that your fastening is strong enough to withstand considerable shaking and other movement, since it will be carried, perhaps with many other papers, at least twice during the process of grading, and may be moved about on other occasions, as well.

---

[259]This book is set in Caslon type, a great font that was created by the greatest of eighteenth-century designers, William Caslon—aspects of whose life contain the material for several wonderful research papers.

Conclusion

Now that you have come to the end of your project, we hope that you have experienced the chief excitement of most educated women and men—the excitement of discovery and exploration. If you have chosen a narrowly-defined topic and have explored what there is to know about it with care, you can rest, for a moment, in the happy knowledge that you are the world's expert on that topic. And, if you have mastered the skills that were necessary to unearth all of the relevant materials about that topic, you have acquired a body of experience which you can, as we promised you at the beginning you would, be able to transfer to any inquiry you take up in the future. Freedom is a state of being, but reaching personal freedom requires the ability to discover—to find out, with real certainty, the nearest approach to the truth about any matter, past or present. The methods we have shown to you in this little book form only the foundation of the structure of skills you must have to pursue serious research, but, we believe, they form a strong foundation indeed. We hope that you will build upon them and advance to enjoy that self-confidence that every master of knowledge enjoys.

Although we know that you understand that the methods of research that we have described in this book will not make you a more intelligent person, they will, if you apply them meticulously and diligently, help you to become a better educated one. And your quality as an educated person, we assert, is not so much determined by what you know, as by your ability to find what you need to know, when you need to know it; and by your ability to bring rational means of consideration to the information that you find—no matter how unfamiliar a subject may be to you, at first. You must remember that you do not need to be an instant expert in a particular field in order to find relevant information on any subject, at any time. But you must know the various resources and retrieval systems, both digital and manual, that will enable you to discover whatever information you may need to begin your inquiry, and then to deepen it and carry it forward to a successful conclusion.

We already have recommended highly Thomas Mann's *A Guide to Library Research Methods*, and do so again. His book, in conjunction with our own, will help you to find your way through the first level of the maze of many resources that are available to you. Later, as you become more experienced, you will discover, on your own, still more resources to support your research—published and on-line guides to research in specific fields, printed bibliographies, on-line and CD-ROM databases, archival finding aids, and many more. As we have said earlier, we think that you should master completely the material in both of these relatively short books to understand and to use effectively the basic procedures and techniques for getting the most that you can from libraries, archives, laboratories, and online resources.

We have saved our expression of sympathy for you until these last pages. As students at the opening of a new millenium, you are plunged into the middle of the greatest revolution in the transmission and manipulation of information since the second half of the fifteenth century. Like all revolutions which are permanent, deep, and profound, it is one which had a sudden beginning but one which will take decades to complete. During this cycle of transformation, you, as users and synthesizers of information, must master both worlds—the older world of the published bibliography, the reference guide, and shelf-browsing; as well as the newer one of online searching, electronic retrieval, and database manipulation. Since so little of the revolution is complete,[260] you must have a mastery of the traditional methods of research that is at least as good as the standard that maintained itself during, shall we say, the period immediately after World War II. Without that mastery, you will not find vast quantities of germane information of great value which simply have not yet been engulfed in the revolution. At the same time, you also must master the new techniques of

---

[260]As we suggested earlier, by the close of 1996, we estimate that there were bibliographical references in some digital form to about forty percent of materials of some intellectual importance, and that only about two percent of such material actually was available online or in another digital form. Giving you an informed guess, at best, we will say that perhaps online bibliographic tools and databases will increase their coverage to about seventy-five percent of what is there to be found by 2010, of which perhaps fifteen percent actually will be available digitally.

online bibliographical searching and other elements of the digital age of information, or there will be yet other large portions of the information and data you will need which you will miss, because it was not enfolded into the older methods of storing information. Indeed, in absolute terms, the overlapping between the two systems is very small. Digital files are seldom retrospective before the date on which they were founded, or, if they are, the retrospective coverage extends backwards for only a few years. At the same time, traditional catalogues and other organized searching aids often have been abandoned hastily and permanently as librarians and bibliographers have embraced the new digital methods with enthusiasm.[261]

We see the bifurcation, and ensuing collapse, in serious research that is taking place around us, as two worlds of research find themselves unable to accommodate, or even talk to, one another. There is our senior colleague on the faculty, a woman of international fame as a scholar in her field with substantial discoveries to her credit, who cannot keep abreast of the work being done in her field by others around the world, because she cannot master the skills to find that information through online methods. Her horizon shrinks, while she still plans to go to London on her next sabbatical leave, in two years, to see materials which she could order digitally tomorrow, and have delivered to her in microform in four weeks. But there also is the young student—especially, in our experience, the entering graduate student—who thinks that everything she needs for her graduate work is available "somewhere on the computer." Never exposed before to sound methods of scholarship, as you have been with this book, she can find some information that is germane to her work but, when she loses the threads of her inquiries, and lost in the world of the library, she resorts to messages on newsgroups and listservers that elicit answers from

---

[261]For example, the Library of Congress itself ceased to maintain its main card catalogue on January 1, 1981. Frozen in time, now, it remains the single largest and most accurate repository of monographic cataloguing in the world in the period from 1898 to 1981. The accuracy of its filings is, in fact, many times greater than that of its digital successor. Fortunately, people who can get to the Library itself still can use the "old catalogue," which lies in heaps of open drawers in a bookstack that is just off the alcove bay of the Main Reading Room in the Thomas Jefferson, or Main, Building.

others as ignorant as she. For her, real inquiry and discovery is truncated, because, while she can and does find the "how" of many processes, scientific and historical, she cannot find the "why" of them—for the explanation of the causes lies in the scholarship of journals and books she does not know how to reach.[262]

Throughout this book, we have emphasized, again and again, how important it is for you to use, with sureness and confidence, the new computerized aids to scholarship and research. Their range is immense, their speed and general accuracy mindboggling. But the computer itself does not teach you anything, nor should it. The computer is, in one sense at least, like a piano. The instrument does not teach you music at all. With it, you can teach yourself first to recreate the music of others and, later — perhaps with additional study of harmony, counterpoint, and orchestration — you can use it as a device to create music of your own. But at no

---

[262]This truncation of inquiry, and its often unfortunate consequence, was revealed to us more fully not long ago, when we chanced upon one of our former students on the sidewalk. She told us that she had lost her scholarship in engineering for the following semester, because she had failed one of the required courses in the subject. When we pressed her for a further explanation, she told us that she had been assigned a project in which she was to take a group of data, which was given to her, and manipulate it with specific Lorentz transforms. She was then to explain not only **how** the transforms operated on that particular data to yield the results she achieved but also **why** they did what they did. The first part of the project went well, but, even with a considerable volume of modern writing on Lorentz transforms, she could not fathom precisely why the transforms operated on that particular group of data in the way that they did. She failed the project, which was forty percent of her grade for the course. When we suggested that she might have considered the origins of the transforms in the mind of Hendrik Antoon Lorentz as he pondered the apparent anomalies in the data from the Michelson-Morley experiments, done to verify empirically the speed of light, she responded that she did not know that Lorentz transforms ever had anything to do with the Michelson-Morley experiments—of which she did know. Later, she called one of us to tell us that she had tracked down the origins of the data she had been given and that it was, in fact, a suite from the second Michelson-Morley experiment. But she was, finally, able to discover this only in journal articles that were published earlier in this century and in the documentation of the experiments themselves. All of this could be traced only with published finding aids in libraries, and she had not paid enough attention in her class with us to realize that traditional methods of library research were her necessary recourse here—something her professor expected as a normal procedure. Her last words on the telephone were, "I should have come and asked you about it." But we teach English, not physics or mathematics.

time did it teach you, rather you used it to teach yourself what you wished to know about music. Similarly, the computer is a tool or device upon which you can "play," like an instrument, to find some information—and, more importantly, a great many other sources of information — which are good beginnings for serious research. It does no good to be able to say that you found two documents, and bibliographical records for eleven books and forty-one articles, on your topic, if you cannot first actually find those books and articles and then determine where the authors got the information they used to write them, and how appropriate that information was to the subject they wrote about. So, the computer, the software, and the databases do not teach you what you need to know, but you can use them to find the materials you need to teach yourself what you need to know.

Learning is a lifelong thing. That is easy to say, and should be understood, self-evidently, to be true. But how you determine what you will learn and how you apply that learning to your life and your work are much more difficult questions, for which you must find your own answers. In that quest, we wish you the joy of discovery, the comfort of understanding, and the strength to help others all the days of your life.

Epilogue: Considering Publication

Now that you have completed your term paper and submitted it for your professor's consideration and grade, you may wish to think about what more you can do with the great volume of research and writing that you have done. The most obvious, and appropriate, choice is to consider revising your text with a view to publishing it in an academic or general-interest journal.

After all, who knows what you do about your topic? Today, only you have experienced the discovery of the new things you have encountered. Others, almost certainly, will be interested in what you have unearthed, especially if you have used your discoveries to tell a well-written story. No one, in our view, put the value of publishing the consequences of every person's serious research better than Theodore Roosevelt:

> What counts in a man or in a nation is not what the man or the nation can do, but what he or it actually does. Scholarship that consists in mere learning, but finds no expression in production, may be of interest and value to the individual, just as ability to shoot well at clay pigeons may be of interest and value to him, but it ranks no higher unless it finds expression in achievement. From the standpoint of the nation, and from the broader standpoint of mankind, scholarship is of worth chiefly when it is productive, when the scholar not merely receives or acquires, but gives.[263]

We urge you to give thought to the idea of making your work available in wider circulation than merely yourself, your instructor, and, perhaps, your friends and family.

---

[263]Theodore Roosevelt, "Productive Scholarship," in *History as Literature, and Other Essays* (New York: Charles Scribner's Sons, 1913; reprinted, Port Washington, New York: Kennikat Press, Incorporated, 1967) 197.

WHERE YOU ARE TODAY

The constraints of time under which you had to do your research, analysis, and writing certainly limited your ability to do a thorough job. In our experience, at the end of a semester, most undergraduate students have completed between thirty and forty percent of all the work they must do in order to have a worthy and publishable contribution to knowledge on the topic upon which they wrote. Generally, it takes several dedicated weeks of effort to explore all of the sources that you had no time to consider while you were rushing to meet the schedule of the course; and to incorporate the additional material seamlessly into your present paper. For example, it took Johanna Cullen, whose paper, in its final form, we have included as Appendix B, between eight and ten weeks of nearly full-time effort beyond the end of the semester to complete a full scholarly exposition of her topic. In fact, she did almost all of this additional research and writing in the following summer, while maintaining a substantial schedule of summer employment. Needless to say, she had little time for recreation in that summer, but we think the consequences of her work, for herself and for her now-established scholarly reputation, were well worth the time and effort.

We have had considerable personal experience with undergraduates who have published revised forms of their term papers. It is possible!

WHO WILL PUBLISH YOUR WORK?

In the course of your research, you probably already have discovered the titles of several scholarly journals that publish articles in the field in which you did your research, just as Ms. Cullen discovered the *Journal of Bacteriology* while searching for material on *Serratia marcescens*. From among these journals, you should have little difficulty in selecting the first candidate to receive your manuscript. Perhaps you have been impressed with the quality of scholarship and writing in one of them more than in others. Perhaps you found another article or two on a very closely related topic, so that you have reason to think that the readers of a particular journal will be interested in what you have written. If you have written on a topic of local or regional interest, perhaps you know of newspapers or local magazines that are for well-informed lay readers that you think will have space for your writing. In any case, we think that you will have little difficulty in determining where you will send your final manuscript first.

THE NEXT STEP

You already have a body of persons who can guide you to the finer points of research that you must do in order to make certain that you have, in fact, covered all the locations and sources that you need to complete your work. Your instructor or professor may be willing to guide you further, by suggesting some additional enhancements to your manuscript, as well as suggesting places where you can get the information you need to accomplish those additions. And the experts with whom you spoke as you collected your original body of data and information also are potential guides towards publication—especially if you send a copy of your paper to each one with a cover letter in which you acknowledge the assistance they gave you in your work. Librarians at the places you did research, too, can be of great help in indicating additional sources on your topic that you may have missed in your first pass through your primary material.

ONCE YOUR REVISION IS DONE

When you have completed your second consideration of your topic, gathered all the additional materials you can, and incorporated your new and expanded analysis into your revised text, you should have several people, from friends and family to scholars and teachers, look at your manuscript with the most critical eye, since you are about to cast your ideas and your writing before a much wider public than was the case when you wrote up your work as a term paper. After you have then enfolded the critical comments you receive, and made one final revision, you are ready for that first exciting step, the trip to the post office to send your manuscript to the editor of the journal you have chosen. Remember to be sure of the name and academic rank and affiliation of the editor, and address your cover letter directly to her, rather than just to the "Editor." This use of a personal communication seldom misses the mark.

WHAT YOU CAN EXPECT NEXT

No editor in any field, no matter how well informed and well educated she may be about the subject that is covered by her journal, can be expected to know every aspect of research and scholarship in that field. Consequently, when she receives your manuscript, she will give it only a preliminary reading to determine whether or not it is, indeed, on a subject which she thinks will be of interest to the readers of her journal. If she decides that your manuscript is a candidate for publication, she will make blind copies[264] of your text and send them to at least one, and perhaps two, outside readers who are recognized scholars in the field.

From them, in a period of about six or eight weeks, she will receive a reader's report, which will contain a critical review of your text with, in some cases, suggestions for a further revision. In addition, the outside readers will make a specific recommendation on whether or not the journal should publish your article. You will receive a copy of these reports, in almost every case, regardless of whether or not that particular journal decides to publish your article. Often, these reports do contain valuable suggestions for further enhancements or revisions, so that, even if your text is rejected on your first try at publication, you may have more guidance for improving your text before you submit it to your second choice. Remember, if your manuscript is returned from the first place to which you send it, do not be discouraged. This is quite common, and has been experienced many times by every scholar in every field.

---

[264]These are copies of your manuscript from which your name and any other significant clues to your identity have been removed, to ensure the intellectual objectivity of the outside readers. In this way, every manuscript is anonymous, and can be judged solely on the basis of its merit as a contribution of knowledge in the field.

GETTING CLOSER TO PRINT

If the reader's reports suggest that you make final emendations and alterations to your text, but still recommend that the journal print your article, by all means hasten to make those changes, unless you think strongly that such changes will violate the integrity of your research or your writing. We believe that intellectual integrity and interior confidence in your own work is more important than having an article appear at a certain time in a certain journal. If you can accommodate the alterations that you are asked to make, by all means do them, however.

After you have done this final re-revision, which you should do as quickly as possible, return the final form of the manuscript to the editor, wait for a notice of acceptance, and then become more and more impatient and anxious as you await the appearance of your work in print. The final satisfaction is well worth the wait.

Once the editor has received your final manuscript, you may have to wait through several issues of the journal before you are published. If the journal is a quarterly—which is the most common cycle of issue for academic journals—you may expect to wait for as long as nine or twelve months before you hold the issue with your article in your hands. In the case of a monthly journal, of course your wait will be less, in most cases. For a submission to a newspaper, you may wait only a week or two.

You probably already know how important publications are to every professional in every field. In the case of undergraduates who do publish, doors to graduate and professional schools swing open a little faster and a little wider, when you can offer specific examples of your own scholarly endeavors. Your future professional standing will be enhanced, when later employers and professional organizations and societies see that you began work in serious scholarship while still an undergraduate. So, publishing your work goes beyond the achievement of personal satisfaction—it can have wide-ranging effects on your professional life and career.

Appendix A:

SOME SAMPLE SEARCHES OF IMPORTANT DATABASES

I. *WorldCat.*

For a topic on how William Morris came to create the great type-face called *Troy*, Beatrice began with several searches for preliminary information on *WorldCat*. Here is one set of her results. She signed-on to OCLC's *FirstSearch* service through the method her college uses, and she saw the first display:

```
* * * * * * * WELCOME TO FIRSTSEARCH ! * * * * * * * *
     Use The FirstSearch service to find books, articles,
theses, films, computer software, and other types of       mate-
rial on the subject you need.

The actions you can take are listed on each screen. Just type the
                ACTION name or first letter.


     OCLC MAKES NO EXPRESS WARRANTIES OR REPRESENTATIONS
     AND DISCLAIMS ALL IMPLIED WARRANTIES WITH RESPECT
     TO THE DATABASES VIA THE FIRSTSEARCH SERVICE,
     INCLUDING ABOUT ITS ACCURACY, MERCHANTABILITY OR
     FITNESS FOR A PARTICULAR PURPOSE.


*** Check out FirstSearch on the World Wide Web! Authorized users
   can go to 'http://www.ref.oclc.org:2000/'. Other users should
       check with your library for FirstSearch WWW access.

             PRESS ENTER TO CONTINUE
```

As she was instructed by the message, she pressed the
ENTER key, and received the next display:

```
* * * * * * * * * * * Topic Area Selection * * * * * * * * * * * * * *
___NO.__TOPIC AREA_____NO.__TOPIC AREA_____
|
|   1   Arts & Humanities         6   General & Reference
|   2   Business & Economics      7   Medicine & Health
|   3   Conferences & Proceedings 8   Public Affairs & Law
|   4   Consumer Affairs & People 9   All Databases
|   5   Engineering & Technology
|_____
HINTS:  Select a topic area . . . . . . . . . . type topic area number.
        Get help . . . . . . . . . . . . . . . . . . . . . . . type H.
        Get News . . . . . . . . . . . . . . . . . . . . type H NEWS.
        See hours of operation . . . . . . . . . . . . type H HOURS.
ACTIONS: Help  Database  BYE  Reset
TOPIC AREA NUMBER (or Action):
```

Now, she entered 9 to see the titles of all the databases that were
available to her, and she saw this display:

```
* * * * * * * * * * * Database Selection * * * * * * * * * * * * * *
TOPIC AREA:  All Databases
  __NO.__DATABASE_____DESCRIPTION_____
|
|   1   WorldCat         Books and other materials in libraries worldwide.
|   2   Article1st       Index of articles from nearly 12,500 journals.
|   3   Contents1st      Table of contents of nearly 12,500 journals.
|   4   FastDoc          Index of articles with text online or by email.
|   5   NetFirst         OCLC database of Internet resources.
|   6   GPO              U.S. government publications.
|   7   MEDLINE          Abstracted articles from medical journals.
|   8   MLA              Literature, languages, linguistics, folklore.
|   9   PapersFirst      An index of papers presented at conferences.
|  10   Pro CD Biz       Pro CD Biz telephone listings.
|_____
HINTS:  See more databases . . . . . . . . . . . . . type F or FORWARD.
        Select a database . . . . . . . . . type database number or name.
        Return to Topic Area screen . . . . . . . . . . just press Enter.
ACTIONS: Help  Forward  BYE  Reset
        DATABASE NUMBER (or Action):
```

Beatrice knew that she wanted to search in *WorldCat*, so she chose item number 1, and saw the following display:

```
* * * * * * * *          WORLDCAT          * * * * * * * * * *
     COVERAGE: Over 35 million records of any type of material cataloged
     by OCLC member libraries. Includes manuscripts written as early as
     the 11th century. Updated daily.
                    Copyright (c) 1996 OCLC.
                    PRESS ENTER TO CONTINUE
```

Again, she pressed the ENTER key and received the next display:

```
* * * * * * * * * * * * * * * Search * * * * * * * * * * * * * * * *
DATABASE: WorldCat
  _SEARCH_____DESCRIPTION_____EXAMPLES_____
 |
 | Subject    Type the label SU: and a word(s).    su:criticism
 |            (Subject headings and titles)         su:freedom of speech
 |
 | Author     Type the label AU: and the author    au:hemingway
 |            name or any part of the name.         au:saul bellow
 |
 | Title      Type the label TI: and the title     ti:estuary
 |            or any word(s) in the title.          ti:love in the asylum
 |_____
HINTS:   Other ways to search . . . . . . . type H <database name> LABELS.
         Include plural (s and es) or possessive . . type + at end of word.
         Return to Database Selection screen . . . . . . . just press Enter.
ACTIONS: Help  Limit  Database  Wordlist  BYE  Reset
SEARCH WORD(S) (or Action):
```

She decided to see if any materials were catalogued under the subject term "Kelmscott Press," since that was the publishing house Morris founded and where the Troy type was used. She entered the search term:

su:kelmscott press

From this one effort alone, she retrieved one hundred seventy-six records, although, as she quickly noticed, some were duplicates. She opened the log-to-file function of her communication software, or the same function on the library terminal she was using, we cannot remember which. She then scrolled through several screens, collecting the following information:

243

RESEARCH GUIDE FOR THE DIGITAL AGE

```
+ * * * * * * * * * * * * List of Records * * * * * * * * * * * * * * * * +
DATABASE: WorldCat                    LIMITED TO:
SEARCH: su:kelmscott press FOUND 176 Records
 _NO._TITLE_____AUTHOR_____YEAR
|
|   1 The Kelmscott Press : an exhibition held ... Carriera, Danie    1996
|   2 The liberty bell on the Kelmscott Goudy p... Lieberman, J. B    1996
|   3 Two proofs of illustrations for the Kelms... Burne-Jones, Ed    1896
|   4 The Kelmscott Press & its legacy : an exh... Bridwell Librar    1996
        . . . . . . . . . . . . . . . . . . . . . . . . .
|  44 The works of Geoffrey Chaucer /              Chaucer, Geoffr    1958
|  45 The Ideal book; four essays.                                   uuuu
|  46 First editions of esteemed American & Bri... Philip C. Dusch    1930
|  47 The Kelmscott Press : a history of Willia... Peterson, Willi    1991
|  48 William Morris exhibition : on the occasi... University of M    1990
        . . . . . . . . . . . . . . . . . . . . . . . . .
|  72 Kelmscott Press, Upper Mall, Hammersmith,... Kelmscott Press    1897
|  73 The Kelmscott Press : a history of Willia... Peterson, Willi    1991
|  74 William Morris and the art of printing.......Chandler, Nancy    1972
|  75 An introduction to the Kelmscott Press : ... Isherwood, Andr    1986
|  76 A note by William Morris on his aims in f... Morris, William    1960
        . . . . . . . . . . . . . . . . . . . . . . . . .
|  99 The typographical adventure of William Mo... William Morris    1958
| 100 Kelmscott revisited /                        Johnson, Ruth.     1966
| 101 A bibliography of the Kelmscott Press /      Peterson, Willi    1985
| 102 Printing specimens.                          Carr, Horace       1900
| 103 A bibliography of the Kelmscott Press /      Peterson, Willi    1984
| 104 Some thoughts on the ornamented mss. of t... Morris, William    1934
        . . . . . . . . . . . . . . . . . . . . . . . . .
| 118 William Morris, en biografi.                 Nordlunde, Carl    1944
| 119 Books printed by William Morris at the Ke... Newberry Librar    1927
| 120 A bibliography of the Kelmscott Press /      Peterson, Willi    1984
| 121 The Kelmscott Press and Japan : an illust... Sekigawa, Sakio    1982
        . . . . . . . . . . . . . . . . . . . . . . . . .
| 176 A bibliography of the works of William Mo... Scott, Temple,     1897
|_____HINTS:
More records . . . type B.    View a record . . type record number.
        Decrease number of records . . . type L (to limit) or A (to 'and').
        Do a new search . . . . . . . . . . . . . . . . type S or SEARCH.
ACTIONS: Help  Search  And  Limit  Print  Email  Database  Back  BYE
RECORD NUMBER (or Action):
```

As she scrolled through the displays, with the forward command
(f), she noticed two citations, numbers 47 and 73, to William S.
Peterson's prize-winning book on the Kelmscott Press, which she
already had found by searching the same subject term in her own
library, which turned out to have a copy. Now, however, she

244

noticed three other citations, numbers **101, 103,** and **120,** to a bibliography about the Kelmscott Press, also by William S. Peterson. This was quite a find, since published bibliographies were high on her list of valuable sources, and Beatrice already knew of one work by Peterson which is highly respected among scholars on the subject. She decided to examine all three entries to see what more she could discover about Peterson's bibliography.

First she chose number **101,** and found:

```
* * * * * * * * * * * * Full Record Display * * * * * * * * * * * * * * *
DATABASE: WorldCat                          LIMITED TO:
SEARCH: su:kelmscott press
 Record   101 of    176_____
 |
 |ACCESSION: 13651852
 |   AUTHOR: Peterson, William S.
 |    TITLE: A bibliography of the Kelmscott Press /
 |  EDITION: Reprinted with corrections.
 |    PLACE: Oxford [Oxfordshire] :
 |PUBLISHER: Clarendon Press,
 |     YEAR: 1985 1984
 | PUB TYPE: Book
 |   FORMAT: xliii, 220 p. : ill. ; 23 cm.
 |   SERIES: The Soho bibliographies ; 24
 |    NOTES: Includes indexes.
 |           "Addenda and errata (August 1985)"--p. [219]-220.
 |  SUBJECT: Morris, William, - 1834-1896 - Bibliography - Catalogs.
 |           Kelmscott Press - Bibliography - Catalogs.
 |           Bibliography - Fine editions - Catalogs.
 |           Privately printed books - Bibliography - Catalogs.
 |_____
 HINTS:   Another page . type F or B.   Another record . type record number.
          See which libraries may own this item . . . . . . . . .type LIB.
          Return to Record List . . . . . . . . . . . . .Just press Enter.
 ACTIONS: Help  Search  Print  Email  Order  LIBraries  Forward  Back
 RECORD NUMBER (or Action):
```

Beatrice then used the LIB command to see which libraries had copies of the book. Her search showed the following collections:

```
* * * * * * * * * * * Library Holdings Display * * * * * * * * * * * * *
_SYM___LIBRARY_____OCLC_ILL_SUPPLIER?_
CA
CLU    UNIV OF CALIFORNIA, LA                          Y
GA
EMU    EMORY UNIV                                      Y
MA
AUM    UNIV OF MASSACHUSETTS AT AMHERST                Y
ACTIONS: Help  Forward  Back
TYPE AN ACTION (or press Enter to return):
```

Still with her log function on, she looked at record **103**:

```
* * * * * * * * * * * * Full Record Display * * * * * * * * * * * * * *
DATABASE: WorldCat                    LIMITED TO:
SEARCH: su:kelmscott press
 Record   103 of   176_____
|
|ACCESSION: 13344105
|   AUTHOR: Peterson, William S.
|    TITLE: A bibliography of the Kelmscott Press /
|  EDITION: Repr. with corrections.
|    PLACE: Oxford [Oxfordshire] :
|PUBLISHER: Clarendon Press,
|     YEAR: 1985 1984
| PUB TYPE: Book
|   FORMAT: xliii, 217 p. : ill. ; 23 cm.
|   SERIES: The Soho bibliographies ; 24
|    NOTES: Includes indexes.
|     ISBN: 019818199X :
|  SUBJECT: Morris, William, — 1834-1896 — Bibliography — Catalogs.
|           Kelmscott Press — Bibliography — Catalogs.
|           Bibliography — Fine editions — Catalogs.
|           Privately printed books — Bibliography — Catalogs.
|_____
HINTS:   Another page . type F or B.   Another record . type record number.
         See which libraries may own this item . . . . . . . . .type LIB.
         Return to Record List . . . . . . . . . . . . just press Enter.
ACTIONS: Help  Search  Print  Email  Order  LIBraries  Forward  Back
RECORD NUMBER (or Action):
```

And, again, she looked for the holdings in other libraries with the LIB command:

```
* * * * * * * * * * * Library Holdings Display * * * * * * * * * * * * *
_SYM___LIBRARY_____OCLC_ILL_SUPPLIER?_
AL
AJB    JACKSONVILLE STATE UNIV                     Y
MA
MTH    MOUNT HOLYOKE COL                           Y
TFW    TUFTS UNIV                                  Y
MO
UMR    UNIV OF MISSOURI, ROLLA LIBR                Y
NY
BUF    SUNY AT BUFFALO                             Y
RRR    UNIV OF ROCHESTER                           Y
SYB    SYRACUSE UNIV                               Y
ZEM    HOBART & WILLIAM SMITH COL                  N
PA
LYU    LEHIGH UNIV                                 Y
SRU    UNIV OF SCRANTON                            Y
TX
TXX    SOUTHWESTERN UNIV                           N
EU
ESU    UNIV OF STRATHCLYDE                         N
ACTIONS: Help  Forward  Back
TYPE AN ACTION (or press Enter to return):
```

She continued onward to examine record 120:

```
* * * * * * * * * * * * Full Record Display * * * * * * * * * * * * * * *
DATABASE: WorldCat                    LIMITED TO:
SEARCH: su:kelmscott press
 Record   120 of  176_____
|ACCESSION: 10207666
|   AUTHOR: Peterson, William S.
|    TITLE: A bibliography of the Kelmscott Press /
|    PLACE: Oxford [Oxfordshire] :
|PUBLISHER: Clarendon Press,
|     YEAR: 1984
| PUB TYPE: Book
|   FORMAT: xliii, 217 p. : ill. ; 23 cm.
|   SERIES: The Soho bibliographies ; 24
|    NOTES: Includes indexes.
|     ISBN: 019818199X :
|  SUBJECT: Morris, William, - 1834-1896 - Bibliography - Catalogs.
|           Kelmscott Press - Bibliography - Catalogs.
|           Kelmscott Press - Catalogs
|           Private press books - Catalogs.
|           Privately printed books - Bibliography - Catalogs.
|           London - Hammersmith and Fulham (London Borough). - Private
|           presses: Kelmscott Press - Publications, to 1898 -
|           Bibliographies
|_____HINTS:
Another page . type F or B.      Another record . type record number.
         See which libraries may own this item . . . . . . . . .type LIB.
         Return to Record List . . . . . . . . . . . . . just press Enter.
ACTIONS: Help  Search  Print  Email  Order  LIBraries  Forward  Back
RECORD NUMBER (or Action):
```

and the holdings for it in other libraries:

```
* * * * * * * * * * Library Holdings Display * * * * * * * * * * * * *
_SYM__LIBRARY_____OCLC_ILL_SUPPLIER?_
DC
DGU    GEORGETOWN UNIV                              Y
DHU    HOWARD UNIV                                  Y
DLC    LIBRARY OF CONGRESS                          N
SMI    SMITHSONIAN INST                             Y
MD
JHE    JOHNS HOPKINS UNIV                           Y
UMC    UNIV OF MARYLAND                             N
VA
VA@    UNIV OF VIRGINIA                             Y
VEH    EMORY & HENRY COL                            Y
VHC    HOLLINS COL                                  Y
VHS    HAMPDEN-SYDNEY COL                           Y
VLW    WASHINGTON & LEE UNIV                        Y
VMW    MARY WASHINGTON COL                          Y
VNS    NORFOLK STATE COL                            Y
VRU    UNIV OF RICHMOND                             Y
VSB    SWEET BRIAR COL LIBR                         Y
VWM    COLLEGE OF WILLIAM & MARY                    Y

ACTIONS: Help  Forward  Back
TYPE AN ACTION (or press Enter to return):
```

OCLC found so many copies of the book in the libraries that participate in its system that *FirstSearch* limited the LIB display for record
103 only to libraries in the general area of Beatrice's college, which
is located near Washington, D. C.

She went back, briefly, to compare the information that she had
found in the three entries. She found, in the EDITION field of both
records **101** and **103** that these entries referred to a reprint of the
original volume with corrections—an important datum. Record
120, by contrast, was the original printing. Even though it could be
found in many more libraries, some of which were nearby, it clearly
was important to use the corrected edition. Since there were more
libraries listed in record **103** than in record **101**, she return to record **103** to place her interlibrary loan order. She used the ORDER
command (O), and she received the display:

```
* * * * * * * * * * * * Text Delivery * * * * * * * * * * * * * * * *
DOCUMENT: A bibliography of the Kelmscott Press
   _NO._METHOD_____DESCRIPTION_____PRICE_RANGE_____
|  1   Interlibrary Loan   Borrow from another library. See library's policy
|_____
HINTS:   To make a selection . . . type the number of a method or supplier.
         To cancel and return to the record display . . . type C or CANCEL.
         For details on text delivery . . . . . . . type H TEXT DELIVERY.
ACTIONS: Help  Cancel  BYE  Reset
METHOD NUMBER (or Action):
```

Beatrice then chose **1**, to enter in the information that was necessary for her to receive the item. She pressed the ENTER key when she had completed typing the requisite information on each line:

```
YOUR NAME (or Cancel): Beatrice Benedick
Business name or street where the item is to be sent.
STREET ADDRESS 1 (or Cancel): Hatshepsut Hall, Campus
Address and street continued. Press Enter to skip to CITY.
STREET ADDRESS 2 (or Cancel): Room 605
CITY (or Cancel): Silver Spring
State or province, such as OH for Ohio (enter 'XX' if not applicable).
STATE/PROVINCE ABBREVIATION (or Cancel): MD
Zip Code or Postal Code (Ex: 76060; 32215-1314; LS23 7BQ).
ZIP OR POSTAL CODE (or Cancel): 20900
Phone Number (Ex: 213-555-1234). Used if questions about loan.
TELEPHONE NUMBER (or Cancel): 807-555-1212
Library card number or number used to check out books.
ID NUMBER (or Cancel): 173-18-9300
Status (Ex: Faculty, Grad, Undergrad, Other).
STATUS (or Cancel): Undergraduate
Department (EX: English, Chemistry, Other).
DEPARTMENT (or Cancel): English
The most you are willing to pay for this loan ($DD.CC).
MAXIMUM COST (or Cancel): $00.00
Latest date you can use this item (Format: MM/DD/YY).
DATE NEEDED (or Cancel): 12/31/99
Brief comments relevant to this Request up to 88 characters.
COMMENTS (or Cancel):
```

On pressing the ENTER key at the end of the last question, she saw the following display:

```
* * * * * * * * Borrow Document: Final Verification * * * * * * * * * *
DOCUMENT: A bibliography of the Kelmscott Press /
InterLibrary Loan
__NO._____IS THIS PAGE OF YOUR ORDER CORRECT?_____
|  1  Patron Name:          Beatrice
|  2  Street Address 1:     Hatshepsut Hall, Campus
|  3  Street Address 2:     Room 605
|  4  City:                 Silver Spring
|  5  State/Province:       MD
|  6  ZIP/Postal Code:      20902
|  7  Phone Number:         807-555-1212
|  8  ID Number:            173-18-9300
|  9  Status:               Undergraduate
| 10  Department:           English
| 11  Maximum Cost:         $00.00
| 12  Date Needed:          12/31/99
| 13  Comments:
| NOTE: If delivery questions, contact your ILL department
|_____
HINTS:    To cancel . . . . type CANCEL. For help . . type H TEXT DELIVERY.
ACTIONS: Help  Cancel  BYE  Reset
TYPE 'Y' IF ORDER IS CORRECT or NUMBER OF LINE TO CHANGE (or Action):
```

She entered "Y" and, after a notice of potential restrictions because of copyright, she received the display:

```
        Processing order. Please wait
```

and then:

```
        Your order has been sent.
```

She then returned to her original index display of 176 items to continue her search.

II. Library of Congress Databases, including the book catalogues [SCORPIO] and the Cross Reference File, LCXR, with a Follow-up to *WorldCat*.

Here is a brief example of how Valeria used the online version of the *Library of Congress Subject Headings*, LCXR — Librray of Congress Cross References, to help her to locate the correct searching term.

Valeria's detailed scholarly report for a class in mathematics was supposed to cover the development one major new analytical function in the past half century. In one article, she came upon a brief mention of "quasientire functions in the sense of Bernstein," a term she had never seen before.

She used *telnet* to **locis.loc.gov**, chose the first item from the menu, LIBRARY OF CONGRESS CATALOGS, and browsed (b or **brws**) the term "quasientire." As you see from the display, below, there is not a title and no subject heading which begins with this word.

CROSSFILE: You browsed: QUASIENTIRE
B01 Quasidifferential calculus//(LOC3=2)
B02 Quasielastic light scattering—//(LOC3=1)
B03 Quasielastic neutron scattering//(LOC3=2)
B04 Quasielastic neutron scattering for the investigat//(LOC2=1)
B05 Quasielastic Neutron Scattering Workshop//(LOC3=1)
B06+Quasigroupes//(PREM=1)
B07 Quasigroups—//(PREM=6; LOC3=18)
B08 Quasigroups and loops//(LOC3=2)
B09 Quasihomogeneous distributions//(LOC3=1)
B10 Quasikonforme Abbildungen//(PREM=1; LOC2=2; LOC3=1)
B11 Quasikonforme Abbildungen und elliptische Systeme//(LOC3=2)
B12 Quasilinear degenerate and nonuniformly elliptic a//(LOC3=1)
B13 Quasilinear elliptic systems//(LOC3=1)
B14 Quasilinear hyperbolic systems and waves//(LOC3=1)
B15 Quasilineare elliptische Gleichungen hoherer Ordn//(LOC3=1)
B16 Quasilinearization//(LOC2=3; LOC3=8)
B17 Quasilinearization and invariant imbedding//(LOC2=1)
B18 Quasilinearization and nonlinear boundary-value pr//(PREM=2; LOC2=1)
B19 Quasilinearization and nonlinear problems in fluid//(LOC2=1)
B20 Quasilinearization and the identification problem//(LOC3=1)

As she looked at this result of her search, she remembered that the *Library of Congress Subject Headings* might help her to solve this problem. While still connected to **locis.loc.gov**, she signed off the catalogue, reëntered it, and chose item seven, LCXR — LIBRARY OF CONGRESS CROSS REFERENCES. Her first screen showed her the following display:

> ***LCXR- THE LIBRARY OF CONGRESS CROSS REFERENCES,
> which was updated on 12/14/96 and contains 438,814 records,
> is now available for your search.
>
> CONTENTS: The LCXR file contains records for terms authorized for
> use as Library of Congress subject headings, as well as
> references to authorized terms from non-authorized forms.
> Records for authorized terms usually include information
> on their use as well as lists of broader, narrower, and
> related terms. This file does not include records for
> actual items in the collections of the Library.
>
> TO START   BROWSE the first words of your subject.
>   EXAMPLES:
> SEARCH: browse cats
>   browse united states. congress—caucuses
>   RETRIEVE key words from a subject heading.
>   EXAMPLE:
>   retrieve shakespeare biography
>
> UPDATE: Index terms are added and updated biweekly.
> HELP: Enter HELP for LCXR info, or HELP COMMANDS for command list.

Once again, Valeria browsed the term "quasientire." The following result appeared:

```
To choose from list, see examples at bottom.          FILE: LCXR
Terms alphabetically close to:QUASIENTIRE
B01 Quasi-uniform spaces//(SUBJ=1)
B02 Quasianalytic functions//(SUBJ=1)
B03 Quasiconformal mappings//(SUBJ=1)
B04 Quasicrystals//(SUBJ=1)
B05 Quasielastic light scattering//(SUBJ=1)
B06+Quasientire functions in the sense of Bernstein//(XREF=1)
B07 Quasigroups//(SUBJ=1)
B08 Quasilinearization//(SUBJ=1)
B09 Quasimodo family//(SUBJ=1)
B10 Quasimolecules//(SUBJ=1)
B11 Quasiparticles (Physics)//(SUBJ=1)
B12 Quasisymmetric groups//(SUBJ=1)
```

She was slightly surprised to see the exact term for which she was searching. She immediately SELECTED (s or slct) the cross-referenced term:

```
SET 1        1: SLCT XREF/Quasientire functions in the sense of Bernstein
```

And then displayed (d) that item:

```
ITEM 1 OF 1             SET 1: BRIEF DISPLAY          FILE: LCXR
                        (ASCENDING ORDER)
   1.  Quasientire functions in the sense of Bernstein          XR00-153395
         USE:  Quasianalytic functions
```

From this she learned that the term "quasianalytic functions" is used for the expression "quasientire functions in the sense of Bernstein." She returned to the catalogue, and browsed the term "quasianalytic functions." Her result was:

CROSSFILE: You browsed: QUASIANALYTIC FUNCTIONS
B01 Quasi-uniform topological spaces//(LOC2=1)
B02 Quasi-war//(LOC2=1)
B03 Quasi-war with France//(PREM=1)
B04 Quasi, fancies for the little ones//(PREM=1)
B05 Quasiaffinitat; rechtshistorische untersuchungen//(PREM=1)
B06+Quasianalytic functions//(LOC3=2)
B07 Quasianalytic functions in the sense of Bernstein//(LOC3=1)
B08 Quasiconformal mappings—//(PREM=4; LOC2=9; LOC3=27)
B09 Quasiconformal mappings and Riemann surfaces//(LOC3=1)
B10 Quasiconformal mappings and Sobolev spaces//(LOC3=1)
B11 Quasiconformal mappings in the plane//(LOC2=1; LOC3=1)
B12 Quasiconformal maps extremal for their boundary va//(LOC3=1)
B13 Quasiconformal space mappings//(LOC3=1)
B14 Quasicristaux—//(LOC3=1)
B15 Quasicrystals—//(LOC3=25)
B16 Quasicrystals and geometry//(LOC3=1)
B17 Quasicrystals and incommensurate structures in con//(LOC3=1)
B18 Quasicrystals, networks, and molecules of fivefold//(LOC3=1)
B19 Quasidifferentiability and nonsmooth modelling in//(LOC3=1)
B20 Quasidifferentiable equations//(LOC3=1)

She again used the SELECT command (s or slct) to choose line B06:

SET 1   2: SLCT LOC3/SUBJ/Quasianalytic functions

Then she used the DISPLAY command (d) to display
SET 1:

FILE:LOC3; TITLE/LINE—SET 1
1. 91-227607: Badalian, G. V. (Gaik Vagarshakovich) Kvazistepennoi riad
   i kvazianaliticheskie klassy funktsii / Moskva : "Nauka," Glav. red.
   fiziko-matematicheskoi lit-ry, 1990. 207 p. ; 20 cm.
   LC CALL NUMBER: QA295 .B24 1990
2. 85-169922: Plesniak, W. Quasianalytic functions in the sense of Bernstein
   / Warszawa : Panstwowe Wydawn. Nauk., 1977. 70 p. ; 24 cm.
   LC CALL NUMBER: QA1 .D54 no. 147

She saw, at once, a title which she thought was exactly the one
which would give her the information she needed. She used the
DISPLAY command to show the second item in a full bibliographic
display (d 1/item 2) and she found:

Plesniak, W.
  Quasianalytic functions in the sense of Bernstein / W. Plesniak. Warszawa :
Panstwowe Wydawn. Nauk., 1977. 70 p. ; 24 cm.

LC CALL NUMBER: QA1 .D54 no. 147 (ALTERNATE CLASS QA331)
SUBJECTS:
  Quasianalytic functions.
SERIES TITLES (Indexed under SERI option):
  Dissertationes mathematicae = Rozprawy matematyczne ; 147
  Rozprawy matematyczne ; 147.
NOTES:
  Bibliography: p. (64)-65.
LCCN: 85-169922 r91

Now, she returned to *WorldCat* to find libraries from which she could either borrow the book, if a collection that had it was near to her, or from which she could order the book through interlibrary loan. She did a combination author (**au:**) and title (**ti:**) search and found two identical records:

```
* * * * * * * * * * * * Full Record Display * * * * * * * * * * * * * * *
DATABASE: WorldCat                          LIMITED TO:
SEARCH: au:plesniak and ti:quasianalytic
 Record  1 of   2_____
|ACCESSION: 14017548
|   AUTHOR: Plesniak, W.
|    TITLE: Quasianalytic functions in the sense of Bernstein /
|    PLACE: Warszawa :
|PUBLISHER: Panstwowe Wydawn. Nauk.,
|     YEAR: 1977
| PUB TYPE: Book
|   FORMAT: 70 p. ; 24 cm.
|   SERIES: Dissertationes mathematicae = Rozprawy matematyczne ; 147
|           Rozprawy matematyczne ; 147.
|    NOTES: Bibliography: p. [64]-65.
|  SUBJECT: Quasianalytic functions.
|_____
HINTS:   Another page . type F or B.    Another record . type record number.
         See which libraries may own this item . . . . . . . . .type LIB.
         Return to Record List . . . . . . . . . . . . . just press Enter.
ACTIONS: Help  Search  Print  Email  Order  LIBraries  Forward  Back
RECORD NUMBER (or Action):
```

Using the LIB command, for the first of the two entries, she found:

```
* * * * * * * * * * * * Library Holdings Display * * * * * * * * * * * * * *
_SYM___LIBRARY_____OCLC_ILL_SUPPLIER?_
DC
DLC    LIBRARY OF CONGRESS                              N
AL
AAA    AUBURN UNIV                                      Y
CA
STF    STANFORD UNIV LIBR                               N
HI
HUH    UNIV OF HAWAII, HAMILTON LIBR                    Y
IL
CRL    CENTER FOR RES LIBR                              Y
ND
NWQ    NORTH DAKOTA STATE UNIV LIBR                     Y
UT
UBY    BRIGHAM YOUNG UNIV LIBR                          Y
ON
CAI    CISTI (CANADA INST SCI TECH INFO)                Y
AS
KJO    JOSAI UNIV LIBR                                  N
ACTIONS: Help  Forward  Back
TYPE AN ACTION (or press Enter to return):
```

For the second record, she found:

```
* * * * * * * * * * * Library Holdings Display * * * * * * * * * * * * *
_SYM___LIBRARY_____OCLC_ILL_SUPPLIER?_
AL
ABC    UNIV OF ALABAMA, BIRMINGHAM                      Y
AZ
AZS    ARIZONA STATE UNIV                               Y
CA
CRU    UNIV OF CALIFORNIA, RIVERSIDE                    Y
FL
FHM    UNIV OF S FLORIDA                                Y
FUG    UNIV OF FLORIDA                                  Y
IL
UIU    UNIV OF ILLINOIS                                 Y
MA
CLS    HARVARD UNIV, CABOT SCI LIBR                     Y
NY
BUF    SUNY AT BUFFALO                                  Y
COO    CORNELL UNIV                                     N
VYF    FORDHAM UNIV                                     Y
TN
TJC    VANDERBILT UNIV LIBR                             Y
WA
WAU    UNIV OF WASHINGTON                               Y

ACTIONS: Help  Forward  Back
TYPE AN ACTION (or press Enter to return):
```

Since no library was close enough for her to travel quickly to retrieve the book, she placed an interlibrary loan order from the second record, because there were more lenders under the interlibrary loan program in that record and because the University of Illinois was the nearest university to her geographically.

She received the book within ten days. She was delighted to find that most of the text was in English, even though it was a doctoral dissertation in mathematics that the author had submitted to a Polish university. She photocopied the whole text for less than four dollars, by copying two pages of text on each photocopy. With a text in hand that she could mark up as she wished, she found a graduate student in the Department of Mathematics to help her with some elements of the notation which were unfamiliar to her and she found a young Polish man, whom she had met while taking a course in economics in the prior semester, to help her with the sense of some of the passages in Polish.[265]

She then used the two-page bibliography in the book to locate four other articles that helped her to understand the material better. She also used the bibliographical citations in two of those articles to find the original published material on these functions, which she examined and cited in her report.

Her professor was surprised by the depth and thoroughness of her report, which was completed in five weeks, since she was a second-semester freshman. The professor also confessed to Valeria that, in fact, she had never heard of quasianalytic functions in the sense of Bernstein before her research. It will not surprise you that Valeria, who is not a native English-speaker, received an A+.

---

[265]We do not have the time here to discuss the further evolution of their relationship, but we will say that their daughter is truly charming.

III. Using the Library of Congress's Databases to Establish Subject Headings, and Getting more References from them.

For a topic on the literary use of the cockney dialect in English poetry up to the Elizabethan period, Regan found a reference to Peter Wright's monograph on *Cockney Dialect & Slang*. She located it without difficulty in the online catalogue of the Library of Congress:

```
CROSSFILE: You browsed: COCKNEY DIALECT
B01 Cockney camera//(LOC3=1)
B02 Cockney campaign//(PREM=1)
B03 Cockney cats//(PREM=1)
B04 Cockney Columbus//(PREM=1)
B05 Cockney Communist//(PREM=1)
B06+Cockney dialect & slang//(LOC3=1)   <<===========
                    Original search term appears on line 6
B07 Cockney dialect and slang//(LOC3=1)
B08 Cockney in Arcadia//(LOC2=1)
B09 Cockney in kilts//(PREM=1)
B10 Cockney in Moscow//(PREM=1)
B11 Cockney on Main street//(PREM=1)
B12 Cockney past and present//(LOC2=1)
B13 Cockney phonology//(PREM=1)
B14 Cockney, past and present//(PREM=1; LOC2=1)
B15 Cockney's farming experiences//(LOC2=1)
B16 Cockneys in California//(PREM=2)
READY FOR NEW COMMAND (FOR NEXT PAGE, XMIT ONLY):
```

She SELECTED **B06** and displayed the resulting set with the command **d 1/item**:

```
81-165873                          ITEM 1 OF 1 IN SET 1
Wright, Peter, 1923-
   Cockney dialect and slang / Peter Wright. London: Batsford,
1981.
   184 p.: ill. ; 23 cm.
LC CALL NUMBER: PE1961 .W7
SUBJECTS:
   English language—Dialects—England—London. <<========
                               Principal Subject Heading
   English language—Slang.
   London (England)—Social life and customs.
OTHER TITLES:
   Cockney dialect & slang.
NOTES:
   Spine title: Cockney dialect & slang.
   Includes index.
   Bibliography: p. 174-175.
GEOG. AREA CODE:  e-uk-en
ISBN:  0713422424 : L8.95
DEWEY DEC.:  427/.1 19
NATL. BIB. NO.:  GB81-15959
LCCN:  81-165873
```

Instead of ending her search with this item, however, she took
note of the first of the listed subject headings, in the hope that this
would guide her to more sources. She then browsed the heading:
English language—Dialects—England—London,
and received the following display:

```
CROSSFILE: You browsed: ENGLISH LANGUAGE-DIALECTS-ENGLAND-LONDON-
B01 English language-Dialects-England-Lancashire//(LOC2=2; LOC3=3)
B02 English language-Dialects-England-Lancashire-G//(LOC2=1)
B03 English language-Dialects-England-Lancashire-T//(LOC3=1)
B04 English language-Dialects-England-Lincolnshire//(LOC2=2; LOC3=1)
B05 English language-Dialects-England-Lindsey//(LOC3=1)
B06+English language-Dialects-England-London//(LOC1=1; LOC2=12; LOC3=10)
B07 English language-Dialects-England-London-Histo//(LOC2=1)
B08 English language-Dialects-England-London-Texts//(LOC1=1; LOC3=1)
B09 English language-Dialects-England-Maps//(LOC2=1; LOC3=6)
B10 English language-Dialects-England-Midlands//(LOC3=2)
B11 English language-Dialects-England-Newcastle upo//(LOC3=1)
B12 English language-Dialects-England-Norfolk//(LOC3=1)
B13 English language-Dialects-England-Northamptonsh//(LOC2=1)
B14 English language-Dialects-England-Northumberlan//(LOC2=2; LOC3=3)
B15 English language-Dialects-England-Northumbria (//(LOC2=1)
B16 English language-Dialects-England-Norwich (Norf//(LOC3=1)
B17 English language-Dialects-England-Nottinghamshi//(LOC3=1)
B18 English language-Dialects-England-Reading//(LOC3=1)
B19 English language-Dialects-England-Rutland//(LOC3=1)
READY FOR NEW COMMAND (FOR NEXT PAGE, XMIT ONLY):
```

Again, she SELECTED **B06**, and then combined (c or **comb**) into one set all of the citations from the subsets of the catalogue, LOC1, LOC2, and LOC3. This operation gave her the following result:

```
SET  8        23: COMB 2R.R7
READY FOR NEW COMMAND:
```

She displayed that set in the short bibliographic form and had twenty-two more monographic titles to add to her preliminary bibliography. A further display of these items in the longer form did reveal three of them to be of potential value to her topic.

FILE:LOC3; TITLE/LINE—SET 8   ITEMS 1-23 OF 23
1. 94-2684: Wright, Laura. Sources of London English :
medieval Thames vocabulary / Oxford : Clarendon
Press ; New York : Oxford University Press, 1996. x, 245 p.;
24 cm.
    LC CALL NUMBER: PE1961 .W69 1996
2. 92-42560: Sebba, Mark. London Jamaican : a case
study in language contact / London ; New York :
Longman, 1993. p. cm.
    CIP - NOT YET IN LC
    . . . .
7. 77-11190: Mackenzie, Barbara Alida. The early London
dialect: contributions to the history of the dialect   of London during the Middle English period / Philadelphia : R. West,
1977. 151 p.; 23 cm.
    NOT IN LC COLLECTION
8. 76-20751: Mackenzie, Barbara Alida. The early London
dialect: contributions to the history of the dialect   of London during the Middle English period/ Norwood, Pa.: Norwood
Editions, 1976. 151 p.;   23 cm.
    LC CALL NUMBER: PE1961 .M23 1976
    . . . .
17. 73-150565: Jones, Jack. Rhyming Cockney slang;
Bristol, Abson Books, 1971. 35 p. illus. 10x16 cm.
    LC CALL NUMBER: PE3724.R5 J6
18. 73-106465: Jacobson, Rodolfo. The London dialect of
the late fourteenth century; a transformational
analysis in historical linguistics. The Hague,
Mouton, 1970. 193 p. fold. 1. 26 cm.
    LC CALL NUMBER: PE525 .J3
20. 71-392184: Stoldt, Peter H. Londoners in word,
sound and pictures. Munchen, Hueber (1968). 46 p.
with illus. 21 cm.
    LC CALL NUMBER: PE1963 .S8
21. 68-30638: Matthews, William, 1905- Cockney, past
and present; a short history of the dialect of
London. Detroit,Gale Research, 1970. xv,245 p.22cm.
    LC CALL NUMBER: PE1961 .M3 1938a
22. 68-25696: Lauder, Afferbeck. Fraffly well spoken:
how to speak the language of London's West End.
Sydney, Ure Smith; London, Wolfe, 1968. 63 p. illus. 19 cm.
    LC CALL NUMBER: PE1963 .L3
23. 32-2701: Chambers, R. W. (Raymond Wilson),
1874-1942, ed. A book of London English, 1384-1425, Oxford,
Clarendon press, 1931. 395,[1] p. 20 cm.
    LC CALL NUMBER: PE1963 .C5
LAST ITEM SHOWN. READY FOR NEW COMMAND OR ITEM NBR:

She was not working with materials about London Jamaican, another dialect. But she did notice, for item 2, the annotation **CIP - NOT YET IN LC**. This is a notice of "cataloging-in- publication" data, which means that the book probably has not yet been published, although it has been assigned an *International Standard Book Number* (ISBN) and has had its preliminary subject cataloguing done by the Library of Congress. Had she been working on a topic for which this book was germane, she would have the name of an author to consult as an expert, as well as the name of the publisher, as a point of contact for locating the author:

```
92-42560          ITEM 1 OF 2 IN SET 1        (BKS3)
  Sebba, Mark.
    London Jamaican : a case study in language contact / Mark
  Sebba. London ;
New York : Longman, 1993. p. cm.

LC CALL NUMBER: PE3313 .S43 1993 *CIP - NOT YET IN LC*
PROJECTED PUBLICATION DATE:   9310

SUBJECTS:
  English language—Dialects—Jamaica.
  English language—Dialects—England—London.
  Creole dialects, English—England—London.
  Languages in contact—England—London.
  Jamaicans—England—London—Language.
  Creole dialects, English—Jamaica.
  Black English—England—London.

SERIES TITLES (Indexed under SERI option):
  Real language series
NOTES:
  Includes bibliographical references and index.
ISBN:   0582080967
        0582080959 (pbk.)
DEWEY DEC.:   427/.97292 20
LCCN:   92-42560
```

After Regan received these three new items through interlibrary loan, she discovered more bibliographical information which gave her, in the end, twelve sources; and, after a careful analysis and presentation of her discoveries, an A+.

IV. Citation Searches with *Arts & Humanities Search*.

Emilia, a student in a freshman composition class, was a dedicated enthusiast for early Baroque music. In addition, three of her four grandparents were of Italian heritage, and one of them, her maternal grandmother, was fluent in Italian. Her maternal grandfather, who was born in Pistoia, had told her, some years before his death, that she was related to the Rospiogliosi family, which gave to the Catholic Church Giulio Rospigliosi, Pope Clement IX. Emilia decided to research the circumstances under which he, as a young bishop, came to write the libretto for the earliest Italian comic opera, *Chi Soffre Speri*. Her instructor thought that the topic was a very good one and appoved it without difficulty, since she also advanced the fact that her grandmother would help her with all the materials she found that were in Italian.

Her first searches on *WorldCat*, and her use of the bibliography in the articles on the composers of the music for the opera, Virgilio Mazzocchi and Marco Marazzoli, in the *New Grove Dictionary of Music and Musicians*,[266] gave her several good sources for starting her research, including a dissertation on Rospigliosi's libretti by Margaret Murata,[267] which later was revsied and published.[268] In addition, Emilia found a photographic reprint of the original manuscript of the opera.[269]

She did have difficulty in finding modern commentaries and criticisms of the opera, so she decided to do a citation search in OCLC's online version of the *Arts and Humanities Citation Index*. She went to the OCLC terminal in her college's library, signed on,

---

[266] *The New Grove Dictionary of Music and Musicians*, reprinted with corrections, 20 vols. (London: Grove, 1995).

[267] Margaret Murata, "Operas for the Papal Court, with texts by Giulio Rospigliosi" (unpublished Ph. D. dissertation, University of Chicago, 1975).

[268] Margart Murata, *Operas for the Papal Court, 1631-1668*, Studies in Musicology, no. 39 (Ann Arbor, Michigan: UMI Research Press, 1981).

[269] Virgilio Mazzocchi and Marco Marazzoli, *L'Egisto, overo, Chi soffre speri* (New York: Garland Publishers, 1982). This musical score has the full text by Giulio Rospigliosi, which is, itself, an adaptation of a story by Giovanni Boccaccio. The published version is a photoreprint of the ms. score in the Biblioteca Apostolica Vaticana (MS Barb. lat. 4386).

and, from the *FirstSearch Extended* menu, chose *Arts & Humanities Search*, and saw the opening display:

```
* * * * * * * *        ARTS & HUMANITIES SEARCH        * * * * * * * * *
  COVERAGE:  Over 1.4 million records referencing more than 1,300 of the
  world's leading arts and humanities journals. 1980 to the present.
  Updated weekly.
    Copyright 1996 by the Institute for Scientific Information (R), Inc.
                    PRESS ENTER TO CONTINUE
```

On pressing the ENTER key, Emilia moved on to the next display:

```
* * * * * * * * * * * * * * Search * * * * * * * * * * * * * * * * * *
DATABASE: A&H Search
   SEARCH_____DESCRIPTION_____EXAMPLES_____
| Subject     Type the label SU: and a word(s).        su:pragmatics
|             (Titles and subject keywords)             su:art of myth
|
| Author      Type the label AU: and the author's      au:harline
|             name or any part of the name.            au:r chametzky
|
| Cited       Type the label CR: and author's          cr:hovius
| Reference   name or words from the cited work.       cr:arch reformation
|_____HINTS:
Other ways to search . . . . . . type H <database name> LABELS.
          Include plural (s and es) or possessive . type + at end of word.
          Return to Database Selection screen . . . . . . just press Enter.
ACTIONS: Help Limit Database Wordlist BYE Reset

SEARCH WORD(S) (or Action):
```

Before she began to search, since citation searching was new to her, she entered h, for **Help**, and then displayed the **labels** which indicated in which ways she could search the database:

A '+' following the name of a kind of search means you can search
simple plurals.

KIND OF SEARCH	LABEL	REMARKS
Subject+	su:	Includes article titles, author keywords, and KeyWordsPlus. The SU: label is not required.
		EXAMPLES: su:monastic reform
Address	ad:	ad:univ idaho
Author	au:	au:harline
Cited Reference	cr:	Example: cr:liebowitz r 1979
Genuine Article Number	ga:	
Journal Information	jn:	
Journal Subject	js:	
Standard Number (ISSN)	sn:	Records added since Sept. 1992.
Keywords	kw:	
Title of Article	ti:	

BOUND-PHRASE SEARCHES		REMARKS
Author	au=	A bound-phrase search looks for
Country	cn=	author, cited reference or work,
Cited Author	ca=	country, or journal name to
Cited Reference	cr=	appear EXACTLY as you type it.
Cited Work	cw=	We recommend that you find your
Cross Reference	xr=	term in the Wordlist first; to
Journal Name	jn=	search, follow the HINTS.
Journal Subject	js=	

She then pressed the ENTER key again, to return to the original
display for accessing the database. She decided upon a direct approach to see if anyone had cited the opera itself in any modern
work. She searched with the title, although she could have
searched by author, as well. At the prompt: SEARCH WORD(S) (or
Action): she entered:

> cr:chi soffre speri

She was surprised to get one record immediately:

```
* * * * * * * * * * * * List of Records * * * * * * * * * * * * * *
DATABASE: A&H Search                LIMITED TO:
SEARCH: cr:chi soffre speri FOUND 1 Records
    NO._TITLE_____AUTHOR_____YEAR_
|
|   1   THE COMIC POPE, ON CLEMENT-IX OPERA-LIBRETTOS  ROMEI D   1990
|_____
```

267

She displayed the full form of the record and found:

```
* * * * * * * * * * * * Full Record Display * * * * * * * * * * * * * * DATABASE:
A&H Search                      LIMITED TO:
SEARCH: cr:chi soffre speri
Record  1 of   1
|Genuine Art. No.:  EQ292
|          Title:  THE COMIC POPE, ON CLEMENT-IX OPERA-LIBRETTOS
|          Author:  ROMEI D
|       Doc. Type:  ARTICLE
|        Language:  ITALIAN
|            Year:  1990
|     No. of Ref.:  0052
|         Journal:  PARAGONE, V41, N482, 1990. P43-62
| Journal Subject:  ARTS & HUMANITIES, GENERAL (BQ)
| Cited Reference:  1639, AVVISO DI ROMA
|                   ADEMOLLO A, 1888, TEATRI ROMA SECOLO 1
|                   ASORROSA A, 1988, STORIA GEOGRAFIA
|                   BALDINUCCI F, 1847, VITA GL BERNINI
|                   BEANI G, 1893, CLEMENTE IX G ROSPIG
|                   BERNINI GL, FONTANA DI TREVI
|                   BRACCIOLINI F, ELETTIONE DI URBANO
|                   BREZZI P, 1967, B STORICO PISTOIESE, V69, P3
|                   BRUMANA BM, 1988, TASSO MUSICA MUSICIS, P137
|                   CALDERONDELABAR. P, EMPENOS DE UN ACOSO
|                   CANEVAZZI G, 1900, CLEMENTE IX POETA
|                   CARDUCCI, 1895, NUOVA ANTOLOGIA, V58
|                   CIANCIARELLI R, 1987, BIBLIOTECA TEATRALE, V7, P1
|                   CLEMENT IX, CANTATA ARMIDA RINAL
|                   CLEMENT IX, CHI SOFFRE SPERI
|                   CLEMENT IX, COMICA DEL CIELO
|                   CLEMENT IX, 1633, COMMUNICATION   0115
|                   CLEMENT IX, ERMINIA SUL GIORDANO
|                   CLEMENT IX, PALAZZO INCANTATO
|                   CLEMENT IX, S EUSTACHIO
|                   CLEMENT IX, SAN BONIFACIO
|                   CLEMENT IX, SANT ALESSIO
|                   CLEMENT IX, SANTA TEODORA
|                   CLEMENT IX, VITA HUMANA
|                   COSTANZO M, 1969, MAFFEO E F BARBERINI
|                   CRISTOFORI R, 1979, STUD ROMANI, V27, P302
|                   DELLACORTE A, 1958, DRAMMI PER MUSICA RI
|                   FAGIOLODELLARCO MM, 1977, EFFIMERO BAROCCO STR
|                   FAGIOLODELLARCO MM, 1977, EFFIMERO BAROCCO STR
|                   HIBBARD H, 1967, DIZIONARIO BIOGRAFIC, V9
|                   LAVIN I, 1980, BERNINI UNITA ARTI V
|                   MANNI A, RAPPRESENTAZIONE ANI
|                   MARIANI F, MERCATO
|                   MARIANI V, 1949, STUDI BIBLIO ARGOMEN, P254
|                   MARITI L, 1978, COMMEDIA RIDICOLOSA
|                   MEROLA A, 1964, DIZIONARIO BIOGRAFIC, V6
|                   MEROLLA R, 1988, STORIA GEOGRAFIA, V2, P1019
|                   MOLINARI C, 1962, CRITICA ARTE, V9, P57
|                   MOLINARI C, 1968, NOZZE DEI SAGGIO GRA
|                   NOVELLI C, 1964, STUD ROMANI, V12, P164
|                   OSBAT L, 1982, DIZIONARIO BIOGRAFIC, V26
|                   PASTOR LV, 1931, STORIA PAPI FINE MED
|                   PIRROTTA N, 1971, STUDI TEATRO VENETO, P341
|                   PRUNIERES H, 1912, SOMMELBANDE MUSIKGES, V14, P218
|                   REINER S, 1961, MUSIC REV, V22, P265
|                   ROLANDI U, 1927, NUOVA ANTOLOGIA, V255, P523
|                   ROSPIGLIOSI G, DISCORSO G ROSPIGLIO
|                   SALVADORI A, REINA SANTORSOLA
|                   SALZA A, 1907, RIV MUSICALE ITALIAN, V14, P437
|                   SOLERTI A, 1905, MUSICA BALLO DRAMMAT
|                   TERLINDEN C, 1904, CLEMENT IX
|_____
```

She was delighted to find this article, because it appeared after both Margaret Murata's dissertation and her subsequent book, which had been Emilia's most recent sources, from 1975 and 1981, respectively. Danilo Romei's article, published in 1990, also provided her with new potential sources which she had not found in any other place, notably:

BEANI G, 1893, CLEMENTE IX G ROSPIG

and

CANEVAZZI G, 1900, CLEMENTE IX POETA

These citations are an example of the "boomerang effect" of citation searching, which we discussed, where a forward search for citations produces other citations to older sources which had not appeared in the original bibliographic searching.

She returned to the opening display for *Arts & Humanities Search* and continued with several other citation searches, including, of course, one on Margaret Murata. After she had completed her citation searching, Emilia signed on to *WorldCat*, where she found a record of bound volumes of *Paragone*.[270] She then ordered volume forty-one of this serial through interlibrary loan.[271]

From the citations in Danilo Romei's original article, she extended the abbreviations for the works by Gaetano Beani and Giovanni Canevazzi, so that she could find these sources, as well.[272] She retrieved them and found additional material for her paper.

---

[270] *Paragone: Rivista Mensile di Arte Figurativa e Letteratura* (Firenze [Florence]: A. Mondadori [*et al.*], 1950-). It is a bimonthly which began with anno 1, no. 1, in January, 1950. The full citation to the article is Danilo Romei, "Il Papa 'Comico': Sui Melodrammi di Giulio Rospigliosi (Clemente IX)," *Paragone: Rivista Mensile di Arte Figurativa e Letteratura* XLI, Nuova Serie, 20 (482) (April, 1990): 43-62.

[271] In this case, it was the library of the Ohio State University, in Columbus, Ohio, which responded to her request.

[272] Gaetano Beani, *Clemente IX (Giulio Rospigliosi Pistoiese)*, in *Notizie Storiche* (Prato: Tipografia Giachetti, Figlio e Compagnia, 1893) and Giovanni Canevazzi, *Papa Clemente IX, Poeta* (Modena: Forghieri e Pellegrini, 1900).

She received the highest mark for her paper, but with some disappointment, since she had planned to extend her paper into a publishable article. Danilo Romei's essay, however, made it unlikely that another journal would be interested in an article that covered much the same ground.

Although she had planned to major in international business, Emilia eventually became a major in music history. Six years after her original freshman term paper, she is writing a master's thesis, at another university, on the place of Pope Urban VIII and his family, the Barberini, as patrons of music in seventeenth-century Rome. Much of her material on Giulio Rospigliosi is now a part of her present work.

V. Searching *Dissertation Abstracts Online*, with a Follow-up to *WorldCat*.

One student in a secton of freshman composition that was taught by Saundra Maley had an earlier version of this book in the form of a handout. She apparently devoured the text in a few days and decided to use online sources to choose a topic for her term paper; one that she thought the professor would like.

Although she was not sure that Saundra Maley had a doctorate, because we do not use our academic titles when we introduce ourselves to our classes, she chose to search for a possible dissertation.

She used her newly-established computer account to access the *FirstSearch Extended* service from her dormitory room, signed on, and chose *DISS*, OCLC's version of *Dissertation Abstracts Online*. She received the opening display:

```
* * * * * *         DISSERTATION ABSTRACTS ONLINE        * * * * * * *

COVERAGE:  The complete range of academic subjects appearing in
dissertations accepted at accredited institutions since 1861.
Updated monthly.

Dissertation Abstracts Online (DAO) is copyrighted by UMI, 1996.

    Data from this file may not be duplicated, except that reproduction
    of limited quantities of reasonable portions of the database is        permit-
ted    for Buyer's internal use but only if Buyer includes a          suitable notice
of database supplier's copyright, in conformity with the
    1976 Copyright Law's standards, on all copies. Under no
    circumstances may copies made under this provision be offered for
    resale in any media. Copying in machine-readable form is not
    authorized. Exceptions to these terms are permitted only with prior
    written permission from UMI. UMI makes no warranties regarding the
    accuracy or completeness of this product although every attempt has
    been made to ensure its accuracy.

                    PRESS ENTER TO CONTINUE
```

After pressing the ENTER key, she received the next display:

```
* * * * * * * * * * * * * * Search * * * * * * * * * * * * * * * * *
DATABASE: Diss
  __SEARCH____  ___DESCRIPTION_____  ___EXAMPLES____|
| Subject      Type the label SU: and a word(s).          su:mania
|              (Descriptors, titles, abstracts)           su:man machine
|
| Author       Type the label AU: and the author          au:geri
|              name or any part of the name.              au:blanchard homer
|
| Title        Type the label TI: and the title           ti:parents
|              or any word(s) in the title.               ti:organ-building
|_____HINTS:
Other ways to search . . . . . . . type H <database name> LABELS.
         Include plural (s and es) or possessive . type + at end of word.
         Return to Database Selection screen . . . . . . just press Enter.
ACTIONS: Help  Limit  Database  Wordlist  BYE  Reset

SEARCH WORD(S) (or Action):
```

She already had consulted the online directory of the faculty to
verify the spelling of the professor's name. Now, she searched with
an author label:

au:maley, saundra

and received the following:

```
+ * * * * * * * * * * * * List of Records * * * * * * * * * * * * * * DATABASE:
Diss                         LIMITED TO:
SEARCH: au:maley, saundra FOUND 1 Records

  _NO.__AUTHOR_____TITLE_____YEAR
|
| 1   MALEY, SAUNDRA ROSE  SOLITARY APPRENTICESHIP: JAMES WRIGHT AND 1994
|_____HINTS:
View a record . . . . . . . . . . . . . . type record number.
         Decrease number of records . . type L (to limit) or A (to 'and').
         Do a new search . . . . . . . . . . . . . . . type S or SEARCH.
ACTIONS: Help  Search  And  Limit  Print  Email  Database  BYE

RECORD NUMBER (or Action):
```

She typed in the number "1" to display the full bibliographic record, and found:

RESEARCH GUIDE FOR THE DIGITAL AGE

Record 1 of   1_____

|
|ACCESSION NO.:   AAG9508009
| TITLE: SOLITARY APPRENTICESHIP: JAMES WRIGHT AND GERMAN POETRY
| (WRIGHT, JAMES)
| AUTHOR: MALEY, SAUNDRA ROSE
| DEGREE: PH.D.
| YEAR: 1994
| INSTITUTION: UNIVERSITY OF MARYLAND COLLEGE PARK; 0117
| ADVISER: Chairman: W. MILNE HOLTON
| SOURCE: DAI, VOL. 55-10A, Page 3191, 00674 Pages
| DESCRIPTORS: LITERATURE, AMERICAN; BIOGRAPHY

| ABSTRACT: This study documents and examines James Wright's interestin
| the German poets, emphasizing his early years. Chapter one
| is a biographical chapter which concentrates on Wright's
| early education—his high school studies, poems, and
| translations; his continued self-education in the army; and
| his intensive undergraduate work at Kenyon College,1948-51,
| where his interest in German poetry formally began.Chapters
| two and three examine Wright's reading and translation of
| Rilke, his primary German interest at Kenyon, and the next
| chapter explores his interest in Heine and Storm. Drafts of
| translations of these three poets, as found among Wright's
| papers, are chronicled. Chapters five and six discuss the
| thirteen additional German poets represented bytranslations
| among the papers from Wright's Kenyon years: Vogelweide and
| the Minnesingers, Goethe, Holderlin, Novalis, Eichendorff,
| Platen, Lenau, Morike, Nietzsche, Dehmel, Hofmannsthal,
| Carossa, and Hesse. Chapter seven examines Wright's
| encounter with the poetry of Georg Trakl while on a
| Fulbright Scholarship at the University of Vienna, 1952-53,
| and extends to include an examination of the many drafts of
| Trakl translations Wright produced with Robert Bly during
| the years immediately preceding the publication of The
| Branch Will Not Break (1963). The conclusion of this study
| suggests the implications this newly-uncovered information
| brings to Wright scholarship while firmly establishing the
| significant role German poetry played in Wright's
| development as a poet. Fair copies of almost one hundredand
| fifty German translations from Wright's Kenyon years and
| beyond are presented in the appendices, along with several
| interesting drafts of original poems, a review, and a short
| story, all previously unrecorded.
|_____

She then turned to *WorldCat*, to determine if she could obtain a copy of the dissertation easily. She found that it had, in fact, already been published as a book.

```
* * * * * * * * * * * Full Record Display * * * * * * * * * * * * * DATABASE:
WorldCat                        LIMITED TO:
SEARCH: au:maley, saundra

  Record 1 of 1_____
  |
  |ACCESSION: 34885922
  |   AUTHOR: Maley, Saundra.
  |    TITLE: Solitary apprenticeship :
  |           James Wright and German poetry /
  |    PLACE: Lewiston, N.Y. :
  |PUBLISHER: Mellen University Press,
  |     YEAR: 1996
  | PUB TYPE: Book
  |   FORMAT: ii, 710 p. ; 24 cm.
  |    NOTES: Includes bibliographical references and index.
  |     ISBN: 0773422579 (alk. paper)
  |  SUBJECT: Wright, James Arlington, — 1927- — Knowledge — Language and
  |           languages.
  |           Wright, James Arlington, — 1927- — Knowledge — Literature.
  |           German poetry — Appreciation — United States — History — 20th
  |           century.
  |           German language — Translating into English — History.
  |           German poetry — Translations into English.
  |           American poetry — German influences.
  |_____
  HINTS: Another page . type F or B.  Another record . type record number.
         See which libraries may own this item . . . . . . . .type LIB.
         Return to Record List . . . . . . . . . . . . just press Enter.
ACTIONS: Help  Search  Print  Email  Order  LIBraries  Forward  Back
  RECORD NUMBER (or Action):
```

She then used the LIB command to see where copies were available:

```
* * * * * * * * * * * Library Holdings Display * * * * * * * * * * * *
_SYM___LIBRARY_____OCLC_ILL_SUPPLIER?_
DC
DLC    LIBRARY OF CONGRESS                            N
OH
OSU    OHIO STATE UNIV, THE                           Y
ON
UWO    UNIV OF WESTERN ONTARIO                        Y
```

274

Because she was in Washington, at The George Washington University, she saw a copy on the next day by taking the subway to the Library of Congress, where she ordered and examined the book.

The whole exercise had taken her about fifteen minutes to search out the material online and about three hours to go to see the book.

She photocopied some of the translations that James Wright had done from the poetry of Rainer Maria Rilke, which appeared in the appendix to the book, and carried them with her to her next class.

In the discussion on that day about choosing topics, she offered to do a paper which explored Wright's translations from Rilke in greater detail. Later, in a further discussion after class, it became clear that she was not truly fascinated by Wright, but rather had chosen her topic because she believed it would please the professor. After she mentioned her enthusiasm for environmental studies, she and the professor both agreed that a study of early efforts to protect the environment of the English Lake District in the nineteenth century would be a better choice.

VI. How to Browse Shelves Digitally,
using the Library of Congress System

For a paper on Robert Somercote, an English churchman of the thirteenth century who became a cardinal, Katherine found one source that she could use to check the dates of his cardinalate, the *Storia dei Cardinali* of *Conte* Francesco Cristofori. She already had found this book and taken data from it when she decided to see if there were any other books which
had been classified by the Library of Congress in the same way. It must be noted that she already had browsed the shelves of her own college's library, but the collection was weak in medieval church history, so she did not find any more potential sources.

She used her computer account to *telnet* to **locis.loc.gov**, chose the catalogues of the Library of Congress, and looked up Cristofori's book again:

```
unk84-20235          ITEM 2 OF 2 IN SET 6      (PREM)

Cristofori, Francesco.
   Storia dei cardinali di santa Roman chiesa dal secolo V all'
anno del Signore MDCCLXXXVIII... [n.p.] 1888- v. obl. cm.

LC CALL NUMBER: BX4664 .C8

LCCN:  unk84-20235
READY FOR NEW COMMAND:
```

From this display, Katherine learned that the Library of Congress had assigned the call number **BX4664.C8** to this volume. This number can be separated into two parts—the *class number* and the *cutter number*. The *class number* is the **BX4664** and the *cutter number* is anything else that follows the right-handmost decimal point, in this case .**C8**. She already had learned that she can use one of the most valuable commands for the Library of Congress's system, the **BRWS CALL** command, to, in effect, browse the shelf where she would find Cristofori's book, were she able to see it physically. She entered the command **BRWS CALL BX4664**, and received the following display:

```
To choose from list, see examples at bottom.
   FILE: X-FILE
Terms alphabetically close to:CALL BX4664

B01 CALL BX4659//(PREM=125; LOC2=16; LOC3=122)
B02 CALL BX4660//(PREM=1; LOC3=10)
B03 CALL BX4661//(PREM=20; LOC2=2; LOC3=16)
B04 CALL BX4662//(PREM=25; LOC2=9; LOC3=38)
B05 CALL BX4663//(PREM=6; LOC3=1)
B06+CALL BX4664//(PREM=3; LOC2=2; LOC3=3) <<====
B07 CALL BX4664.2//(PREM=1; LOC2=1; LOC3=3)
B08 CALL BX4665//(PREM=13; LOC2=1; LOC3=6)
B09 CALL BX4666//(PREM=12; LOC3=5)
B10 CALL BX46678//(PREM=13; LOC2=2; LOC3=8)
B11 CALL BX4668//(PREM=182; LOC1=1; LOC2=13; LOC3=110)
B12 CALL BX4668.15//(LOC3=1)
```

Katherine then SELECTED B06 (s b6) and received the following display:

```
SET 1          3: SLCT PREM/CALL/CALL BX4664
   THE TERM, (B06)"CALL BX4664", IS NOT USED IN LOC1.
SET 2          2: SLCT LOC2/CALL/CALL BX4664
SET 3          3: SLCT LOC3/CALL/CALL BX4664
READY FOR NEW COMMAND:
```

She then combined all of the listings in the catalogue for works that have the *class number,* BX4664, by using the COMBINE command with the Boolean operator OR: c 1 o 2 o 3. Now she had a new set of items:

```
SET 4          8: COMB 14 O 15 O 16
READY FOR NEW COMMAND:
```

She displayed the combined set in the short bibliographic form (d 4). Now could "read the shelf," just as if she were standing in front of it:

```
ITEMS 1-8 OF 8      SET 4: BRIEF DISPLAY      FILE: LOC3
                    (DESCENDING ORDER)
1. 95-149221: Rossi, Agnelo, 1913-  Cardinali santi /   Roma :
Pontifical Universitas Urbaniana, 1994. 94 p. ; 21 cm.
     LC CALL NUMBER: BX4664.2 .R67 1994
2. 82-114728: I Testamenti dei cardinali del Duecento / Roma :
Presso la Societa, 1980. clviii, 572 p.; 25 cm.
     LC CALL NUMBER: DG402 .S635 n. 25
3. 78-17845: MacEoin, Gary, 1909- The inner elite : dossiers
of papal candidates / Kansas City, Kan. : S. Andrews and
McMeel, c1978. xxx, 300 p., [8] leaves of plates : ill. ; 24
cm.
     LC CALL NUMBER: BX4664.2 .M32
4. 72-314712: Muhr, Alfred, 1903- Das Kabinett Gottes. Politik
in d. Wandelgangen d. Vatikan. Dusseldorf, Wien, Econ-Verl.
(1971). 496 p., several l. of illus. 22 cm.
     LC CALL NUMBER: BX4664.2 .M8
5. 70-134119: Morgan, Thomas B. (Thomas Brynmor), 1886- Speak-
ing of cardinals, Freeport, N.Y., Books for Libraries Press
[1971, c1946] 264 p. 23 cm.
     LC CALL NUMBER: BX4664 .M6 1971
6. unk84-20235: Cristofori, Francesco. Storia dei cardinali di
santa Romana chiesa dal secols V all' anno del Signore
MDCCLXXXVIII... [n.p.] 1888- v. obl. cm.
     LC CALL NUMBER: BX4664 .C8
7. 64-7964: Novak, Michael, ed. The men who make the Council.
[Notre Dame, Ind., University of Notre Dame Press, 1964-65. 8
v. 18 cm.
     LC CALL NUMBER: BX4664.2 .N6
8. 47-1261: Morgan, Thomas Brynmor, 1886- Speaking of cardi-
nals,   New York, G. P. Putnam's sons [1946]  4 p.l., 264 p. 21
cm.
     LC CALL NUMBER: BX4664 .M6
```

From this list, Katherine found one item that piqued her interest, because the subject of her present research was a thirteenth-century cardinal and so a book about their testaments might well have something of use to her. She DISPLAYed item 2 of the eight she had found (d 17/item 2), and received the following screen:

```
82-114728          ITEM 2 OF 8 IN SET 17      (BKS3)

I Testamenti dei cardinali del Duecento / [a cura di] Agostino
Paravicini Bagliani. Roma : Presso la Societa, 1980. clviii,
572 p. ; 25 cm.

LC CALL NUMBER: DG402 .S635 n.25
  (ALTERNATE CLASS BX4664.2)

SUBJECTS:
  Cardinals.
  Civilization, Medieval—13th century.
  Wills.
OTHER NAMES:
  Paravicini Bagliani, Agostino.
SERIES TITLES (Indexed under SERI option):
  Miscellanea della Societa romana di storia patria; 25
NOTES:
  Italian and Latin.
  Includes bibliographical references and index.
LANGUAGE CODE:  italat
NATL. BIB. NO.:  It82-Jan
LCCN:  82-114728 r96
```

Since she could not go to the Library of Congress to see the book,
she searched *WorldCat* to see if she could order it through interlibrary loan from another source. She found the book with a title
search, **ti:testamenti and ti:duecento.**

```
* * * * * * * * * * * * Full Record Display * * * * * * * * * * * * * * DATABASE:
WorldCat                    LIMITED TO:
SEARCH: ti:testamenti and ti:duecento
  Record 1 of 1_____
|ACCESSION: 7827310
|     TITLE: I Testamenti dei cardinali del Duecento /
|     PLACE: Roma :
|PUBLISHER: Presso la Societa,
|      YEAR: 1980
|  PUB TYPE: Book
|    FORMAT: clviii, 572 p. ; 25 cm.
|    SERIES: Miscellanea della Societa romana di storia patria ; 25
|     NOTES: Italian and Latin.
|            Includes bibliographical references and index.
|   SUBJECT: Cardinals.
|            Civilization, Medieval — 13th century.
|            Wills.
|     OTHER: Paravicini Bagliani, Agostino.
|_____
```

And, with the LIB command, she found many libraries that had copies of the book, including:

```
* * * * * * * * * * * Library Holdings Display * * * * * * * * * * * *
_SYM___LIBRARY_____OCLC_ILL_SUPPLIER?_
DC
DLC    LIBRARY OF CONGRESS                              N
IN
IND    UNIV OF NOTRE DAME                               Y
MA
HLS    HARVARD UNIV                                     Y
SNN    SMITH COL                                        Y
MI
EYM    UNIV OF MICHIGAN LIBR                            Y
MO
XII    SAINT LOUIS UNIV, PIUS XII LIBR                  Y
NY
BNG    STATE UNIV OF NEW YORK, BINGHAMTON LIBR          Y
OH
OSU    OHIO STATE UNIV, THE                             Y
PA
PAU    UNIV OF PENNSYLVANIA                             Y
EU
CUD    CAMBRIDGE UNIV                                   N
EQO    UNIV OF OXFORD                                   N
LHR    UNIV OF LONDON, INST OF HIST RES                 N
QCL    GLASGOW UNIV LIBR                                N
WG2    UNIV OF LONDON, WARBURG INST                     N
```

She ordered the book, which she received in about a week. It proved not to have material that was useful for her research, but she had learned the ability to browse the shelves of the largest library in the world digitally. Thus, she had a new tool on which she could rely to show her items that were related to one another by the proximity of their shelving according to their classification. Notice that, if she wished to broaden her search, she could go back to the original BRWS CALL display and select BX4663 and BX4665, and so forth, until she had widened her search to cover everything in which she might be interested, just as if she had looked backward and forward along the shelves of the library itself.

Appendix B: An Undergraduate Term Paper

"The Microbiological Miracle of Bolsena"

Johanna C. Cullen

In 1263, a German priest on a pilgrimage to Rome, stopped in Bolsena,[273] Italy, to celebrate mass at the church of Santa Cristina. As he bent over the host at the moment of consecration, he became troubled with doubt over whether or not the host truly became the body of Christ.[274] His temptation disappeared, however, as "the blood that Christ had sweated in His agony in Gethsemane oozed from the Host and dripped down upon the linen of the altar."[275] As the priest attempted to clean his fingers and the altar, the blood stained the corporal, purificators, and the marble.[276]

At that time, Pope Urban IV (Jacques Pantaléon, 29 August 1261 - 2 October 1264) was staying in Orvieto,[277] and the repentant

---

[273] A town of the province of Rome situated on the northeast bank of the Lago di Bolsena (Lake Bolsena). Karl Baedeker, *Central Italy and Rome*, 15th ed., (New York: Charles Scribner's Sons, 1909), 105.

[274] The Lateran Council, in 1215, had defined the doctrine of transubstantiation, which holds that, at the moment of consecration the bread and wine do become, in fact, the body and blood of Christ, without changing the natural appearance, however.

[275] John Ayscough, *Saints and Places* (New York: Benziger Brothers, 1912), 166. The blood-stained altar linens were a corporal and purificators (see footnote 7). The corporal is a square piece of cloth resembling a napkin in size and appearance. During the mass, the corporal is spread out on the altar and the chalice is placed on it. The purificator is a linen cloth used for wiping the chalice, and the fingers and mouth of the celebrant after Communion. For details, see Rev. F. X. Lasance, *The New Roman Missal* (New York: Benziger Brothers, Inc., 1950), 60-62.

[276] Andrea Lazzarini, *Miracolo di Bolsena: Testimonianze e Documenti dei Secoli XIII e XIV* (Rome: Edizioni di Storia e Letteratura, 1952), 1-3, 23; translated by Brigitte Cullen [1993]; and Pietro Barbieri and Ulisse Pucci, eds. *Guide to Catholic Italy*, (Rome: Holy Year 1950 Publishing Co., ED.A.S., 1950), 953.

[277] Orvieto is a small town with an episcopal residence, twelve miles ENE of Bolsena, on an isolated tufa rock. It occupies what was probably the site of Volsinii, one of the twelve capitals of the Etruscan League. In the Middle ages it was a great stronghold of the Guelphs and often afforded refuge to the popes. Baedeker, *Central Italy*, 100.

priest took up the blood-stained altar linens and went immediately to confess his now-resolved doubts and to seek absolution for them. Urban already had received word of the miracle and, attended by his cardinals, met the priest and the relics of the miracle at the bridge over the Chiaro. This miraculous event hastened Urban's decision to make the festival which honored the real presence of Christ in the Eucharist an obligation for the whole Church. In the following year, 1264, he issued the bull *Transiturus de hoc mundo* which instituted the feast of Corpus Christi[278] in memory of the miracle of the Mass of Bolsena.[279] Urban further ordered the construction of a new cathedral at Orvieto. Here, the host and corporal[280] are enshrined to this day.

---

[278]"Hujus memorialis continuam debemus celebrare memoriam, ut illius, cujus ipsum fore memoriale cognoscimus . . .. Licet igitur hoc memoriale Sacramentum in quotidianis missarum solemnis frequentetur, conveniens . . . arbitramur & dignum, ut de ipso semel saltem in anno . . . memoria & celebrior habeatur." Laertii Cherubino, *Magnum Bullarum Romanum, a beato Leone Magno usque ad S. D. N. Benedictum XIII* (Luxembourg: Andreæ Chevalier, 1727), 121. "This memorial ought to be continually celebrated, that we may be ever mindful of Him . . .. Therefore, although this memorial Sacrament is already celebrated in the daily observance of Mass, . . . we think it fitting and worthy that at least once in the year, . . . there be a more solemn and notable memory." Darwell Stone, *A History of the Doctrine of the Holy Eucharist* (London: Longmans, Green, and Co., 1909), 345.

[279]Ayscough, *Saints and Places*, 167.

[280]In the cathedral of Orvieto, near the rear wall of the chapel of the Holy Corporal, is a large tabernacle which contains the reliquary of the host, corporal, and other relics from Bolsena. The reliquary was made by order of Bishop Bertrand dei Monaldeschi, by Ugolino di Maestro Vieri of Sienna (1337). *The Catholic Encyclopedia*, Vol. XI (New York: Robert Appleton Company, 15 volumes, 1911), 331-332. In 1658, Bishop Giuseppe della Corgna (1656-1676), a Dominican, conducted the first detailed examination of these relics and recorded the presence of the corporal, two blood-stained purificators, and a third cloth covered with several spots of blood. Although Della Corgna reported the presence of a blood-stained host, the *Liber Ecclesiasticus* stated simply: "Inventio fragmenti ostie ss.mi Corporalis." A more recent inventory of the relics of Bolsena, published in 1950, identified the host and corporal, as well as four pieces of linen; several small pieces of linen, silk, and gauze of various colors (white, red, and yellow); a small wooden box; a small silver urn decorated with crystals; a burse of gold brocade; and three scrolls inscribed as follows: "Reliquie sanguinis isti;" "Sanguis isti sparsus fuit super hoc corporale et // ideo cum summa diligentia debet custodiri;" and "Benda in qua fuit involutum corporale et residuum Corporalis // cum guttis sanguinis isti et figuris." The inscriptions were validated as

Soon, the event at Bolsena became the most celebrated miracle of the century and was commemorated and recommemorated in art and legend. The most famous of its depictions is found in the Vatican, on the right wall as one enters from the Stanza di Elio-doro. It is the celebrated fresco by Raphael — the last he painted for Pope Julius II (Giuliano della Rovere, 31 October 1503 - 21 February 1513). Here, forever anachronistically, the pope and his cousin, Cardinal Raphael Riario, observe the "Mass of Bolsena."[281]

The purpose of this paper is not to challenge the doctrine of transubstantiation, the miraculous nature of the Mass of Bolsena, nor the faith of the priest, but to demonstrate that the physical manifestations during the miracle of the Mass of Bolsena may have a more microbiological basis than a metaphysical one. By review-ing the description of the historical event of the Mass of Bol-sena,[282] other examples of "bleeding" throughout history, and the relevant research conducted by Bartolomeo Bizio,[283] Vincenzo

having been written in the fourteenth, thirteenth, and thirteenth centuries, re-spectively. Lazzarini, *Miracolo di Bolsena*, 1-3, 23.

[281] Ayscough, *Saints and Places*, 165-166; Giovanni Pietro Bellori, *Descrizione delle Immagini Dipinte da Raffaelle d'Urbino nel Palazzo Vaticano, e nella Farnesina alla Lungara: con alcuni ragionamenti in onore delle sue opere, e della pittura, e scultura, di Gio. Pietro Bellori. In questa nuova edizione accrescuita anche della vita de medesimo Raffaelle. descritta da Giorgio Vasari* (Rome: Appresso gli eredi del q. Gio. Lorenzo Barbiellini, 1751): xxii-xxiv and 88-92; text translated by Richard Cullen; and Joseph Cundall, ed., *The Great Works of Raphael Sanzio of Urbino; A Series of Thirty Photographs from best Engravings of his most celebrated Paintings; with Descriptions, translated from Passavant's "Rafael von Urbino und sein Vater," Vasari's Life of Raphael, translated by Mrs. Jonathon Foster: and an Appendix, con-taining a classified list of the principal paintings of the artist* (London: Bell and Daldy, 1870): 27-28

[282] The miracle of Bolsena is not supported by contemporary evidence. The oldest historical record is contained in a long inscription preserved in the church of Santa Cristina, in the chapel of the Corporal. This inscription, which states, *Mi-raculi Sanctissimi Corporalis Descriptio* ["Description of the Miracle of the Most Holy Corporal"], was validated as having been written between 1323 and 1344. Lazzarini, *Miracolo di Bolsena*, 43. Another historical reference is found in Anto-nio Forcilioni [St. Antonius of Florence], *Chronica*. III., tit. XIX., c. 13. and Ludwig von Pastor, *Geschichte der Päpste seit dem Ausgang des Mittelalters: Mit Be-nutzung des Päpstlichen Geheim-Archives und vieler anderer Archive bearbeitet* (Freiburg im Breisgau: Herder & Co. G.m.b.H., 1926), III:1030, n. 2.

[283] Bartolomeo Bizio was an Italian pharmacist who first attempted a natural ex-planation of the blood phenomenon. Robert S. and Margaret E. Breed, "The Type Species of the Genus Serratia, Commonly Known as *Bacillus prodigiosus*,"

Sette,[284] and Christian Gottfried Ehrenberg,[285] we can see that the event at Bolsena may, in fact, have been but a single link in a chain of events that began in historical antiquity. The unexplained appearance of "blood" on foodstuff has been a matter of observation for centuries.[286] In one of his dialogues, Lucian[287] allows Pythagoras[288] to give, as a reason for forbidding

Journal of Bacteriology 9 (1924): 548.

[284]Vincenzo Sette was a physician and surgeon from Piove, Italy, whose efforts toward a natural explanation for the blood phenomenon paralleled those of Bizio. Sette's work, along with that of Bizio, was of a "high order for the period in which it was done." *Ibid.*

[285]Christian Gottfried Ehrenberg (1795-1876) was a biologist, micropaleontologist, and a member of the Berlin Academy of Sciences and of the Academie des Sciences of Paris. See Ilse Jahn, "Ehrenberg, Christian Gottfried" in Charles Coulston Gillespie, ed., *Dictionary of Scientific Biography* (New York: Charles Scribner's Sons, 1981) 288-292. Although Ehrenberg's scientific work was less complete than the earlier Italian work of Bizio and Sette, he studied the history of the blood phenomenon much more completely. Breed and Breed, "Type Species of the Genus Serratia," 552.

[286]For accounts of this history, see: E. Scheurlen, "Geschichtliche und experimentelle Studien über den Prodigiosus," *Archiv für Hygiene* (1896), 2-12; translated by Brigitte Cullen [1993]; and Mary Hefferan, "A Comparative and Experimental Study of Bacilli Producing Red Pigment," *Centralblatt für Bakteriologie, Parasitenkunde und Infektionskrankheiten* 11 (1903), 313-314. Their accounts are largely taken from the more complete information developed by Ehrenberg in the following articles:Christian Gottfried Ehrenberg, "Forsetzung der Beobachtung des sogenannten Blutes im Brode als Monas prodigiosa," *Bericht über die zur Bekanntmachung geeigneten Verhandlungen der Königl. Preuß. Akademie der Wissenschaften zu Berlin* (16 October 1848), [1849], 354-362. Christian Gottfried Ehrenberg, (Observations on the so-called bleeding bread caused by *Monas prodigiosa*), *Bericht über die zur Bekanntmachung geeigneten Verhandlungen der Königl. Preuß. Akademie der Wissenschaften zu Berlin* (26 October 1848), [1849], 349-353. Christian Gottfried Ehrenberg, "Fernere Mittheilungen über Monas prodigiosa oder die Purpurmonade," *Bericht über die zur Bekanntmachung geeigneten Verhandlungen der Königl. Preuß. Akademie der Wissenschaften zu Berlin* (15 March 1849), [1850], 101-116. Christian Gottfried Ehrenberg, "Höchst wahrscheinlicher Grund d. Verbotes d. Bohnengenusses bei d. Pythagoräern," *Bericht über die zur Bekanntmachung geeigneten Verhandlungen der Königl. Preuß. Akademie der Wissenschaften zu Berlin* (17 January 1850), [1851], 5-9. Christian Gottfried Ehrenberg, "Eine Centurie historischer Nachträge zu den blutfarbigen Meteoren und sogenannten Prodigien," *Bericht über die zur Bekanntmachung geeigneten Verhandlungen der Königl. Preuß. Akademie der Wissenschaften zu Berlin* (27 June 1850), [1851], 215-246.

[287]Lucian of Samosata was a Syro-Greek satirist of the second century, A. D..

[288]Pythagoras was a Greek philosopher and mathematician of the sixth century B.

the consumption of beans by his disciples, the fact that white cooked beans, if placed in the moonlight, change into blood.[289] Since forbidding beans as food was common in antiquity, *e.g.*, by Egyptian priests and by the Zoroastrians,[290] from whom Pythagoras may have obtained the notion, the appearances of blood on foodstuffs may be as old as mankind's consumption of stored starches.[291] The first documented occurrence dates from 332 B.C., during Alexander the Great's siege of Tyre. According to Quintus Curtius, in *The History of Alexander*,[292] Alexander's soldiers were frightened when they broke open their bread and found "blood" inside. Aristander, a priest, quieted the terrified soldiers and turned the appearance into a beneficial event by telling them "that as long as the blood was inside the bread, a bloody fate would fall upon those inside, not outside, the city."[293] Alexander, however, was to sit before the gates of Tyre for seven months before that city surrendered.[294]

C.. He was a native of Samos.

[289]Lucian, "Sale of Creeds," *The Works of Lucian of Samosata*, trans. H. W. Fowler and F. G. Fowler, (Oxford: Clarendon Press, 1949), 192.

[290]Zoroastrians are adherents of the teachings of Zarathustra, a Persian religious teacher and monotheist of the fifth or sixth century B. C..

[291]Ferdinand Julius Cohn, a botanist and the founder of the journal *Beiträge zur Biologie der Pflanzen*, in a letter to Ehrenberg, as quoted in Ehrenberg, "Höchst wahrscheinlicher Grund," 5-9.

[292]Quintus Curtius *History of Alexander*, trans. John C. Rolfe, (Cambridge, Massachusetts: Harvard University Press, 1931) 4.2.

[293]*Ibid.*

[294]Edwyn Robert Bevan, "Alexander III," *Encyclopædia Britannica*, 11th ed., (New York: The Encyclopædia Britannica Company, 29 volumes, 1910) I: 552. Later, noteworthy examples include: In 91 B.C., Paulus Orosius, historian and theologian born in Spain toward the close of the fourth century, wrote that in Aretium, during the consumption of bread at banquets, "blood flowed from the middle of the loaves as if from bodily wounds." Paulus Orosius, *The Seven Books of History against the Pagans*, trans. Roy J. Deferrari (Washington, D.C.: Catholic University Press, 1964), 207. In 583, blood was seen to have run from bread in Tours, France. Ehrenberg, "Observations," 351. In 1093, in the Duchy of Namur, bread baked in ash also appeared to be spotted with blood. Lycosthenes, Conrad [Conrad Wolffhart], *Prodigiorum ac Ostentorum Chronicon* (Basileae: per Henricum Petri, 1557) 416. In 1104, near Speier [Spier], blood flowed from bread and also that bread baked in fire on the grill, when broken, showed flowing drops of blood. Ehrenberg, "Observations," 351. A list of the events in which blood was reported to have appeared on foodstuffs appears in Appendix I.

The first instance of blood appearing on a host occurred in 1169. In his record of the event, Lycosthenes[295] wrote that a priest on the island of Als, Denmark, saw blood on a host.[296] Written records reveal similar manifestations from the thirteenth through the fifteenth centuries.[297] Although the phenomena may not have disappeared, knowledge replaced superstition and caused the events to be less noteworthy.

Perhaps the most significant and well documented event in which "blood" appeared on starchy foods, and that one of the greatest importance to understanding the Mass of Bolsena, occurred at Legnaro, a small town about six miles southeast of Padua.

On August 3, 1819, a farmer named Antonio Pittarello discovered that a bowl of polenta,[298] which he had left overnight in a cupboard, was covered on the following morning with droplets of "blood." He discarded the polenta. However, on the following day, the blood appeared again on fresh polenta. Antonio and his neighbors, now frightened, called a priest to bless the site, but the situation grew worse by the day.[299] Later, a bowl of rice soup and a

---

[295]Conrad Wolffhart (1518-1561), a Swiss philologist and theologian, wrote under the pseudonym Lycosthenes.

[296]Lycosthenes, *Prodigiorum*, 419. Other appearances before the Mass of Bolsena include: In 1171, during celebration of mass on Easter Sunday, blood flowed from the host in Ferrara, Italy. A. Achilli and Q. Galli, *Riti Feste Primaverili e il Lago di Bolsena Atti del Convegno Tenutosi a Bolsena il 7-8 Giugno 1986*, volume 6 of *Vita Cultura Storia Delle Classi Subalterne Dell' Alto Lazio* (Viterbo: [Tipolitografia Quatrini], 1988), 20. In 1198, during mass, a priest saw that the wine had transformed into blood and the bread into flesh. Lycosthenes, *Prodigiorum*, 427. In 1199, blood appeared on hosts in Augsburg, Germany. Caesar Baronius, *Annales ecclesiastici* [1199], as cited in Ehrenberg, "Fernere Mittheilungen," 106. In 1200, blood flowed from a host during communion in Halle, Germany. *Ibid.* In 1218, blood appeared on a host in Cologne. *Annales ecclesiastici*, as cited in *Ibid.*, 107. In 1239, blood appeared on host in Schloss Chum in Valencia. *Ibid.* In 1247, blood appeared on a host in Beelitz near Potsdam. *Brandenburg Geschichte*, as cited in *Ibid.*, 108. In 1249, blood appeared on a host in Zehdenick. *Ibid.*

[297]A noteworthy observation is the change in the popular reaction to the appearances of blood on hosts. Before the Mass of Bolsena and Urban IV's Bull, the appearances were considered to be miraculous. On several occasions, the hosts were enshrined in reliquaries and preserved in chapels. In the fourteenth and fifteenth centuries, however, the persecution of Jews frequently followed the appearances of bloody hosts.

[298]An Italian dish — a mush made of barley, chestnut meal, or cornmeal.

bread dish took on the same coloration, and half a cooked chicken which hung in a cupboard appeared to be "dripping with blood."[300] The villagers marveled at the "bloody polenta," and considered the coloring to be of supernatural origin. For some, the fear was so great that they would not even live under the same roof where such "supernatural influences were operating."[301] Quite often, the families in whose homes the phenomenon occurred were charged with "all sorts of evil doings."[302] Many horrified villagers went to the local priests and begged them to banish "such maleficent spirits."[303] In response to such requests, Father Pietro Melo was asked to visit a farmer in the district of Padua to free the house of evil spirits. Melo, who was not a chemist but was rather the Director of the Botanical Garden at Savonara, examined the phenomenon, and, in a report published in the *Giornale dell'italiana letteratura del Da Rio*, asserted that the reddish substance was a product of fermentation.[304]

The incident caused such a disturbance[305] that the police were forced into action[306]— so they appointed a commission of several

---

[299]By mid-August, the phenomenon had spread to the neighboring villages of Ponte Longo, Abano, Correzola, Udine, and La Motta. In the district of Padua, more than one hundred families were affected. Ehrenberg, "Forsetzung der Beobachtung," 356.

[300]*Ibid.*, 354.

[301]Bartolomeo Bizio, "Lettera di Bartolomeo Bizio al chiarissimo canonico Angelo Bellani sopra il fenomeno della polenta porporina," *Journal of Bacteriology* 9 (1924): 529.

[302]*Ibid.*

[303]*Ibid.*, 533.

[304]*Ibid.*, 527. Bizio later disagreed with Melo's idea that the reddish substance was a product of fermentation. Bizio said, in his letter to Father Angelo Bellani, that Melo had based his assumption solely on the results of observations with the microscope. "[B]ut this method of inspection should be only accessory, when more exact methods are available which allow us to distinguish organic beings from ordinary matter." He continued, "I do not say that he was mistaken . . . but I do think that having a better method for elucidating the phenomenon, this ought to be preferred. . . .. I therefore chose another method, taking as my guide the original experiments of that very brilliant scholar, Spallanzani." *Ibid.*, 529, 533.

[305]The authorities felt "compelled to intervene because of the threatening behavior of the crowds who spoke of a punishment by God."E. Scheurlen, "Geschichtliche und experimentelle Studien," 6.

[306]Mary Hefferan, "A Comparative and Experimental Study," 314.

physicians and professors from the University of Padua to investigate.[307] With the introduction of these "scientists," the mystery surrounding the strange appearance of blood on foodstuffs began to unravel.

On August 10, the district administration requested that Vincenzo Sette examine the matter and furnish a report on the appearance of the "bloody polenta."[308] Sette was a surgeon and the district physician of Piove. He was described as "a uniquely enlightened man, to whom we owe the precise recording of this epidemic."[309]

When the commission from the University of Padua arrived at Legnaro on August 15, Sette already was prepared to present the results of his examinations.[310] Sette described Pittarello's kitchen as extremely damp—"The utensils are old and smell musty. There is little care for cleanliness in the entire area."[311] Sette subjected several specimens to microscopic examination, but with poor results because of the quality of his microscope. Based upon the observations he had made, however, he felt the phenomenon was a fungus[312] and named it *Zoagalactina imetrofa* ("living slime" "sitting on foods").[313] Although Sette's work was presented before the Athenæum at Treviso on the evening of April 28, 1820, it was not published until 1824.[314]

On August 20, Bartolomeo Bizio, a young pharmacist who studied the matter independently, observed the phenomenon, conducted two experiments, and found, as Sette had, that the "reddish matter of the polenta is produced in a very damp and warm atmosphere. If, in addition to this, there are putrid exhalations in the air, then it is still more conducive to the production of the phenomenon."[315] He felt that, although this was the first time the town of

---

[307]Breed and Breed, "Type Species of the Genus Serratia," 548.
[308]Scheurlen, "Geschichtliche und experimentelle Studien," 6.
[309]*Ibid.*
[310]Sette's examinations included a variety of foods which he had injected with the organism that was responsible for the reddening. These foods were polenta, rice soup, dried fish, fried chicken, boiled chicken, beef, and bread. *Ibid.*
[311]*Ibid.*, 7.
[312]Ehrenberg, "Observations," 351.
[313]Breed and Breed, "Type Species of the Genus Serratia," 548.
[314]*Ibid.*, 548-549.
[315]Bizio, "Lettera," 531.

Padua had observed such a phenomenon, the reddening of polenta had "manifested itself at other times in the warm season."[316] The reason that no one had ever noticed the phenomenon before the incident at Legnaro was, according to Bizio, that the whole surface of Pittarello's polenta was covered with a bright red color, while in the earlier cases, only small red spots appeared and went unobserved by the peasants.[317] Bizio found that the reddish substance had "seeds" that could germinate several years later. He performed several experiments with polenta and paper that had been soaked with the substance. New growth arose from the paper years later, suggesting that it — the paper — effectively could preserve the "seeds." He found that wood also could preserve these "seeds," which explained ". . . how in the home of Pittarello of Legnaro and other farmers the polenta became colored in the period of a few hours. Indeed, in addition to supplying the conditions necessary for the development of the plant, these farmers, without realizing it, were sowing it by placing the polenta on the same board and in the same cupboard. In such a case, the wood must receive some of the seeds, whereby the phenomenon was reproduced on the polenta that came in contact with it."[318] At the same time, Bizio noted that the conditions were such that they provided for the very noticeable effect.[319] Finally, Bizio thought that the phenomenon had been going on for years because "the causes that produce it and the substance on which it manifests itself show conclusively that the phenomenon must have had its origin at the time when corn meal or the flour of other cereal grains came to be used as food."[320]

Bizio decided to name this new genus *Serratia*, in memory of a celebrated physicist of the preceding generation, Serafino Serrati,[321] "whose memory is neglected so that we attribute to the foreigner that which exclusively belongs to us."[322] Bizio

---

[316] *Ibid.*, 527.

[317] *Ibid.*, 528.

[318] *Ibid.*, 541.

[319] *Ibid.*, 528.

[320] *Ibid.*, 529.

[321] *Ibid.*, 538. Bergey's Manual states: "Serratia named for Serafino Serrati, the Italian physicist who invented a steamboat at Florence before 1787." Robert S. Breed, E. G. D. Murray, Nathan R. Smith, *Bergey's Manual of Determinative Bacteriology*, 7th ed. (The Williams and Wilkins Co. Baltimore: Waverly Press, 1957), 360.

distinguished the genus *Serratia* with the species name, *marcescens*,[323] because "as it reaches maturity (which is effected in a few hours) it decays immediately, dissolving into a fluid and viscous matter which has a mucilaginous appearance."[324] On August 22, Bizio reported his findings to the governmental authorities, and, on August 24, he anonymously published the report of his experiments in the *Gazetta privilegiata di Venezia*.[325]

According to Breed and Breed,[326] "it was a result of fine work by Bizio and Sette at this time that it was first recognized that this phenomenon was caused by a living organism (fungus) similar in many of its manifestations to the little plant (alga) causing the red snow of the Alpine districts."[327]

That which Bartolomeo Bizio called *Serratia marcescens*, and Vincenzo Sette called *Zoagalactina imetrofa*, later became the object of intensive historical and biological studies by Christian Ehrenberg.[328] Ehrenberg had studied the history of similar outbreaks and had the advantage of studying the material under the improved microscopic lenses of the period.[329] In 1848, Ehrenberg's attention was called to red spots on a cooked potato from a home in Berlin where there had been a fatal case of cholera.[330] He performed several tests on the blood-producing organism and reported the results to the Berlin Academy of Sciences.[331] Ehrenberg remained thoroughly ignorant of Bizio's work and obtained a copy of Sette's report only after having arrived at his own conclusions. He regarded the phenomenon that he observed as identical with that seen by Sette. From his own microscopic examinations,

---

[322]Bizio, "*Lettera*," 538.

[323]*Marcescens*, the present participle of the Latin verb, *marcescere*, to wither or decay.

[324]*Ibid.*

[325]*Ibid.*, 530.

[326]Breed and Breed, "Type Species of the Genus Serratia," 547.

[327]*Ibid.*

[328]It was Ehrenberg's interest in the appearances of blood (about which he had written since 1830) and the historical record of blood appearing on bread (which he had never seen personally) that caused him to take an interest in the event in Berlin. *Ibid.*, 551.

[329]*Ibid.*, 552.

[330]*Ibid.*, 551.

[331]Ehrenberg, "Forsetzung der Beobachtung," "Observations," and "Fernere Mittheilungen."

however, he stated that the red material was made up of tiny, isolated, oval animalcules which he regarded as animals.[332] Because of his erroneous assumption that the bacterium in question was of animal nature and had a single polar flagellum, Ehrenberg assigned this organism to the animal kingdom and named it *Monas prodigiosa*,[333] although he knew that Sette had named it *Zoagalactina imetrofa* in 1824.[334] Nonetheless, Ehrenberg was the first to see the organism and to recognize it as the cause of the alleged blood formation.[335]

In his report to the Berlin Academy of Sciences, on October 16, 1848, Ehrenberg described three characteristics of the historical blood phenomena which are significant to the Mass of Bolsena: "1) the truly intensive blood color, 2) the rapid growth of the first round spots, and 3) the dripping effect, completely foreign to molds and fungi, with clear liquid, rather than a gel-like character."[336] Equally important was his observation that "in the days of the warm Scirocco wind, it was the most pronounced;" and that "by the end of September, the appearance stopped completely."[337]

Ehrenberg "was able readily to reproduce the appearance on host bread,"[338] and believed that whenever we read about bloody food, it

---

[332]Breed and Breed, "Type Series of the Genus Serratia," 552.

[333]Scheurlen, "Geschichtliche und experimentelle Studien," 9.

[334]"Thus, on Ehrenberg's shoulders lies the blame for confusing a situation that was already confused, in that Sette's name had been proposed in ignorance of the fact that Bizio had named the organism *Serratia marcescens* in the previous year." Robert S. and Margaret E. Breed, "The Genus Serratia Bizio," *Centralblatt für Bakteriologie, Parasitenkunde und Infektionskrankheiten* 71 (1927): 435. The problems of nomenclature are presented in detail in Breed and Breed, "The Type Species of the Genus Serratia," 545-557; and "Genus Serratia Bizio," 435-440. In 1918, Robert Earle Buchanan, a professor of bacteriology at Iowa State College, and a bacteriologist at the Ames, Iowa, Agricultural Experiment Station, reached the conclusion that the proper name was *Serratia marcescens* Bizio. After reviewing the work of Bizio and Sette, Breed and Breed, in 1923, supported Buchanan and recommended including *Serratia marcescens* in Bergey's *Manual of Determinative Bacteriology*. Breed and Breed, "Type Species of the Genus Serratia," 545.

[335]Breed and Breed, "Type Species of the Genus Serratia," 551-552.

[336]Ehrenberg, "Forsetzung der Beobachtung," 359.

[337]*Ibid.*, 356.

[338]*Ibid.*, 362. Ehrenberg said that prodigiosus "is most beautiful on cooked rice. In covered containers and plates it develops surprisingly quickly in warm air." *Ibid.*

was the organism, *Monas prodigiosa*, that produced the "blood." Scheurlen supported this belief, because "we do not know of a second microorganism which produces, under the circumstances present,. . . such a deceptive blood red as the *prodigiosus* does."[339]

In Scheurlen's examination of the history of the organism, he discovered that hosts were made of a "particularly agreeable amylum-rich [starchy] and acid-free medium," thereby explaining the increase in the number of miracles of transubstantiation during the Middle Ages.[340] He stated further that, because of the host's dry condition, when they were moistened they supported "the growth of a bacteria, and, since they usually [were] always stored in a dry place, it was necessary to reach this condition to have a special coincidence, for which in this unhygienic age there was ample opportunity."[341] These circumstances, combined with the superstitions of the time, contributed to elevating this natural occurrence to the status of a phenomenon.[342]

Scheurlen made an important observation about the role of temperature, climate, and environment in furthering the growth of the organism: "The epidemic lasted the entire period of the hot Scirocco wind. When [the wind] abated at the end of August and a dry Northeasterly wind came, it abated only to spread again during the occurrence of the hot, damp Southeasterly wind. Only at the end of September did it stop entirely."[343] High temperatures

---

[339]Scheurlen, "Geschichtliche und Experimentelle Studien," 2, translated by Brigitte Cullen. The chemical nature of bacterial pigment has been discussed at length by: F. Cohn, "Untersuchungen über Bakterien, *"Beiträge zur Biologie der Pflanzen*, Bd. I. Heft 2. (1872) 155 ff.; A. B. Griffiths, "Sur la matiere colorante du Monas prodigiosa," *Comptes rendus de l'Academie de Science*. CXV. (1892) 321; E. Kraft, "Beiträge zur Biologie des B. prodigiosus und zum chemischen Verhalten seines Pigments," Ph.D. diss., Würzburg (1902); W. W. Rosenberg, "Beiträge zur Kenntnis der Bakterienfarbstoffe, insbes. der Gruppe des *B. prodigiosus*," Ph.D. diss.,Würzburg (1899); Scheurlen, "Geschichtliche und experimentelle Studien," 1; P. Schneider, "Die Bedeutung der Bakterienfarbstoffe für die Unterscheidung der Arten," Ph.D. diss., Basel (1894); J. Schroeter, "Über einige durch Bakterien gebildete Pigmente", *Beiträge zur Biologie der Pflanzen*, Bd. I. Heft 2. (1872) p. 109.
[340]Scheurlen, "Geschichtliche und experimentelle Studien," 4, translated by Brigitte Cullen.
[341]*Ibid.*, translated by Brigitte Cullen.
[342]*Ibid.*
[343]*Ibid.*, 7, translated by Brigitte Cullen.

combined with high humidity in the air of a damp, unventilated room, were appropriate conditions under which the epidemics of *prodigiosus* [*Serratia marcescens*] appeared.[344]

As shown below, the conditions present during the Mass of Bolsena compared closely to those observed in Padua and those that were necessary for the propagation of *Serratia marcescens*:

1) *Manifested in putrid exhalations and epidemics.* Bolsena is located on the north-eastern shore of the Lake of Bolsena. The outlet to the lake is the river Marta, which flows for approximately thirty kilometers to the Tyrrhenian Sea below Corneto, at Porto San Clementino. "In winter, the small seaport is alive and busy; in summer the maremme[345] fever empties it. The shores of the Lake of Bolsena suffer from the same dread enemy."[346]

2) *Manifested in unhygienic surroundings.* The Mass of Bolsena was celebrated in 1263, at a time when the concept of the proper storage of food was unknown.[347]

3) *Manifested in damp and unventilated surroundings.* The Mass of Bolsena was celebrated in a "gloomy" chapel in the church of Santa Cristina.[348]

4) *Manifested during the summer months.* The Mass of Bolsena was celebrated in the month of June.[349]

5) *Manifested during warm, damp weather.* Bolsena was subject to the warm, moist, southwesterly Scirocco winds.

6) *Manifested readily on amylum-rich [starchy] and acid free medium.* Blood appeared on a host during the celebration of mass.[350] Sacramental bread is rich in starch and poor in acids.[351]

---

[344] *Ibid.*, 16, translated by Brigitte Cullen. In reference to the recorded observations of large and small epidemics, Scheurlen stated that "whenever a date is given for the appearance of *prodigiosus*, it is in the months of July, August, and September." *Ibid.* [translated by Brigitte Cullen].

[345] The *maremme* (from the Latin root, *mare*: the sea) are low, unhealthful, but fertile marshy lands near the sea, especially in Italy.

[346] Ayscough, *Saints and Places*, 173.

[347] Ayscough, *Saints and Places*, 166-167; Ehrenberg, "Observations," 361; Lazzarani, *Miracolo di Bolsena*, 39-41; *Dictionnaire d'Histoire et de Géographie Ecclésiastiques* (Paris: Librairie Letouzey et Ane. 1937) IX:680; and Gaetano Moroni, *Dizionario di Erudizione Storico-Ecclesiastica* (Venezia: Tipografia Emiliana, 1840) V:312.

[348] Ayscough, *Saints and Places*, 167.

[349] A. Achilli and Q. Galli, *Riti, Feste Primaverili*, 15.

[350] Lazzarani, *Miracolo di Bolsena*, 1-3, 23.

7) *Manifested as a blood-red liquid.* The blood was sufficiently liquid to stain the altar linen.[352]

8) *Manifests itself at other times.* In 1171, in the city of Ferrara, blood appeared on a host during the celebration of mass on Easter Sunday.[353]

Since the conditions at the Mass of Bolsena closely paralleled those described by Bizio, Sette, and Ehrenberg, the following experiments were conducted to test whether blood appearances were reproducible in a contemporary laboratory setting. The media selected for the experiments were polenta and sacramental bread.[354]

On May 20, 1993, a small amount of nutrient broth containing *Serratia marcescens* was transferred aseptically to a petri dish which contained fresh polenta. The petri dish then was placed in an incubator that was set at 30° C. On the following day, the polenta was covered partially with a light red growth.[355] By the second day, the growth had become blood red. Subsequently, with each passing day, the growth became a darker more intense red.[356] It was evident that *Serratia marcescens* grew quite well on polenta at 30° C. The cultures survived several days before desiccating.

On June 22, 1993, a similar experiment was performed to see if *Serratia marcescens* would produce similar results on sacramental bread (priest's hosts). A small amount of *Serratia marcescens* was then aseptically transferred directly onto each of the priest's hosts. The petri dishes were then placed into a plastic bag which contained damp paper towels—in order to maintain the moist environment that is favorable to the growth of *Serratia marcescens*. The cultures were incubated at 30°C. As was the case with the previous

---

[351]Mary Hefferan, "A Comparative and Experimental Study," 314.

[352]Ayscough, *Saints and Places*, 166 and Lazzarani, *Miracolo di Bolsena*, 1-3, 23.

[353]Achilli and Galli, *Riti, Feste Primaverili*, 77.

[354]The polenta was an Italian product produced by Fattorie & Pandea [Quaker-Chiari & Forti S.p.A. (Societa per Azioni), Parma, Italy]. The sacramental hosts were supplied by Christian Wolf, Inc.,(Troy, Illinois) and were fine traditional hosts made of wheat flour and water. The Biology Department of George Mason University provided the *Serratia marcescens* and the laboratory facilities and equipment.

[355][Figure 1, a photographic illustration with the caption, "Serratia on Polenta (24 Hours)," was inserted here.] [*our note*]

[356][Figure 2, a photographic illustration with the caption, "Serratia on Polenta (72 Hours)," was inserted here.] [*our note*]

experiment, within three days, the cultures of *Serratia marcescens* had become a dark, intense red — indeed blood-like.[357] The colonies of *Serratia marcescens* on the modern host are quite in keeping with the way in which Raphael illustrated the miracle in his famous fresco.[358] His understanding of the apperance may have been based on a description of the event published in 1466.[359]

The photographs of these experiments reveal an appearance that is identical to that in Padua and Bolsena. Both the polenta and the sacramental bread produced a rich blood-like growth which very easily could be mistaken for blood.[360]

The results of the contemporary experiment, the historical record, and the research conducted by Bizio, Sette, and Ehrenberg, all serve as circumstantial evidence to support the conclusion that the miracle of the Mass of Bolsena was simply another manifestation of *Serratia marcescens*. The truth of this assertion can be obtained only by testing the desiccated DNA of the corporal and purificators from Bolsena currently located in the cathedral of Orvieto.

---

[357][Figure 3, a photographic illustration with the caption, "Serratia on Sacramental Bread," was inserted here.] [*our note*]

[358][Figure 4, a photograph of the fresco by Raphael in the Stanza d'Eliodoro, in the Vatican, with the caption, "Raphael's 'Mass of Bolsena,'" was inserted here.] [*our note*]

[359]See Pastor, *Geschichte der Päpste*, III:1030, n. 2.

[360]The differences in the color of the bacterial pigment apparent in the photographs are attributable to the influences of preliminary cultivation, reaction of the media, and ages of the two cultures used. For a more complete discussion of pigmentation in bacterial cultures, see Mary Hefferan, "A Comparative and Experimental Study," 462.

Appendix I: Chronology of Appearances on Food

Date Location	Time of Year	Type of Event	
530 (bc) (Pythagoras)		Beans	
332 (bc) Rome, Italy		Unknown	
332 (bc) Tyre [Soûr, Lebanon]		Bread	
91 (bc) Aretium [Arezzo, Italy]		Bread	
100 (Pythagoras)		Beans	
260 (Pythagoras)		Beans	
583 Tours, France		Bread	
1004 Duchy of Namur [Belgium]		Bread	
1091 Zweifalten [Germany]		Bread	
1093 Namur [Belgium]		Bread	
1104 Speier [Spier, Netherlands]		Bread	
1163 La Rochelle [France]		Bread	
1169 Als [Denmark]		Host	
1171 Ferrara, Italy	Spring	Host	
1192 Erfurt in Thüringen [Germany]		Host	
1198 Rosetum [Germany]		Host	
1199 Augsburg, Germany		Host	
1200 Halle, Germany		Host	
1201 fenshagen [Germany]		Host	Stef-
1218 Cologne [Germany]		Host	
1233 *Not specified*		Host	
1239 Valencia [Spain]		Host	
1247 Beelitz [Germany]		Host	
1249 Zehdenick [Germany]		Host	
1251 *Not specified*		Bread	
1264 Bolsena [Italy]	June	Host	
1290 Paris [France]	Summer	Host	
1296 Rotil [unknown]		Host	
1299 Röttingen [Germany]		Host	
1330		Host	

296

Location / Date	Item	
Güstrow [Germany]		
1338	Host	
Polka [unknown]		
1355	Host	
Krakow [Germany]		
1369 June	Host	
Brussels [Belgium]		
1379 July	Host	
Brussels [Belguim]		
1383 August	Host	
Wilsnak [Germany]		
1399	Host	
Posen [Poznan, Poland]		
1489	Host	
Cologne [Germany]		
1492 July	Host	
Sternberg [Germany]		
1492	Host	Water-
sleben in Stollberg		
1503	Bread	
Germany		
1503	Bread	
Germany		
1510 Summer	Host	
Berlin [Germany]		
1550	Bread	
Siena [Italy]		
1555	Bread	
Neuendorf [Germany]		
1556 July	Bread	
Unknown		
1556	Bread	
Frankfort an der Oder [Germany]		
1583	Bread	
Teltow [Germany]		
1616	Food	
Wurtzen in Meißen [Germany]		
1617	Bread	
Mähren [Czechoslovakia]		
1618	Corn meal	
St. Palais [France]		
1627	Bread	
Brieg [Brzeg, Poland]		
1630	Bread	
Frankfort an der Oder [Germany]		
1634	Meat	
Lützen [Poland]		
1634	Meat	
Eulenberg [Germany]		
1651	Bread	
Birchheim [unknown]		
1652 July	Meat	
Leipzig [Germany]		
1662	Bread	
Mark Brandenburg [Germany]		
1667	Bread	
Eiderstedt [Germany]		
1667	Bread	
Flensburg [Germany]		
1693 July	Cake	
Stennwitz [Germany]		
1694	Poppy Cake	
Cüstrin [Germany]		
1792 September	Bread	
Chalons [France]		
1819 August	Polenta	
Legnaro [Italy]		
1820-24	unknown	
Padua [Italy]		

1821	August	Bread	Ger-
hardtsmühle [Germany]			
1832	Summer	Bread	Phila-
delphia, Pa.			
1843		Bread	
France			
1846	September	unknown	
Hamburg [Germany]			
1846	September	unknown	
Berlin [Germany]			
1847		unknown	
Breslau [Poland]			
1847		Bread	
Algiers [Algeria]			
1848	September	Potato	
Berlin [Germany]			
1849	Summer	unknown	
India			
1849	September	unknown	
Halle [Germany]			
1851	August	Bread	
Berlin [Germany]			
1852	July	Chicken	
Rouen [France]			
1866	August	Bread	
Berlin [Germany]			
1872	September	unknown	
Danzig [Gdansk, Poland]			
1874	July	unknown	
Danzig [Gdansk, Poland]			
1910-11		Host	
Naples [Italy]			

Select Bibliography

Achilli, A. and Q. Galli. *Riti Feste Primaverili e il Lago di Bolsena Atti del Convegno Tenutosi a Bolsena il 7-8 Giugno 1986.* Volume 6 of *Vita Cultura Storia Delle Classi Subalterne Dell' Alto Lazio.* Viterbo: [s.n.] Tipolitografia Quatrini. 1988.

Ayscough, John. *Saints and Places.* New York: Benziger Brothers, 1912.

Baedeker, Karl. *Central Italy and Rome.* 15th ed. New York: Charles Scribner's Sons, 1909: 100-105.

Barbieri, Pietro and Ulisse Pucci, eds. *Guide to Catholic Italy.* Rome: Holy Year 1950 Publishing Co., ED.A.S., 1950.

Bellori, Giovanni Pietro. *Descrizione delle Immagini Dipinte da Raffaelle d'Urbino nel Palazzo Vaticano, e nella Farnesina alla Lungara: con alcuni ragionamenti in onore delle sue opere, e della pittura, e scultura, di Gio. Pietro Bellori. In questa nuova edizione accrescuita anche della vita de medesimo Raffaelle. descritta da Giorgio Vasari.* Rome: Appresso gli eredi del q. Gio. Lorenzo Barbiellini, 1751.

Bevan, Edwyn Robert. "Alexander III." *Encyclopædia Britannica.* 11th ed. (New York: Encyclopædia Britannica Company, 29 volumes, 1910), 563.

[Bizio, Bartolomeo]. *Nuovo Osservatore Veneziano,* August 24, 1819, no. 101, 4.

_____. "Trovata della precisa cagione, che produce il fenomeno del superficiale coloramento in rossa della polenta." *Gazzeta privilegiata di Venezia,* 24 August 1819, no. 190, 3-4.

Bizio, Bartolomeo. "Lettera di Bartolomeo Bizio al chiarissimo canonico Angelo Bellani sopra il fenomeno della polenta porporina." *Biblioteca Italiano o sia Giornale di Letteratura, Scienze e Arti.* 30 (1823): 275-295. Translated by C. P. Merlino, in *Journal of Bacteriology* 9 (1924): 527-543.

_____. "Del fenomeno della polenta porporina." *Oposculi Chimicofisici,* Tomo 1, Parte 2, Richerche e spiegazioni di alcuni fenomeni, Articolo 1 (1827): 261-298, Giuseppe Antonelli, Venezia.

Breed, Robert S. and Margaret E. Breed. "The Genus Serratia Bizio." *Centralblatt für Bakteriologie, Parasitenkunde, und Infektionskrankheiten* 71 (1927): 435-440.

_____. "The Type Species of the Genus Serratia, Commonly Known as Bacillus prodigiosus." *Journal of Bacteriology* 9 (1924): 545-557.

Breed, Robert S., E. G. D. Murray, Nathan R. Smith. *Bergey's Manual of Determinative Bacteriology.* 7th ed. The Williams and Wilkins Co. Baltimore: Waverly Press, 1957.

Bulloch, William. *The History of Bacteriology.* Oxford: Oxford University Press; reprint, Dover Publications, Inc., 1979.

The Catholic Encyclopedia. Vol. XI (New York: Robert Appleton Company, 15 volumes,1911), 331-332.

Cherubino, Laertii. *Magnum Bullarum Romanum, a beato Leone Magno usque ad S. D. N. Benedictum XIII.* Luxembourg: Andreæ Chevalier, 1727.

Cohn, Ferdinand. "Untersuchungen über Bakterien." *Beiträge zur Biologie der Pflanzen,* Bd. I. Heft 2. (1872): 127-224.

Cundall, Joseph, Ed. *The Great Works of Raphael Sanzio of Urbino; A Series of Thirty Photographs from best Engravings of his most celebrated Paintings; with Descriptions, translated from Passavant's "Rafael von Urbino und sein Vater;" Vasari's Life of Raphael, translated by Mrs. Jonathon Foster: and an Appendix, containing a classified list of the principal paintings of the artist.* London: Bell and Daldy, 1870.

Curtius, Quintus. *History of Alexander.* Translated by John C. Rolfe. Cambridge: Harvard University Press, 1971.

Dictionnaire d'Histoire et de Géographie Ecclésiastiques. (1937), vol. 9, p. 680, s. v. "Bolsena."

Ehrenberg, Christian Gottfried. "Forsetzung der Beobachtung des sogenannten Blutes im Brode als Monas prodigiosa." *Bericht über die zur Bekanntmachung geeigneten Verhandlungen der Königl. Preuß. Akademie der Wissenschaften zu Berlin* (16 October 1848) [1849]: 354-362.

_____. (Observations on the So-called Bleeding Bread caused by *Monas prodigiosa*). *Bericht über die zur Bekanntmachung geeigneten Verhandlungen der Königl. Preuß. Akademie der Wissenschaften zu Berlin* (26 October 1848) [1849]: 349-353.

_____. "Fernere Mittheilungen über Monas prodigiosa oder die Purpurmonade." *Bericht über die zur Bekanntmachung geeigneten Verhandlungen der Königl. Preuß. Akademie der Wissenschaften zu Berlin* (15 March 1849) [1850]: 101-116.

_____. "Höchst wahrscheinlicher Grund d. Verbotes d. Bohnengenusses bei d. Pythagoräern." *Bericht über die zur Bekanntmachung geeigneten Verhandlungen der Königl. Preuß. Akademie der Wissenschaften zu Berlin* (17 January 1850) [1851]: 5-9.

_____. "Eine Centurie historischer Nachträge zu den blutfarbigen Meteoren und sogenannten Prodigien." *Bericht über die zur Bekanntmachung geeigneten Verhandlungen der Königl. Preuß. Akademie der Wissenschaften zu Berlin* (27 June 1850) [1851]: 215-246.

Forcilioni, Antonio [St. Antonius of Florence]. *Chronica.* III., tit. XIX., c. 13.

Fortineau, M. Louis. "L'Erythrobacillus pyosepticus." *Comptes Rendus Hebdomadaires des Séances et Mémoires de la Société de la Biologie* 58 (1905): 104-106.

Gascoigne, Robert Mortimer. *A Chronology of the History of Science, 1450-1900.* New York: Garland Publishing, Inc., 1987.

Griffiths, A. B. "Sur la matiere colorante du Monas prodigiosa," *Comptes rendus de l'Academie de Science.* CXV. (1892): 321.

Hefferan, Mary. "A Comparative and Experimental Study of Bacilli Producing Red Pigment." *Centralblatt für Bakteriologie, Parasitenkunde und Infektionskrankheiten* 11 (1903): 311-317, 397-404, 456-475, 520-540.

Howard, Arthur V. *Chamber's Dictionary of Scientists.* London: W. & R. Chambers, 1951.

Index Biologorum: Investigatores, Laboratoria, Periodica. Edited by Gottwald C. Hirsch. Berlin: J. Springer, 1928.

Jahn, Ilse. "Ehrenberg, Christian Gottfried." in *Dictionary of Scientific Biography.* New York: Charles Scribner's Sons, 1981, pp. 288-292.

Kraft, E. "Beiträge zur Biologie des B. prodigiosus und zum chemischen Verhalten seines Pigments." Ph. D. dissertation, Würzburg (1902).

Lasance, F. X. *The New Roman Missal.* New York: Benziger Brothers, Inc., 1950.

Lazzarani, Andrea. *Miracolo di Bolsena: Testimonianze e Documenti dei Secoli XIII e XIV.* Roma: Edizioni di Storia e Letteratura, 1952.

Livius, Titus. *Livy, with an English Translation.* Volume IV. Translated by B. O. Foster. Cambridge, Mass.: Harvard University Press, 14 vols., 1963.

Locy, William Albert. *Biology and It's Makers.* New York: H. Holt and Company, 1915.

Lucian. "Sale of Creeds." *The Works of Lucian of Samosata.* Translated by H. W. Fowler and F. G. Fowler. Oxford: Clarendon Press, 1949.

Luciani Samosatensis: *Opera Græce et Latine.* Vol. 3. Biponti: Typographia Societatis, 1790.

Lycosthenes, Conrad [Conrad Wolffhart]. *Prodigiorum ac Ostentorum Chronicon.* Basileæ: per Henricum Petri, 1557.

Melo, Pietro. "Memoria sulla polenta rossa." *Giornale dell'italiana letteratura del Da Rio* 49 (1819): 333-341.

Moroni, Gaetano. *Dizionario di Erudizione Storico-Ecclesiastica.* Venezia: Tipografia Emiliana, 1840, vol. 5, p. 312, *s.v.* "Bolsena."

Orosius, Paulus. *The Seven Books of History against the Pagans.* Translated by Roy J. Deferrari. Washington, D.C.: Catholic University Press, 1964.

Pastor, Ludwig von. *Die Fresken der Sixtinischen Kapelle und Raffaels Fresken in den Stanzen und den Loggien des Vaticans.* Freiburg im Breisgau: Herder & Co. G.M.B.H., 1925.

_____. *Geschichte der Päpste seit dem Ausgang des Mittelalters: mit Benutzung des Päpstlichen Geheim-Archives und vieler anderer Archive bearbeitet.* Vol. 3, Part 2. Freiburg im Breisgau: Herder & Co. G.M.B.H., 1926.

Redig De Campos, D[eoclecio]. *Rafael in den Stanzen*. Trans. into German by Dora Mitsky. 2nd Edition. Milano: Aldo Martello Editore, [1971].

Rosenberg, W. W. *Beiträge zur Kenntnis der Bakterienfarbstoffe, insbes. der Gruppe des B. prodigiosus*. Ph.D. diss. Wuerzburg (1899).

Scheurlen, E. "Geschichtliche und experimentelle Studien über den Prodigiosus." *Archiv für Hygiene* (1896): 1-31.

Schmidt, Johs. and Frederik Weis. *Die Bakterien*. Jena: Verlag von Gustav Fischer, 1902.

Schneider, P. *Die Bedeutung der Bakterienfarbstoffe für die Unterscheidung der Arten*. Ph. D. diss. Basel (1894).

Schroeter, J. "Über einige durch Bakterien gebildete Pigmente." *Beiträge zur Biologie der Pflanzen*, Bd. I. Heft 2. (1872): 109-126.

Sette, Vincenzo. "Memoria storico-naturale sull'arrossimento straordinario di alcune sostanze alimentose osservato nella provincia di Padova l'anno MDCCCXIX." *Lettera all'Ateneo di Treviso nella sera 28 Aprile 1820*. Alvisopoli, Venezia.

Spica, P. "Sulla materia colorante prodotta dal Micrococcus prodigiosus. Rivendicazione di priorita par Bartolomeo Bizio." *Atti del Reale Istituto Veneto di Scienze, Lettere ed Arti* 59, Parte 2, (1899-1900): 1025-1031.

Stone, Darwell. *A History of the Doctrine of the Holy Eucharist*. London: Longmans, Green, and Co., 1909.

World Who's Who in Science: A Biographical Dictionary of Notable Scientists from Antiquity to the Present. Edited by Allen G. Debus. Chicago, Illinois: Marquis-Who's Who, Incorporated, 1968.

Appendix C

Logical Fallacies That You Must Avoid in Analysis and Argument[361]

Of course, in daily speech, people use the word "fallacy" to refer to mistaken beliefs, as well as to the faulty reasoning that leads to those beliefs. In logic, the term is restricted specifically to a form of technically incorrect argument—especially if the argument appears to be valid or convincing. So, for the purposes of this discussion, a fallacy is some element of a supposedly-logical argument which looks correct, but one which you can see to be incorrect when you examine it more carefully. If you will learn to recognize logical fallacies, you can avoid being misled by them—which is one of the greatest mental assets of the educated person.

Below is a list of some common fallacies, and also a short discussion of some of the rhetorical devices that people often use in debate. The list is not exhaustive, but it does cover those fallacies which are the most common. The best general discussion of fallacies, from the point of view of the serious researcher and writer, we believe to be that in David Hackett Fischer's *Historian's Fallacies*, which we discussed above.[362]

ANECDOTAL EVIDENCE

One of the simplest fallacies is to rely on anecdotal evidence. For example:

> *"Violent crime is increasing, because you hear much more about it on the news these days."*

It is quite valid for you to use a personal experience to illustrate a point; but anecdotes, of themselves, do not prove anything to

---

[361]The following text is modified from the text of part 3 of the frequently-asked-questions [FAQ] for the alt.atheism USENET newsgroup. The version upon which we base this text is the revision of November 14, 1996.
[362]The Nizkor Project, at the URL: http://www.nizkor.org, has another excellent list of logical fallacies.

anyone. Your friend may say that she met George Washington, general and first president of the United States, in her local supermarket, but those who have not had the same experience will need much more than your friend's anecdotal evidence to persude them that this event actually occurred.

ARGUMENTUM AD BACULUM / APPEAL TO FORCE

You commit an APPEAL TO FORCE when you resort to force, or the threat of force, in you attempt to push others to accept your conclusion. This fallacy is often used by politicians, and can be summarized as "might makes right." The threat does not necessarily have to come directly from the person who is making the argument. For example:

> "... Thus, there is ample proof of the truth of the capitalist system. All those who refuse to accept that truth will, inevitably, collapse into ruin."

> "... In any case, I know your phone number and I know where you live."

ARGUMENTUM AD HOMINEM

The phrase ARGUMENTUM AD HOMINEM literally means "an argument directed at the man." There are two types of this false argument, *abusive* and *circumstantial*. If you argue against some assertion by attacking the person who made the assertion, then you have committed the *abusive* form of the ARGUMENTUM AD HOMINEM. A personal attack is not a valid argument, because the truth of an assertion does not depend on the virtues of the person who asserts it. For example:

> "Catholicism is an evil form of Christianity. It was the creed of Adolf Hitler."

Sometimes, in a court of law, attorneys will try to cast doubt on the testimony of a witness. For example, the prosecution may show that a particular witness is a known perjurer. This is a valid way to reduce the credibility of the testimony given by that witness, and is not a form of the ARGUMENTUM AD HOMINEM. However, casting that doubt does not demonstrate, in itself, that the witness's testimony is false.

If you argue that someone should accept the truth of an assertion because of that person's particular circumstances, then you have committed the *circumstantial* form of the ARGUMENTUM AD HOMINEM. For example:

> *"It is perfectly acceptable to kill animals for food. How can you argue otherwise when you are quite happy to wear leather shoes?"*

This also is an abusive charge of inconsistency, which is used as an excuse for dismissing an opponent's argument. The fallacy also can be used to reject a particular conclusion. For example:

> *"Of course, you argue that reducing the government's expenditure for welfare for children is a bad thing. You receive government benefits."*

But, of course, so does every person who takes a deduction from her income tax for the interest she pays on her mortgage. This particular form of ARGUMENTUM AD HOMINEM, when you allege that someone is rationalizing a conclusion for selfish reasons, also is known as *"poisoning the well."*

ARGUMENTUM AD IGNORANTIAM

The phrase ARGUMENTUM AD IGNORANTIAM means "an argument from ignorance." You commit this fallacy when you argue that something must be true because it has not been proved to be false; or the corrolary. that something must be false, because it has not been proved to be true. Note carefully, however, that this is not the same as assuming that something is false until it has been proved to be true—that is a basic principle of both the scientific and historical methods of research. For example:

"Of course, the Bible is true. Nobody can prove otherwise."

"Of course, telepathy does not exist. Nobody has produced any proof that they are real."

Note that this fallacy does not apply in American courts of law, where you are supposed to be presumed innocent, until you are proven to be guilty.

Also, in both scientific and historical investigation, if you know that some event, as described or defined, would produce certain evidence of its having occurred, you can use the absence of such evidence validly to infer that the event did not, in fact, occur in the manner in which it is defined or described. For example:

"A world-engulfing flood, as described in the Bible, would require an enormous volume of water to be present on the earth. The earth does not have a tenth as much water as would be needed, even if we count that which is frozen into ice at the poles. Therefore, the flood which is described in the Bible, if it occurred, must have been one of smaller proportions than the Biblical description states."

In the correct application of the scientific and historical methods of research, **we can assume** validly that the lack of any evidence that something did occur is an indication that it did not occur, but **we cannot conclude**, with absolute certainty, that it did not occur.

See also SHIFTING THE BURDEN OF PROOF.

ARGUMENTUM AD MISERICORDIAM

This fallacy also is called the *Appeal to Pity*, or *Special Pleading*. You commit this error when you appeal to pity for the sake of getting your conclusion accepted by others. For example:

"I did not murder my mother and father! Please do not find me guilty. I am suffering enough because I am an orphan."

ARGUMENTUM AD POPULUM

This is known also as *Appealing to the Gallery*, or *Appealing to the People*. You commit this fallacy if you attempt to win acceptance of an assertion by appealing to a large group of people. This form of fallacy is often characterized by emotive language. For example:

> *"Pornography must be banned. It is violence against women."*

> *"For thousands of years people people believed that comets were harbingers of disaster. This belief had a great effect on their lives. What more evidence do you need that comets are, indeed, harbingers of disaster? Would you tell all those people of the past that they were all mistaken fools?"*

ARGUMENTUM AD NUMERUM

This fallacy is related closely to the ARGUMENTUM AD POPULUM. You commit this fallacy when you assert that the more people who support or believe a proposition, the more likely it is that the particular proposition is true. For example:

> *"The vast majority of people in this country believe that capital punishment deters crime. To suggest that it does not, in the face of so much evidence, is ridiculous."*

> *"Thousands of people believe in pyramid power, so there must be something to it."*

ARGUMENTUM AD VERECUNDIAM

You commit this fallacy, which also is called the *Appeal to Authority*, when you use an overt admiration of a famous person to try to win support for an assertion. For example:

> *"Isaac Newton was a genius and he believed in alchemy. Therefore, serious scientists should pay more attention to alchemy today."*

This line of argument is not always completely false. For example, it may be relevant to refer to a widely-regarded authority in a particular field, if you are discussing material from that subject. For example, we can distinguish quite clearly between:

> *"Stephen Hawking has concluded that black holes give off radiation."*

and

> *"Sir Roger Penrose has concluded that it is impossible to build an intelligent computer."*

Stephen Hawking is the physicist who elucidated the whole general nature of black holes for us, so we can reasonably expect his opinions on the radiation of energy from black holes to be informed ones.[363] Sir Roger Penrose is a mathematician, so you are entitled to question whether he is or is not well-qualified to speak on the subject of intelligent machines.[364]

---

[363]Stephen William Hawking was born January 8, 1942, at Oxford. He received his B. A. from University College, Oxford, in 1962, and his Ph. D. from Trinity Hall, Cambridge, in 1966. Before he had completed his doctorate, he contracted amyotrophic lateral sclerosis, the incurable degenerative neuromuscular condition that often is called Lou Gerhig's Disease. In spite of it, he has become perhaps the most distinguished physicist of the later twentieth century. Hawking works primarily on the physics of black holes. In 1974, he suggested that, in accordance with the predictions of quantum theory, black holes emit subatomic particles until their energy is spent and then they finally explode.

In the same year, he became one of the youngest fellows in the history of the Royal Society. In 1977, he was appointed professor of gravitational physics at Cambridge and, two years later, he became the Lucasian Professor of Mathematics at Cambridge. The last occasion on which he was able to write with his own hand was his phenomenal exercise of will in signing the register of Lucasian professors, just below the signature of Isaac Newton, his predecessor.

[364]Sir Roger Penrose was born August 8, 1931, at Colchester. He received his Ph. D. in algebraic geometry from Cambridge in 1957. Since 1973, he has been the Rouse-Ball Professor of Mathematics at Oxford. He was knighted in 1994. In 1969, while working with Stephen Hawking, he demonstrated that all matter in a black hole collapses to a geometric point in space where the mass is compressed to both an infinite density and a zero volume.

ARGUMENTUM AD ANTIQUITATEM

You commit this fallacy when you assert that something is right or good simply because it is old or traditional—because "that's the way it has always been." It is the opposite of the ARGUMENTUM AD NOVITATEM. For example:

> *"For many hundreds of years, many people have believed that the number thirteen was an unlucky one. It must, therefore, be right to believe that, since that belief has persisted for all of that time, even in the face of mockery and derision."*

ARGUMENTUM AD NOVITATEM

This is the opposite of the ARGUMENTUM AD ANTIQUITATEM. You commit this fallacy when you assert that something is more correct simply because it is new, or newer, than something else.

ARGUMENTUM AD CRUMENAM

In committing this fallacy, you assert that money is a criterion of correctness, so that those with more money are more likely to be right. It is the opposite of the ARGUMENTUM AD LAZARUM.

Many people, in spite of the obvious fallaciousness of this argument, find that it is one that is very easy to accept. In the later nineteenth century, this fallacy was often advanced as a reason for electing millionaires to the Senate and the House of Representatives, simply because they were millionaires. It was in this way that men such as Leland Stanford[365] and George Hearst[366]

---

[365]Leland Stanford was born in Watervliet, New York, on March 9, 1824. He studied law and began to practice in 1848 in Port Washington, Wisconsin. In 1852, he moved west and opened a general store at Michigan Bluff, California. Three years later, he moved to Sacramento and began to built a mercantile business on a large scale. His wealth brought him access to political power, and he served as governor of California from 1861 to 1863. He branched out into railroading, and became one of the "big four" who constructed the Central Pacific Railroad, the western half of the first transcontinental line. He was elected to the Senate in 1885, and reëlected in 1891—serving from March 4, 1885, to his death, June 21, 1893. Today, he is perhaps best remembered as the founder of Leland Stanford, Junior, University, in Palo Alto, California, which he did as a

came into the Senate. Thus, in the Fiftieth and Fifty-first Congresses, California was represented in the Senate by the two men who were, almost certainly, the two wealthiest men in the state.

ARGUMENTUM AD LAZARUM

In this fallacy, you advance the assumption that someone who is poor, or whose origins were in poverty, is sounder or more virtuous than someone else who is wealthier. This fallacy is the opposite of the ARGUMENTUM AD CRUMENAM.

Again, this fallacious argument is one which many people find easy to accept. It is often advanced in politcal rhetoric to support the candidacy of a person of humble or poor origins over that of an opponent who comes from a wealthier background. In this form, it is the fallacy that the "log cabin" candidate is, by virtue of being just that, superior to the "silver spoon" candidate.

ARGUMENTUM AD NAUSEAM

This is the incorrect belief that an assertion is more likely to be true, or is more likely to be accepted as true, the more often it is heard. So, in an ARGUMENTUM AD NAUSEAM you assert something;

---

memorial to his dead son.

[366]George Hearst was born near Sullivan, Franklin County, Missouri, on September 3, 1820. After he was graduated from the Franklin County Mining School in 1838, his career was uneventful until he moved to California, in 1850. Within a decade, first in Eldorado County, and then in Nevada County, he elevated himself through mining and ranching to a position of tremendous wealth. He moved to San Francisco in 1862 and served in the California State Assembly in 1865 and 1866. In 1880, he became the owner of the San Francisco Examiner, a newspaper which he gave to his son, William Randolph Hearst, six years later—and which the younger man turned into the nucleus of the great Hearst chain of newspapers and magazines. George Hearst was unsuccessful as the Democratic candidate for governor of California in 1882. Early in 1886, however, he was appointed to the Senate to fill the vacancy that was caused by the death of John F. Miller. He served from March 23, 1886, to August 4, 1886, when he gave place to Abram P. Williams, who was chosen in a special election to fill the seat. His taste for being a senator was whetted, however, and he was elected in his own right when he challenged Williams in the following general election. He served agin in the Senate from March 4, 1887, to his death, in Washington, D. C., on February 28, 1891.

constantly and repeatedly, until your readers or auditors are, literally, nauseated when they read it or hear it again. When you use this fallacy, you hope that your readers or hearers will accept your argument just to avoid hearing it again. Of course, constant repitition does not establish truth, or the validity of an argument. Consider, however, the following successful example:

> *"Mommy, I'm only saying again that I have been a good girl, so I deserve that chemistry set."*

> *"All right, you can have the chemistry set, as long as I do not have to hear abut it any more."*

THE FALLACY OF ACCIDENT / SWEEPING GENERALIZATION / DICTO SIMPLICITER

You construct a sweeping generalization when you apply a general rule to a particular situation, but when the features of that particular situation mean that the general rule is inapplicable to that situation. It is an error that you make when you go, in **deduction**, from a general condition to a specific circumstance. For example:

> *"People generally dislike snakes. You are a person, so you must dislike snakes."*

This fallacy is often committed by people who try to decide moral and legal questions by applying general rules mechanically.

CONVERSE ACCIDENT / HASTY GENERALIZATION

This fallacy is the reverse of the FALLACY OF ACCIDENT. In is an **inductive** error, when you form a general rule by examining only a few specific cases which are not, in fact, representative of all the possible cases.For example:

> *"Jim Bakker was an insincere Christian. Therefore, all Christians are insincere."*

313

NON CAUSA PRO CAUSA

You commit the fallacy of NON CAUSA PRO CAUSA, which is one example of a *false cause* fallacy, when you identify something as the cause of an event, but you do not, in fact, show that it was the cause. For example:

> *"I took an aspirin and prayed to the Egyptian god, Anubis.*
> *My headache disappeared.*
> *So Anubis cured me of my headache."*

POST HOC ERGO PROPTER HOC

You commit the fallacy of POST HOC ERGO PROPTER HOC, which is another type of *false cause* fallacy, when you assume that something (A) caused something else (B), just because A happened before B. For example:

> *"The Roman Empire fell after the rise of Christianity to be the principal religion of the Empire, therefore Christianity was the cause of the collapse of the Roman Empire."*

CUM HOC ERGO PROPTER HOC

This fallacy is similar to POST HOC ERGO PROPTER HOC. You commmit this fallacy when you assert that, because two events occured together in time, they must be related to one another in causation. It is a fallacy because it ignores other factors that may be the cause, or the causes, of the events.

PETITIO PRINCIPII / BEGGING THE QUESTION

You commit this fallacy when you premises are at least as questionable as the conclusion you reach through them. For example:

314

"Aliens are abducting innocent victims every week. The government must know what is going on. Therefore the government is in league with the aliens."

CIRCULUS IN DEMONSTRANDO

You commit this fallacy if you assume as a premise the conclusion that you wish to reach. Often, people rephrase the proposition so that the fallacy appears to be a valid argument. For example:

"Homosexuals must not be allowed to hold government office. Hence any government official who is revealed to be a homosexual will lose his job. Therefore, homosexuals will do anything to hide their secret, and will be open to blackmail. Therefore homosexuals cannot be allowed to hold government office."

Note that the argument is entirely circular, because the premise is the same as the conclusion. Another example:

"We know that God exists, because the Bible tells us so. And we know that the Bible is true, because it is the word of God."

Circular arguments are surprisingly common. If you already have reached a particular conclusion once yourself, it is to make it, often accidentally or unintentionally, an assertion when you explain your reasoning to someone else.

COMPLEX QUESTION / FALLACY OF INTERROGATION / FALLACY OF PRESUPPOSITION

This is the interrogative form of BEGGING THE QUESTION. One example is the classic question:

"Have you stopped beating your children?"

The question presupposes a definite answer to another question which has not even been asked. This trick is often used by lawyers in cross-examination, when they ask questions such as:

315

"Where did you hide the money you stole?"

Similarly, politicians often ask loaded questions such as:

"How long will this interference in our affairs by foreign nationals be allowed to continue?"

or

"Does the president plan four more years of ruinous foreign policy?"

Another form of this fallacy is to ask for an explanation of something which is untrue or not yet established.

IGNORATIO ELENCHI / IRRELEVANT CONCLUSION

The fallacy of the IRRELEVANT CONCLUSION occurs when you claim that an argument supports a particular conclusion when it is actually, logically, has nothing to do with that conclusion. For example, a Marxist may begin by saying that she will argue that the teachings of Marxism undoubtedly are true. If she then argues, at length, that Marxism has been of great help to many people, no matter how well she argues that point, she will not have shown that Marxist teachings are true. Sadly, such fallacious arguments are often successful, because they arouse emotions which may cause others to view the supposed conclusion in a more favourable light.

EQUIVOCATION / FALLACY OF FOUR TERMS

You commit EQUIVOCATION when you use a key word that has two or more different meanings in the same argument. For example:

"What could be more affordable than free software? But to make sure that it remains free, that users can do what they like with it,

316

we must place a license on it to make sure that will always be redistributable freely."

One way you can avoid this fallacy is to choose your terminology carefully before you begin your argument, and avoid words, like "free," which can have many meanings.

AMPHIBOLY

Amphiboly occurs when you use premises in an argument that are ambiguous or confusing because you have phrased them carelessly or ungrammatically.

ACCENT

ACCENT is another form of fallacy which you can cause by a shift in the meaning of the words you use. In this case, the meaning is changed by altering the emphasis of different parts of a statement. For example, consider:

*"We should not **speak** ill of our friends"*

and

*"We should not speak ill of our **friends**"*

Be particularly wary of causing this fallacy for yourself when you are reading any printed matter, whether on a published page, in a letter or other handwritten document, or in digital form. In each of these cases, it is easy—very easy indeed—to mis-read the emphasis of what actually was written.

FALLACIES OF COMPOSITION

One FALLACY OF COMPOSITION is to conclude that some property that is shared by the parts of something must apply to the whole of that thing. It is the logical misapplication of the rhetorical device of **synecdoche**. For example:

"The bicycle is made entirely of low mass components, and is, therefore, very lightweight."

The other FALLACY OF COMPOSITION is to conclude that a specific property of a number of individual items is shared by a collection of those items. For example:

"A car uses less gasoline and causes less pollution than a bus. Therefore, cars do less damage to the environment than busses do."

FALLACY OF DIVISION

The FALLACY OF DIVISION is the opposite of the FALLACY OF COMPOSITION. Like the latter, it exists in two varieties. The first is to assume that a property of some particular thing must apply to the parts of that particular thing. We dedicate this example to all the students who have burdened themselves, or whose families have burdened themselves, with a mountain of debt in order to attend an expensive college in their search for an excellent education:

"You are studying at an expensive college. Therefore, you must be rich."

The other form of the FALLACY OF DIVISION is to assume that a property of a collection of items is shared by each item. For example:

"Ants can destroy a tree. Therefore, this ant can destroy a tree."

SLIPPERY SLOPE ARGUMENT

In this argument, you state that, if one event occurs, other harmful events certainly will follow. But your argument offers no proof that any later harmful events will be caused by the first event. For example:

318

"If we legalize marijuana for any purpose, medical or otherwise, then more people will start to use crack cocaine and heroin, and, eventually, we will have to legalize those drugs, too. Soon, we will have a nation full of drug-addicts on welfare. Therefore, we cannot legalize marijuana for any reason."

"A IS BASED ON B" FALLACIES / "...IS A TYPE OF..." FALLACIES / FALLACY OF THE UNDISTRIBUTED MIDDLE

These fallacies occur if you attempt to argue that certain things are in some way similar, but you do not actually specify in what way they are similar. For example:

"Cats are a form of animal based on carbon chemistry; dogs are a form of animal based on carbon chemistry. So are not dogs a form of cat?"

AFFIRMATION OF THE CONSEQUENT

This fallacy is an argument of the form "A implies B, and, since B is true, therefore A is true." To understand why this is a fallacy, examine the truth table for implication which we included earlier in the text of our book. For example:

"If I fall into the swimming pool, then I will get wet. I am wet, so, therefore, I must have fallen into the swimming pool."

This fallacy is the converse of the DENIAL OF THE ANTECEDENT.

DENIAL OF THE ANTECEDENT

This fallacy is an argument of the form "A implies B, so, since A is false, therefore B also is false." The truth table for implication, presented in the text of the book, makes it clear why this is a fallacy.

Note that this fallacy differs from NON CAUSA PRO CAUSA. The latter has the form "A implies B, so, because A is false, therefore B also is false," where A does not, in fact, imply B at all. In the case here, the problem is not that the implication is invalid; rather it is that the falseness of A does not allow you to deduce anything about B. For example:

> *"If I fall into the swimming pool, I will get wet. I did not fall into the swimming pool, therefore, I am not wet."*

This is the converse of the fallacy of the AFFIRMATION OF THE CONSEQUENT.

CONVERTING A CONDITIONAL

This fallacy is an argument of the form "If A then B, therefore if B then A." For example:

> *"If educational standards are lowered, the quality of argument seen on the Internet will worsen. So if we see the level of debate on the 'net get worse over the next few years, then we will know that our educational standards are still falling."*

> *"If it is raining outside and I do not have an umbrella, I will get wet if I go outside. So, if I get wet when I go outside, then it is raining outside and I do not have an umbrella."*

This fallacy is similar to the AFFIRMATION OF THE CONSEQUENT, but, in this case, it is phrased as a conditional statement.

BIFURCATION

Sometimes called the *black or white* fallacy, BIFURCATION occurs if you present a situation as having only two alternatives, when, in fact, other alternatives do exist or can exist. For example, the statement:

> *"Napoleon lost the battle of Waterloo either because he was suffering from an acute attack of piles or because he had lost his strategic understanding of the situation."*

is obviously false, because it takes no notice of the Duke of Wellington, nor of Marshal Blucher, nor of their armies, nor of hundreds of other factors which contributed, or can have contributed, to Napoleon's defeat.

PLURIUM INTERROGATIONUM / MANY QUESTIONS

This fallacy occurs when someone demands a simple, or simplistic, answer to a complex question.

NON SEQUITUR

A NON SEQUITUR is an argument in which you draw a conclusion from premises which are not connected logically to it. The NON SEQUITUR is among the easiest fallacies to identify, which is why it is an important element in humor. For example:

"Since the ancient Egyptians did so much excavation to construct the pyramids, they were well versed in paleontology."

RED HERRING

You commit this fallacy if you introduce irrelevant material into to the issue you are discussing, so that you intentionally divert your reader's, or auditor's, attention away from the actual subject under consideration and towards a different conclusion.

REIFICATION / HYPOSTATIZATION

REIFICATION occurs when you mistakenly treat an abstract concept as a concrete thing.

SHIFTING THE BURDEN OF PROOF

The burden of proof is always on you, when you assert that something is true. Shifting the burden of proof, a special case of ARGUMENTUM AD IGNORANTIAM, is the fallacy of putting the burden of proof on the person who denies or questions your assertion. The source of the fallacy is the assumption that something is true unless proven not to be so. For example:

> *"Very well, if you do not think that little green women have taken control of the American government, can you prove it?"*

STRAW MAN

The STRAW MAN fallacy occurs when you misrepresent someone else's position so that it can be attacked more easily, then you attack that misrepresented position successfully, and then you conclude that the original position has been demolished. It is fallacious because it fails to deal with the actual arguments that have been made. For example:

> *"To be a true Marxist, you have to believe with absolute certainty that there is no God. In order to convince yourself with absolute certainty, you must examine all the universe and all the places where God could possibly be. Since you obviously have not done this, your position is indefensible."*

EXTENDED ANALOGY

The fallacy of the EXTENDED ANALOGY often occurs in arguments about some general rule or circumstance. The fallacy is to assume that mentioning two different situations, in an argument about a general rule, constitutes a claim that those two separate situations are analogous to each other. Consider this example from a debate about anti-cryptography legislation:

> A: *"I believe it is always wrong to oppose the law by breaking it."*
> B: *"Such a position is odious: it implies that you would not have supported Doctor Martin Luther King."*
> A: *"Are you saying that cryptography legislation is as important as the struggle to achieve equality in civil rights? How dare you!"*

322

TU QUOQUE

This is the famous *you too* fallacy. It occurs if you argue that an action is acceptable because your opponent has performed it. For instance:

> *"You're just being randomly abusive."*
> *"So? You've been abusive too."*

Because this is a personal attack, it is, therefore, a special case of ARGUMENTUM AD HOMINEM.

AUDIATUR ET ALTERA PARS

Often, people will argue from assumptions which they have not bothered to state. The principle of AUDIATUR ET ALTERA PARS is that all of the premises of an argument should be stated explicitly. While it is not strictly a fallacy to fail to state all of your assumptions, people may view your thinking with suspicion, and may reject your argument, if you do not do so.

AD HOC

There is a difference between argument and explanation. If we're interested in establishing **A**, and **B** is offered as evidence, the statement **A because B** is an argument. If we're trying to establish the truth of **B**, then **A because B** is not an argument, it is an explanation. The AD HOC fallacy occurs when you offer an after-the-fact explanation which does not apply to other situations. Often, people present AD HOC explanations in the form of arguments, when they emphatically are not. For example, if we assume that the law treats all people equally, then the following is an AD HOC explanation:

> A: *"I was found 'not guilty' of the false charge that was levelled against me."*
> B: *"The principles of the law saved you. The law was your salvation, as it is the great guardian of all human rights"*

A: *"So, will the law save others who have been charged falsely?"*
B: *"Er. . . The law is a fallable human institution, and its ways are mysterious."*

ARGUMENTUM AD LOGICAM

This is the *fallacy fallacy* of arguing that a proposition is false because it has been presented as the conclusion of a fallacious argument. Remember always that fallacious arguments can arrive at true conclusions.

> *"Take the fraction 16/64. Now, cancelling a 6 on top and a six on the bottom, we get that 16/64 = 1/4."*
> *"Wait a second! You cannot just cancel the six!"*
> *"Oh, so you are telling us that 16/64 is not equal to 1/4, are you?"*

THE "NO TRUE SCOTSWOMAN. . ." FALLACY

Suppose that I assert that no Scotswoman puts sugar on her porridge. You counter this by pointing out that your friend Margaret likes sugar with her porridge. I then say "Ah, yes, but no true Scotswoman puts sugar on her porridge."

This is an example of an AD HOC change being used to shore up an assertion, combined with an attempt to shift the meaning of the words used in the original assertion. It is, in fact, a combination of fallacies.

Appendix D

Abbreviations to be Used in Footnotes

abbr., abbreviated, -ion
ab init., *ab initio*, from the beginning
abr., abridged; abridgment
add., addendum
ad inf., *ad infinitum*, to infinity
ad init., *ad initium*, at the beginning
ad int., *ad interim*, in the meantime
ad lib., *ad libitum*, at will
ad loc., *ad locum*, at the place
æt., *aetatis*, aged
anon., anonymous
app., appendix
art., article
b., born; brother
bibl., *bibliotheca*, library
bibliog., bibliography, -er, -ical
biog., biography, -er, -ical
bk., block; book
c., chapter (in law citations); *circa*
ca., *circa*, about, approximately
Cantab., *Cantabrigiensis*, of Cambridge
cf., *confer*, compare
chap., chapter
Cia, *Compañia*, Company (no period)
Cie, *Compagnie*, Company (no period)
col., column
colloq., colloquial, -ly, -ism
comp., compiler (*pl.* comps.); compiled by
cont., continued
copr., cop., or ©, copyright
cp., compare
d., died; daughter
dept., department
d.h., *das heisst*, namely

d.i., *das ist*, that is
dial., dialect
dict., dictionary
dim., diminutive
div., division; divorced
do., ditto (the same)
dram. pers., *dramatis personæ*
Dr. u. Vrl., *Druck und Verlag*, printer and publisher
D.V., *Deo volente*, God willing
ea., each
ed. editor (*pl.* eds.); edition; edited by
e.g., *exempli gratia*, for example
encyc., encyclopedia
engr., engineer; engraved, engraving
esp., especially
et al., *et alii*, and others
etc., &c., *et cetera*, and so forth
et seq., *et sequentes*, and the following
ex., example (*pl.* exx. *or* exs.)
f., and following (*pl.* ff.)
fasc., fascicle
fig., figure
fl., *floruit*, flourished
fol., folio
fr., from
f.r., *folio recto*, on the front of the page
fut., future
f.v., *folio verso*, on the back of the page
ibid., *ibidem*, in the same place[367]
id., *idem*, the same
i.e., *id est*, that is

---

[367]A wonderful bird is the *ibid*.
In appearance it's pale and insibid.
It stands as a sage
At the foot of the page
To tell where the passage was cribbed.

See Richard D. Altick, *The Art of Literary Research*, 3d. ed., rev John J. Fenstermaker (New York: W. W. Norton & Company, 1981) 226; quoting *A News Letter of the Institute of Early American History & Culture* (June 1958), no. 13.

incl., inclusive; including; includes
inf., *infra*, below
inst., instant, this month; institute, institution
introd. or intro., introduction
irreg., irregular
l., left; line (*pl.* ll.)
lang., language
lit., literally
loc., locative
loc. cit., *loco citato*, in the place cited
loq., *loquitur*, he or she speaks
m., married; male; measure (pl. mm.)
marg., margin, -al
med., median; medical; medieval; medium
memo, memorandum
misc., miscellaneous
m.m., *mutatis mutandis*, necessary changes being made
MS (*pl.* MSS), *manuscriptum* (-*a*), manuscript(s)
mus., museum; music, -al
n., *natus*, bom; note, footnote (*pl.* nn.); noun
N.B., *nota bene*, take careful note
n.d., no date
no., number (*pl.* nos.)
non obs., *non obstante*, notwithstanding
non seq., *non sequitur*, it does not follow
n.p., no place; no publisher; no page
N.S., New Style (dates)
n.s., new series
ob., *obiit*, died
obs., obsolete
op. cit., *opere citato*, in the work cited
O.S., Old Style (dates)
o.s., old series
Oxon., *Oxoniensis*, of Oxford
p., page (*pl.* pp.); past
par., paragraph
pass. *passim*, throughout; here and there; passive
perf., perfect; perforated

perh., perhaps
pers., person, personal
pinx., *pinxit*, painted by
pl., plate; plural
PPS, *post postscriptum*, a later postscript
pres., present
pro tem., *pro tempore*, for the time being
prox., *proximo*, next month
PS, *postscriptum*, postscript
pt., part
pub., publication, publisher, published by
quart., quarterly
q.v., *quod vide*, which see
R., *rex*, king; *regina*, queen; right (in stage directions)
r., right; reigned; recto
repr., reprint, reprinted
rev., review; revised, revision
s.a., *sine anno*, witbout year; *sub anno*, under the year
sc., scene; *scilicet*, namely; *sculpsit*, carved by
sec., section; *secundum*, according to
ser., series
s.l., *sine loco*, without place
s.n., *sine nomine*, without name
st., stanza
subj., subject; subjective; subjunctive
sup., *supra*, above
supp. *or* suppl., supplement
s.v., *sub verbo*, *sub voce*, under tbe word (*pl.* s.vv.)
ult., *ultimatus*, ultimate, last; *ultimo*, last month
univ., university
usw., *und so weiter*, and so forth
ut sup., *ut supra*, as above
v., verse (*pl.* vv.); verso; versus; *vide*, see
viz., *videlicet*, namely
vol., volume
vs. *or* v., versus
yr., year; your

Appendix E

How You Can Evaluate the Information That You Find on the Internet

The Internet offers you the opportunity to find information and data from all over the world.[368] In addition, the development of the *World Wide Web* has made the Internet easier to use, both for finding information and for publishing it electronically. Because so much information is available, and because that information can appear to be fairly anonymous, you must develop the ability to evaluate what you find. When you use a research or academic library, the books, journals and other resources already have been evaluated by a librarian or scholar. When you use an index or a database to find information on a specific topic, that index or database often is produced by a professional or scholarly organization that selects the journals to be indexed on the basis of their quality. If the index or database is not produced by such an organization, it is usually the work of a commercial indexing and abstracting business that qualifies as part of the information industry. In other words, every resource you find has been evaluated in one way or another before you ever see it. When you use the *World Wide Web*, none of this is true. There are no filters between you and the Internet. In addition, because it is so easy to construct *Web* documents, you will find information across the widest range of quality, written by authors of the widest range of authority, all available on an even playing field. Thus, you will find excellent resources beside the most dubious. The Internet epitomizes the concept of *caveat lector: let the reader beware.*

This little section discusses the criteria by which scholars in most fields evaluate information in print, and shows you how you can use the same criteria to assess the information you find on the Internet.

---

[368]We are indebted for the outline of this section, and for some material, to URL: http://milton.mse.jhu.edu:8001/research/education/net.html.

BASIC CRITERIA FOR EVALUATING INFORMATION, AND HOW THEY APPLY TO THE INTERNET

There are certain criteria that you should apply whenever you evaluate information, whether it is in print, on film, or electronic. These criteria include:

> Authorship
> Publisher
> Reference to, and knowledge of, other sources
> Accuracy and verifiability
> Currency

Authorship is perhaps the best criterion you can use to evaluate information. Who wrote this? When you look for information with some type of critical value, you want to know the basis of the authority with which the author speaks. Here are some possible ways to judge:

In your own field of study, the author is a well-known and well-regarded name you recognize. When you find an author you do not recognize:

> &☙ The author is mentioned in a positive fashion by another author or another person you trust as an authority;

> &☙ You found, or linked to, the author's *Web* or Internet document from another document you trust;

> &☙ The *Web* or Internet document you are reading gives biographical information, including the author's position, institutional affiliation and address;

> &☙ You can find biographical information about the author by linking to another document; this enables you to judge whether the author's credentials allow her to speak with authority on the topic at hand;

> &☙ If none of these, then there is an address and telephone number, as well as an e-mail address, for the author, so that you can request further information on her work and professional background. Remember, an e-mail address alone gives you no more information than you already have.

330

The publisher also helps you to evaluate any kind of document you may be reading. In the world of publishing, this generally means that the author's manuscript has been screened to verify that it meets the scholarly standards and aims of the organization that serves as the publisher, which almost certain includes a peer review. On the Internet, ask the following questions to assess the role and authority of the publisher, which, in this case means the server where you found the document:

અ Is the name of any organization given on the document you are reading?

અ Are there headers, footers, or a distinctive watermark that show the document to be part of an official academic or scholarly Web site?

અ Can you contact the site's Webmaster by a link from this document? If not, can you link to a page where such information is listed?

અ Can you tell that it is on the same server and in the same directory--by looking at the URL?

અ Is this organization recognized in the field in which you are studying?

અ Is this organization suitable to address the topic at hand?

અ Can you ascertain the relationship of the author to the publisher or server?

અ Was the document that you are viewing prepared as part of the author's professional duties--and thus, by extension, within her area of expertise? Or is the relationship of a casual or for-fee nature, which tells you nothing about the author's credentials within an institution?

અ Can you verify the identity of the server where the document resides? You can use Internet programs such *dnslookup* and *whois* to do this.

અ Does the document reside in a person's Internet account, rather than as a part of an official Web site? If so, you should approach this type of information resource with the greatest caution.

The author's references to, and knowledge of, the literature refers to the context in which the author situates her work. This reveals what the author knows about her discipline and its practices. This allows you to evaluate the author's scholarship and knowledge of the subject she discusses in the document. The following criteria will help you to judge the value of all forms of information:

> ঌ The document includes a bibliography.
> ঌ The author alludes to, and displays her knowledge of, related sources, with proper attribution.
> ঌ The author displays her knowledge of theories, schools of thought, or techniques that are considered to be appropriate in the treatment of her subject.
> ঌ If the author is using a new theory or technique as a basis for research, she discusses the value and the limitations of this new approach.
> ঌ If the author's treatment of the subject is controversial, she knows this and acknowledges it openly.

The accuracy and verifiability of details are important parts of your process of evaluation, especially when you are reading the work of an unfamiliar author presented by an unfamiliar organization, or a work that is presented in a non-traditional way. For an Internet document that purports to be the result of research, among the criteria you can use to evaluate accuracy are:

> ঌ The author includes the all the significant data that she gathered, and she offers an explanation of the research methods she used to gather and interpret that data.
> ঌ The methods that are outlined in the document are appropriate to the topic and, in the case of scientific materials, allow the study to be duplicated for purposes of verification. In historical, linguistic, literary, aor artistic studies, the author presents her full range of sources so clearly that you will have no difficulty in locating them.
> ঌ All of the other sources upon which the document relies are listed in a bibliography, and there are links to the documents themselves, wherever possible.

332

ə The document names all those persons who provided un-published data and guidance that the author used to prepare the document.

ə You can verify for accuracy all the background information that the author used.

In the sciences, the currency, or timeliness, of the information you find is of great importance. In printed documents, of course, the date of publication and the date of copyright, if it is different, are the principal indicators of currency. For some types of information, currency is not an issue, and authorship or the place of the information in history is more important. This is always true in the arts and humanities, where an article or book published more than a century ago may be of far more importance to your research than anything published since. For many types of data, however, currency is extremely important, as is the regularity with which the data is updated. You can apply the following criteria to determine the currency of the document at which you are looking:

ə The document includes the dates on which the author gathered the information.

ə The document refers to information that is dated clearly. For example, a document with tables of demographic data has a note that states the source, such as "Based on 1990 US Census data."

ə Where a document must have data added to it periodically, or where it must be updated regularly, the author has included in the document some information on the regularity of updates.

ə The document includes a publication date or the date on which the author last updated it.

ə The document includes a date of copyright.

ə If you can find no date in an electronic document, can you view the directory in which it resides and read the date of the latest modification to it there?

If you found information by using one of the search engines for the Internet, such as ALTAVISTA or EXCITE; or a directory of the

Internet, such as YAHOO; or any of the services that rate *World Wide Web* pages, you need to know how that site looks for information and how the information is rated, as well as how often the site's information is updated. Most sites of this nature will have a link to a text which tells you about the site and what criteria must be met to have a document included there.

Remember, you must evaluate all information, whether in print or by byte, for its authority, appropriateness, and value. If you find information that is "too good to be true," it probably is. Never use information that you cannot verify. You must establish and learn criteria to examine the information you find on the Internet. This is essential, if you are to become a critical user of digital information. Look at every item you find with a cold, critical, and skeptical eye. Question it! And then look for other sources of information that can authenticate or corroborate what you find.

PRACTICAL STEPS YOU CAN TAKE TO EVALUATE INTERNET RESOURCES

Of the five principal evaluative criteria for evaluating the information you find on the Internet, you can investigate three of them by electronic means: **authorship, publisher,** and the **currency** of the document itself.

While this appendix gives you a variety of ways to look for each kind of information, always remember that there other, non-electronic, methods that you can use—many of which are more accurate—to get much of the information we discuss here.

AUTHORSHIP

What do you need to know about the author? When the author is someone unknown to you, ask the following questions:

- ❧ Is the document signed?
- ❧ Can I get more information on the author by linking from this page to other documents?
- ❧ Was there information about the author on the page from which I linked to this one?

If you can answer "yes" to the second or the third question, it is possible that you will have enough information to do a preliminary evaluation of the document. At least, you should have enough information to help you find the author's telephone number or e-mail address, so that you may contact her with any questions you have about the document. If you can answer "yes" to the first question only, you need to find further information on the author. There are a number of ways in which you may do this, quite apart from using sources beyond the Internet:

    ⁚ Go to the home page of the *web* site where the document resides and search for the author's name with any available internal search engine or directory. This approach works best at academic *web* sites. This sort of search may help you to establish the author's academic or profesional affiliation.

    ⁚ Try searching the author's name, enclosed in quotation marks, in ALTAVISTA. This may lead you to other information on, or other web pages by, the same   author.

    ⁚ Try using an e-mail address finder, such as http://www.switchboard.com or http://www.excite.com.

These are not the ideal means for finding an author's credentials, which is often easy to do with the affiliation note in printed matter, but they may help you to identify the person more precisely and, perhaps, locate her.

If you can find no information on the author, or if there is no signature or attribution on the page, consider the publisher. Where are you, in the geography of cyberspace? Look at the web page you are trying to evaluate. Does it include any of the following:

    ⁚ A header or footer that shows its affiliation as part of a larger web site.

    ⁚ A watermark or wallpaper that fulfills the same function.

    ⁚ A link at the bottom or top of the page that allows you to go to the home page of the web site where the document resides.

   ❧ A link that allows you to send a message to the site's *webmaster*.

These characteristics will help you to judge something of the professional quality of a *web* page. They act to assure you that the page you are evaluating is a part of some type of institutional setting. Judging the official nature of a web page is extremely important, if the page is not signed. Some web sites do not include attributions to individual authors, so you will have to rely on your ability to evaluate the institution, or the Internet domain, where the page resides. If the page at which you are looking gives no clues as to its identity, you will need to focus on the URL.

   ❧ Can you find the web site's home page by deleting all the information in the URL after the server's name?
   ❧ Can you tell if the page is actually part of someone's personal account, rather than being a part of an official site?
   ❧ If all else fails, can you find some information on the server or the Internet domain?

To do this this last task, you must query the database of the *InterNIC Registration Services Host*. Try typing *whois* followed by the name of the Internet domain (for example: **whois umd.edu**) at your account's system prompt. If you college or university has implemented the *whois* server locally, you will receive a response that shows considerable detail about the domain name you entered. If you receive no response with this procedure, *telnet* to **rs.internic.net** and, once you receive its prompt, type the same query and press enter.

Once you find the name of the organization that owns the server, you may have enough information to judge its reputation as a source of information. Remember that this is only of value for official pages from a web site. If the page you are evaluating comes from someone's personal account, you really have no idea of their place in the organization, or if they are in a position to represent it. If you are not familiar with the organization, try searching for its name, enclosed in quotation marks, in ALTAVISTA.

If you cannot determine something about either the author or the publisher of the page you are trying to evaluate, you are looking at information that is as anonymous as a page torn from a book. You cannot evaluate information that you cannot verify. And, of course, it is very unwise to use information of this nature, for you will sacrifice all scholarly credibility if you do so. Look for another source!

CURRENCY OF THE DOCUMENT ITSELF

Even when you can find information on the author and the publisher of a web page, you still must consider how fresh the document is. This is especially critical if the document discusses time-sensitive information, such as statistical or mathematical information, scientific data in the biological sciences, or other data from fields whose body of information is expanding, and changing in value, quickly. First, look for some form of internal text or note that tells you directly about the currency of the data or information:

> ☙ Does the presentation of the data have a caption that cites both a source and a date, such as "Based on data in *Jane's Fighting Ships*, 1941"?
> ☙ Does it include information, within the document, about the source of the information and where you can find it, such as "Closing Dow-Jones Averages, September 1, 1928, to August 31, 1933, reprinted from . . ."?
> ☙ Is the source of the data or information listed in a bibliography that is appended or linked to the page?

If you cannot determine the source and the age of the information, you are, once more, looking at anonymous information of no scholarly value. It also is important to know when a *web* page, or other Internet document, was last updated. Has it been revised recently, or has it been sitting on the Internet, unaltered, for a considerable time? Notice that almost all bibliographic records in online catalogues have an *update field* which shows when the record was last reviewed.

❧ Look at the bottom of the page. Does it have a date that shows when it was last updated?

❧ Use the *document information* feature in you *web* browser, if it has one. Does it tell you the date of the document or page at which you are looking?

❧ Change the URL by backing up to the last slash (/) in the address. This may reveal to you the details of the directory or subdirectory of the server, including your page. Usually the last date on which the material was modified is included in the data that is displayed by this query.

❧ Search the title of the page in ALTAVISTA. There should be a date in italics included in the information that the search engine presents on the page in which you are interested.

It is very important for you to know the age of the information that you find, and, consequently, its currency, because you may be looking at a document whose data or information has been superseded or replaced by other information. Do remember that **the best counterfeit looks the most like the authentic object.** The question you must ask yourself with every new source on the Internet is, how trustworthy is this information?

For Further Reading

Instead of presenting you with a mammoth list of works to consult, which we could do easily, because of the vast scope of the topic of research and writing, we have included here only the few fundamental books which constitute — together with this volume — the books we regard as essential for mastering the basic elements of research, analysis, and writing. If you know the arts and skills presented in these books, you can research fully, analyze sensibly, and write lucidly on almost any topic that interests you or is important to you.

Altick, Richard D[aniel]. *The Scholar Adventurers*. Revised edition. New York: Macmillan, 1966.

Altick, Richard D[aniel]. *The Art of Literary Research*. 4th ed. Edited by John J. Fenstermaker. New York: W. W. Norton and Company, 1993.

Barker, Stephen Francis. *The Elements of Logic*. 5th ed. New York: McGraw-Hill, 1989.

Barzun, Jacques, and Henry F[ranklin] Graff. *The Modern Researcher*. 4th ed. New York: Harcourt Brace Jovanovich, 1977.

Burkle-Young, Francis A., and Saundra Rose Maley. *The Art of the Footnote: The Intelligent Student's Guide to the Art and Science of Annotating Texts*. Lanham, Maryland: University Press of America, 1996.

Fischer, David Hackett. *Historians' Fallacies: Toward a Logic of Historical Thought*. New York: Harper & Row, 1970.

Fowler, H[enry] W[atson]. *A Dictionary of Modern English Usage*. Oxford: Clarendon Press, 1926.

Gordon, Karen Elizabeth. *The New Well-Tempered Sentence: A Punctuation Handbook for the Innocent, the Eager, and the Doomed.* Revised and expanded. New York: Ticknor & Fields, 1993.

Lanham, Richard A. *A Handlist of Rhetorical Terms.* 2nd ed. Berkeley: University of California Press, 1991.

Mann, Thomas, *A Guide to Library Research Methods.* New York: Oxford University Press, 1987.

Mann, Thomas. *Library Research Models: A Guide to Classification, Cataloging, and Computers.* New York: Oxford University Press, 1993.

Opdycke, John B[aker]. *Harper's English Grammar.* New York: Warner Books, 1983.

Winks, Robin W., ed. *The Historian as Detective: Essays on Evidence.* New York: Harper & Row, 1970.

General Index

A

abbreviations, 213;
  in footnotes, 325-328
accent (fallacy), 161, 317
accident (fallacy), 160, 313
accident, converse (fallacy), 313
acetylsalicylic acid, 20
acknowledgements (footnotes)
  224-226
Acronyms, Initialisms & Abbreviations Dictionary, 226
ad hoc (fallacy), 323
Adams, Franklin P[ierce], 11
affirming the consequent, 162, 319
Age of Romanticism, 11
Agricola, 121
ALTAVISTA, 82-83, 333, 336, 338
Altick, Richard D., 209-210, 339
America: History and Life, 41
American Library Directory, 37
amphiboly (fallacy), 161, 317
analogy, extended (fallacy), 322
analysis, principles of, 134-162
anecdotal evidence (fallacy), 305-306
annotated bibliography, 96-98
annotations, 207-226
anonymous authority (fallacy), 159
Antiquarian Catalogues of Musical Interest, 64
appeal to authority (fallacy), 159, 309
appeal to force (fallacy), 159, 306
appeal to pity (fallacy), 159, 308
appeal to the gallery (fallacy), 309
appeal to the people (fallacy), 309
appeals to motives (fallacies), 159
Applied Science and Technology Index, 84
archival collections

argument, logical, 150, 154-156
argumentum ad antiquitatem, 311
argumentum ad baculum, 306
argumentum ad crumenam, 311-312
argumentum ad hominem, 306-307, 323
argumentum ad ignorantiam, 307-308
argumentum ad lazarum, 312
argumentum ad logicam, 324
argumentum ad misericordiam, 308
argumentum ad nauseam, 312-313
argumentum ad novitatem, 311
argumentum ad numerum, 309
argumentum ad populam, 309
argumentum ad verecundiam, 309-310
ARGUS CLEARINGHOUSE, 81
ARL Member Libraries' Information Servers, 51
Arnold, Matthew, 11, 142
ARPAnet, 130
Art Index, 84
Arthur, Chester Alan, 88
Art of Literary Research, 209-210, 326, 339
Arts & Humanities Index, 93, 265-270
Arts & Humanities Search, 94, 265-270
asides & commentaries (footnote), 220
ASM News, 33
Austen, Jane, 60

B

Bacon, Francis, 11, 18-19, 40
Ballard, Robert D., 24-25
Barker, Stephen F., 149, 339
baryton, 29
Barr, Catherine, 112
Barzun, Jacques, 40, 339
Baskerville (font), 230
because, 197-198
begging the question, 161, 314-315
Besterman, Theodore, 61

Besterman World Bibliographies, 63
Beyond Legal Information, 76
Bibliographic Index, 62, 84
bibliographies, descriptive, 89
bibliographies, subject, 89
bibliographies of bibligraphies, 61-64
*Bibliography of Bibliographic Services of
  European Parliamentary Libraries*, 64
*Bibliography of Bibliographies in
  American Literature*, 64
Bibliophile Research Tools, 51
bifurcation (fallacy), 320-321
biographical footnotes, 213-214
Biography Index, 84
Biology and Agriculture Index, 84
BIOSYS, 44
blue sheets (DIALOG), 71
Bolsena, see Mass of Bolsena
Book Review Digest, 84
Boölean algebra, 52, 113, 150
boomerang effect, 92, 269
Bottle, R. T., 64
Bowers, Fredson Thayer, 90
*Bowker Annual Library and Book Trade
  Almanac*, 112
Brian Yoder's Fallacy Zoo, 150
browsing shelves, 90-91; digitally,
  276-280
brws call, 91, 276-277
Bucky balls, 20
Budget of the United States, 7
Burkle-Young, F. A., 138, 139, 207
Business Index, 84
BUSREF, 74

C
Cambridge University, 12
Carlyle, Thomas, 66, 68
Case, Thomas, 163
Caslon, William, 230
Cate, George Allan, 68, 97-98

categorical errors (fallacies), 161
cause and effect, 103, 134, 197
CD-ROM, 61, 84, 93, 116
Cederblom, J. B., 149
Century Schoolbook (font), 230
changing the subject, 159-160
Chesterton, Gilbert Keith, 11
Chicago Manual of Style, 201, 212
chromosome 11, 70
circulus in demonstrando (fallacy), 315
citation searching, 91-95, 265-270
clarity, in writing, 187-189, 205-206
Class Z, 37
CMC Information Sources, 81
Coddington, Edwin B., 26
Cohen, Carl, 149
complex cause (fallacy), 161
complex question, 159, 315-316
composition (fallacy), 161
conclusions, logical, 154
consequences (fallacy), 159
contrasting views (footnote), 217-220
converse accident (fallacy), 160
converting a conditional (fallacy), 320
coördination (outline), 179-180
Coover, James, 64
Copernicus, Nicolaus, 143-144
Copi, Irving M., 149
copyright laws, 100
Cor-Ten, 29
Courier (font), 230
Critical Reasoning, 149
cross-references (footnote), 223-224
Cullen, Johanna C., 32, 211, 237, 281
Culture and Anarchy, 142
cum hoc ergo propter hoc (fallacy),
  314

D
DAO, 127-128, 133, 271-275; display,
  129

Darwin, Charles,173-174
data, significance of, 13-15
De Quincey, Thomas, 11
December, John, 81-82
December List, 81-82
deductive argument, 154-155
deduction, logical, 140-141
DeLashmitt, Eleanor, 77
denying the antecedent, 162, 319-320
descriptive bibliographies, 89
descriptive footnotes, 215-216
Dewey Decimal Classification System, 36, 117
diction, standard, 199-201
Dictionary of Modern English Usage, 190, 201, 339
dicto simpliciter (fallacy), 313
Directory of Genealogical and Historical Society Libraries, Archives, and Collections, 29
Directory of Heritage Organizations and Resources, 29
Directory of Historical Organizations in Ohio, 29
Directory of Special Libraries and Collections in New Mexico, 29
Discovering WESTLAW, 76
DISS, 271-275
Dissertations Abstracts International, 43, 127; see also DAO.
Dissertations Abstracts Online, see DAO
division (fallacy), 161, 318
division (outline), 181-183
documentation, original, see primary sources
dotted quad address, 49
Doyle, Sir Arthur Conan, 141

E
Eagle Eye, 66
Education Index, 84

Einstein, Albert, 178
Elements of Ethics, 170
Elements of Logic, 149, 339
e-mail, 38, 330
ENASSC, 74
Encyclopædia Britannica, eleventh edition, 37, 163-164, 170
Encyclopedia of Associations, 29, 37, 74, 124-125; display, 126
Epsewasson, 6
equivocation (fallacy), 316-317
ERIC, 66
errors, digital, 67
Esdaile, Arundell J. K., 90
essay, Baconian, 11, 18-19
essay, expository, 10
essay, formal, 2, 10-11, 20, 209
Essay and General Literature Index, 84
Euclid, 164
EUREKA, 77-78
evaluating Internet information, 329-338
EXCITE, 82, 333
expanding information (footnote), 216
explication de texte, 20
extended analogy (fallacy), 322

F
fallacies, logical, 158-162, 305-324
fallacies of ambiguity, 161
fallacies of composition, 317-318
fallacies of distractions, 158-159
fallacy fallacy, 324
fallacy of exclusion, 160
fallacy of four terms, 316-317
fallacy of interrogation, 315-316
fallacy of presupposition, 315-316
false analogy (fallacy), 160
false dilemma (fallacy), 160
festschrift, 98
field (digital), 107

films, 5, 78, 98, 110
FirstSearch, 41-45, 127; see also
  WorldCat, OCLC
FirstSearch Extended service, 44,
  47-48, 84, 95
FirstSearch Standard service, 47
Fischer, David Hackett, 140, 168-169,
  179, 305, 339
Fisher, John H., 63
folio shelves, 111
fonts, typographical, 230
footnotes, 207-226
foreign languages, texts in, 131-133
format field (digital cataloguing), 110
format, term paper, 229-230
Fowler, H. W., 190, 201, 339
Freud, Sigmund, 167
ftp, 38, 46
fuzzy logic, 150

G
*Gale Database of Publications and
  Broadcast Media*, 74
*Gale Directory of Publications and
  Broadcast Media*, 74
Garfield, Eugene, 91
Garamond (font), 230
Garraghan, Gilbert Joseph, 104
Gaskell, Philip, 90
General Science Index, 84
geographical footnotes, 215
gerunds, 190-192
Getting Started on DIALOG, 72
Gettysburg, Battle of, 26-28, 34
Gibbon, Edward, 210
glossing words and phrases (footnote),
  216-217
Goddard, Robert, 218
gopher, 46, 60
Gordon, Karen Elizabeth, 195, 340

government documents, 5, 7, 47, 65,
  66, 78, 183
Government Printing Office, 7
Graff, Henry F., 40, 339
grammatical construction, 198-199
Gray, Richard A., 63
Gregorian calendar, 6
Guide to Historical Method, 104
Guide to Library Research Methods, 40,
  61, 65, 104, 224, 232, 340
Guide to Published Library Catalogs, 62
*Guide to Serial Bibliographies for
  Modern Literatures*, 63

H
Hammond, William Alexander, 54
Handlist of Rhetorical Terms, 340
Hanlon's Corollary, 18, 148-149
Harper's English Grammar, 185, 340
hasty generalization, 160, 164, 165,
  313
Hawking, Stephen William, 310
Hazlitt, William, 11
Hearst, George, 311-312
Hegel, Georg Wilhelm Friedrich, 167
Henige, David P., 63
Hippocratic Oath, 87-88
Historian as Detective, 340
Historian's Fallacies, 140, 168-169, 305
historical method, 1-2, 18, 33,
  103-104, 158, 307, 308
Hugo, Victor, 168
Humanities Index, 84
H. W. Wilson Company, 84
hypostatization, 321
hysteron proteron, 134
HYTELNET, 51

I
ignoratio elenchi (fallacy), 316
implication, logical, 156-158

inconsistency (fallacy), 162
inference, logical, 152-153
induction (logic), 140-141
inductive argument (logic), 154
inductive fallacies, 160
information, significance of, 13-15
Information Sources in Chemistry, 64
INKTOMI, 82
insignificant cause (fallacy), 161
Institute for Scientific Information, 91
interlibrary loan system, 2, 4, 7, 32, 35, 36, 43, 96, 105, 108, 112, 132, 249; ordering, 250-251, 256, 258, 269, 279
International Standard Book Number, see ISBN
International Standard Serial Number, see ISSN
InterNIC Registration Services Host, 336
Internet, 2, 48, 60, 68, 329
Introduction to Bibliography for Literary Students, 90
Introduction to Logic, 149
irrelevant conclusion (fallacy), 161, 316
ISBN, 112, 117
ISSN, 112

J
James, Henry, 87
Jefferson, Thomas, 14, 148, 175
Jenner, Edward, 144-146
John Ruskin: A Reference Guide, 97, 98
Johnson, Nancy P., 76
joint effect (fallacy), 161
Jonson, Ben, 199, 200
Journal of Bacteriology, 32
Julian calendar, 6

K
Keynes, John Maynard, 167
knowledge, significance of, 13-15
Kohl, Ernst, 64
KrzyÔanowski, Wladimir, 26-28

L
Lamb, Charles, 11
Lanham, Richard A., 340
Lawrence, D. H., 85-86
LCCN, 36, 117
LCXR, 55, 252-256
Learning LEXIS, 75
Legal Periodical & Books (index), 84
Les Miserables, 168
LEXIS/NEXIS, 30, 40, 70, 74-75
LEXIS/NEXIS *Companion*, 75
LEXIS/NEXIS *Product Guide*, 75
Library Literature, 84
Library of Congress, 2, 40, 48
Library of Congress Card Number, see LCCN
Library of Congress Catalog, 55, 71, 78, 91, 108, 233
Library of Congress Classification System, 36
Library of Congress Cross References, see LCXR
Library of Congress Information System (LOCIS), 50, 116-118
Library of Congress Subject Headings, 36, 48, 51, 52-54, 118, 252-253, 260-264
Library Research Guide to Philosophy, 64
Library Research Models, 340
Linnæan classification, 114
List, Charles J., 64
LISTSERVS, 60
literature reviews, 101
literature surveys, 101

log-to-file (function), 38-39, 56
Lorentz, Hendrik Antoon, 234
Lusitania, 23-25
LYCOS, 82
lynx, 38, 56, 81, 83; commands,
  58-59, 60

M
Maley, Saundra, 138-139, 207, 339
Mann, Thomas, 40, 61, 65, 104, 224,
  232, 340
*Manual for Writers of Term Papers,
  Theses, and Dissertations*, 201, 212
many questions (fallacy), 321
Marx, Karl, 167
Mass of Bolsena, 32, 98, 211, 281-304
master's theses, 116
mbu, 148
McKerrow, Ronald, 90
McKnight, Jean Sinclair, 75
MEDLINE, 44, 66, 79-80; display, 80
MELVYL, 78-79
Michelson-Morley experiment, 234
Microsoft Explorer, 39, 56
MLA International Bibliography, 44, 66
*MLA Style Citations of Electronic
  Sources*, 202
Modern Researcher, 40, 339
Monel metal, 20
Monet, Claude, 7
Montaigne, Michel de, 10
Morison, Stanley, 230
Morris, William, 108-114
Mount Vernon, 6
Muirhead, John Henry, 170
MUMS, 2, 50, see also Library of
  Congress Information System
Murphy's Law, 35
musical scores, 5, 64, 78

N

Napoleon I, 22, 79-80, 137
National Library of Medicine, 79-80,
  see also MEDLINE
Nelmes, Sarah, 145
Nelson, Bonnie R., 62
NetFirst, 60
Netscape, 39, 56, 81
newsgroups, 60, 82, 132, 150, 305
New Introduction to Bibliography, 90
New Well-Tempered Sentence, 195, 340
New York Public Records Guide, 30
New York Times, 65
newspaper morgues, 66
Newton, Isaac, 7
Nilon, Charles H., 64
non causa pro causa (fallacy), 314
non sequiturs (fallacies), 162, 321
notes, digital, 111-112
"no true Scotswoman" (fallacy), 324
noun-noun-noun constructions,
  195-197
nouns, use of precise, 192-193

O
Occam, William of, 15
Occam's Razor, 15-16, 142-144
OCLC, 30, 40, 41-45, 94, 107, 115, 127;
  see also *FirstSearch, WorldCat*
Official Museum Directory, 30
Okuno, Takashi, 64
*Online Legal Research for College
  Students*, 75
online writing laboratories, 177, 203
Opdycke, John B., 185, 340
ophecleide, 29
Origin of Species, 173-174
outline, model, 184
outline, sentence, 177
outline, topical, 177
OWLS, see online writing laboratories

Oxford English Dictionary, 10, 37, 86, 120, 134, 140, 141, 150, 198-199
Oxford University, 12

P

parallelism (outline), 178-179
Parsons, Charles Algernon, Sir, 106
passive voice, 189-190
Pater, Walter Horatio, 167-168
Paulsen, David W., 149
Penrose, Walter, Sir, 167-168
Periodical Directories and Bibliographies, 63
Peterson, William S., 108-114, 117
petitio principii (fallacy), 161, 314-315
Petrie, William Matthew Flinders, 110
Phipps, James, 145
Play Index, 84
Plum, Stephen H., 64
plurium interrogationum (fallacy), 321
Pocket Guide to DIALOG, 72
post hoc ergo propter hoc (fallacy), 135, 160, 314
prejudicial language, 159
premise (logical), 152, 153
primary sources, 4-5, 7-9. 12, 13, 21-22, 23, 25, 26, 28, 29, 31, 52, 84, 88, 89, 98, 101, 111, 136, 137, 158, 220, 238
Principles of Bibliographical Description, 90
PRO CD BIZ, 41
PRO CD HOME, 41
ProCite, 103
ProComm Plus, 39
profession, nature of, 120
propositions (logical), 151
Pruett, James W., 64
publication, future, 236-240
punctuation, 194-195

Purdue University, 177, 203

R

Readers' Guide to Periodical Literature, 84
record (digital), 107
records, public, 5, 30
recto, 99
red herring (fallacy), 321
relationships and associations (footnote), 220-221
Religious Bibliographies in Serial Literature, 64
The Renaissance: Studies in Art and Poetry, 167-168
Research Guide to Musicology, 64
Research Guide to Philosophy, 64
Research Libraries Information Network, see RLIN
Resources for Rhetoric and Composition, 203
Rhetoric Page at the South Dakota School of Mines and Technology, 203
Rhetoric Resources at Tech, 203
RLIN, 77-78
Roe *v.* Wade, 9
Roosevelt, Eleanor, 11
Roosevelt, Theodore, 236
Rosenberg, John D., 97
Rouse, Richard H., 64
Rowland, J. F. B., 64
Russell, Bertrand, 221

S

Sanderson, Rosalie Massery, 76
Sauers, Richard, 27
Scholar Adventurers, 339
Science Citation Index, 93-94
scientific method, 1-2, 18, 103, 158, 307, 308
SciSearch, 93

SCORPIO, 2, 50, 56; searching,
    252-256; see also Library of
    Congress Information System
screen snapshots, 38-39
search engines, see ALTAVISTA, EXCITE,
    INKTOMI, LYCOS, YAHOO
Search Tips: LEXIS/NEXIS, 75
secretaries, departmental, 123
SelectPhone, 123
self-editing, principle of, 205
Serial Bibliographies and Abstracts in
    History, 63
Serial Bibliographies for Medieval
    Studies, 64
Serial Bibliographies in the Humanities
    and Social Sciences, 63
Shaw, George Bernard, 200
shelf browsing, 90-91; digital, 276-280
Sherlock Holmes's Rule, 16-17,
    144-148
shifting the burden of proof (fallacy),
    308, 321-322
Sholes, Christopher Latham, 135
Short Story Index, 84
sitzfleisch, 85-86
Skinner, Burrhus Frederic, 167
Slavens, Thomas P., 64
slippery slope argument, 159, 318-319
slothful induction (fallacy), 160
Smith's Guide to the Literature of the
    Life Sciences, 64
so, 197-198
Social Sciences Citation Index, 93-94
Social Sciences Index, 84
source, primary, see primary sources
source, secondary, 5-6, 7, 20, 28, 52,
    84, 86, 89, 116, 137, 208
source, tertiary, 6-7, 208
Sourcebook of County Asset/Lien Records,
    30
Sourcebook of County Court Records, 30

special pleading (fallacy), 308
Stanford, Leland, 311-312
Stanford University, 83
statements (logical), 151
statistical syllogisms (fallacy), 160
Stevenson, Robert Louis, 11
Stokes, Roy Bishop, 90
stolen concept (fallacy), 162
straw man (fallacy), 161, 322
Streit, Christian, 31
Student's Manual of Bibliography, 90
style over substance (fallacy), 159
subject bibliographies, 89
subject cataloguing, digital, 112-114
subordination (outline), 180-181
Supreme Court (U. S.), 9
sweeping generalization (fallacy), 313
Swift, Jonathan, 201
synthesis, of ideas, 138, 163-174

T
Tarbert, Gary C., 63
telnet, 38, 46, 48-50, 56
ten hour rule, 7-8
Textile Technology Digest, 41
thesis statement, 175-176
Thurber, James, 11
Tice, Terrence N., 64
The Times (London), 65, 230
Times Roman (font), 230
Toomey, Alice F., 61
translations (footnote), 221-222
Trumpet Winsock, 41
Tsukuba Studies in Human Geography,
    64
Tsukuba Daigaku jimbun chirigaku
    kenkyu, 64
tu quoque (fallacy), 323
Turabian, Kate L., 201, 212

U
undistributed middle (fallacy), 319
Uniform Resource Locator, 45
University of California, 78-79;
    see also MELVYL
University of Victoria, 149
unrepresentative sample (fallacy), 160
Unternehmensbeteiligungsgesellschaft
    Baden-Württemberg
    Aktiengesellschaft, 196
usage, standard American, 199-201
Using Computers in Legal Research, 75

V
verbs, 193-194
verso, 99
Vertical File Index, 84
Vipera berus, 21
Voyage of the Beagle, 173

W
Walker, Janice R., 202
Walpole, Sir Robert, 136
Walsh, Michael J., 64
Warner, Ezra, 27, 28
Washington, Augustine, 140
Washington, George, 6, 31, 136-137,
    140, 148
Washington, Mary Ball, 140
Washington Post, 65
Waterloo, Battle of, 22, 79-80
Watson, Gary, 75
Watt, James, 106
WESTLAW, 40, 75-77
WESTLAW *Database List*, 76
WESTLAW *Desktop Command Reference*,
    76
WESTLAW *User Guide*, 76
White, E[lwyn] B[rooks], 11
Whitehead, Alfred North, 221
whois, 336

Wilson indexes and abstracts, 84
Windows (Microsoft), 39, 48
Winks, Robin W., 340
Winning Research Skills, 76
Winterhalter, Franz Xaver, 72-73
wisdom, nature of, 13-15
Wordsworth, William, 134
World Bibliography of Bibliographies, 61
*World Bibliography of Geographical
    Bibliographies*, 64
World War I, 23; see also *Lusitania*
World Wide Web, 2, 38, 39, 43, 44,
    45, 50, 56, 57, 60, 68, 74, 81, 83,
    84, 151, 329, 334
*World Wide Web Resources for Rhetoric
    and Composition*, 203
WorldCat, 2, 41-43, 48, 55, 56, 67,
    92, 108, 117, 133; display, 107;
    labels, 115; searching, 241-251,
    256-259; see also *FirstSearch*, OCLC
Wortman, William A., 63
Wren, Christopher G., 75
Wren, Jill Robinson, 75
Wright, James, 272-275
Wyatt, Tristram, 125

Y
YAHOO, 83-84, 203-204, 334; *People
    Search*, 123
Yoder, Brian, 150

Index of URLs

ftp://ota.ac.uk/pub/ota/public/english/Darwin/origin1783, 174
ftp://uiarchive.cso.uiuc.edu/pub/etext/gutenberg/etext94/lesms10.txt, 168
ftp://wiretap.spies.com/Library/Classic/beagle.txt, 173
http://arl.cni.org/members.html, 51
http://inktomi.berkeley.edu, 82
http://lcweb.loc.gov/catalog, 51
http://library.usask.ca/hytelnet, 51
http://lynx.browser.org, 60
http://milton.mse.jhu.edu:8001/research/education/net.html, 329
http://owl.english.purdue.edu. 177
http://uts.cc.utexas.edu/~churchh/janeinfo.html#janetoc, 60
http://webserver.maclab.comp.uvic.ca/writersguide/Logic/logicToc.html,
    149-150
http://www.altavista.digital.com, 82
http://www.altavista.digital.com/cgi-bin/query?pg=aq&what=web&text=yes,
    82
http://www.bis.dowjones.com, 82
http://www.bis.dowjones.com/clipping/custom-clips/publications
    /publications.html, 82
http://www.cas.usf.edu/english/walker/mla.html, 202
http://www.clark.net/pub/rmharris/research.html, 51
http://www.clearinghouse.net, 81
http://www.contractjobs.com/tel, 123
http://www.december.com, 81
http://www.december.com/cmc/info, 81
http://www.december.com/net/tools, 81
http://www.dialog.com, 72
http://www.dla.ucop.edu/welcome.html, 79
http://www.dla.utexas.edu/depts/drc/othersites.html, 203
http://www.english.purdue.edu, 203
http://www.excite.com, 82, 335
http://www.gatech.edu/lcc/lcc1001/rhetoric.html, 203
http://www.grainger.uiuc.edu/ugl/howlcsh.htm, 53
http://www.ind.net/Internet/comp.html, 203
http://www.isinet.com, 91
http://www.nizkor.org, 150, 305
http://www.oclc.org/oclc/menu/t-doc.htm#fs, 45
http://www.ovid.com, 77

http://www.primenet.com/~byoder/fallazoo.htm, 150
http://www.sagrelto.com/sagrelto/tutorial/snewusr.htm, 45
http://www.sagrelto.com/sagrelto/tutorial/urlintro.htm, 45
http://www.sdsmt.edu/www/rhetoric/rhetoric.html, 203
http://www.switchboard.com, 123, 335
http://www.tcp.com/~prime8/Orbit/MDCR/argument1.html, 150
http://www.thomson.com/gale/default.htm, 74
http://www.uvm.edu/~xli/reference/estyles.html, 201
http://www.yahoo.com, 83
http://www.yahoo.com/search/people, 123
http://www.yahoo.com/Social_Science/Linguistics_and_Human_Languages/
    Languages/English, 204
news://alt.atheism, 150
news://soc.culture groups, 132
news://soc.culture.ukranian, 132
telnet://locis.loc.gov, 50, 55, 253, 276
telnet://melvyl.ucop.edu, 79